The Buddha from Dolpo

The Buddha from Dolpo

A Study of the Life and Thought of the Tibetan Master Dolpopa Sherab Gyaltsen

Cyrus Stearns

MOTILAL BANARSIDASS PUBLISHERS
PRIVATE LIMITED • DELHI

First Indian Edition: Delhi, 2002

First Published by State University of New York Press, Albany, USA.

ISBN: 81-208-1833-4 (Cloth)
ISBN: 81-208-1936-5 (Paper)

Also available at:

MOTILAL BANARSIDASS

41 U.A. Bungalow Road, Jawahar Nagar, Delhi 110 007
8 Mahalaxmi Chamber, 22 Bhulabhai Desai Road, Mumbai 400 026
236, 9th Main III Block, Jayanagar, Bangalore 560 011
120 Royapettah High Road, Mylapore, Chennai 600 004
Sanas Plaza, 1302 Baji Rao Road, Pune 411 002
8 Camac Street, Kolkata 700 017
Ashok Rajpath, Patna 800 004
Chowk, Varanasi 221 001

Printed in India
BY JAINENDRA PRAKASH JAIN AT SHRI JAINENDRA PRESS,
A-45 NARAINA, PHASE-I, NEW DELHI 110 028
AND PUBLISHED BY NARENDRA PRAKASH JAIN FOR
MOTILAL BANARSIDASS PUBLISHERS PRIVATE LIMITED,
BUNGALOW ROAD, DELHI 110 007

Table of Contents

Preface and Acknowledgments

This book is the product of a lingering fascination with several topics that have remained largely unexplored by Western students of Tibetan religion and history. When I first began my own study of Tibetan literature in the early 1970s I occasionally came across brief references to an intriguing fourteenth-century figure known as Dolpopa, or the Buddha from Dolpo, and usually hostile descriptions of his unique vision of the nature of reality. The fact that his tradition had been effectively censured by the Tibetan government in the seventeenth century only served to pique my curiosity. My teacher, the late Dezhung Tulku Rinpoche, was at first somewhat reticent to speak about Dolpopa's theories, no doubt in large part due to my obvious lack of the necessary skills to engage in such a discussion. Rinpoche was a peerless example of the nonsectarian approach to realization, and as the years passed I was fortunate to learn from him an appreciation of the wide range of views contained in all the ancient traditions of Tibet, including that of Dolpopa's Zhentong lineage. I am deeply grateful for Dezhung Rinpoche's inspiring example.

While living in Nepal in the 1980s I found a large volume of Dolpopa's miscellaneous writings for sale in the monastery of my teacher, the late Dilgo Khyentse Rinpoche, who had recently published it in Bhutan. This collection contained both of the texts that I have translated in the present work. I am particularly thankful to Khyentse Rinpoche for personally encouraging me to read Dolpopa's writings.

During the following years in Nepal I continued to be nagged with curiosity about Dolpopa and his ideas, and returned periodically to the volume of his writings. Then in 1988 my teacher Chogye Trichen Rinpoche begin teaching the Kālacakra Six-branch Yoga of Dolpopa's tradition according to the instruction manual written by Jonang Tāranātha. During the next two years Rinpoche taught the Six-branch Yoga in Nepal, Borneo, and the United States, and as his interpreter I had the unique opportunity to study these teachings and have many conversations with him about their practice. I then began to delve more deeply into Tāranātha's other writings, which led me back to Dolpopa, his great predecessor. I am extremely indebted to Chogye Rinpoche for his exceptional kindness, and for sharing his profound insight into the practice of Buddhist tantra.

After my return to the United States in 1991 I gradually began to concentrate on the study of Dolpopa's life and teachings. This became much more feasible with the 1992 publication of Dolpopa's voluminous Collected Works, which had been recovered from eastern Tibet by Professor Matthew Kapstein. In addition, Prof. Leonard van der Kuijp graciously made available to me copies of a number of extremely important rare manuscripts from his own collection, and carefully read through an earlier version of this book. Without access to the works recovered by Professors Kapstein and van der Kuijp a study of this type would have been impossible. I should also like to thank Dr. Jeffrey Schoening for his thoughtful reading of this work, and his many helpful comments and suggestions. The insightful suggestions and references from Mr. Hubert Decleer are also very much appreciated. I am likewise grateful to Professor Collett Cox, Professor Richard Salomon, and Dr. Dan Martin for their helpful readings of an earlier manuscript. Professor John Newman, Professor David Germano, and Dr. Franz-Karl Ehrhard were also very generous with their comments and references. I would also like to thank Khenpo Apey, Guru Lama, Mr. Kurtis Schaeffer, Ms. Marilyn Kennell, Mr. Jérôme Edou, and Mr. Jan-Ulrich Sobisch for providing copies of rare texts, directing me to references, or making editorial suggestions. I am also grateful to Professor David Jackson for his helpful comments and for locating photographs of an old image and painting of Dolpopa. Mr. Michael Henss, Mr. Ulrich von Schroeder, and Mr. Andy Quintman all deserve my thanks for kindly allowing their photographs to be used in this book. And finally, I must acknowledge that much of this work was written under the influence of the divine music of Franz

List, Frank Zappa, Ludwig van Beethoven, Miles Davis, and Johann Sebastian Bach.

This book is based on my Ph.D. dissertation entitled "The Buddha from Dolpo and His Fourth Council" (University of Washington, 1996). However, many corrections, revisions, and additions have been made for the present work, most significantly the study and translation of Dolpopa's *A General Commentary on the Doctrine*, which was not included in the dissertation.

In the main text of this book all Tibetan names have been phoneticized for the convenience of the reader, but in the annotations the correct Tibetan spellings have been retained. Both forms are listed in the Index. The phonetic rendering of Tibetan words is a problematic area. No great effort has been made here to establish a fixed phonetic system, since this would presuppose a standard pronunciation for terms whose actual pronunciation varies widely in different regions of Tibet. When a passage from an original Tibetan text has been translated from an unpublished manuscript the Tibetan has usually been reproduced in italicized transliteration in the annotations. No attempt has been made to "correct" the spellings found in the original texts. All Sanskrit terms are transliterated in the standard fashion.

I hope that some of the charismatic force of Dolpopa's character may be glimpsed in the following description of his life and ideas, and that this initial attempt to present a small portion of his controversial and inspiring insights will contribute toward further investigations by others in the future. Since even Dolpopa's own Dharma heirs were said to have experienced difficulties in grasping the full range of their master's genius, I am certain the present work is far from perfect. But at least in the eyes of interested students of Buddhism, Dolpopa and his spiritual legacy may now begin to emerge from the long shadows of official Tibetan history.

Introduction

One of the major sources of tension in the interpretation of late Indian Buddhism as it was received in Tibet was the apparently contradictory descriptions of emptiness (*śūnyatā*, *stong pa nyid*) found in scriptures and commentaries identified with different phases of the tradition.[1] The notion of an enlightened eternal essence, or Buddha-nature (*tathāgatagarbha*, *bde bzhin gshegs pa'i snying po*), present within every living being, was in marked contrast to the earlier traditional Buddhist emphasis on the lack of any enduring essence in sentient beings. For followers of Mahāyāna and Vajrayāna Buddhism in Tibet, the interpretation and reconciliation of these two themes in the doctrinal materials they had inherited from India, and elsewhere, was of crucial importance.

In fourteenth-century Tibet the concern with these issues seems to have finally reached a point of critical mass. There was a burst of scholarly works dealing in particular with the question of the Buddha-nature and the attendant implications for the Buddhist traditions of practice and explication. What forces were primarily responsible for the intense interest surrounding these issues at this specific point in Tibetan history is not yet clearly understood. What can be seen is that many of the prominent masters of this period who produced the most influential works on these subjects were both intimately involved in the practice and teaching of the *Kālacakra tantra*, and either personally knew each other or had many of the same teachers and disciples. Among the most important of these masters were the third Karmapa hierarch Rangjung Dorje (1284–1339), Budön Rinchen Drup (1290–1364), Dolpopa

Sherab Gyaltsen (1292–1361), Longchen Rabjampa (1308–1364), Lama Dampa Sönam Gyaltsen (1312–1375), and Barawa Gyaltsen Balzang (1310–1391).[2]

Without question, the teachings and writings of Dolpopa, who was also known as "The Buddha from Dolpo" (Dol po sangs rgyas), and "The Omniscient One from Dolpo Who Embodies the Buddhas of the Three Times" (Dus gsum sangs rgyas kun mkhyen Dol po pa), contain the most controversial and stunning ideas ever presented by a great Tibetan Buddhist master. The controversies that stemmed from his teachings are still very much alive today among Tibetan Buddhists, more than six hundred years after Dolpopa's death.

When attempting to grasp the nature and significance of Dolpopa's ideas and their impact on Tibetan religious history, it is important to recognize that he was one of the towering figures of fourteenth-century Tibet. He was not a minor figure whose strange notions influenced only the members of his own Jonang tradition, and whose maverick line of hermeneutic thought died out when that tradition was violently suppressed by the central Tibetan government in the middle of the seventeenth century. Although this is perhaps the orthodox version of events, there is, on the other hand, abundant evidence that Dolpopa's legacy spread widely, and had a profound impact on the development of Tibetan Buddhism from the fourteenth century to the present day.

Whenever Dolpopa's name comes up, whether in ancient polemic tracts, or in conversation with modern Tibetan teachers, it is obvious that he is remembered first and foremost for the development of what is known as the Zhentong (*gzhan stong*) view. Until quite recently this view has been familiar to modern scholars largely via the intensely critical writings of later doctrinal opponents of Dolpopa and the Jonang school.[3] As such, in the absence of the original voice for this view—that is, Dolpopa's extensive writings, which have only been widely available for the last few years—even Dolpopa's name, and the words *Jonang* and *Zhentong,* have come to often evoke merely the image of an aberrant and heretical doctrine, which thankfully was purged from the Tibetan Buddhist scene centuries ago.[4] In this way an extremely significant segment of Tibetan religious history has been swept under the rug. One of the main aims of the present work is to allow Dolpopa's life and ideas to speak for themselves.

Dolpopa used the Tibetan term *gzhan stong*, "empty of other," to describe absolute reality as empty only of other relative phenomena. This view is Dolpopa's primary legacy. And there is always a strong reaction to it, whether positive or negative. Although there were no doubt others before him who held much the same opinion, in both India and Tibet, Dolpopa was the first to come out and directly state what he thought in writing, using terminology which was new and shocking for many of his contemporaries. His new "Dharma language" (*chos skad*), which included the use of previously unknown terms such as *gzhan stong*, "empty of other," will be discussed in chapter 2.

In Dolpopa's view the absolute and the relative are both empty, as Buddhism has always proclaimed, but they *must* be empty in different ways. Phenomena at the relative level (*saṃvṛti*, *kun rdzob*) are empty of self-nature (*svabhāvaśūnya*, *rang stong*), and are no more real than the fictitious horn of a rabbit, or the child of a barren woman. In contrast, the reality of absolute truth (*paramārtha*, *don dam*) is empty only of other (**parabhāva-śūnya*, *gzhan stong*) relative phenomena, and not itself empty. With the recent availability of a large number of writings by Dolpopa it is now becoming clear that he was not simply setting up the viewpoints of an emptiness of self-nature (*rang stong*) and an emptiness of other (*gzhan stong*) as opposed theories located on the same level.[5] He obviously viewed the pair as complementary, while making the careful distinction that the view of an "emptiness of other" applied only to the absolute, and an "emptiness of self-nature" only to the relative. Both approaches were essential for a correct understanding of the nature of saṃsāra and nirvāṇa. Dolpopa's quarrel was with those who viewed *both* the absolute and the relative as empty of self-nature (*rang stong*), and who refused to recognize the existence of anything which was not empty of self-nature. From this point of view the notion of an emptiness of other relative phenomena (*gzhan stong*) did not fit the definition of emptiness.

Dolpopa further identified the absolute with the Buddha-nature (*tathāgatagarbha*), which was thus seen to be eternal and not empty of self-nature, but only empty of other. The Buddha-nature is perfect and complete from the beginning, with all the characteristics of a Buddha eternally present in every living being. It is only the impermanent and temporary defilements veiling the Buddha-nature that are empty of self-nature, and that must be removed through the practice of a spiritual path in order to allow the ever-present Buddha-nature to manifest in its full splendor.

This view was in accord with many Mahāyāna and Vajrayāna scriptures, but most of the scholars in Tibet during Dolpopa's life disagreed with him. They viewed such scriptural statements to be of provisional meaning (*neyārtha*, *drang don*), and in need of interpretation for the true intended meaning to be correctly comprehended. This was, for example, the opinion of the mainstream Sakya tradition, to which Dolpopa belonged before he moved to the monastery of Jonang. As such, for some time Dolpopa tried to keep his teachings secret, realizing that they would be misunderstood and cause great turmoil and uncertainty for those who had closed minds and were accustomed to certain styles of interpretation that differed greatly from his own. Dolpopa often remarked that the majority of buddhas and bodhisattvas agreed with his viewpoint on these issues, but that the majority of scholars in Tibet were opposed to him.[6] For instance, the general Sakya position is that the Buddha-nature is present in living beings as a potential, or seed. This seed can be caused to ripen through the various practices of the spiritual path and come to final fruition as perfect buddhahood. If left in a box without any water, light, warmth, soil, and so forth, the seed will never bear fruit. However, if it is planted in the proper soil, receives the right amount of sunlight, water, and so forth, it will grow into a healthy plant and finally bear its fruit. From this viewpoint, the Buddha-nature is a fertile seed in every living being, which has the potential to expand and manifest as a result of spiritual practice but is not complete and perfect already, as Dolpopa maintained.[7]

In regard to the two truths, the absolute and the relative, Dolpopa saw no difference between speaking of the absolute as totally unestablished and saying that there is no absolute. He asked whether a relative is possible without an absolute, the incidental possible without the primordial, and the entities of existence (*dharma*, *chos*) possible without a true nature (*dharmatā*, *chos nyid*). If, he asked, their existence is possible without an absolute, then would those relative, incidental entities of existence themselves not constitute an omnipresent reality or true nature? There would, in such a situation, be nothing else. This, of course, is an unacceptable conclusion, and Dolpopa's doctrinal opponents would have to respond by saying that everything is not the relative, for there is of course an absolute truth as well. But, Dolpopa would respond, if it is impossible for there to be no absolute, does that not contradict the notion of an absolute which is totally unestablished?[8] Everything cannot be simply empty of self-nature, for then there would be no difference between the absolute and the relative. As Dolpopa stated in his autocommentary to *The Fourth Council* (*Bka' bsdu bzhi pa*):

> Why is the realization that everything is empty of self-nature not the same as no realization?
> Why is the explanation of everything as empty of self-nature not the same as no explanation?
> Why is writing that everything is empty of self-nature not the same as not writing?[9]

Dolpopa saw the only solution to these sorts of problems to be the acceptance of the absolute as a true, eternal, and veridically established reality, empty merely of extraneous relative phenomena.

Descriptions of reality, or the Buddha-nature, in these terms are common in a number of scriptures which the Tibetan tradition places in the Third Turning of the Dharma Wheel,[10] and in the Buddhist tantras. Nevertheless, no one before Dolpopa in Tibet had ever simply said that absolute reality was not empty of self-nature. This was what caused all the trouble. In answer to the objections of his opponents, Dolpopa noted that his teachings, and the Dharma language (*chos skad*) he was using, were indeed new, but only in the sense that they were not well-known in Tibet. This was because they had come from the realm of Shambhala to the north, where they had been widespread from an early date.[11] He explicitly linked his ideas to the *Kālacakra tantra* and its great commentary, the *Vimalaprabhā*, composed by the Shambhala emperor Kalkin Puṇḍarīka, which were not translated into Tibetan until the early eleventh century. Dolpopa clearly felt that earlier interpreters of the Kālacakra literature had not fully comprehended its profound meaning. As will be discussed in the first chapter, he even ordered a new revised translation of the *Kālacakra tantra* and the *Vimalaprabhā*, for the purpose of making the definitive meaning (*nītārtha*, *nges don*) more accessible to Tibetan scholars and practitioners. In this respect he was attempting through a revised translation to remove the results of accumulated mistaken presuppositions that had informed the earlier translations in Tibet, and thus provided the basis for many erroneous opinions concerning the true meaning of the *Kālacakra*.[12]

The views of Dolpopa and the Jonang tradition, and their influence in Tibet, have attracted only modest attention in the published research of modern scholars. D. S. Ruegg has touched upon these topics more than anyone else, although usually from the viewpoint of the determined Geluk and Zhalu opponents of the Jonang position. M. Kapstein has both summarized the life of Dolpopa and briefly discussed his ideas in his recent catalogue to the newly discovered collection of Dolpopa's complete works. S. Hookham has studied the Zhentong approach to the interpretation of the *Uttaratantra*, and M. Broido has very briefly outlined some of Dolpopa's views on Madhyamaka as found in Dolpopa's major work, *The Ocean of Definitive Meaning* (*Nges don rgya mtsho*).[13] Until now there has been no detailed study of Dolpopa's life and the Zhentong tradition in Tibet, nor any translations of his major works.

The following work is divided into two parts. Part 1 deals with Dolpopa's life and teachings. In chapter 1 Dolpopa's life is discussed in a more complete fashion then has been the case to date. This has been made possible by the recent publication of one full-length Tibetan biography of Dolpopa and the recovery of another unpublished manuscript biography, both by direct disciples who witnessed much of what they describe. Numerous other Tibetan sources have also been utilized for this discussion. The presentation of a somewhat detailed version of Dolpopa's life provides essential background for an appreciation of his spiritual and intellectual development and his personal character, as well as his tremendous influence in fourteenth-century Tibet.

Chapter 2 provides a summary of the historical development of the Zhentong tradition in Tibet. Some of the earlier Tibetan precedents for the view of ultimate reality as an emptiness only of other relative phenomena are briefly discussed. Dolpopa's unique use of language and the major influences on his development of the Zhentong theory are presented in some detail. The fate of the Jonang tradition after Dolpopa is described, as well as the significance of several of the most important adherents to the Zhentong view from the fourteenth through the twentieth centuries.

Chapter 3 is a discussion of Dolpopa's view of the nature of absolute reality as empty of phenomena other than itself (*gzhan stong*), and of the relative as empty of self-nature (*rang stong*). In connection with these ideas, there is also a discussion of Dolpopa's attempt to redefine the views of Cittamātra and Madhyamaka in Tibet, and his own definition of what constitutes the tradition of the Great Madhyamaka (**mahāmadhyamaka, dbu ma chen po*). Finally, there is a brief presentation of two opposing views of what actually brings about enlightenment. Dolpopa maintained that enlightenment occurs only when the vital winds (*vāyu, rlung*) normally circulating through numerous subtle channels in the body are drawn into the central channel (*avadhūtī*) through the practice of tantric yoga. He strongly objected to the view that enlightenment could be achieved merely through a recognition of the nature of the mind, without the necessity for the accumulation of the assemblies of merit and gnosis through the practice of the spiritual path. These topics are discussed with the intention of providing the reader with background information necessary for an understanding of the following translations.

Part 2 contains the first translations of two major works by Dolpopa, both originally composed in verse. The first work is *A General Commentary on the Doctrine* (*Bstan pa spyi 'grel*), one of the earliest texts composed by Dolpopa to present his unique vision of the entire structure of the Buddhist tradition.[14] An introduction to the translation will discuss the circumstances of the composition and the reasons for its significance. The translation of *A General Commentary on the Doctrine* is annotated from the detailed commentary by Nyaön Kunga Bal (1285–1379), who was one of Dolpopa's most important disciples.[15] The second translation is of a work entitled *The Fourth Council* (*Bka' bsdu bzhi pa*).[16] The circumstances surrounding the actual composition of the text at the request of the Sakya hierarch Lama Dampa Sönam Gyaltsen are discussed in the introduction to the translation. *The Fourth Council* itself was composed in the last years of Dolpopa's life, and may be viewed as a final verse summation of the ideas he considered most important. The entire text of his own condensed commentary (*bsdus don 'grel pa*) on the work is included here with the translation. Annotations to the translation are drawn from a number of sources, but particularly from Dolpopa's own autocommentary (*rang 'grel*) to *The Fourth Council*.

Part One

The Life and Teachings of the Omniscient Dolpopa

1

The Life of the Buddha from Dolpo

> The Buddhist tradition is steeped in the marvelous. Belittled by some schools and exaggerated by others, the marvelous is ubiquitous. We have accepted it as such without attempting to eliminate it in the name of western rationalism. To disregard it would be to offer the reader a caricature of Buddhism and still not attain historical truth. It is not enough to discard the legend in order to discern the reality of the facts. By leaving the marvelous the place it has always occupied in the sources, we believe we have given a more faithful image of the mentality of the Buddha's disciples. And it is this mentality which is the true object of our research and not a fleeting and elusive historical certainty.
>
> —*History of Indian Buddhism*, É. Lamotte[1]

In the year 1309 a seventeen-year-old novice monk ran away from home in the Dolpo area of present-day Nepal and endured a harrowing journey north to the region of Mustang (Glo) in quest of spiritual guidance from a great Buddhist master. No one could have imagined that in less than twenty years he would be enthroned as the leader of Jonang monastery in the Tibetan province of Tsang, where he would soon construct the largest stūpa temple (*sku 'bum*) ever seen in Tibet, and proclaim his vision of the nature of reality in a series of treatises that would rock the Tibetan Buddhist world. As an indispensable foundation for understanding Dolpopa's ideas and influence, the first thing that is required is a clear picture of his life and the cultural environment in which he lived.[2] Fortunately, two primary sources provide us with crucial information. These are the biographies of Dolpopa composed by two of his main disciples, Gharungwa Lhey Gyaltsen (1319–1401) and Kunpang Chödrak Balzang (1283–1363?), both of whom were witnesses to many of the events they describe and who record Dolpopa's own statements about his life and experiences. Later sketches of Dolpopa's life in historical works by Jetsun Tāranātha (1575–1635) and Mangtö Ludrup Gyantso (1523–1596) also supply interesting material, although they are sometimes at odds with the earlier sources.[3]

1. Childhood and Early Education

In 1292 Dolpopa was born into a clan that practiced the tantric tradition of the Nyingma, especially the cycles connected with the deity Vajrakilāya, of which he became an expert as a boy.[4] As early as 1297, when he was only five years old, he received the initiation of Red Mañjuśrī, and in meditation was graced by a vision of the deity, from whom he is said to have gained great powers of discriminating awareness.[5] After receiving ordination as a novice monk in 1304, when he was twelve years old, he had the strong desire to study the sūtras on the perfection of transcendent knowledge (*prajñāpāramitā*) and the treatises on logical reasoning (*pramāṇa*), but there was no institute for their study in his home region. These subjects were the specialty of the Sakya tradition, which was not as strong as the Nyingma school in Dolpopa's homeland. He had by this time met and received teachings and tantric initiations, such as *The Rosary Trilogy* (*'Phreng ba skor gsum*) of the Indian master Abhayākaragupta, from Gyidön Jamyang Trakpa Gyaltsen, a Sakya teacher who would become one of his two most important spiritual masters. Overcome with faith in his teacher, Dolpopa wished to follow Gyidön to Mustang but was prevented by his parents, who insisted that he study the tantras of the Nyingma tradition.

In 1309, when Dolpopa was seventeen, he fled alone in secret, without the permission of his parents, and after enduring great hardships, arrived in the presence of the master Gyidön in upper Mustang. There he received many teachings, such as the treatises on the sūtras concerned with the perfection of transcendent knowledge (*prajñāpāramitā*), the manuals on logical reasoning (*pramāṇa*), and the texts on cosmology and psychology (*abhidharma*). After only a month of intense study Dolpopa quickly mastered the specific Dharma language (*chos skad*) associated with each of those genres of Buddhist learning and was able to enter into informed discussions, thereby attracting attention for the first time.[6] At that point Gyidön received an urgent message from his uncle Shakya Bum, insisting that he come to the great monastery of Sakya, in the Tibetan province of Tsang, where he was teaching.[7] Gyidön assured his sponsors and students in Mustang that he would soon return and left for Sakya, which was at that time the most prestigious center of learning in Tibet.[8] In the meantime Dolpopa continued his studies in Mustang under two other learned masters.

2. Studies at the Great Monastery of Sakya

When Gyidön prepared to return to Mustang after about two years, his uncle Shakya Bum, and other teachers in Sakya, would not allow him to do so. He sent an explanation to Mustang and a message to Dolpopa telling him to come to Sakya. Dolpopa arrived in Sakya in 1312, when he was twenty years old, and resumed his studies with his former master. By this point Dolpopa had clearly been recognized as a most precocious student. He continued to concentrate on the simultaneous study of the sūtras concerned with the perfection of transcendent knowledge, the manuals on logical reasoning, and the texts on cosmology and psychology. His friends tried to dissuade him from this approach, advising that he focus on one area at a time in order to master it, but he ignored their advice and even added on the study of the *Bodhicāryāvatāra* and several tantric texts such as the *Vajrāvalītantra (Rdo rje 'phreng ba'i rgyud)* and the *Buddhakapālitantra (Sangs rgyas thod pa'i rgyud)*. In only a year and a half he would master the above four Mahāyāna subjects and their commentaries.[9]

During this period of intense study Dolpopa continued to receive many special teachings from his main preceptor, Gyidön Jamyang Trakpa. Little is known of this teacher who was so instrumental in Dolpopa's early development. Gyidön had studied the Kālacakra under Rongpa Sherab Senge (1251–1315) and the translator named Chokden,[10] and it was the tradition of this tantra that he apparently emphasized. Dolpopa received countless teachings from him at Sakya, the most important of which seem to have been the *Kālacakra tantra*, *The Bodhisattva Trilogy* (*Sems 'grel skor gsum*),[11] the ten *Sūtras on the Buddha-nature* (*Snying po'i mdo*),[12] the five *Sūtras of Definitive Meaning* (*Nges don mdo*),[13] and the five *Treatises of Maitreya* (*Byams chos*).[14] These are foremost among the scriptures and treatises that Dolpopa himself would constantly teach throughout the last half of his life and which he would cite as scriptural sources for his controversial theories.

Gyidön himself was a consummate expert on all subjects of sūtra and tantra, as well as the related esoteric instructions for meditation, and would praise any authentic teaching system without bias. In particular, he highly praised the Kālacakra and the practice of meditation. Specifically, he had the greatest faith in the Six-branch Yoga (*ṣaḍaṅgayoga*), and would repeatedly praise it.[15] This caused many academically oriented monks to actually engage in the practice of tantric meditation.[16] The influence of his teacher's highest regard for this particular system must have been great on the young Dolpopa. Having received all of the initiations, textual explanations, and esoteric instructions of the Kālacakra from Gyidön, Dolpopa became an expert in this tradition and also served as Gyidön's teaching assistant for several years.[17]

During this period Dolpopa also received many teachings and tantric initiations from other great masters, such as the Sakya throne holder Daknyi Chenpo Zangpo Bal (1262–1323) and Gyidön's uncle Shakya Bum. From Kunpang Trakpa Gyaltsen (1263?–1347?) he again received teachings on the sūtras concerned with the perfection of transcendent knowledge (*prajñāpāramitā*), the manuals on logical reasoning (*pramāṇa*), and the texts on cosmology and psychology (*abhidharma*). But perhaps most significantly, he received the *Vimalaprabhā* commentary on the *Kālacakra tantra* by Kalkin Puṇḍarīka, which he had already studied under Gyidön.[18] Two masters of the Sharpa family line of Sakya were also important teachers for Dolpopa. These were the brothers Senge Bal, with whom he studied logical reasoning (*pramāṇa*), and Kunga Sönam (1285–1346), from whom he received the extensive teachings of the Path and Result (Lam 'bras), the most important Sakya system of tantric practice, as well as the textual transmission of many tantras of the Hevajra cycle.[19] In this way Dolpopa pursued intensive study of both the Mahāyāna and Vajrayāna traditions as taught at Sakya and became a great expert in these fields, but especially in the sūtras concerned with the perfection of transcendent knowledge, the manuals on logical reasoning, and the texts on cosmology and psychology.

In 1313, when Dolpopa was twenty-one years old, he received a generous offering from his parents (who had by now forgiven him for running away) for the purpose of holding his first public teaching. Jetsun Tāranātha states that while the preparations for his teaching debut were being made, Dolpopa went to the monastery of Danak and for about three months studied *The Five Treatises of Maitreya* (*Byams pa'i chos lnga*), as well as various techniques for the practice of austerities, with the master Rinchen Yeshe. This is a very interesting statement, because Tāranātha's predecessor Jetsun Kunga Drolchok (1507–1566) had earlier remarked that Budön Rinchen Drup (1290–1364) felt that Dolpopa had enhanced a previous Tibetan philosophical system held by one Rinchen Yeshe of Danak.[20] The question of possible influences such as this on Dolpopa's later formulation of the Zhentong theory will be dealt with in detail in chapter 2.

Upon his return to Sakya, and at the invitation of his teacher Sharpa Senge Bal, Dolpopa gave an extensive exposition to a large audience on the four major subjects of the perfection of transcendent knowledge, logical reasoning, cosmology and psychology, and monastic discipline. In the morning he taught cosmology and psychology, as well as the perfection of transcendent knowledge, and then after midday tea he taught both logical reasoning and monastic discipline. His teachings were received with unprecedented acclaim, although some criticized him for teaching too many texts at once.[21] By this time Dolpopa had obviously become a very promising young scholar of the Sakya school, and there would have been great expectations about his future career as a Sakya teacher.

In 1314, when Dolpopa was twenty-two years old, he embarked upon a tour of the teaching institutes of Tsang and Ü provinces, for the purpose of rounding out his education and meeting the best teachers in other regions of Tibet.[22] He had discussions and interviews with many masters, all of whom were very impressed with his intelligence and learning, and he received many predictions of future greatness. During this period he began to become famous and first received the epithet "Omniscient" (Kun mkhyen) because of his mastery of scriptures such as the *Śatasāhasrikā prajñāpāramitā*, the one-hundred-thousand line scripture on the perfection of transcendent knowledge. He continued to be known by this title for the rest of his life.[23] During this trip Dolpopa received full monastic ordination from the great abbot Sönam Trakpa (1273–1352) of Chölung monastery, who had earlier participated in the ordination of Budön Rinchen Drup and would later ordain the Sakya master

Lama Dampa Sönam Gyaltsen and his elder brother Dönyö Gyaltsen (1310–1344).[24] Dolpopa also made the vow at that time to never eat slaughtered meat for the rest of his life.

Dolpopa received numerous teachings of the Kagyü and Nyingma traditions during this journey, as well as the instructions of Severance (Gcod) and the Pacification of Suffering (Zhi byed).[25] While practicing these instructions, he continued to travel around to many temples and shrines in Ü and Tsang. In particular, he went to Lhasa and made prayers in the most holy temple of Tibet, the Jokhang. While there he composed a text for the ritual awakening of the enlightenment thought, as well as a verse praise to the Jowo image. He also made various special offerings in the Jokhang, some of which apparently became customary thereafter.[26] Perhaps it was on the return route through Tsang that Dolpopa visited the monastery of Trophu and made offerings and prayers at the great Maitreya image and the large stūpa there, both constructed by the Trophu translator Jampa Bal (1172–1236). In front of the great stūpa Dolpopa prayed that he would be able to build one like it, or even larger.[27] This prayer would be fulfilled in the near future.

According to Tāranātha, sometime at the end of this journey Dolpopa went back home to Dolpo and visited his family for about one year. Then he returned to Sakya, where he gave many initiations and spiritual instructions and performed the Hevajra retreat, which resulted in a vision of Hevajra and the eight goddesses. Up to the age of twenty-nine (1321) he had studied with more than thirty teachers, the most important of whom, Gyidön Jamyang Trakpa Gyaltsen, had bestowed upon him some seventy initiations and teachings.[28]

3. The Move to Jonang

In the year 1321, when he was twenty-nine years old, Dolpopa visited the monastery of Jonang for the first time.[29] In later years he often told his disciple and biographer Lhey Gyaltsen about his initial experience during that visit:

> However many scholars might gather, I had never been humbled, and my confidence just grew greater and greater. But when I went to Jonang and [saw] that every man and woman who was seriously practicing meditation had realized

the nature of reality through meditation, I was extremely humbled. An uncontrolled faith and pure vision was born towards them.[30]

According to Jetsun Tāranātha, Dolpopa then traveled to the central province of Ü. At the monastery of Tsurphu he met the third Karmapa, Rangjung Dorje (1284–1339), and had extensive discussions about Buddhist doctrine. Dolpopa's earlier experience at Jonang apparently acted as a catalyst, for in 1322, when he was thirty years old, he left Sakya and returned to Jonang to meet the master Yönden Gyantso (1260–1327) and request the complete transmission of the *Kālacakra tantra* and the many lineages of its perfection-stage practices, the Six-branch Yoga.[31] Dolpopa was by now a widely recognized master himself and was accompanied by an entourage of eight monks when he traveled to Jonang. In Sakya, on the night before Dolpopa arrived at Jonang, his teacher Kunpang Trakpa Gyaltsen dreamed of the bodhisattva Avalokiteśvara, surrounded by many monks, traveling to Jonang enveloped by light rays of the Dharma. And that same night, in Jonang itself, the master Yönden Gyantso dreamed of the Shambhala emperor Kalkin Puṇḍarīka raising the victory banner of the Buddhist teachings at Jonang. This auspicious dream caused Yönden Gyantso to give Dolpopa the complete Kālacakra initiation, the transmission of *The Bodhisattva Trilogy*, and the profound instructions (*zab khrid*) of the Six-branch Yoga.[32] He then offered the use of the hermitage of Khachö Deden to Dolpopa, who immediately entered into a meditation retreat.

Soon after this retreat Dolpopa's future disciple and biographer, Kunpang Chödrak Balzang, first met him at the monastery of Dzum Chölung, where Dolpopa was receiving instructions on the Great Perfection (*rdzogs chen*) and the Six Teachings of Nāropa (*nā ro chos drug*). Kunpang recognized that Dolpopa was very special and, upon his return to Jonang, invited him to the hermitage of Gyiphuk and requested many teachings from him, such as the great commentary on the *Kālacakra tantra*. He also stayed with Dolpopa constantly for the next year, serving as his personal attendant. That spring the master Yönden Gyantso convinced Dolpopa to teach in the assembly at Jonang and also bestowed upon him many more systems of esoteric knowledge, such as the Path and Result (Lam 'bras), the *Pañcakrama* of the *Guhyasamāja tantra* and of the *Cakrasamvara tantra*, the Pacification of Suffering (Zhi byed), the Severance Cycle (Gcod skor), and so forth. Then Dolpopa was invited to Sakya by Tishri Kunga Gyaltsen (1310–1358) of the Khön family line, and bestowed upon him the Kālacakra initiation.[33]

Upon returning to Jonang, Dolpopa began another strict retreat at Khachö Deden, meditating on the Six-branch Yoga for one year.[34] During this period of intense meditation he experienced the realization of the first four of the six branches. Kunpang describes the results of this retreat:

> On the basis of both Individual Withdrawal [*pratyāhāra*] and Mental Stability [*dhyāna*], he beheld innumurable figures of the buddhas and pure lands. On the basis of Breath Control [*prāṇāyāma*] and Retention [*dhāraṇā*], exceptional experience and realization was born due to the blazing of a blissful spiritual warmth.[35]

It was during this period that the realization of the Zhentong view first arose in Dolpopa's mind. However, according to Jetsun Tāranātha's guidebook to the Khachö Deden hermitage, Dolpopa stayed there for two to three years and perfected just the first three branches of the Six-branch Yoga. For the meditation practice, which requires total darkness for the detachment of the sense faculties from their objects, he no doubt used the dark room (*mun khang*) there.[36] Elsewhere Tāranātha describes the circumstances as follows:

> [Dolpopa] made the instructions on the Six-branch Yoga into experience. Except for when requesting the specific teachings, he stayed at Khachö Deden without meeting anyone. Since he perfected the experience and realization of Individual Withdrawal [*pratyāhāra*] and Mental Stability [*dhyāna*], the master [Yönden Gyantso] remarked, "I should give the instructions quickly," but [Dolpopa] asked to be guided carefully. When he meditated he gained the signs of the perfection of Breath Control [*prāṇāyāma*] just as explained in the [*Kālacakra*] *tantra.*[37]

Later in the same text Tāranātha makes this very significant statement:

> Although the exceptional view and meditation of the Zhentong was born in his mind while staying at Khachö Deden, he did not speak of it to others for several years.[38]

This retreat was the pivotal event in Dolpopa's spiritual development. But he would not communicate the Zhentong view to others until at least five more years had passed.[39]

At some time in 1325, after this retreat was over, the master Yönden Gyantso urged Dolpopa to become his Dharma heir and accept the leadership of Jonang monastery. This was completely at odds with Dolpopa's own desire to practice intensive meditation in isolated hermitages, without the responsibilities and restrictions that a monastic position would entail.[40] Before making his decision, he decided to travel to Lhasa in the spring of 1326, where he would make prayers in the Jokhang cathedral, requesting guidance from the holy image of Avalokiteśvara as to whether he could be of more benefit to the Buddhist tradition if he went into extended meditation retreat or took over the leadership of Jonang monastery. Miraculously, light rays in the form of a garland of lotus flowers shown forth from the heart of the image, which also spoke verses urging him to become the leader of Jonang in order to benefit the Doctrine.

Dolpopa returned to Jonang in the fall of 1326, and was formerly installed there as Yönden Gyantso's successor on the teaching throne.[41] From then on he assumed the lifestyle of his predecessors at Jonang, remaining only in meditation retreat throughout the summer and winter, and bestowing extensive teachings during the autumn and spring. He especially taught the *Kālacakra tantra*, *The Bodhisattva Trilogy (Sems 'grel skor gsum)*, the ten *Sūtras on the Buddha-nature* (*Snying po'i mdo*), the five *Sutras of Definitive Meaning* (*Nges don mdo*), the five *Treatises of Maitreya* (*Byams chos*), certain works of Nāgārjuna, and many esoteric instructions.[42] It is interesting to note that he is said to have taught all these texts in accord with Kalkin Puṇḍarīka's great commentary on the *Kālacakra tantra*.[43]

4. Raising Mt. Meru and Revealing the Zhentong View

Many years earlier, Kunpang Tukje Tsöndrü (1243–1313), the founder of Jonang monastery, had told his disciple Yönden Gyantso:

> At this hermitage of mine, there will come a grandson better than the son, and a great-grandson even better than the grandson. In the future [the great-grandson] will teach Dharma at upper Zangden and build a great stūpa at lower Zangden.[44]

When his master Yönden Gyantso passed away in 1327, Dolpopa decided to build a monumental stūpa in fulfillment of the prayer he had made before the great stūpa at Trophu, and in particular to repay his master's kindness. He also felt that the stūpa would become an object of worship for people who were not fortunate enough to engage in study, contemplation, and meditation, and therefore provide them with the opportunity to accumulate virtue.[45]

A large stūpa was first quickly built at upper Zangden in the spring of 1329, but it collapsed.[46] In the spring of 1330 the dimensions of the foundation for a gigantic stūpa were marked off at the new site of lower Zangden. Everyone around Dolpopa exclaimed that the dimensions were much too large and that it would be impossible to ever finish such an over-ambitious project. They were afraid that it would end up being a ruin of earth and stone and provide only a basis for ridicule from others.[47] In part, Dolpopa replied like this:

> When I first went on a tour of teaching institutes, I saw Trophu Lotsawa's stūpa and made many prayers with the force of intense faith. I saw many quotations in many sūtras and tantras [which stated] that the assemblies [of merit and gnosis] are perfected if one constructs huge images and stūpas. It is an exceptional basis of virtue for achieving meditative concentration on the nature of reality. There are few such individuals. If I think about the actual condition of sentient beings in general, an infinite compassion arises. There is no doubt that anyone who even sees, hears, or touches this stūpa will be freed, that the seed of liberation will be planted, and that vast benefit for others will occur. Those who oppose it will later be regretful.[48]

The construction of the stūpa was carried out in an atmosphere of incredible activity. Many skilled artisans and laborers of all description gathered from different regions of Tibet to contribute to the great work. Building materials and foodstuffs were brought in from all directions.[49] Kitchens and refreshment areas were set up for the many hundreds of workers who did the physical labor while chanting maṇis and praying to the masters of the lineage. Dolpopa himself sometimes carried earth and stones and sometimes worked on the building of the walls. He had a ramp built from the west side of the stūpa so donkeys could carry earth and stone up onto the main body of the structure, and long ramps made on the south and north sides so that those carrying loads could come up one side and then go down without their loads on the other. The artisans continually circled the structure, and if the work was even a little out of alignment it was completely torn down and rebuilt. As word of Dolpopa's project spread, great offerings of gold, silver, copper, iron, silk, tea, cloth, medicines, and so forth began to flow in to Jonang from all over the Tibetan world.[50]

By this time Dolpopa had gathered an exceptional group of yogins, scholars, and translators around him, among whom were Kunpang Chötrak Balzang, Mati Panchen Jamyang Lodrö (1294–1376), Lotsawa Lodrö Bal (1299–1353), and the great abbot Choley Namgyal (1306–1386). They all participated in the construction of the stūpa. Nyaön Kunga Bal (1285–1379) was probably also in attendance, since it seems that he completed his commentary on Dolpopa's *A General Commentry on the Doctrine* (*Bstan pa spyi 'grel*) at Jonang before the consecration of the stūpa in 1333.[51]

The intense physical labor of the external construction of the stūpa was accompanied by many extraordinary discourses by Dolpopa on the ultimate significance of the Buddha's doctrinal message. According to Kunpang, who witnessed the events, prior to the winter of 1330 the long central poles were placed in the stūpa and Dolpopa taught *The Bodhisattva Trilogy* to a huge assembly. On this occasion he took great pleasure in making, for the first time, the clear distinction between the relative as empty of self-nature (*rang stong*) and the absolute as empty of other relative phenomena (*gzhan stong*). Tāranātha, however, says that after laying the foundation for the stūpa and ascending the teaching throne of upper Zangden, Dolpopa first spoke of the Zhentong theory to an audience of about ten persons, and this was in the context of giving a detailed explication of the ten *Sūtras on the Buddha-nature*.[52] Whichever the case, it is clear that it was during the building of the stūpa, which Dolpopa himself linked to his realization, that he first openly taught the Zhentong and related topics.

The construction of the stūpa at Jonang was carefully based on descriptions found in the *Vimalaprabhā*, so that upon its completion it fulfilled all the criteria necessary to be considered the same as the Glorious Stūpa of the Lunar Mansions (*dpal ldan rgyu skar gyi mchod ldan*), in which the Buddha had first taught the *Kālacakra tantra*.[53] Dolpopa stated that his realization of "the absolute as empty of other, which was previously unknown in Tibet,"[54] arose due to the kindness of his teachers and the Triple Gem, whose blessings he had received because of his devotion to them and their representations, and because he had done what was to be done for the benefit of the Buddhist teachings. His biographer Lhey Gyaltsen is more specific, stating that Dolpopa's precise realization of the nature of absolute reality was due to "the blessings of his construction of inconceivable marvelous three-fold representations, such as those of the masters, buddhas, bodhisattvas, and the great stūpa (*sku 'bum chen po*)."[55] The connection between his realization of the Zhentong, the teachings of the *Kālacakra tantra*, and the stūpa of Jonang are made explicit by Dolpopa in a short series of verses speaking of his discovery:

> Alas, my share of good fortune may be inferior, but I think a discovery such as this is good fortune.
>
> Is this discovery by a lazy fool due to the blessing of the Kalkin emperor?
>
> Although I have not physically arrived at Kalāpa [court], has the Kalkin entered my faithful mind, or what?
>
> Although my intelligence has not been refined in three-fold knowledge, I think the raising of Mt. Meru has caused the Ocean to gush forth.[56]
>
> I bow in homage to the masters, buddhas, and kalkins by whose kindness the essential points which are difficult for even the exalted ones to realize are precisely realized, and to their great stūpa.[57]

The raising of Mt. Meru is a reference to Dolpopa's construction of the massive stūpa, and the Ocean that flowed forth from the blessings and energy awakened during that endeavor was his most famous work, *The Ocean of Definitive Meaning*: *A Mountain Dharma* (*Ri chos nges don rgya mtsho*). Although not itself dated, this great treatise was perhaps completed even before the final consecration of the stūpa on October 30, 1333, since it is mentioned in the commentary to Dolpopa's *A General Commentary on the Doctrine* (*Bstan pa spyi 'grel*), apparently completed by his disciple Nyaön Kunga Bal on May or June 30, 1333.[58] Thus it is clear that the external construction of the great monument was for Dolpopa a reflection of the simultaneous internal process, which produced a number of his most significant literary works.

5. The Initial Reception of the Zhentong Teachings

Following his first proclamation of the Zhentong view, Dolpopa wrote a number of minor works to explain it. But according to Tāranātha, when these works were first circulated they were incomprehensible to most scholars because of the unusual Dharma language (*chos skad*) Dolpopa was introducing. The scholars no doubt experienced a degree of hermeneutical shock when confronted with writings that they could not easily fit into any familiar category.[59] However, in another text Tāranātha states that when Dolpopa proclaimed the Zhentong doctrine, all who were fortunate and courageous were delighted by it. It was not until much later that the adherents of the Sakya, Geluk, Gadam, Zhalu, Bodong, and some followers of the Nyingma tradition experienced heart seizure (*snying gas*) and scrambled brains (*klad pa 'gems pa*) upon hearing about the Zhentong philosophical system (*grub mtha'*).[60]

Writing some three hundred years after the event, the Sakya master Jamgön Amey Zhap (1597–1659) claimed that a large part of the negative reaction was outrage on the part of Sakya scholars who felt betrayed when Dolpopa began to teach the unprecedented Zhentong position, which contradicted the teachings of the founding fathers of Sakya. In this context, it should be remembered that Jonang was considered an affiliate monastery of the Sakya school. Dolpopa had been educated as a Sakya monk, and up until this point in his career had accepted the ancient teachings of that tradition.[61] Amey Zhap's opinion that all Sakya scholars totally rejected Dolpopa's theories is certainly an exaggeration, since it is known that his own ancestors, Tishri Kunga Gyaltsen and his two sons Da En Chögyi Gyaltsen (1332-1359) and Da En Lodrö Gyaltsen (1332-1364), as well as Dönyö Gyaltsen and his brother Lama Dampa Sönam Gyaltsen, all requested teachings from Dolpopa. Tāranātha, the seventeenth-century leader of the Jonang tradition, remarks that all those who came to Jonang to discuss the issues with Dolpopa gained confidence in his theories and faith in him. Others who sent written objections and refutations were said to have gained understanding upon receiving his well-reasoned replies.[62]

A very clear example of this is related by Barawa Gyaltsen Balzang (1310–1391), who studied with both Dolpopa and Budön Rinchen Drup. Barawa had doubts about some points concerning Dolpopa's distinction between the universal ground gnosis (*kun gzhi ye shes*) and the universal ground consciousness (*kun gzhi rnam shes*) and sent written questions to Dolpopa and some of his main disciples. He received answers from the disciples but his doubts were not resolved. Later he received a response from Dolpopa which was much more satisfying but different from what the great disciples had said. Finally, he was able to meet with Dolpopa at the hermitage of Sakya Chuzang to discuss the points in question.[63] Dolpopa's explanations were consistent with his previous written answer and Barawa realized the true import of his teachings.[64] In this way, after establishing his viewpoint through discussion with many different scholars, Dolpopa composed his major works, such as *The Ocean of Definitive Meaning: A Mountain Dharma* (*Ri chos nges don rgya mtsho*).[65]

6. The New Jonang Translation of the *Kālacakra Tantra* and the *Vimalaprabhā*

In 1334, while staying in the Jonang hermitage of Dewacen, Dolpopa ordered his disciples Lotsawa Lodrö Bal and Mati Panchen Jamyang Lodrö Gyaltsen to prepare a revised translation of the *Kālacakra tantra* and its commentary, the *Vimalaprabhā*.[66] At the request of his disciple and biographer Kunpang Chötrak Balzang, Dolpopa himself then composed a topical outline (*sa bcad*) and annotations (*mchan bu*) to the *Vimalaprabhā*. Unfortunately, Dolpopa's annotations and topical outline are not found in his recently published writings.[67] Further important information about the circumstances of the new Jonang translation (*jo nang gsar 'gyur*) is found in the colophon to the Jonang revision of Shongdön Dorje Gyaltsen's earlier translation:[68]

> Later the splendid and excellent master, the Omniscient Dharma Lord, and Dharmakīrtiśrībhadra, a great adept of Śrī Kālacakra, carefully pondered the meaning of this [tantra]. Compelled by their orders, and according to their teachings, Lodrö Gyaltsen and Lodrö Balzangpo, Buddhist monk translators who know how to correctly translate due to the kind-

> ness of the great scholar Sthiramati,[69] consulted many Indian mansucripts of the tantra and commentary, and translated, checked and established it in agreement with those which were correct.[70]

Some years after this new revised translation was completed, a translator by the name of Sherab Rinchen asked Dolpopa some questions about the Kālacakra tradition in Tibet, and Dolpopa made this comment about the Jonang translation:

> The pair of translators [named] Lodrö also revised the translation, once again discovering many excellent [points] in addition to the previous excellent ones. And from establishing it again and again through much explication, study, and meditation, there were many discoveries of the profound intent of the tantra commentary, as well as of the esoteric instructions. From the construction and supplication of the stūpa of all the masters, Victors, and spiritual sons, the natural language of the profound ultimate became perfectly obvious, and the secret wording of the profound tantras became perfectly obvious.[71]

A very interesting discussion of the Jonang translation of the *Kālacakra tantra* and its commentary is provided by Jonang Kunga Drolchok, one of Dolpopa's successors on the throne of Jonang monastery. In his biography of Rikden Namgyal Trakzang (1395–1475), the master physician, Kālacakra adept, and religious king of the northern province of Chang, Kunga Drolchok records the opinions of Chamling Panchen Sönam Namgyal (1400–1475) in regard to the revision ordered by Dolpopa:[72]

> The Omniscient Budön also took the Shong translation [of the *Kālacakra tantra* and *Vimalaprabhā*][73] as the fundamental text for explication, and made the statement, "There are about thirty points here which are unsuitable to leave uncorrected."[74] Accordingly, the great Omniscient Buddha from Dolpo gave the order to the two translators, and when they were making the new translation all the revisions which had been made in the earlier annotations by Budön were left alone.[75] Other than that, they perfected the natural language of the definitely ultimate [points] by virtue of reliance upon the

> meaning.[76] After nailing it down with the Dol annotations themselves, [Dolpopa] opened up the clearest of the clear chariot-ways with extensive commentaries upon the essential meaning, such as *The Ocean of Definitive Meaning* [*Nges don rgya mtsho*], *A General Commentry on the Doctrine* [*Bstan pa spyi 'grel*], and *The Fourth Council* [*Bka' bsdu bzhi pa*].[77] I am confident there is certainly no one who has commented upon the *Śrī* [*Kālacakra*] *tantra* better than this, even to the north in Shambhala. The production of explication and composition in regard to all the general fields of the Doctrine was somewhat greater for Budön, but in the context of gathering together the definitive secrets of the *Kālacakra* alone, he certainly did not match the rain of Dolpopa.[78]

The new Jonang translation (*jo nang gsar 'gyur*) was certainly an important part of Dolpopa's attempt to establish and spread his Zhentong theory and the related interpretations of doctrine and practice.[79] The *Kālacakra tantra* and the *Vimalaprabhā* were the ultimate scriptural basis for Dolpopa's innovative teachings, and in discussions with his bilingual disciples, he had no doubt found reason to feel that the earlier Tibetan translation of Dro Lotsawa Sherab Trak as revised by Shongdön Dorje Gyaltsen, did not allow the true meaning of the most profound definitive sense (*nītārtha, nges don*) to shine forth. Dolpopa had just finished the construction of the great stūpa at Jonang in 1333. The composition of his most influential work, *The Ocean of Definitive Meaning: A Mountain Dharma* (*Ri chos nges don rgya mtsho*), had perhaps only recently been completed. Dolpopa, who was not himself ignorant of Sanskrit, was surrounded by capable translators (*lo tsā ba*), such as his disciples Mati Panchen, Lotsawa Lodrö Bal, Kunpang Chötrak Balzang, and Drikung Lotsawa Maṇikaśrī, all of whom were great practitioners of the Six-branch Yoga and scholars of the Kālacakra. Pang Lotsawa Lodrö Denpa (1276–1342), often regarded as the most influential master of Sanskrit grammatical studies in Tibet, had also expressed the greatest admiration for Dolpopa.[80]

It is striking that two of the greatest masters of the Kālacakra in Tibetan history, Dolpopa and Budön, were exact contemporaries, and lived in the same general area of Tsang, with many of the same teachers, and many of the same disciples. Some time before the new Jonang translation in 1334 Budön had completed his own extensive annotations to Shongdön's translation of the *Kālacakra tantra* and the *Vimalaprabhā*, and was teaching these texts and annotations every year.[81] Dolpopa decided to order a new revised translation in which the points he was trying to illustrate were more clearly brought forth, and then composed annotations. He clearly stated his motivations for composing both the annotations and the synopsis of the *Vimalaprabhā*:

> Since all the essential points of the profound definitive meaning were discovered in the great commentary of the *Kālacakra*, it has been remarkably kind. To prevent mistakes in regard to the basic treatise [of the *Vimalaprabhā*] I have also composed a synopsis and exceptional annotations, as well as many other texts.[82]

Dolpopa's annotations to the *Vimalaprabhā* were substantial enough to be referred to first among all his works in a list compiled by Lhey Gyaltsen, implying that they were the most important of his thirty-eight works on the *Kālacakra*.[83] Dolpopa apparently felt that his annotations to the *Vimalaprabhā* were an awesome accomplishment. The following quotation reveals more about Dolpopa himself than about the annotations.

> Looking at the annotations to the great commentary upon the [*Kālacakra*] *tantra*, the Dharma Lord [Dolpopa] himself exclaimed, "Ah la la! Whose work are all these? They're incredible!"
>
> Joining his palms together again and again, he said, "When I look at this kind of an understanding of the profound definitive meaning, I wonder who I [really] am."[84]

This is not simple arrogance. Dolpopa was a master adept of the Six-branch Yoga, the perfection stage of the *Kālacakra tantra*. He was inspired by the Kalkin emperors of Shambhala, and was generally viewed as an incarnation of the Shambhala emperor Kalkin Puṇḍarīka, the author of the *Vimalaprabhā*. It is also quite certain that Dolpopa believed himself to be Puṇḍarīka reborn.[85]

7. Years of Retreat and Teaching

In the years following the completion of the Jonang stūpa, Dolpopa traveled to many different areas, where he mostly stayed in meditation retreat. But he also constructed a large number of shrines, closely examined the scriptures in the Tibetan canon, and wrote many significant treatises. During this period he experienced a number of visions, both of pure lands and specific tantric deities.[86] In particular, he directly beheld the pure land of Shambhala, the source of the Kālacakra teachings, and on another occasion claimed to have actually gone there by visionary means.[87] Kunpang states that Dolpopa also composed a large number of texts while staying in the hermitage of Gyiphuk at Jonang.[88]

By now Dolpopa was acknowledged as one of the paramount Buddhist masters in Tibet. Letters of praise had been received from the master Dönyö Gyaltsen of the Sakya Khön family, and he had received offerings of gold from the Sakya Tishri Kunga Gyaltsen, and a golden maṇḍala from the third Karmapa, Rangjung Dorje.[89]

In the fall of the Mouse year (1336) Dolpopa was invited to return and teach at Sakya monastery. There he gave extensive teachings to several thousand people, at the end of which he engaged in much debate about philosophical viewpoints. Using the sūtras and tantras as witnesses, especially the set of *Prajñāpāramitā sūtras*, he distinguished between relative and absolute truth by means of the categories of an emptiness of self-nature (*rang stong*) and an emptiness of other (*gzhan stong*).[90]

In the Earth-Tiger year (1338) Dolpopa retired from the leadership of Jonang monastery, and appointed Lotsawa Lodrö Bal as his successor. Lodrö Bal would remain on the teaching throne of Jonang for the next seventeen years.[91]

8. Invitation to China by the Yüan Emperor Toghon Temür

In the ninth month of the Monkey year (1344), when Dolpopa was fifty-two years old and Lotsawa Lodrö Bal had held the throne of Jonang for seven years, the Mongolian imperial envoys Dzambhala Tushri and Bhate Tshe En arrived in Tsang with imperial decrees issued by the Yüan dynasty emperor Toghon Temür to invite both Dolpopa and Budön to China.[92] Neither Dolpopa nor Budön accepted the imperial invitations, and both retreated to isolated hermitages for meditation. According to Lhey Gyaltsen, Toghon Temür was extremely displeased with the refusal, and Dolpopa was very much afraid that another summons would come.[93] To avoid such a possibility, he stayed in different isolated areas for the next four years.[94] At the end of that period a message came from the emperor allowing him to remain in Tibet, and telling him to work for the Buddhist Doctrine in his own country.[95]

The version of these events according to Lhey Gyaltsen is quite straightforward, but Kunpang introduces an entirely different tone into his narration. In fact, it is very difficult to determine whether the events he describes are to be understood as referring to the established invitation of 1344, or to a later and otherwise unknown invitation from the Chinese emperor.[96] According to this very extensive account, an eminent Chinese scholar named Dzala Kara heard about Dolpopa during a visit to Lhasa.[97] Upon his return to China he was summoned to the Keshamkara Palace by the emperor Jampey Khorlo, and asked about who was the most famous scholar in Ü and Tsang. Dzala Kara praised Dolpopa above all. The emperor sent a large party, including Dzala Kara, Lopön Tsakura, fifty couriers led by Dzakara, four athletes such as Langchen Padma, and a great deal of offerings, to secretly invite Dolpopa to China. When they arrived in Jonang, Dolpopa conversed with Dzala Kara in Chinese, and finally agreed to come. He told them to meet him in Lhasa after three months, and the Chinese traveled there without anyone knowing.

According to this version, in a Monkey year (which may be understood as 1344) Dolpopa is said to have told his senior disciples Kunpang Chötrak Bal, Sazang Mati Panchen, Changtse Lotsawa, and Maṇika Shri to accompany him on a visit to Lhasa to pray before the famous images of the Jowo and the Shākyamuni.[98] He told Lotsawa Lodrö Bal to uphold the leadership position at Jonang until his return[99] and set off for Lhasa in a sandalwood chariot. In Lhasa prayers were directed to the sacred images, and the replies indicated that it would be disastrous for Dolpopa to go to China. But out of compassion for the Chinese he agreed to go. During this time Dolpopa's senior disciple Rintsulwa (1297-1368) made an exceptional image of Dolpopa, which the master himself agreed to consecrate.[100] There is then a lengthy description of events which culminate in the Depa Tsenyi and Changpa king mobilizing the armies of Ü and Tsang to prevent the Chinese from taking Dolpopa away to China. Finally Dolpopa gives a long and very interesting versified teaching on the specific philosophical views of the non-Buddhists and the Buddhists, to be taken back to China for the edification of the emperor, whom he refers to as Mandzu Gyalpo Chenpo, the Great Mañjuśrī King.[101] Later Dolpopa is said to have taken pity upon the distraught Chinese, and traveled to the imperial court by magical means and pleased the emperor.

There are many problems with this story, which cannot be dealt with in detail here. It would seem that the actual events of the invitation of 1344 and a later trip by Dolpopa to Ü in the years 1358-1360 have been conflated, and then a good deal of extra material added from unknown sources. For example, the final events of Dolpopa's chariot being stuck in the mud and the Chinese strongmen being unable to move it has distinct overtones of the nearly mythic events found in *The Compilation of Manis* (*Ma ṇi bka' 'bum*), where the chariot of the Chinese princess which is carrying the Jowo image is stuck in the sand outside of Lhasa and cannot be budged by the Chinese strongmen.[102]

9. Changes in the Jonang Leadership and the Beginning of the Journey to Lhasa

In the Wood-Horse year (1354) Lotsawa Lodrö Bal passed away. He had occupied the teaching throne at Jonang for seventeen years. Dolpopa returned to Jonang and led the funeral services, after which he appointed his disciple Choley Namgyal (1306–1386) to the leadership position. He would remain on the teaching throne for the next four years.[103] Choley Namgyal was already the Dharma master at the Ngamring institute which had been apparently founded, or perhaps expanded, earlier the same year by Dolpopa, with the support of the Chang ruler Dai En Namkha Denpa (b. 1316). Namkha Denpa insisted that Choley Namgyal also retain the leadership position of the Ngamring institute for as long as he was on the teaching throne at Jonang.[104]

During the preceding years Dolpopa had given religious teachings to many of the greatest luminaries of the Tibetan intellectual and political world. Among them were the Sakya master of the Zhitok line,[105] Kunpang (d. 1357),[106] the Grand Governer (*dpon chen*) Gyalzang (d. 1357), Changpa Siddhi, and Yakde Panchen (1299–1378).[107] During the tenure of Choley Namgyal on the Jonang teaching throne, Dolpopa mostly stayed in the Jonang area.[108] On one occasion he sent out word that he was growing old, and that those who wished to receive his last teachings should gather at Jonang. Foremost among the many hundreds who came were Kunpang Chötrak Balzang, Sharpa Rinchen Gyaltsen (1306?–1355?),[109] Mati Panchen Lodrö Gyaltsen, the great abbot Choley Namgyal, the abbot of Nedruk, the master Gyaltsen Jungney, and the Kālacakra master Dorje Nyingpo.[110]

Soon thereafter Dolpopa was invited by the abbot Chimdön Lozang Trakpa (1299–1375) to teach at the ancient Gadam monastery of Nartang.[111] He gave to the dialecticians there an extensive explanation of the distinction between the two truths, emphasizing that true experts do not cling to the nonexistent relative as existing, nor to the existing absolute as nonexisting, but abide in the middle beyond extremes.[112]

By the end of 1358 the burden of being the head of both Jonang monastery and the institute at Ngamring was too heavy for Choley Namgyal. With the permission of Dolpopa he gave up both positions at the same time. Another of Dolpopa's senior disciples, Gönchok Gyaltsen, was then enthroned as Choley Namgyal's successor at Jonang in the first month of the Pig year (1359).[113]

Dolpopa had become increasingly disturbed by the extensive damage to the Buddhist communities, temples, and shrines in Tibet due to the great political turmoil that had swept through the land during the protracted power struggle between the Sakya rulers in Tsang and the newly arisen Phagmodru in Ü. He decided that the only thing that would help was to travel to Lhasa and make prayers to the Jowo image there, which he felt to be the same as the Buddha himself.[114] Dolpopa was now sixty-six years old, and had become extremely heavy (*sku sha lcis pa*) in his later years, so that it was very difficult for him to travel. His body was about twice the size of an average person (*phal pa nyis 'gyur tsam gyis sku che*), and his physical presence dominated any gathering, even when there were hundreds of people. Important and charismatic figures became like children when they arrived before him. When he departed from Jonang on the sixteenth day of the fifth month of the Earth-Dog year (1358), he traveled by boat down the Tsangpo river, stopping at different places along the banks, and giving extensive religious teachings. He stayed for one year at the monasteries of Neysar and Chölung, where he gave many teachings.[115] Lama Dampa Sönam Gyaltsen, the fifteenth Patriarch of Sakya, came to meet Dolpopa at Chölung, received teachings, and asked him to compose *The Fourth Council* (*Bka' bsdu bzhi pa*) and its autocommentary.[116]

When further invitations to Ü arrived from the Tshalpa ruler and Dolpopa's senior disciples such as the masters Tangpoche and Bumchenpa, he set off by palanquin in the fourth month of the Earth-Pig year (1359).[117] He proceeded slowly through Tsang and into Ü, receiving lavish welcomes from all the people and the clergy, who lined up in the roads to greet him and escort him into the different monasteries. The crowds were often so large that people at the edges could not hear the teaching, so it had to be relayed through an interpreter (*lo tstsha ba cug gin gsungs*). When he taught at Dölung Namgyal monastery in Ü, where his disciple Rintsulwa had been abbot since 1354, the Duensha Zhönu Gyaltsen and his entourage received teachings at the head of a crowd of many hundreds of people.[118]

10. Teachings in Central Tibet and the Return to Tsang

At the end of the sixth month of the same year, Dolpopa finally arrived in Lhasa. He offered gold for the guilding of the images of the Jowo and the Shākyamuni, and used three hundred loads of butter to offer butter lamps in the shrines. He stayed for about six months at Marpori, Traklha Luphuk, and the Ramoche.[119] In particular, Dolpopa gave the instructions of the profound path of the Six-branch Yoga many times to countless teachers who came from many different monasteries. It was obviously an incredible scene. So many people came to request Dharma teachings that they could not fit into the buildings. When some persons who had never received instructions were unable to hear, the newcomers were allowed to come in first. Then as many others as could fit into the building were allowed to enter. Since there were too many requesting teachings, and too many having strange physical experiences (*lus nyams*), Dolpopa had to come out from the Ramoche Khangsar and stay at Zhol. There were so many people listening to the teachings that doors were broken and stairways collapsed. Even the extreme measure of tying dogs at the head of the stairways to prevent too many people from entering was ineffective in controlling the crowds.[120]

On one occasion Dolpopa was invited with great ceremony to the nearby monastery of Tshal Gungtang. There he gave the great initiation of Kālacakra, and many other teachings, to the ruler

Delek. Then he taught outside of the monastery, again utilizing an interpreter to relay the teachings to the outskirts of the huge crowd. At another time, when Dolpopa was sitting before the precious Jowo image in the cathedral of Lhasa, the ruler Geway Lodrö (d. 1364) came and requested initiation. But when the ruler Lhundrubpa invited him to Lagong the crowds were so great in the daytime that Dolpopa had to go in secret at night, and bestow the Hayagrīva initiation to a group led by Gewey Lodrö. He also had to go to request blessings from the Jowo image at night because there were more people than could fit into the marketplace crowded around the temple during the day.[121]

At the end of the first month of the Mouse year (1360), a party arrived to invite Dolpopa back to Jonang. The people of Lhasa were distraught at the thought of his departure. When he reached Garchung Gyede, the plain of Gyang was filled with a crowd of people and horses. His palanquin could not even get through, so that many members of the Sangha had to join hands in a circle around it and the crowd of people requesting blessings had to join hands and go single-file under his palanquin. It was like this up until he reached Chukha. The members of the Sangha were reciting supplications, such as *A General Commentary on the Doctrine (Bstan pa spyi 'grel),*[122] while the entire mass of people were hysterically wailing. Most of the crowd had lost their senses, and many could not even walk. The sun was warm and the sky was clear, but the atmosphere was filled with rainbows. When Dolpopa got into a boat to cross the river, many people jumped into the water after him, and had to be saved by others.

After passing through the lower Sang valley, where he was hosted by the leaders and Sangha of the upper and lower colleges of Sangphu monastery, he crossed the river at the ferry landing of Nyan Kharnak. At the instruction of Lama Dampa Sönam Gyaltsen, he was then escorted with music and a procession of monks to Nyetang. There again the crowds were so large that when he went to visit the stūpa of Atiśa in the monastery the gate to the courtyard was blocked with people, and his palanquin was lifted up and the crowd scrambled under it to receive his blessings. Then he crossed the Gyi river and worshiped at the obelisk of Üshang Do. At Chushul Drugu Gang he was welcomed by Lama Bado, and many of the shrine objects of Sinpori were brought down to Chushul for Dolpopa to receive their blessings.[123]

Then Dolpopa was invited to Rabtsun by a procession of monks, and according to the advice of Lopön Situpa (1302-1364), Lopön Balrin and his attendants came and received Dharma teachings.[124] From there Dolpopa was escorted to Yamdrog Nagartse by Lopön Lochenpa and stayed for about one month, giving teachings and initiations. The people of Yamdrog bore his palanquin and escorted him through the Kharo pass and as far as the Om plain. There he was welcomed by the ruler Phakpa (1318–1370) and escorted by the monks to Ralung monastery, where he gave many teachings. He spent several days at the medicinal springs of Nyingro and then stopped to teach at Nenying and other monasteries along the way.

According to Tāranātha's history of the Nyang region, the ruler Phakpa Balzang and his younger brother Phakpa Rinchen (1320-1376) had for some time wished to request Dharma teachings from Dolpopa, and so they now invited him to Jangra. Because of his weight (*sku sha 'byor pa*), it was too difficult for Dolpopa to climb the long stairs up to Jangra, so he stayed for a long time below on the battlefield (*g.yul thang*) of Dzingka, where he spread out a huge silk maṇḍala of Kālacakra, performed the preliminary offering rites, and then bestowed a very extensive Kālacakra initiation. At this time Dolpopa also had a vision of the nearby mountain slope of Tsechen as the palace of Shambhala, and prophesied that in the future there would be a monastery there in which only the Six-branch Yoga would be practiced. When Dolpopa left Jangra, he was escorted to Neysar by Phakpa Balzang, during which time he instructed the ruler, "Honor the Buddha as permanent, the Dharma as true, and the Sangha as infallible! It will always be beneficial, now and in the future, and your realm will also be stable."[125]

11. The Aborted Meeting with Budön Rinchen Drup

Dolpopa was next invited to Zhalu and Tshokdü, where he taught a massive gathering, utilizing an interpreter to relay the teachings as he had before in Ü.[126] Several Tibetan sources mention that when Dolpopa arrived at Zhalu the master Budön was unable to debate with him. For example, in his history of Buddhism written in 1581, Drukchen Payma Garpo says:

> There is the story that when Budön was staying at Riphuk [Dolpopa] came to debate, but Budön was unable. [Dolpopa]

> enunciated the opening exclamation for debate, which cracked [the wall of Budön's] residence. This is not in other sources. I think it is from the experiences of Jonang meditators.[127]

Jetsun Tāranātha later refers to the same story, but places it in a less confrontational context, saying that it is known that Dolpopa wished to hold discussions with Budön, the "Second Omniscient One," but that the great Budön was unable to debate. Tāranātha then states that this story is in fact true (*don la gnas*).[128]

Kunpang's biography of Dolpopa is certainly the original source for these accounts.[129] He says that Dolpopa went to Zhalu after receiving a letter from Budön. He was well received there and also made generous gifts in return. Then he sent a message to Budön, who was apparently at his nearby residence of Riphuk and not in Zhalu itself, saying that he had received his previous letter, had arrived in Zhalu, and now felt that the time had come to hold discussions for the benefit of the Buddhist Doctrine and sentient beings. Those at Zhalu, such as Jamyang Garpo, were frightened, and spoke to Budön. He was also apprehensive, and told one of his attendants to pick a volume of scripture at random and open it in order to divine the auspices of the situation. The volume was opened in the *Mahāberī sūtra ('Phags pa rnga bo che)*. When Budön asked for it to be read, it turned out to be the very passage that was considered to be the prophecy of Dolpopa's appearance in the world. In the situation, this was considered very inauspicious. Everyone was frightened by this event, and after some discussion, three white conch shells, two gold images, and many other offerings were presented to Dolpopa, and he was told that Budön was not in good health. But Dolpopa knew what was going on, and enunciated the opening exclamation for debate (*thal skad*), the force of which was said to have produced a crack in the wall of Budön's residence.

After leaving the Zhalu area Dolpopa was again invited to Nartang, and taught *The Small Lotus Commentary* (*'Grel chung padma can*) to the abbot and others.[130] On that occasion the abbot rose and made an impassioned speech about his undivided faith in Dolpopa. Then the party from Jonang, led by the throne-holder, arrived to escort him back home.[131] Dolpopa continued to stop along the way and give teachings. In particular, he stayed for a while at the monastery of Trophu, and offered butter lamps at the huge image of Maitreya and at the stūpa that had inspired him to build his own at Jonang. In front of the Maitreya image he asked for the biography of Trophu Lotsawa to be read, which caused him to weep for a long time. As the procession of about one hundred persons continued towards Jonang, he taught in all the large and small monasteries. It was clearly a very emotional scene, with great crowds of people escorting him through the valleys, chanting the six-syllable mantra of Avalokiteśvara, making prayers, and weeping from faith. Along the road people usually received Dolpopa's blessing by going under his palanquin, instead of being touched on the head by the hand of the master.[132]

12. The Last Months at Jonang

On the sixteenth day of the fifth month of the Mouse year (1360) Dolpopa arrived back at the great hermitage of Jonang in excellent health. The large offerings that had been received in Ü were used for the decoration of the stūpa and various temples. Dolpopa stayed in meditation at his residence of Dewacen, after bestowing gifts and teachings upon the many persons who came from all directions to see him, such as the great master Drung Zhitokpa, the splendid Panchenpa, the great abbot Namkha Yeshe, the master abbot, and the great ruler.[133] Then Dolpopa went to Dzum Chölung, and built a Victory Stūpa (*rnam rgyal mchod rten*). He also experienced a vision of the Indian adept Śavaripa, who gave him a direct transmission of the Six-branch Yoga.[134] Then he returned to Jonang in the sixth month.

In the autumn of the Iron-Ox year (1361), when Dolpopa was sixty-nine years old, the Jonang throne-holder left for a visit to Sakya.[135] Dolpopa gave various instructions to his senior disciples, and made some comments about the cold weather in Tibet, and how he would not be bothered by it in a warm place. One of his attendants asked him where he was going that was warm. He replied that he was going to Dewacen (Sukhāvatī), where it was warm. Some of those in attendance understood this to mean that he was just going to his residence, which was called Dewacen, but some understood him to mean the pure land of Dewacen, and their hairs stood on end.[136]

On the fourth day of the eleventh month Dolpopa began to teach his great work *The Ocean of Definitive Meaning* (*Nges don rgya mtsho*) to those in the monastic assembly. He also began to give instructions on the preliminary practices to a group of newcomers. On the sixth day he had finished about half of *The Ocean of Definitive Meaning*, and when the teaching session was over he told the students that this was all he would teach, and to take good care of the text. To the newcomers, he taught all four of the preliminaries that day, in great detail. He seemed more radiant and healthy than ever before. He gave them extensive advice, and everyone wept from faith. After dispersing, they said to each other, "Why was the master gazing up into space, and why did he seem so energized?"[137]

Then Dolpopa said he was going to the stūpa. His attendants told him that snow had fallen and the path was not safe. He told them they didn't understand, that it was necessary for him to go.[138] But they insisted that it was unsafe, and assisted him to his residence. Tea was served, and his attendant was sent to summon the elder disciples for some private conversation. They gathered before him, and he gave them a detailed explanation of the "powerful tenfold anagram."[139] That evening he was pleased with everyone, and there was much joking and laughing. Then he went to sleep. After one period of the night had passed he asked his attendant, the monk Ngödrup, "Is it dawn yet?"

The attendant told him the night was not even half over. Dolpopa said, "It should be dawn soon," and went back to sleep.

When the attendant got up, he said, "Now it's dawn."

Dolpopa replied, "Yes. Help with my robes."

The attendant served him, and after a little while said, "Will you stand up now?"

Dolpopa didn't say anything. The attendant thought he was in meditation and didn't ask again. When the sun came up, the attendant pulled at Dolpopa's hand, and said "Will you stand up now?"

Dolpopa sat staring straight ahead, appearing to be in deep meditation, and didn't say anything. When this happened the attendant called for some of the elder and more experienced disciples. They thought maybe he was affected by the intense cold, and took him out into the sun and massaged him. After about midday his eyes closed, and without any sign of illness he passed into deep meditation. He was then taken back into his quarters and attended to in every way. After a few minutes he adjusted his position into that of Vajrasattva and passed away into bliss.

When he heard the news, the great abbot Choley Namgyal sent word that he was coming to see Dolpopa's body. The body was kept on Dolpopa's bed for several days, and some senior disciples, such as Drung Zhitokpa, visited and made offerings.[140] There were offerings, prostrations, and circumambulations made throughout the day and night. After Choley Namgyal arrived, Dolpopa's body was put into a wooden casket, which was anointed with perfume and adorned with silk and precious ornaments and placed inside the crematorium. The body was extemely flexible, like a piece of cotton-wool.[141] From the twenty-first day until the full moon, services were conducted by more than one hundred masters, led by Lama Panchenpa, the great abbot, the throne-holder, and others.[142]

On the evening of the sixth day of the first month of the Tiger year (1362), the cremation ceremony was performed. When the corpse was offered into the fire, the smoke rose up only about the length of a spear, then went to the stūpa like a streaking arrow, circled it many times, and finally disappeared to the west. At that time huge offerings of incense, butter lamps, music, and so forth were made. In particular, the men and women practitioners offered butter lamps on the roofs of their individual meditation huts, so that all the valley sparkled. Until the smoke had faded away, each of them made prayers with tears flowing down their faces.

The next morning the crematorium was sealed. When it was later opened on the tenth day, some remains were distributed to the disciples who had received the transmission of the *Vimalaprabhā* from Dolpopa. Among the ashes were many relics (*ring bsrel*) that were clear like crystal. Later countless others appeared. Then many votive images (*tsha tsha*) covered with gold leaf were made from the remains.

When many of the votive images and relics were taken to Sakya, they were welcomed with music and a great yellow procession of the Sangha led by the master of the Sharpa family of Sakya. Offerings were made to the relics by all of Dolpopa's disciples and patrons in the Genden Temple, and a fine memorial ceremony was held in the main Sakya assembly. Similar ceremonies were held in many monasteries throughout Ü and Tsang, such as Nartang, Chölung, Neysar, and Tshal Gungtang.[143] At Jonang, ashes from the cremation were gathered and put along with other relics into an image of Dolpopa that was placed in the great stūpa he had built.[144]

By the end of his life Dolpopa's influence on the Tibetan spiritual and intellectual scene was immense. Although his teachings were extremely controversial he had taught them to others with an attitude of great love and compassion. Eyewitness accounts mention that even when he was criticizing perverse philosophical opinions he never did so in an angry manner, and in Dharma discussions which entailed the identification of opponents, wrong positions, and so forth, he never used harsh words, or made physically aggressive gestures.[145] Moreover, although he lived during a time in which there was great political turmoil in Tibet, he had never taken sides, except to take a strong stand against all prejudice and bias. He had once commented: "Here at Jonang we do not take any sides. Buddhahood is not reached through prejudicial Dharma. And thus we do not take part in worthless evil. Like the clouds in the sky, we do not take any sides."[146] This sentiment is further indicated at the end of many of his works, which often ended with the phrase "composed by the impartial and unbiased author endowed with the four reliances."[147] Due to this attitude he is said to have become an object of worship for everyone. In short, he was a great Buddhist saint whose main goal in life was to revive the definitive meaning of the Buddha's message, which he felt was in great danger of being lost. Fully conscious of the risks involved in such an attempt to redirect the dominant trends in the Buddhism of his time, he tried to accomplish his aim with love and compassion, while emphasizing a lack of sectarian bias. Nevertheless, his tradition would suffer greatly in the future from some of the very forces he sought to counter during his lifetime.

2

A Historical Survey of the Zhentong Tradition in Tibet

> This advice by the Omniscient Dolpopa should be kept as the essential point in our hearts: "If buddhahood will be reached merely as a result of having heard the word 'Buddha-nature,' what need to mention what will happen from actualizing it by means of faith and devotion, and meditating upon it? Therefore, compassionate experts should teach it even though they may lose their lives, and so forth, and those who strive for liberation should seek it out and listen to it even though they must cross through a great pit of fire."
>
> —Jamgön Kongdrul[1]

Very little is known about the early Tibetan proponents of philosophical points of view which would later come to be known as Zhentong (*gzhan stong*). According to Lhey Gyaltsen, many persons with partial realization of the teachings of definitive meaning had appeared in Tibet before the fourteenth century, most of them serious meditators, but no one until Dolpopa had mastered all the teachings of definitive meaning found in the various scriptures, treatises, and esoteric instructions, and then formulated that realization into a coherent philosophical system.[2] Tāranātha traces a transmission lineage for what he refers to as "the instructions on the view of the Zhentong Middle Way," as well as a separate lineage for the transmission of the Kālacakra teachings passed down in the Jonang tradition.[3] The first of these lists is concerned with the transmission of the practical instructions which epitomize the intentions of all the sūtras and commentaries of the Third Turning of the Dharma Wheel. This lineage is primarily traced through Maitreya and the Indian brothers Asaṅga and Vasubandhu, who are considered to be the originators of the doctrine, but another list is also given for the transmission from Nāgārjuna.[4] This text may be considered a record of the names of teachers who taught the Zhentong view based upon the teachings of the Mahāyāna scriptures and commentaries. Tāranātha's second text, concerned with the lineage of the Kālacakra as transmitted in the Jonang school, may be considered a record of the names of teachers who taught the Zhentong view based upon the teachings found in the tantras, and specifically as articulated in the Kālacakra tantra and the related literature. Examples of the teachings of only one Tibetan master in each of these lineages before the time of Dolpopa are available at the present time.

1. The Zhentong Tradition in Tibet before Dolpopa

According to Tāranātha, one of the earliest Tibetan masters in the Zhentong lineages based upon Mahāyāna teachings was Drimey Sherab, better known as Tsen Khawoche (b. 1021), who was most intimately connected with the transmission of the *Uttaratantra*.[5] In his important collection of one hundred different instructions from a variety of lineages, Jonang Kunga Drolchok (1507-1566) preserved some instructions of this teacher, which are the earliest extant materials dealing with the Zhentong tradition in Tibet.[6] The first excerpt he provides gives some historical context for the issue of the origins of the Zhentong position:

> In regard to the instructions on the view of an emptiness of other, Tsen Khawoche said, "Sañjana, the paṇḍita of Kashmir, made the very significant statement that 'The Victor turned the Wheel of Dharma three times. The first Wheel [proclaimed] the Four Truths, the Middle [proclaimed] the lack of defining characteristics, and the Final made careful and thorough distinctions. From among them, the first two did not distinguish between the real and the artificial. The final one, at the point of certainty concerning the absolute, taught by distinguishing between the middle and the extreme, and distinguishing between phenomena and true nature. Although just the original manuscripts of the *Dharmadharmatāvibhaṅga* and the *Uttaratantra* were re-

discovered, if these two texts were lost it would be equivalent to the demise of Maitreya.'"

This [statement] appearing in an old notebook of Tsen Khawoche himself which bears the title *The Lotus Hook* [*Padma lcags kyu*], is informative concerning the later claim that the distinction of an "emptiness of other" was totally unknown in India, and only appeared later in Tibet with the Omniscient Dolpopa. Please also carefully examine the statement appearing in one of the Omniscient Budön's replies to questions [*dris lan*], in which he states that there was earlier a philosophical system of Danakpa Rinchen Yeshe which appears to have been later enhanced and maintained by Dolpopa.[7]

Kunga Drolchok regards this statement by Tsen Khawoche as an extremely important example of an early precedent for the philosophical distinctions later formulated by Dolpopa. Tsen Khawoche refers to his teacher Sañjana's opinion that only the Third Turning of the Dharma Wheel, wherein clear distinctions are made between phenomena and their true nature, represents the definitive meaning of the Buddha's teachings. Kunga Drolchok feels that this is enough to refute the criticism made by Tibetan critics who claimed that the Zhentong tradition was completely unknown in India and Tibet until the time of Dolpopa. He further remarks that even the great Budön commented that Dolpopa had enhanced an earlier Tibetan philosophical system held by one Danakpa Rinchen Yeshe, and refers the reader to one of Budön's replies to questions (*dris lan*). This is an extremely interesting comment, but unfortunately there is no mention of Dolpopa in the replies of Budön that have been preserved.[8] However, it is quite certain that Dolpopa did study with the Danak master Rinchen Yeshe. When he was still quite young, and just before his teaching debut at Sakya in 1313, Dolpopa spent about three months at Danak, where he studied with Rinchen Yeshe, and received from him an explanation of *The Five Treatises of Maitreya*, one of which is, of course, the *Uttaratantra*.[9] The question of important influences on Dolpopa's formulation of the Zhentong doctrine will be dealt with in detail below.

In the lineage of the *Kālacakra tantra* transmissions in the Jonang school, the definitive aspect of the teaching was being emphasized long before the time of Dolpopa. This is most obvious in the collection entitled *Four Clear Lamps* (*Gsal sgron skor bzhi*) by the eleventh-century Kālacakra master Yumowa Migyö Dorje, which has only recently become available. In these texts Yumowa is clearly dealing with some of the same themes that Dolpopa later elaborated. In fact, Tāranātha identifies Yumowa as having "initiated the tradition of the philosophical system of tantric Zhentong."[10] It is very significant, however, that none of the key terms associated with Dolpopa's theories, such as *gzhan stong*, "emptiness of other," or *kun gzhi ye shes*, "universal ground gnosis," appear in the extant writings of Yumowa, nor does he use any of the terminology that Dolpopa apparently borrowed from certain Mahāyāna sūtras and treatises.

Nevertheless, the Geluk master Thukan Lozang Chögyi Nyima (1737–1802) much later states in *A Crystal Mirror of Philosphical Systems* (*Grub mtha' shel gyi me long*) that Yumowa was the originator of the Zhentong teachings, which he so named, and that they were passed down orally until the time of Dolpopa as a hidden doctrine (*lkog pa'i chos*) without any written texts. Although it is known that Dolpopa actively taught Yumowa's *Four Clear Lamps* (*Gsal sgron skor bzhi*), he neither mentions Yumowa in his own writings, nor quotes from his texts.[11]

Yumowa's four brief treatises are ultimately concerned with the correct practice of the Six-branch Yoga, the perfection-stage meditation system grounded in the *Kālacakra tantra*. The four texts have as their topic matter total integration (*zung 'jug*), the Great Seal (*phyag rgya chen po*), radiant light (*'od gsal*), and emptiness (*stong nyid*). That the extant manuscript was passed down in the Jonang tradition is indicated by the fact that a prayer to the masters in the transmission line of the Kālacakra teachings according to the Jonang lineage is appended to the first of the four texts.[12]

In these texts Yumowa focuses upon the discussion of tantric topics which are beyond the scope of this book. But it may be observed that one of his recurring concerns is to show that he does *not* accept the opinion of most scholars that the spiritual path is a process of realization in which emptiness is recognized as the ultimate nature of all phenomena, not established by any essential nature of its own, and free from the extremes of existence, nonexistence, both, and neither. He sees this view of emptiness as only the presentation of the philosophical system in which emptiness is established as the ultimate nature of all entities. This is *not* what is to be meditated upon as the path according to the stages of esoteric instruction. In short, he feels that emptiness in the context of the path of meditation must be experiential. That which is emptiness by nature (*rang bzhin gyi stong pa nyid*) cannot be directly experienced. In making these statements Yumowa is alluding to specific experiences which occur during the practice of the Six-branch Yoga, when what are known as "empty forms" (*śūnyabimba*, *stong gzugs*) are seen with the eyes. This is the direct experience of emptiness as the path according to the teachings of the *Kālacakra tantra*. So when Yumowa says that emptiness arrived at through logical analysis, and emptiness that is inconceivable, are not the path, he is indicating that it is the emptiness seen with the eyes during the experience of meditation that is the subject of his work.[13] Echoes of this point of view will also be found in the works of Dolpopa.

The teachings of Dolpopa were also solidly grounded in the doctrine of the tantras, especially the *Kālacakra tantra*, and his treatises do not simply follow established philosophical tenets, but represent a synthesis of the view and practice of Mahāyāna and Vajrayāna Buddhism. This will become clear when his views are actually encountered in the texts translated in part 2.

2. Dolpopa and the Zhentong View

It seems quite certain that the teachings of Tsen Khawoche, Yumowa, and others who taught what was later referred to as the Zhentong view did so only to small groups in the context of private instruction. No treatises written by any of the later members of their lineages, from the eleventh century until the fourteenth century, have survived. It was not until Dolpopa later proclaimed his realization, and gave his doctrine the name Zhentong, that this term and the teachings now associated with it became widely known in Tibet. The circumstances surrounding Dolpopa's initial proclamation of the Zhentong were already described in chapter 1, and the nature of his controversial theories will be treated below in chapter 3 and in part 2. Here some of the influences behind his theories, his innovative use of language, his motivation, and the method by which he approached the Buddhist scriptures will be discussed.

It is clear from Dolpopa's own statements that the most important scriptural sources for his controversial theories were *The*

Bodhisattva Trilogy (*Sems 'grel skor gsum*), which are the definitive commentaries on the *Kālacakra tantra*, the *Hevajra tantra*, and the *Cakrasaṃvara tantra*. For example, in a text which he sent to the ruler of the northern principality of Chang, he credits these three texts as being the key scriptural factors in his conversion from the the view of absolute reality as an emptiness of self-nature (*rang stong*).[14] From among them, the *Vimalaprabhā* of Kalkin Puṇḍarīka held special significance for him. He once remarked, "Since I discovered all the essential points of profound definitive meaning from the great commentary of the *Kālacakra tantra*, it has been very kind."[15]

It is important to keep in mind that Dolpopa was a consummate practitioner of the Six-branch Yoga, the perfection-stage practices of the *Kālacakra tantra*, and although he based his doctrinal discussions upon scripture, in particular the *Kālacakra*-related cycles, his own experience in meditation was crucial to the formation of his theories. Indeed, as George Tanabe has recently emphasized in his study of the Japanese master Myōe, "Buddhists have long insisted that the primary experience—and experience is primary—is that of meditation and practice."[16] Dolpopa obviously felt that he had experienced a special insight into the definitive meaning of the Buddha's message as known in the land of Shambhala, but not understood in Tibet. As mentioned in chapter 1, Dolpopa once claimed to have actually gone to Shambhala during an evening meditation session. The next morning he gave an extensive teaching about the layout of Shambhala, its relation to the rest of the universe, and the esoteric instructions of the *Kālacakra tantra*. After directly seeing Shambhala, he composed versified praises of it, in one of which he declared that he had discovered the precise manner in which Shambhala and Kailash exist, which was previously unknown to Indian and Tibetan scholars.[17]

When giving personal meditation advice to his students Dolpopa most often spoke of the special knowledge that he had discovered. He emphasized that although many in Shambhala understood the experiences arising from meditation upon the Six-branch Yoga, no one in Tibet did except for him, and that his own awareness was due solely to the kindness of the Kalkin emperors. For example, he wrote the following verses in an instruction to one of his disciples.

In general, if I speak frankly others do not like it. If I said what others say it would deceive my disciples.
It is hard to be a master in the present times. Even so, I will speak to you frankly.
The Kalkin resides in Shambhala to the north. In the Dharma Palace of Kalāpa many reside who understand experiences like this. In the kingdom of snowy Tibet only I understand experiences like this.[18]

And to another disciple he wrote:

> These days most of those who are known as experts, who assert that they have fine meditation and high realization, and who are proud in being great adepts, are not aware of this method, but I have discovered it by the kindness of the Kalkin.[19]

The combination of Dolpopa's experience in meditation on the Six-branch Yoga and his visionary contact with the land of Shambhala, its Kalkin emperors, and their special blessings, certainly provided the primary inspiration for his theories. But there is also evidence that many of the themes of interpretation that came to fruition in his teaching had been present within the Buddhist tradition in Tibet for centuries. The teachings of Tsen Khawoche and Yumowa touched upon in the previous section are just two examples of earlier Tibetan teachers whose views certainly provided a precedent for some of Dolpopa's theories.[20]

It is of considerable interest that some Tibetan sources speak of Dolpopa's contemporary, the third Karmapa, Rangjung Dorje, as a possible influence, or even as the first adherent of the Zhentong.[21] The earliest available account of the meeting between these two teachers is by the sixteenth-century Sakya master Mangtö Ludrup Gyantso, who remarks:

> Moreover, this lord [Dolpopa] met with Karma Rangjung Dorje, and it is said that since [Dolpopa] upheld the philosophical system of the emptiness of self-nature [*rang stong*], the Karmapa prophesied that he would later become an adherent of the emptiness of other [*gzhan stong*]. In general I think the tradition of the emptiness of other was first upheld

> by Karma Rangjung Dorje. The emptiness of other [was accepted] at Jonang following the Great Omniscient [Dolpopa].[22]

According to Tāranātha this meeting seems to have taken place when Dolpopa was twenty-nine or thirty years old, just prior to his trip to Jonang to meet Yönden Gyantso in 1322. He describes it like this:

> Then [Dolpopa] traveled to Lhasa, Tsurphu, and so forth. He had many discussions about Dharma with the Dharma Lord Rangjung. Although Rangjung could not match the scriptural reasoning of this lord [Dolpopa], he had fine clairvoyance, and prophesied, "You will soon have a view, practice, and Dharma language [*chos skad*] much better than this which you have now."[23]

Tāranātha seems to directly quote the Karmapa's prophecy, but makes no mention of him as a possible source for Dolpopa's development of the Zhentong view. Unfortunately, there is no record of this meeting in any of the extant early biographies of either teacher.[24] There is, however, mention of it in the late history of the Karma Kamtsang tradition written by Situ Panchen Chögyi Jungney (1700-1774), who specifies that Dolpopa still adhered to the view of reality as an emptiness of self-nature (*rang stong*) at the time of the meeting. According to the chronology of this work the meeting between these two masters can be dated to between 1320 and 1324.[25]

One of the most innovative aspects of Dolpopa's philosophical enterprise was his development of a new Dharma language (*chos skad*), which he utilized to express a wide range of themes found in Mahāyāna and Vajrayāna scripture. Tāranātha mentions that when Dolpopa first taught the Zhentong he wrote a number of texts containing a certain Dharma language which was incomprehensible to many scholars, who upon reading them experienced a state of what might be termed "hermeneutical shock."[26] As mentioned above, Rangjung Dorje also prophesied that Dolpopa would soon develop a new and superior terminology.

Dolpopa did two things in regard to language that were largely unprecedented in Tibet. Although much research into these points needs to be done, it seems probable that he first developed a special terminology, or Dharma language, that involved the appropriation of a number of terms from certain Mahāyāna sūtras and treatises; terms that were acceptable in their original context within scripture but were almost never used in ordinary scholarly discourse. Then he created, or a least made first extensive use of, several Tibetan terms, such as *gzhan stong* and *kun gzhi ye shes*, to express scriptural themes he wished to emphasize. He also drew into his vocabulary some key terms such as *dbu ma chen po* (**mahāmadhyamaka*), "Great Madhyamaka," which had been in use in Tibet for centuries, but are not found in any Indian scriptures or commentaries. In this second phase he employed what may be referred to as source-alien terminology, utilizing previously unknown terms to explicate ideas and themes found in many Buddhist scriptures.[27]

In his unique use of language Dolpopa first borrowed loaded terminology from Mahāyāna sūtras and treatises and incorporated it into his own compositions. A few examples will illustrate this unusual facet of his work. One of the controversial points in his teaching is the assertion that ultimate truth, referred to by terms such as *tathāgathagarbha* (Buddha-nature), *dharmadhātu* (expanse of reality), and *dharmakāya* (buddha-body of reality), is a permanent or eternal state. Of course, statements to this effect are not unusual in certain Mahāyāna sūtras and treatises, but for most scholars in Tibet the hermeneutical approach was to view those statements as provisional, and in need of interpretation (*neyārtha*, *drang don*).[28] For Dolpopa, all such statements in the scriptures and commentaries were of definitive meaning (*nītārtha*, *nges don*), and were to be understood literally. He began to freely use the terminology of these scriptures, in a manner suggesting that no interpretation was required, and this was no doubt shocking. For instance, the Tibetan terms *bdag* (*ātman*), *rtag pa* (*nitya*), and *brtan pa* (*dhruva*), as well as *ther zug*, *g.yung drung*, and *mi 'jig pa* (all three of which were used to translate Sanskrit *śāśvata*), are found in the Tibetan translations of treatises such as the *Uttaratantra*, and sūtras such as the *Laṅkāvatāra*, *Gaṇḍavyūha*, *Aṅgulimālīya*, *Śrīmālā*, and *Mahāparinirvāṇa*, where they are used to describe the buddha-body of reality (*dharmakāya*), the Tathāgata, and the Buddha-nature (*tathāgathagarbha*).[29] These terms, which may be translated as "self," "permanent," "everlasting," and "eternal," are used by Dolpopa throughout his writings, not just when discussing the meaning of a passage in scripture. Budön's refutations of the Jonang position in regard to the interpretation of these very terms as used in scripture, clearly shows that this was one of the areas in which Dolpopa's contemporaries reacted strongly.[30]

In one of his early short texts, *A General Commentary on the Doctrine* (*Bstan pa spyi 'grel*), which is nevertheless considered a major work, most of the terms in question are already in use. In another early and important work, *Exceptional Esoteric Instructions on the Middle Way* (*Dbu ma'i man ngag khyad 'phags*), which he wrote at the request of the master Sönam Trakpa, from whom he received ordination, several of these terms are also found, and a number of themes he would later develop more fully may be seen in embryonic form. These terms continue to be found in all of his later writings. In his last major work, *The Fourth Council* (*Bka' bsdu bzhi pa*), Dolpopa frequently used all the terms listed above, as well as other unusual compounds, such as "eternal buddha-body" (*g.yung drung sku*, *ther zug sku*; **śāśvatakāya*).[31]

Unfortunately, Dolpopa never dated his major works, but it may be possible in the future to establish an approximate chronology of his writings through analysis of the terminology used in the different texts. For example, *A General Commentary on the Doctrine* and *Exceptional Esoteric Instructions on the Middle Way* do not contain the terms *gzhan stong* ("emptiness of other") or *kun gzhi ye shes* ("universal ground gnosis"). This gives the impression that they are very early works, and that the borrowing of vocabulary from scriptural sources, which is present in these works, was the first step in the evolution of his use of language, later to be followed by the creation of his own Dharma language.

The term *gzhan stong* is most often associated with Dolpopa, who is usually thought to have coined it.[32] There is, however, some evidence of at least a few isolated occurrences of this term before his time. Dolpopa himself quotes a master whom he identifies as Lord Poripa, who makes a statement that could have come from Dolpopa:

> Relative truth is empty of self nature [*rang gis stong pa*]
> and absolute truth is empty of other [*gzhan gyi stong pa*].
> If the mode of emptiness of the two truths is not understood
> in this way, there is danger of denigrating perfect
> buddhahood.[33]

Although this is certainly the most significant occurrence of the term by a writer who may predate Dolpopa, there is very little information about any earlier master know as Poripa, or Phoripa, as the name is also spelled. The single possible identification is with the obscure early Kagyü teacher Phoriwa Gönchok Gyaltsen.[34]

Another example of the use of the term *gzhan stong* is found in the biography of Ra Lotsawa Dorje Trak (eleventh to twelfth century), who uses it in contrast to the term *rang stong* in a spiritual song. There are, however, quite definite grounds on which to conclude that this biography was extensively reworked in the seventeenth century, and so the occurrence of the term *gzhan stong* is probably not significant.[35]

Dolpopa's contemporary, the esteemed Nyingma master Longchen Rabjampa, also mentions the term on one occasion in the context of a discussion of the "three-nature" (*trisvabhāva*) theory of the Yogācāra school. He contrasts the three categories of "empty of self-nature" (*rang gis stong pa*), "empty of other" (*gzhan gyis stong pa*), and "empty of both" (*gnyis kas stong pa*), but with none of the connotations inherent in Dolpopa's usage. During a discussion of the Buddha-nature, the expression *gzhan stong* is also used once in a text attributed to Padmasambhava in *The Heartdrop of the Dakinis* (*Mkha' 'gro snying thig*), which was revealed in the thirteenth century by Payma Lendrel Tsel.[36] Once again, the usage of the term is not similar to that found in Dolpopa's works.

This evidence shows that the term *gzhan stong* had been used in Tibet before the time of Dolpopa, albeit only in isolated instances, and without the same connotation that he attached to it. Although the tradition itself certainly considers him as the one who coined the term, it is probably more accurate to say that Dolpopa made use of an obscure term that had very limited use before him, and gave it a place of fundamental importance in the expression of his philosophy.

Another central theme of Dolpopa's thought is the contrasting of *kun gzhi rnam shes*, (*ālayavijñāna*), the "universal ground consciousness," with *kun gzhi ye shes* (**ālayajñāna*), "universal ground gnosis." The term *kun gzhi ye shes* is not known to have occurred in the writings of any earlier Tibetan authors. Dolpopa includes *kun gzhi ye shes* in a listing of the various topics previously unknown in Tibet that he felt he had realized and explicated.[37] As noted above, Karmapa Rangjung Dorje may have had some role in the development of Dolpopa's ideas. Although there is no occurrence in Rangjung Dorje's extant works of the terms *gzhan stong* or *kun gzhi ye shes*, the latter term may have been used in a work which is not available at the present time. In his commentary to Rangjung Dorje's *The Profound Inner Meaning* (*Zab mo nang don*), Jamgön Kongdrul Lodrö Tayey (1813–1899), himself an adherent to the Zhentong view, speaks of Rangjung Dorje's own use of the contrasting terms *kun gzhi rnam shes* and *kun gzhi ye shes* in his autocommentary to *The Profound Inner Meaning*. Unfortunately, Kongdrul does not directly quote Rangjung Dorje's text.[38] Rangjung Dorje wrote the *Profound Inner Meaning* in 1322, apparently the year after his meeting with Dolpopa. According to the chronology in the sketch of Rangjung Dorje's life as found in *The Blue Annals*, he wrote the autocommentary before 1326. This is considerably before the writings of Dolpopa began to circulate in Tibet. However, a short text in the collected spiritual songs of Rangjung Dorje, which is devoted to defining the nature of *kun gzhi*, the "universal ground," uses neither the term *kun gzhi rnam shes* nor *kun gzhi ye shes*, and the ideas expressed are definitely incompatible with Dolpopa and the Zhentong doctrine.[39]

The phrase "mirror-like universal ground gnosis" (*kun gzhi me long lta bu'i ye shes*) is found in one of the works of Longchen Rabjampa. He uses this term to characterize the buddha-body of reality (*dharmakāya*), and contrasts it with the "universal ground consciousness" as one of the eight modes of consciousness. In this one instance there are some similarities with Dolpopa's ideas, but Longchenpa's usual position is to identify the *kun gzhi* only with impure states of mind.[40]

Until 1322, when he was thirty years old, Dolpopa had spent almost all of his life in the study of Buddhist literature, philosophy, and practice according to the Sakya tradition. For most of the previous decade he had studied and taught at Sakya monastery itself. It is absolutely certain that he had thoroughly examined and mastered the works of Sakya Pandita Kunga Gyaltsen (1182-1251), such as *Distinguishing the Three Vows* (*Sdom gsum rab dbye*), which were fundamental to the education of a Sakya scholar and practitioner. The similarities between Sakya Pandita's statements concerning his motives for the composition of his controversial works, such as *Distinguishing the Three Vows*, and Dolpopa's own statements about his motives, are as striking as the fact that the two masters were at opposite ends of the spectrum of doctrinal interpretation.

A small example of Dolpopa's familiarity with Sakya Pandita's work, and his sympathy for the sentiments expressed in it, is found at the end of his autocommentary to *The Fourth Council*. In this instance Dolpopa has taken a couplet directly from *Distinguishing the Three Vows*, and then extended Sakya Pandita's metaphor by repeating it as a refrain for several pages.[41] The gist of Sakya Pandita's verse is that no matter how many traditions of Dharma there may be, if they are not linked to an authentic source, they are worthless, like gaming pieces which are off the board and irrelevant, like dead men. Dolpopa used the first couplet of Sakya Pandita's verse as a point of departure, and through its repetition addressed a number of further related issues. For example, he states that there may be numerous teachings of the degenerate Tretayuga, but if they are not linked to the perfect Kṛtayuga they are worthless, like dead men.[42] He continues in this vein, contrasting the fully established nature (*pariniṣpanna*, *yongs grub*) to the imagined nature (*parikalpita*, *kun brtags*), the absolute to the relative, emptiness of self-nature to emptiness of other, and so forth.[43] This borrowing was certainly done on purpose, and would have called to mind the themes and tone of Sakya Pandita's treatise, especially considering the fact that it was one of his descendants, Lama Dampa Sönam Gyaltsen, who had requested Dolpopa to compose *The Fourth Council*.

One of the clearest extended statements of motivations and sentiments by Dolpopa is found at the end of *A Brief Analysis* (*Gshag 'byed bsdus pa*), which he sent to the ruler of the principality of Chang to explain his doctrinal views.[44] It is an extremely informative spiritual and literary autobiographical testament:

> These investigations have been made by laying down a plumb line straight upon the true nature of reality just as it is, and are not contaminated with impurities such as prejudice, partiality, and presumptions. This is because I have taken as witnesses the opinions of the omniscient Blessed One, the Buddha, and the excellent lords on the tenth spiritual level, such as the Lords of the Three Spiritual Races,[45] Vajragarbha, and Maitreyanātha, as well as the great originators [of philosophical systems] and the excellent realized experts, such as noble Asaṅga, the great brahmin Saraha, and the great paṇḍita Nāropa. And because I have avoided

exaggeration and denigration, and have written after thoroughly mastering their intentions exactly as they are.

It may be thought, "You are arrogant in having realized their intentions exactly as they are, but aren't your ideas in disagreement with those of other Tibetan masters precisely because you haven't actually realized them?"

That is not the way it is. The causes for a lack of realization are certainly inferior intelligence, a lack of the oral instructions of an excellent [master], little study, no experience and realization in meditation, being filled with pride and arrogance, determining truth and falsehood on the basis of presumptions and quantity of talk, and so forth. But I first engaged in much study of the great scriptural traditions, and then engaged in the practice of the oral instructions of India and Tibet which are known to be profound, and the precise experience and realization of each of them actually arose.

Then, as a result of the entrance of a little of the blessing of having encountered the definitive meaning of the great root tantras, the oral instructions of glorious Kalāpa,[46] the uncommonly profound heart-advice of the Kalkins on the tenth spiritual level, I discovered many profound essential points which have not been discovered, have not been realized, and have not been mastered by egotistical scholars, most great meditators endowed with experience and realization, and most of those who are arrogant as great upholders of secret mantra. Because a fine realization burst forth from within, and because I have an exceptional certainty untainted by doubts, not only most great meditators endowed with experience and realization, and those who are arrogant as great upholders of secret mantra, but even the Buddha definitely could not turn me back from this.

It may also be thought, "All that certainty is from blurred and dim meditation, or from misunderstanding; there are no perfect scriptural quotations for proof."

There is no lack [of such proof], because there are a great many clear quotations, as well as reasoning and esoteric instructions, from those upon the twelfth spiritual level, those upon the tenth spiritual level, and excellent realized experts such as Nāgārjuna and his spiritual sons, and the great paṇḍita Nāropa. Although that is the case, I have not written them here from fear of being overly verbose, but if you wish and are interested, I will write and offer them later.[47]

Among these points [which I have written about], there are certainly several exceptional ones which are in disagreement with some that have been previously known in Tibet. But you have been accustomed to the previous philosophical system for a long time, so that the propensity for it has become firm, and many in Tibet adhere to that tradition. Therefore, although there is a difference of firm and unstable propensities for these previous and later philosophical systems, and a difference in the numbers of adherents, without giving in to the influence of those differences, please take as witnesses the scriptures of the Buddha and bodhisattvas, and then examine them with an attitude of unbiased honesty as to which [system] is true.[48]

As this and many other passages make clear, there was certainly considerable opposition to Dolpopa's theories. Specifically, he felt that most people had already closed their minds to the teachings of definitive meaning. He often mentions the presumptions and prejudice inherent in the established traditions of his time as one of the greatest factors inhibiting the widespread acceptance of his ideas. He was presenting his case to a prejudiced jury. It is therefore curious that not a single contemporary text has survived in which hostile testimony against Dolpopa is preserved. It may well be that the full reaction to his doctrine did not find open expression until after his death.

3. The Zhentong Tradition after Dolpopa

Dolpopa was surrounded by a group of scholars as formidable as any in fourteenth-century Tibet. His most influential successors in the Jonang tradition were his senior disciples Nyaön Kunga Bal, Mati Panchen Jamyang Lodrö, and the great abbot Choley Namgyal. Major works by both Nyaön and Mati Panchen are extant, and demonstrate the extent to which they followed Dolpopa's example when dealing with crucial doctrinal questions. In particular, it was apparently the teachings of Nyaön that provoked polemic responses and negative reactions.[49]

The best known and most influential early opponent of the Jonang tradition was the Sakya scholar Rendawa Zhönu Lodrö (1348-1413). Scholarly tradition generally credits Rendawa for establishing the Prāsaṅgika form of Madhyamaka philosophy in Tibet.[50] He became one of the most important teachers of the great Tsongkapa Lozang Trakpa (1357–1419), but was viewed by the Jonang tradition as a vicious opponent of the teachings of definitive meaning (*nītārtha*, *nges don*) which had been spread so successfully by Dolpopa. For example, in the pseudo-prophecy, which was attributed to Dolpopa as a last testament but which was surely composed much later by a Jonang follower and added to his biography, there is a very strong condemnation of Rendawa. There he is described as an evil demon who would spread the nihilistic view (*med par lta ba*). Moreover, he would refute the doctrine of the Buddha-nature as the ultimate ground, denigrate the Six-branch Yoga as the ultimate path, and deny the existence of the ultimate result as a separation from all taints. He would also criticize the *Kālacakra mūla tantra* because it did not begin with the words "Thus have I heard," as do other sūtras and tantras, and would make various criticisms of the *Condensed Kālacakra tantra*. Finally, he would gather together copies of the *Vimalaprabhā* and have them thrown into rivers.[51]

These are very serious allegations, but in all fairness it seems that they are also tainted with a considerable degree of hysteria.[52] Rendawa's biography specifically points out that he was famous in Tibet for having said that the *Kālacakra tantra* was not Dharma, but that this was incorrect. While he did see internal contradictions in a literal reading of the *Kālacakra*, he did not dismiss it as a non-Buddhist teaching (*chos min*). This is made clear in a statement by Rendawa himself at the end of *The Jewel Rosary* (*Nor bu'i phreng ba*), the text in which he voiced his objections to specific points in the *Kālacakra tantra*:

> Nevertheless, whether or not [the *Kālacakra*] was composed
> by a Noble One, it is easy to see that it also has many
> fine explanations,
> And therefore I have not denigrated this totally by saying
> "It is not an entryway for those who wish liberation."[53]

That Rendawa's main quarrel was not actually with the content of the *Kālacakra tantra* itself, but with the prevalent practice of understanding its words literally (*sgra ji bzhin pa*), is specified in *My Own Reply to the Jewel Rosary* (*Nor bu'i phreng ba'i rang lan*), a text in which he specifically defends the *Kālacakra tantra* against some of his own earlier objections:

> Nowadays arrogant scholars in the land of glacial mountain ranges have become passionately attached to the literal meaning of the words in the *Kālacakra* and its commentary, which present the profound by means of implicit language.
>
> After seeing the spread of many perverse distinctions which contradict the collection of pure sūtras and tantras, I have written this by means of objection and analysis, as though straightening a crooked stick.[54]

Rendawa is indeed the most famous (or infamous) critic of the Kālacakra tradition in Tibet.[55] But he had first studied with some of Dolpopa's greatest disciples, such as Nyaön Kunga Bal and Mati Panchen, and had been extremely impressed with the Jonang philosophical system. He then decided to investigate thoroughly the scriptures upon which the Jonang teachers based their doctrine, such as the *Kālacakra tantra*, the *Laṅkāvatāra sūtra*, the *Uttaratantra*, the *Dharmadhātu stotra*, and so forth. He analyzed these scriptures three times. After the first reading he was certain that the Jonang position was correct. On the second reading he became uncertain as to whether it was correct or incorrect. After the third reading he was sure that the Jonang interpretations were incorrect.[56] Following this Rendawa went to Sakya and reported to another of his teachers, the great abbot Sangye Phel, that he had determined that the Jonang doctrine was erroneous, and was encouraged in this conclusion. Rendawa then apparently embarked on a crusade to discredit the Jonang tradition and to call into question the internal contradictions he perceived in a literal reading of the *Kālacakra tantra*. First he sent a message to his teacher Nyaön, telling him what he had decided. Nyaön was very displeased at this turn about in Rendawa's view. Nevertheless, Rendawa felt that because of Nyaön's great intellectual powers, and specifically his consummate knowledge of logical reasoning, he could be convinced that the Jonang view was wrong if Rendawa could demonstrate this through logic and scriptural quotations. He was sure that once Nyaön was converted, all the other members of the Jonang school would change their views.[57] Nyaön is certainly portrayed here as the leading proponent of Dolpopa's tradition.

However, when Rendawa went to Tsechen monastery to speak to Nyaön, his old teacher indicated in many ways that he was displeased with him, and Rendawa recognized that there was no point in broaching the subject. Instead, he returned to Sakya and composed *The Jewel Rosary* (*Nor bu'i phreng ba*), his famous critique of the *Kālacakra*.[58] In front of a huge assembly presided over by Drung Zhitokpa at Sakya, Rendawa then debated against a certain Karmapa Gönzhön on the question of internal contradictions in the *Kālacakra tantra*. Then he was invited to Jonang itself, where he debated on the status of the Buddha-nature. All of this would have been happening before the year 1379, when Nyaön passed away. According to Rendawa's biography, he was successful in converting many Jonang monks, caused others to doubt their views, and prevented still others from joining the Jonang tradition.[59] In short, he does seem to have led a strong reactionary movement against the Jonang philosophical system less than fifteen years after the death of Dolpopa.

Nevertheless, it now seems clear that Rendawa's attitude was considerably more ambivalent than the later Tibetan historical sources would have us believe. In the latter part of his life Rendawa lived in semiseclusion at a hermitage in the region of Kangbuley, where he composed his most substantial work on the *Kālacakra*, entitled *A Jewel Lamp Illuminating the Definitive Meaning of the Glorious Kālacakra* (*Dpal dus kyi 'khor lo'i nges don gsal bar byed pa rin po che'i sgron me*).[60] Unlike his two earlier polemic works, the first of which was certainly written while Rendawa was not yet thirty years of age, this fascinating treatise is a thorough and positive analysis of the meditation practices of the *Kālacakra*. The work is obviously an attempt to extract the profound essence of the *Kālacakra* teachings, while correcting some errors of interpretation made by others. In light of the historical material presented above and Rendawa's reputation as an opponent of the Jonang tradition and a critic of the *Kālacakra*, it is nothing less than a major shock to find the following passage in this final work:

> According to the tradition of this [*Kālacakra*] *tantra* the classification of the two truths is like this: all the phenomena

of the incidental stains that arise from the delusive circumstances of ignorance are the relative truth, because they obscure the perception of reality and are reference points for the totally afflicting emotions. Furthermore, because it is not established as the object of a perfect gnosis, it is empty of self-nature [*rang stong*], a nihilistic emptiness [*chad stong*], and an inanimate emptiness [*bems po'i stong pa nyid*].

All the primordial phenomena of the true nature of mind, natural radiant light, are the absolute truth. And that is not the case because it has been proven able to withstand analysis by logical reasoning. . . . It is the absolute because it is the object of a nonconceptual perception. It is empty of other [*gzhan stong*] because the incidental stains are absent, and it is not a nihilistic emptiness [*chad stong*] and an inanimate emptiness [*bems stong*] because it is experienced through a specific self-cognizing intrinsic awareness. . . .

In regard to that, the emptiness of self-nature [*rang stong*] falls into the extreme of nihilism, and therefore its realization is not the perfect path of liberation; only the emptiness of other [*gzhan stong*], the true nature of mind, radiant light, an immutable interior intrinsic awareness experienced through the force of meditation and through a specific self-cognizing intrinsic awareness is accepted as the perfect path.[61]

Can it be that Rendawa actually came to accept that the definitive meaning of the *Kālacakra* was compatible with the Zhentong view held by the Jonang tradition? And yet, at other points in this important text he continues strongly to condemn the view of a permanent and eternal absolute reality, which he equates with the teachings of the Vedic scriptures.[62] Without a more careful study of Rendawa's works it is very difficult to reach a final conclusion about how he was apparently able to admit the validity of the Zhentong in the context of the definitive view of the *Kālacakra*, but reject the various other aspects of the theory, such as the permanent and eternal status of the Buddha-nature. Whatever the case, it is certain that later generations of Tibetan scholars continued to view Rendawa as a determined enemy of both the Jonang tradition and the teachings of the *Kālacakra*, despite the obvious evidence to the contrary in his final work on the subject.[63]

In spite of the doctrinal backlash against the Jonang tradition in the late fourteenth century, Dolpopa's legacy remained powerful for many decades in the province of Tsang before other influences gained the upper hand. Jonang Tāranātha later remarked that the prophecy about Dolpopa found in the *Mahāberī sūtra* (*Rnga bo che mdo*)[64] was correct in that the stream of the practice of the Six-branch Yoga which he spread throughout Tibet, and the teaching of the *Sūtras on the Buddha-nature*, the *Uttaratantra*, and other scriptures of the Third Turning of the Dharma Wheel which proclaimed the Buddha-nature, remained strong in all teaching institutes for more than eighty years. After that point, the teaching of those scriptures was not as influential as before, due to the appearance of many who were obsessed with the provisional meaning (*neyārtha*, *drang don*) and were concerned with having the highest view, and gaining reputation, power, and large entourages.[65] This is quite clearly a negative reference to the rise of the Geluk tradition founded by Lord Tsongkapa, whose main disciples Khedrup Gelek Balzang (1385-1438) and Gyaltsab Darma Rinchen (1364-1431) led the attack against the Jonang tradition in the fifteenth century. But, Tāranātha continued, even in his own time the practice of the Six-branch Yoga and the tradition of the teachings about the Buddha-nature had still managed to survive.[66]

From the point of view of the Jonang tradition itself, information about this lineage and the teachings of the Zhentong and other related topics is very scarce from the time of Dolpopa's immediate disciples until the period of Jonang Kunga Drolchok (1507–1566). In fact, from the late fourteenth century until Tāranātha began to revive the tradition around the beginning of the seventeenth century, there are no extant writings by Jonang masters which are concerned with issues originally raised by Dolpopa. For that matter, the few available writings of Kunga Drolchok are all that have survived from the Jonang school for a period of almost 150 years, and none of his works even mention the Zhentong.[67]

Therefore there is a period of more than two hundred years in which almost all available information about the Jonang tradition is found in polemic passages from members of other traditions, nearly universally hostile, with the notable exception of the Sakya master Serdok Panchen Shakya Chokden (1428–1507). As far as can be known from the presently available sources, Shakya Chokden was the most influential advocate of the Zhentong in the fifteenth and early sixteenth centuries. This impression is strengthened by Tāranātha, who composed a fascinating text comparing the views of Dolpopa and Shakya Chokden on twenty-one profound points of Mahāyāna and Vajrayāna doctrine.[68] In the late eighteenth century the Geluk critic Thukan Lozang Chögyi Nyima does not mention any Zhentong masters after Dolpopa's direct disciples until he singles out Shakya Chokden with particular venom. This role as an important upholder of the Zhentong view is all the more remarkable when it is remembered that Shakya Chokden was, with the possible exception of his contemporary rival Goram Sönam Senge (1429–1489), the greatest Sakya scholar of his time.[69]

Where did Shakya Chokden get the Zhentong teachings? And how did he manage to remain a staunch Sakya master while upholding this view? There is not total agreement about the source of the Zhentong received by Shakya Chokden. One of his main teachers was the Sakya master Rongdön Sheja Kunrik (1367-1449). In his survey of the recently recovered writings of Shakya Chokden, the modern Tibetan scholar Dhongthog Rinpoche states that Shakya Chokden followed the example of his teacher Rongdön in professing the Zhentong in secret, and refuting the exegetical tradition of Lord Tsongkapa through logical reasoning.[70] Although this is not the place to examine the thought of Rongdön, there is probably some truth to Dhongthog Rinpoche's statement. For example, a eulogy to Dolpopa composed by Rongdön has survived, which at least indicates that this Sakya teacher had great respect for Dolpopa and his views.[71]

In the Kagyü tradition, however, the seventh Karmapa, Chötrak Gyantso (1454–1506), is credited as having inspired Shakya Chokden to accept the Zhentong point of view. As was mentioned above, the third Karmapa, Rangjung Dorje, is sometimes named as an influence on Dolpopa's initial development of the Zhentong doctrine. Although at the present stage of research the dynamics of how the Zhentong came to be accepted by many members of the Kagyü tradition, especially in the Karma Kamtsang branch, is not well understood, it is certain that it was a powerful force within this lineage, probably from the time of the third Karmapa.[72]

In the earliest available source on the life of Shakya Chokden, written by Jonang Kunga Drolchok, it is stated that he met the seventh Karmapa, Chötrak Gyantso, on two occasions. These meetings can be dated to the year 1502. The most significant event was the second meeting, at the Rinpung court of Dönyö Dorje, at that time the most powerful ruler in Tibet. According to the Kagyü historian Bawo Tsukla Trengwa (1504–1566), who was writing between the years 1545 and 1564, from twenty to thirty thousand people are said to have gathered from throughout Tsang province to welcome the Karmapa upon his arrival in Rinpung. Shakya Chokden stayed with the Karmapa for about one month. During this period he received many of the Kagyü hierarch's uncommon profound instructions, which greatly enhanced his experience of renunciation and realization in meditation, and caused him to accept the Karmapa as his main spiritual master. A late history of the Karma Kagyü tradition elaborates further, stating that the Karmapa accorded Shakya Chokden the incredible honor of sitting upon a throne of equal height in the midst of the assembly, and that they spent the month in discussion of the most profound topics. On this occasion the Karmapa said that he and Shakya Chokden were of the same mind (*thugs rgyud gcig pa*). A passage later in the same work finally mentions the fact that in his writings Shakya Chokden maintained, as did the Karmapa, that the ultimate view of the two great traditions of the Mahāyāna was the Zhentong view of the absolute as only empty of other relative phenomena.[73] Although Shakya Chokden was already seventy-three or seventy-four years old, this event is often considered to have been the deciding factor in his acceptance of the Zhentong.[74] It seems more likely that Shakya Chokden had upheld the Zhentong view for a long time, and that this lengthy discussion with the Karmapa was more of a validation and enrichment of his realization than a complete change of view; otherwise it would have to be accepted that all of his works dealing with the questions of an emptiness of self-nature (*rang stong*) and an emptiness of other (*gzhan stong*) were composed in the remaining five years of his life.

The works of Shakya Chokden were later banned in Tibet during the middle of the seventeenth century. Bigoted supporters of the Geluk tradition, who held political power, sealed the printery where the blocks for Shakya Chokden's works were kept, and ordered copies of his works to be confiscated.[75] What was perhaps a unique copy survived in Bhutan, and was recently used to publish the now-available *Collected Works*. The banning of his works no doubt had a lasting effect on the later doctrinal development of the Sakya tradition.

Shakya Chokden's works often focus on a theme of reconciliation and synthesis between traditions that have become polarized over doctrinal issues. His brand of Zhentong differed in many respects from that of Dolpopa, although they agreed about the ultimate import of the view.[76] In one brief work Shakya Chokden compares the views of Dolpopa and Budön, both of whom he considers to be Sakya, and comes to the startling conclusion that in the ultimate sense there is no basis for disagreement between the Jonang and Zhalu traditions on the subject of the emptiness of self-nature (*rang stong*) and the emptiness of other (*gzhan stong*), because in the context of the definitive meaning of the tantras, Budön's tradition also maintained the view of the emptiness of other (*gzhan stong*).[77]

The theme of synthesis, or at least maintaining that there is no contradiction between these two points of view, was also the approach of the seventh Karmapa, Chötrak Gyantso, as recorded by his disciple Karma Trinlepa (1456–1539). The text which best exemplifies this is Karma Trinlepa's brief verse response to some written questions he had received. This text, which must surely be the one referred to much later by Belo Tsewang Kunkyab as "the brief treatise which illustrates that there is no contradiction between an emptiness of self-nature and an emptiness of other," specifically summarizes the view of the seventh Karmapa on this topic. As several modern writers have already noted, the eighth Karmapa, Migyö Dorje (1507–1554), also wrote a text on the Zhentong view, although later in his life he changed his mind, and wrote refutations of Dolpopa and Shakya Chokden.[78]

Another figure also wrote a very interesting brief text attempting to bring the views of the emptiness of self-nature (*rang stong*) and the emptiness of other (*gzhan stong*) into harmony. This is the sixteenth- to seventeenth-century yogin Shongchen Denpey Gyaltsen, who was responsible for codifying the teachings on Severance (Gcod) which had been passed down in an oral transmission from the great adept Tangtong Gyalpo (1361-1485), who claimed to be the rebirth of Dolpopa. Shongchen's text is a versified presentation of the essential points involved in the philosophical system of the Great Madhyamaka.[79]

The picture of the Sakya position in regard to the Jonang doctrine of the Zhentong and related questions is extremely complex from the late fifteenth century through the late sixteenth century. With the exception of Shakya Chokden and Gorampa, there are no extant writings by Sakya masters of the period specifically devoted to these issues. There are, however, a number of brief passages in biographies and in some minor texts that give indications of the situation. Important information is found in the biographies of Gorum Kunga Lekpa (1477–1544), who was the Jonang throne-holder for many years as well as a leading exponent of the Sakya teachings of the Path and Result (Lam 'bras); the great Tsarchen Losel Gyantso (1502–1566), who was the most highly regarded of all the masters of the Path and Result in the sixteenth century and who received many teachings from Gorumpa; Jonang Kunga Drolchok, who should definitely be considered representative of a major lineage of Sakya explication and practice; and Jamyang Khyentse Wangchuk (1524–1568), who studied with Gorumpa, Tsarchen, and Kunga Drolchok.

The biography of Gorumpa is one of the major sources for information about the situation at Jonang from the late fifteenth century to the middle of the sixteenth century. In this work it is obvious that the tradition was still strong, and that Dolpopa's major treatises, such as *The Ocean of Definitive Meaning*, the basic text and the autocommentary of *The Fourth Council*, and *A General Commentary on the Doctrine* were still being transmitted and studied at Jonang. In 1516 Gorumpa ascended the teaching throne at Jonang, and held the leadership position until 1527. During this time, and during the tenure of his hand-picked successor Namkha Balzang, who held the position from 1527 to 1543, Dolpopa's teachings of definitive meaning were preserved without any corruption.[80] Gorumpa taught not only the Jonang specialties, but also many tantric instructions of the Sakya school, such as the Path and Result. During these years Gorumpa was clearly a very prominent example of what must have been a not uncommon situation—the practice and study of both Jonang and Sakya teachings without the existence of any serious obstacles to such an approach. The followers of the Jonang school were still considered to be in the Sakya tradition, but with a special emphasis on the practice of the Six-branch Yoga and the peculiar teachings which had been passed down from Dolpopa.

Jonang Kunga Drolchok was certainly the best known leader of the Jonang tradition in the sixteenth century and left the most lasting legacy. In reading Kunga Drolchok's extensive autobiographies, the *One Hundred Instructions of Jonang* (*Jo nang khrid brgya*), and his other miscellaneous writings, three things are immediately apparent. He was very much a product of the Sakya tradition, which he upheld through practice and teaching, he was an excellent model of a completely unbiased upholder of nonsectarian (*ris med*) sentiments, and there is extremely little evidence that he felt any special allegiance to the Jonang tradition, which he led, over that of others that he also taught and practiced.

The three main lineages of tantric practice which seem to have been the most important for Kunga Drolchok were the Sakya teachings of the Path and Result, the esoteric instructions of the Shangpa Kagyü school, and the Jonang tradition of the Six-branch Yoga.[81] He constantly bestowed these teachings throughout his life. In the present context, what is most striking is the total lack of any aggressive attempt to spread the Zhentong teachings of Dolpopa. Kunga Drolchok was much more interested in creating an atmosphere of tolerance for all lineages of explication and practice than furthering that of only one. This is probably indicative of the situation in which the Jonang tradition now found itself.

Due to the great influence of the Geluk sect, which was very antagonistic toward the Jonang views, the mainstream of Sakya scholars had increasingly distanced themselves from the doctrinal position of the Jonang school, even though there seems to have been no such gulf between the two traditions in regard to practice. There is considerable evidence in both the writings of Shakya Chokden and Kunga Drolchok that many representatives of the Sakya school during the fifteenth and sixteenth centuries had been deeply influenced by the unique views of Lord Tsongkapa, whose supporters had continued to increase in number. This may have happened in large part because many Sakya scholars following the time of Rendawa had rejected the theories of Dolpopa, and perhaps gone to the other extreme and allied themselves with the new Geluk school, founded by Rendawa's disciple Lord Tsongkapa, whose views were very questionable in light of the ancient teachings of the original Sakya masters.[82] Shakya Chokden and Kunga Drolchok referred to this trend among some followers of the Sakya school as the "lately arisen Sakya tradition" (*phyis byung sa skya pa*), and to a tension between the "new and old Sakya traditions" (*sa skya pa gsar rnying*), especially in regard to the teachings of the Path and Result.[83] They viewed this as an extremely serious corruption of the teachings of the original Sakya masters, whose ultimate intentions they felt were more in agreement with those of the Jonang tradition. Kunga Drolchok saw these adherents to a "new Sakya" movement as wolves in sheep's clothing who were destroying the true Sakya teachings. In short, they were Geluk followers masquerading as members of the Sakya tradition.[84] On the other hand, it may also be the case that some Sakya followers were attracted toward the Zhentong orientation precisely in order to counteract the dominant Geluk influence in Tibetan spiritual matters of that time.

One of Kunga Drolchok's great strengths was an exceptional ability to focus on the specific teachings of a given lineage, and not let its views be influenced by those of any other tradition, even those of the Jonang school which he represented.[85] If he was writing about the Sakya teachings of the Path and Result, he would carefully distinguish its view from that of traditions that had different approaches, and when discussing the Jonang teachings of the Six-branch Yoga he kept precisely to Dolpopa's interpretation as the ultimate authority.[86] In the latter context he once referred to himself as Dolpopa, the embodiment of the buddhas of the past, present, and future, once again returned to sit upon his teaching throne and preserve his tradition:

> As the physical embodiment of the three regal masters, and the single protector of maternal living beings in the three worlds,
>
> Wasn't Sherab Gyaltsen the name of the splendid Dolpopa, the Buddha of the Three Times?
>
> Sitting upon that lord's Dharma throne, and maintaining that lord's tradition, am I not the yogin Rangdrol, the Lord Buddha from Dolpo returned once again?[87]

Also, when teaching instructions in a lineage that came from Dolpopa, Kunga Drolchok did not hesitate to use the terminology characteristic of his great predecessor.[88]

During this period Jonang itself was flourishing. Tsarchen Losel Gyantso, considered the greatest Sakya master of tantra in the sixteenth century, received the Jonang instructions of the Six-branch Yoga from Gorumpa, as well as many teachings of the Sakya Path and Result. In 1539 Tsarchen visited Jonang, and in what is reminiscent of Dolpopa's initial experience there, looked up at the stone meditation huts on the mountainside and was filled with awe at the tradition of continuous meditation retreat that had been maintained there. Two years later he revisited Jonang and was warmly greeted by his elder friend and teacher, Kunga Drolchok.[89] Generally speaking, there were clearly very cordial relations between the Sakya and Jonang sects at this time.

Jamyang Khyentse Wangchuk, whose instruction manuals for major tantric practices in the Sakya tradition are authoritative to the present day, studied with Gorumpa as a youth, and then later with Tsarchen and Kunga Drolchok. In particular, from Gorumpa he received the full transmission of the Jonang teachings of Dolpopa, as well as the Sakya teachings of the Path and Result, and other esoteric instructions. Then he became the principal Dharma heir of Tsarchen, and was later the abbot of Zhalu monastery. It is very clear from his autobiography that he was deeply committed to meditation practice, of both the Jonang and Sakya variety, in contrast to scholastic studies. On one occasion he expressed his deep wish to go into isolated retreat far from everyone, and practice the (Sakya) Naro Khachöma for the creation stage meditation (*bskyed rim*) and the (Jonang) Six-branch Yoga for the perfection stage (*rdzogs rim*).[90] This is indeed remarkable for a master who would later ascend Budön's teaching throne at Zhalu.

One revealing episode occurred when Khyentse Wangchuk visited the Kagyü monastery of Ralung in 1550. He listened quitely one day as a group of scholars were discussing points of doctrine and practice, and heard one of them declare that Dolpopa had maintained that a permanent entity existed (*rtag pa'i dngos po yod*), and that it was the Buddha-nature. No one disputed this. Khyentse Wangchuk thought to himself that while Dolpopa certainly did accept that the Buddha-nature was permanent, he did not accept that it was an entity (*dngos po*).[91] In all his writings Dolpopa had said that the ground of emptiness was naturally noncomposite radiant light (*stong gzhi rang bzhin 'od gsal 'dus ma byas*), and while one could object to this, it was not something which could be proven or refuted through vain argumentation. In any case, Khyentse Wangchuk commented, Budön had said the same thing![92] Once again the impression is that there was really no serious disagreement between the ultimate intention of the greatest masters; only between later interpreters who did not fully comprehend their doctrines.

Unlike the works of Kunga Drolchok, in which evidence of Dolpopa's theories is very scarce, the writings of Kunga Drolchok's reincarnation, Jonang Tāranātha, are replete with the teachings of the Zhentong and related themes. In the history of the Jonang tradition Tāranātha is second in importance only to Dolpopa himself. He was responsible for the short-lived renaissance of the school as a whole in the late sixteenth and early seventeenth centuries, and the widespread revitalization of the Zhentong theory in particular. Like Kunga Drolchok, Tāranātha also practiced and taught a wide variety of tantric teachings from different lineages, and was nonsectarian (*ris med*) in his approach to realization. He was also one of the last great Tibetan translators of Sanskrit tantric texts.[93] Tāranātha was respectful of all forms of authentic Buddhism, including the tradition of Budön, and that of the Geluk, which were antagonistic toward the Jonang school.[94] He also emphasized the practice of the Sakya teachings of the Path and Result and the esoteric instructions of the Shangpa Kagyü, as had Kunga Drolchok, but he focused on the explication of the Kālacakra and the practice of the Six-branch Yoga as the most profound of all the teachings given by the Buddha. It is especially clear throughout his writings that he considered Dolpopa to be the ultimate authority in matters of doctrine and practice.

Tāranātha's autobiography provides unique access to the actual condition of the Jonang tradition from the point of view of its leader. He took upon himself the responsibility of causing Dolpopa's insights to once again reach a wide audience, and was determined to revive what he saw as a priceless transmission lineage in danger of being lost. For example, in the early 1590s Tāranātha stated that it had been many years since the complete instructions of the Six-branch Yoga had been given at Jonang. In addition, although the instruction manual of Dolpopa's Dharma heir Choley Namgyal was still being used at Jonang to teach the Six-branch Yoga as it had been transmitted from Dolpopa, there were very few who understood the philosophical system of Dolpopa and his spiritual sons. Of even more concern was the fact that some of the previous leaders of Jonang, such as Lord Orgyan Dzongpa, had given initiations and instructions according to the Jonang tradition, but then criticized and refuted Dolpopa's adamantine proclamations of the ultimate view of Zhentong, which was the secret teaching of all the buddhas and bodhisattvas. As a result, many unfortunate things had occurred. Even though Tāranātha personally disavowed any ability to refute another system, on this occasion he felt the necessity to defend the original views of Dolpopa through refutation of erroneous opinions, and to establish the correct interpretations according to his lineage.[95]

In the year 1604, after a decade of great effort to revive the original teachings of the Jonang sect, all of Tāranātha's work was threatened by serious political conflict between the regions of Chang and Tsang. The monastery of Jonang itself was in immediate danger of being attacked by hostile armies. While meditating at Dolpopa's great stūpa Tāranātha became very despondent, and seeing all of his efforts about to be wiped out and the tradition itself perhaps destroyed, he felt only like going into retreat to practice far away from all the troubles created by deluded and impassioned individuals. At this point Dolpopa himself appeared to Tāranātha in a vision, encouraged him to continue as before, and assured him that his efforts would not be fruitless. The next night Tāranātha prayed to Dolpopa, and experienced another vision, of a bodhisattva who spoke a quatrain of verse to him. As a result of these events Tāranātha himself stated that he gained realization of the true intentions of Dolpopa as expressed in his Zhentong doctrine, and all his uncertainties and doubts were completely removed. He felt that a great key had been placed in his hands with which to open the doors of all the Buddha's teachings.[96] As an expression of his realization he then composed the versified text entitled *An Ornament of the Zhentong Middle Way* (*Gzhan stong dbu ma'i rgyan*), one of his most important works devoted solely to the explication of the Zhentong view, and a companion text of quotations from scripture in support of the ideas therein.[97] Describing the same vision of Dolpopa in another of his autobiographical writings, Tāranātha mentions that he received several prophecies from him, and from that time on met him many times, both actually and in dreams. And he comments, "This is the reason I am now an expert in the great Omniscient Dolpopa's view, and preserve his true intentions."[98]

Throughout Tāranātha's life he often encountered resistance and opposition to the Jonang doctrine of the Zhentong. For example, he once spent considerable energy trying to explain the Zhentong view to the ruler of Chang, the abbot of Ngamring monastery, and a group of scholars who had gathered at Trompa Lhatse.

There was some interest, but absolutely no comprehension of the actual nature and significance of the teachings he gave. The main cause for the scholars' inability to understand was that they identified the Zhentong doctrine with the tradition of the Cittamātra which did not accept the validity of a cognitive image (*sems tsam rnam rdzun pa*). They were completely unable to comprehend the great differences between the Zhentong and the Cittamātra.[99] Even great masters such as the Zhamar hierarch of the Kagyü school, with whom Tāranātha communicated in about 1620, had mistaken assumptions about the Jonang views.[100]

Following the death of Tāranātha in 1635, his successor Kunga Rinchen Gyantso led the Jonang tradition for the next fifteen years.[101] Then a series of events occurred which were crucial for the future of the Jonang tradition, but which have not yet been clearly explained. It has generally been stated in Western works on Tibetan history that the suppression of the Jonang sect and the conversion of their monasteries to the Geluk school came about in 1658.[102] This is only partially correct. The political situation of the seventeenth century was extremely complex, and to the future misfortune of the Jonang school Tāranātha was one of the main spiritual advisors to the rulers of Tsang province during their struggle against the Geluk powers of Central Tibet for political supremacy. Some modern authors have blamed Tāranātha's role for the downfall of the Jonang tradition.[103] In light of the following information, this also seems unlikely. Although the details are still quite sketchy, a somewhat more complete picture of the situation may now be drawn.

In 1642, seven years after the death of Tāranātha, an alliance of Mongol armies led by Gushri Khan finally defeated the Tsang rulers and enthroned the fifth Dalai Lama, Ngawang Lozang Gyantso (1617–1682), as the supreme political ruler of all Tibet. In his autobiography, the Great Fifth himself briefly touches upon the fate of the Jonang sect. At the instigation of a certain Jamyang Trulku, a Geluk teaching institute (*bshad grwa*) was established at Dakden Tamchö Ling, the monastery built by Tāranātha near the original site of Jonang.[104] The philosophical system (*grub mtha'*) of the monastery was thus converted from Jonang to Geluk in the Iron-Tiger (*lcags stag*) year (1650).[105] This may then be understood as the point at which the Zhentong doctrine was banned at Jonang by order of the victorious Geluk authorities. The year 1650 also matches the end of the tenure of Tāranātha's successor Kunga Rinchen Gyantso, who then went to live for the latter part of his life at the monastery of Sangak Riwo Dechen.[106]

It was originally the prompting of the Jamyang Trulku that provided the pretext for the Fifth Dalai Lama to intervene at the Jonang establishment of Dakden Tamchö Ling. Who was this figure? Fortunately, much earlier in his autobiography the Dalai Lama provides the necessary information to identify him. Jamyang Trulku was the son of the Khalha Tusheyetu king.[107] Now the situation becomes much more interesting. Jamyang Trulku was the son of the Mongol Khalka Tushiyetu Khan, Gönpo Dorje, and the grandson of Erke Mergen Khan. Better known by the names Yeshe Dorje and Lozang Denpey Gyaltsen (1635–1723), Jamyang Trulku had actually been recognized by the Fifth Dalai Lama, the first Panchen Lama Lozang Chögyi Gyaltsen (1567–1662), and the Tibetan State Oracle (*la mo chos skyong*) as the rebirth of Tāranātha himself, and the first of the series of Mongol incarnations known as the Khalka Jetsun Tampa.[108] It is of further interest that he was generally referred to as Jamyang Trulku, "the emanation of Jamyang," because he was also believed to be the rebirth (*sku skye*) of Jamyang Chöje (1357–1419), the founder of the great Geluk monastery of Drepung. After that he was said to have appeared as Tāranātha's reincarnation (*yang srid*).[109] Of course, the earlier life as Jamyang Chöje was understandably emphasized by the Geluk authorities in order to establish a profound prior connection with the Geluk tradition, and indeed with Lord Tsongkapa himself. However, the 156-year gap between the death of Jamyang Chöje and the birth of Tāranātha was not explained, and there is no mention of Jonang Kunga Drolchok, Tāranātha's predecessor, in the incarnation line of Jamyang Trulku, the Khalka Jetsun Tampa. Clearly, the reasons for his recognition as the reincarnation of Tāranātha were political, enabling the Geluk establishment to eliminate the possibility of a Tāranātha rebirth as the new leader of the Jonang tradition. Although the Jonang school itself certainly did not accept this enforced recognition of its great master as a new Geluk teacher who demanded the conversion of Jonang monastery into a Geluk establishment, they had no choice in a country now ruled by Geluk political administration and Mongolian military might.

In the biography of the Khalka Jetsun Tampa there is some interesting material presented to rationalize his recognition as

Tāranātha's reincarnation. According to one source, just before Tāranātha passed away his Jonang disciples and patrons prayed for him to reincarnate for the purpose of spreading his Jonang doctrine. In this source he is quoted as having given the following reply:

> Be satisfied with just this much expansion of our Jonang doctrine. Through the force of supplications by the Genden [i.e., Geluk] protectors, and the force of previous prayers, I will now spread the doctrine of Lord Tsongkapa in a barbarian borderland.[110]

Tāranātha's own extensive autobiographical writings, as well as his voluminous religious works, are filled with evidence of his devotion to Dolpopa and the special teachings of definitive meaning which characterized the Jonang tradition. It seems highly unlikely that he would have made such a statement, or chosen to be reborn in the very tradition which became the instrument for the destruction of Dolpopa's Jonang school as a viable independent tradition. Not surprisingly, this statement is not recorded in the Jonang accounts of Tāranātha's last days.[111]

In addition to the alleged final statement by Tāranātha, a passage from one of his own secret autobiographies was also cited by Geluk authors as proof that he had intended to take birth in the Geluk tradition. Tāranātha himself describes a vision he had as a young man:

> At Yamdrog a man who had an aura of blessing, and who was said to be Budön, put a yellow scholar's hat [on my head], and said, "Now you should wear only this."
>
> This was also the placing of the true crown. And that is the reason I now wear a yellow hat with long ear-flaps.[112]

Budön Rinchen Drup was one of the most important spiritual ancestors for the Geluk transmission lineages, especially that of the Kālacakra. Tāranātha's vision does not necessarily lend itself to the Geluk interpretation. Tāranātha had great respect for Budön, and had received the transmission of his Kālacakra teachings. His autobiographies also record visions of a number of other great teachers, both Indian and Tibetan. A yellow scholar's hat (*paṇ zhwa ser po*) was earlier worn by Budön, and later became a trademark of the Geluk tradition. But Budön and the Geluk teachers after him were by no means the only ones to wear yellow ceremonial teaching hats in Tibet. Dolpopa himself had worn a yellow hat, and it is clear in the account of the vision that Tāranātha wore a yellow hat while he was still obviously a Jonang teacher.[113] As mentioned above, the Sakya master Jamgön Amey Zhap claimed that Dolpopa himself repented of the Zhentong view toward the end of his life, and the Geluk teacher Thukan Lozang Chögyi Nyima would make the same spurious claim in regard to Shakya Chokden.[114] A final and more effective ploy by the enemies of Jonang was to simply accomplish through political power the actual recognition of the rebirth of Tāranātha as a Geluk teacher.

It now seems clear that arrangements were made for the fifteen-year-old incarnation, who had received a strict Geluk education in Mongolia from disciples of the Fifth Dalai Lama, to request the Great Fifth to establish the institute at Dakden, providing the opportunity for the conversion of Tāranātha's monastery into a Geluk center. Later in 1650 the young Khalka Jetsun traveled to Tashi Lhunpo monastery, and received novice vows and a number of teachings from the first Panchen Lama.[115] At this point the Panchen Lama was urgently asked to go to Dakden, undoubtedly for the purpose of accomplishing the conversion into a Geluk monastery. There the Panchen Lama gave a number of initiations for the major tantric lineages followed by the Geluk tradition, and the textual transmissions for many of the ritual texts required for the liturgical practices of that school. He also gave teachings to the nuns at nearby Jonang during the same visit.[116] It is significant that the Khalkha Jetsun himself did not visit Jonang or Dakden at the same time, as would certainly have been expected if he were accepted there as Tāranātha's rebirth.

According to the Fifth Dalai Lama's own account, Tāranātha's monastery of Dakden Phuntsok Ling was taken over by the Geluk tradition in 1650, but the monks who had been there from before did not actually change their views and practices, and even the newly arrived ones were predisposed toward the original teachings of the Jonang sect. The Dalai Lama used the example of brass coated with gold to refer to them as Jonang with only a Geluk veneer. As a result, the Geluk authorities expelled them to other monasteries, made harsher regulations concerning the Geluk conversion, and gave the monastery the new name of Genden Phuntsok Ling. This was all done in 1658.[117]

From this time the Jonang tradition was suppressed as an independent school in Central and Western Tibet. Nevertheless, the teachings of the Zhentong and the Kālacakra according to the Jonang lineage was continued even in those areas, although the far eastern Amdo monastery of Dzamtang and its affiliates now became the sole remaining centers which were openly Jonang.[118]

The Jonang teachings of the Zhentong view and the Kālacakra instructions have continued to be transmitted and practiced up to the present day. However, their survival in mainstream Tibetan religion has not been due to the presence of the Dzamtang enclave of Jonang followers in the relative isolation of Amdo, but to the influence of several great Nyingma and Kagyü masters from the Kham region of eastern Tibet who came to accept and actively teach Dolpopa's controversial views.

The Nyingma master Katok Rikzin Tsewang Norbu (1698–1755) was responsible for bringing about a sort of renaissance of the Jonang teachings of the Zhentong and the Kālacakra by introducing them to some of the leading Kagyü teachers of his time. In one of his versified autobiographical accounts, Tsewang Norbu notes that even as a child he felt great faith whenever he heard the names of Dolpopa and his immediate disciples.[119] His natural affinity for the Zhentong view and the Kālacakra teachings became understandable later when the master from whom he received the transmission of the Jonang teachings recognized him as the rebirth of Dolpopa's disciple Mati Panchen Lodrö Gyaltsen, one of the pair of translators responsible for the Jonang translation of the *Kālacakra tantra* and the *Vimalaprabhā*.[120]

In 1726, as he was passing through Tsang province in route to the Kathmandu valley in Nepal, Tsewang Norbu first made an effort to obtain the Jonang teachings from the great yogin Kunzang Wangpo, one of whose teachers had been a direct disciple of Tāranātha. Kuzang Wangpo was in strict retreat at the hermitage of Rulag Drepung, now renamed Genden Khachö due to its enforced change into a Geluk establishment, and Tsewang Norbu was not even able to see him, although he spent three days trying. He was very impressed with this master's serious meditation practice, and became even more determined to receive the Jonang transmissions from him.[121]

On his return to Tibet toward the end of 1728, Tsewang Norbu again approached Kunzang Wangpo, and this time succeeded in receiving the entire transmission of the Jonang teachings. Kunzang Wangpo bestowed upon him the instructions of the view of the Zhentong approach to the realization of the Great Madhyamaka (*gzhan stong dbu ma chen po'i lta khrid*), the full Kālacakra initiations, as well as the complete teachings of the Six-branch Yoga, and many nonsectarian (*ris med*) teachings. He also received *The One Hundred Instructions of Jonang* (*Jo nang khrid brgya*) compiled by Kunga Drolchok, and the textual transmissions for the collected works (*gsung 'bum*) of both Dolpopa and Tāranātha. From this information it can be seen that although the Jonang institutions had been converted to the Geluk tradition, the original teachings from Dolpopa were still taught and practiced in those same monasteries even in the middle of the eighteenth century. The fifth Dalai Lama's earlier attempts to stamp out the Jonang teachings had been successful only on the surface, as had indeed been the case in the initial phases of the conversion operation discussed above. Contrary to the general impression, the teaching transmissions had survived not only in the far eastern region of Amdo but in the original Tsang areas near Jonang. In fact, this picture becomes even clearer when it is taken into account that Tsewang Norbu himself went to Jonang in 1734, ascended the teaching throne previously occupied by Dolpopa and Tāranātha, and gave many initiations, textual transmissions, and esoteric instructions of the original Jonang teachings to a large gathering.[122] At least during this period the Geluk authorities were obviously not exerting great efforts to prevent the teachings of the Jonang tradition from being spread or revived even in Tsang.

Tsewang Norbu later spread these teachings in Central Tibet, where he gave a number of Jonang transmissions to the thirteenth Karmapa, Düdül Dorje (1733–1797), and the tenth Zhamar, Chödrup Gyantso (1742–1792).[123] But Tsewang Norbu's most significant role in terms of the continuation of the Jonang lineages was as a teacher of the great Situ Panchen Chögyi Jungney (1770–1774). Situ Panchen had already been to Dakden and Jonang in 1723, several years before Tsewang Norbu's first visit. From the description in Situ's autobiography, it was an important event. From his account it is known that Tāranātha's silver stūpa reliquary at Dakden had already been destroyed long before. According to Situ this had been done when the Geluk conversion had been ordered by the Fifth Dalai Lama at the instigation of his teacher Möndropa. Situ noted that although Dakden was now a Geluk institute, there were some old monks who had not given up the original Jonang tradition.[124] He made attempts to obtain copies of Jonang works, but they had been placed under seal by the order of the central government.[125] Situ felt great sadness at what had so quickly befallen Tāranātha's center, and lamented the degenerate times. But when he went to Jonang itself the next day he found about seven hundred Jonang nuns there who had not changed their tradition to that of the Geluk.[126]

Twenty-five years later, in 1748, Tsewang Norbu and Situ spent time together in the Kathmandu valley of Nepal. Although Situ had clearly been very interested in the Jonang tradition for many years, it was his teacher Tsewang Norbu who now insisted that he accept the Zhentong view, which he taught him in great detail, apparently at the great stūpa of Bodhnāth.[127] Situ relates that Tsewang Norbu ordered him to uphold the profound view of the Zhentong, and that the acceptance of this view would create an auspicious pattern of events (*rten 'brel*) which would lead to Situ's longevity, and the vast spread of his activities.[128] Situ further mentions that there were several different brands of Zhentong, among which he adhered most closely to that of the Seventh Lord and Zilungpa, which was somewhat different than that of Dolpopa.[129] In the end it would be Situ, more than anyone, who would create the environment for the widespread acceptance of the Zhentong theories in the next century. As Smith already mentioned in 1970, "It was Si-tu who had blended the seemingly irreconcilable *gzhan stong* and Mahāmudrā positions and spread them throughout the Dkar-brgyud-pa traditions of Khams."[130]

The eventual result of this revival initiated by Tsewang Norbu and Situ Panchen was the crucial role of the Zhentong and other Jonang teachings in the phenomenal nonsectarian (*ris med*) movement of the nineteenth century in Kham.[131] This movement included such great masters as Dza Baltrul (1808–1887), Jamgön Kongdrul (1813–1899), Jamyang Khyentse Wangpo (1820–1892),[132] and later Mipham Gyantso (1846-1912).[133] From among them, Jamgön Kongdrul was the most assertive in his advocacy of the Zhentong viewpoint, which he fully incorporated into his own immensely influential works.[134] Kongdrul was also extremely devoted to the Six-branch Yoga of the Kālacakra, in which he carefully followed the tradition of Dolpopa and Tāranātha.[135]

The Zhentong teachings and the Jonang practice of the Six-branch Yoga have thus come down to the present day in large part through the transmission lineages of Kongdrul, Khyentse, and Mipham. It is this tradition which has reached a widespread audience, whereas the Jonang tradition proper, which has been preserved in the Amdo monastery of Dzamtang and its affiliated establishments, has remained quite isolated.

From the turn of the twentieth century until the present day the Zhentong tradition has been maintained by several of Tibet's greatest teachers, all from eastern Tibet, and all followers of the lineages taught by Kongdrul, Khyentse, and Mipham. Jamyang Chögyi Lodrö (1896–1959), the great heir to the nonsectarian movement, was sympathetic to the Zhentong view, and wrote a guruyoga text focused upon Dolpopa.[136] The Nyingma master Dilgo Khyentse Rinpoche, Rabsel Dawa (1910–1991), the most important disciple of Jamyang Chögyi Lodrö, was very partial to the Zhentong, as were the Kagyü master Kalu Rinpoche, Rangjung Kunkyab (1905–1989), and the Nyingma master Dudjom Rinpoche, Jikdral Yeshe Dorje (1904–1987).[137] Nowadays most Kagyü and Nyingma teachers follow the lines of explication and practice passed down by these three masters. As a result, among those Kagyü and Nyingma teachers who accept the Zhentong view, the Zhentong interpretations of Kongdrul and Mipham in particular are now the most widespread.[138] Outside of the Jonang tradition now centered in Dzamtang, none of Dolpopa's own treatises are still being transmitted. Not even the minimal reading transmission (*lung*) of the writings of Dolpopa himself seems to be current among present-day leading representatives of the Kagyü and Nyingma brands of the Zhentong.[139] When the Zhentong is taught by these teachers, the different works of Kongdrul and Mipham, which vary a great deal from the original teachings of Dolpopa, are the treatises of choice.[140] What is now taught as the Zhentong view in the Kagyü and Nyingma traditions represents a synthesis that has developed over the centuries, primarily in order to enable Dolpopa's most vital insights to be incorporated into the already established doctrines of the Great Seal and the Great Perfection. In the following chapter some of the most essential aspects of Dolpopa's own doctrine will be presented as a preface to the translations of his works that appear in part 2.

3

The Doctrine of the Buddha from Dolpo

> Existence and nirvāṇa are not identical,
> but like a shadow and the sun.
>
> —Bhagavān Avalokiteśvara[1]

The title alone of Dolpopa's *The Great Calculation of the Doctrine Which Has the Significance of a Fourth Council* (*Bka' bsdu bzhi pa'i don bstan rtsis chen po*) would have been enough to rankle those who were opposed to his interpretations of Buddhist Doctrine. In Tibet it was universally accepted that there had been three great councils (*bka' bsdu*) in India for the purpose of gathering and accurately preserving the teachings of the Buddha after his final nirvāṇa.[2] Dolpopa's audacious claim that his text served as a fourth such council would obviously have provoked incredulous reactions among many of his contemporaries. That he anticipated certain objections is clear from the following comments at the end of his autocommentary to *The Fourth Council*:

> Having realized that the Doctrine of the Buddha remains in a superior, a middling, and an inferior [form, it is realized that] the superior is the Kṛtayuga Dharma, which is the witness and authority. The middling is the Tretayuga Dharma and the inferior is the Dvāparayuga Dharma. Those two are not witnesses. This realization by the great experts who stand guard over the Doctrine is very important.
>
> To establish the path of perfect view, meditation, and conduct after cleansing the flawless Doctrine of flaws which have

been mixed in, and contamination which has been imposed by the flawed intellects of ordinary persons, is also the purpose of a council. There were three councils before, and this is the fourth. It is also a great calculation of the Doctrine.[3] It is called impartial and unbiased because all the faithful respect, pure vision, expressions of disagreement, appeals, love, compassion, and so forth, remain impartial and unbiased, without falling into any prejudice.

Objection: While it is known that many arhats [destroyers of the enemy] gathered for the previous councils, here the gathering is just to destroy [your] enemies.

[Reply:] In the sublime Kṛtayuga teachings there are many thousands of profound quotations by the great arhat, the Blessed One, the Buddha, which very clearly present the meaning of this. Since those [quotations] are the same as the [actual presence of] the great arhat, this has been compiled according to his tradition.

Future compilers please also do likewise, and if there is disagreement in regard to the interpretation of the quotations, please use the autocommentaries of the Buddha himself as witnesses.[4]

In addition to clarifying the meaning of the title of his text, these remarks also touch upon the first major point raised by Dolpopa in *The Fourth Council* itself. In this work, and many of his earlier compositions as well, Dolpopa speaks of a fourfold division of the Buddhist teachings according to four eons (*yuga*). Basing himself upon the teachings of the *Vimalaprabhā*, Dolpopa mentions two sets of four eons (*yuga*), the first of which is the greater, referring to the quality of the eons which make up a cosmic age (*kalpa*), while the lesser set refers to the quality of the different periods of the Buddhist teachings.[5] In the autocommentary he states his criteria for this classification, and makes it obvious that he is speaking of a doxographical scheme in regard to the eons of the Doctrine. This has recently been noted by M. Kapstein, who has said that Dolpopa was "allocating philosophical doctrines to 'aeons' according to purely dogomatic criteria."[6] According to Dolpopa, the teachings of the perfect Kṛtayuga are those which apply directly to the truth just as it is, whereas the teachings which belong to the Tretayuga,

Dvāparayuga, and Kaliyuga are progressively contaminated and filled with flaws, due to the nature of the individuals who have composed them. Thus the Kṛtayuga teachings are the only ones which should be regarded as valid testimonies to the enlightened intentions of the Buddha.[7]

This classification of the historical degeneration of the Buddhist teachings is indeed found in full form in the *Vimalaprabhā*, primarily in the section of commentary upon verses 22 and 23 of the *Lokadhātupaṭala* of the *Kālacakra tantra*.[8] Budön's annotations to these passages make it clear that Dolpopa was not here making any innovative interpretations of the original treatise.[9] What is less clear is what the *Vimalaprabhā* and Dolpopa both consider to be the teachings of the Kṛtayuga. As indicated by quotations found throughout his writings, Dolpopa certainly considered the Kṛtayuga Dharma to include many, if not all of the highest tantras, as well as *The Trilogy of Bodhisattva Commentaries*, *The Ten Sūtras on the Buddha-nature*, *The Ten Sūtras of Definitive Meaning*,[10] and the works of Maitreya, Nāgārjuna, Vasubandhu, Asaṅga, Nāropa, and Saraha. As Kapstein has mentioned, Dolpopa seems to have considered Ārya Vimuktisena, Haribhadra, Yaśomitra, and other late Indian masters to represent the Tretayuga.[11]

It will become obvious in the translation of *The Fourth Council* in part 2 that Dolpopa identified his own tradition with the teachings of those scriptures and writers which he viewed as truly portraying the Kṛtayuga tradition. This was also a motivating factor behind his wish to redefine what had until his time been accepted as the orthodox lines of scriptural interpretation in Tibet.

1. Emptiness of Self-Nature and Emptiness of Other

The key to Dolpopa's approach was to link his doctrine of the absolute as empty only of other relative phenomena (*gzhan stong*) to the teachings of the Kṛtayuga, as opposed to the teachings of the Tretayuga and later eons which emphasized that even absolute reality was empty of self-nature (*rang stong*). This he makes clear early in *The Fourth Council*:

> Thoroughly understanding each of those divisions, I wish to purge the Doctrine,

And wishing for myself and others to enter upon a fine path, I honor the sublime Kṛtayuga Dharma as a witness.

The Tretayuga and later [eons] are flawed, and their treatises which have been diluted like milk in the marketplace are in every case unfit to act as witnesses.

The higher refutes the lower, as the higher philosophical systems refute the lower.

The Kṛtayuga Dharma is the immaculate words of the Victor, and those well spoken by the lords on the tenth spiritual level, and by the great originators of systems which are flawless and endowed with sublime qualities.

In that tradition all is not empty of self-nature. Finely distinguishing empty of self-nature and empty of other, whatever is relative is all stated to be empty of self-nature, and whatever is absolute is stated to be precisely empty of other.[12]

Dolpopa maintained that there are two modes of emptiness that can be correlated with the two truths, and with phenomena and reality. He emphasized that absolute truth is not empty of itself (*rang stong*), but is the ground or substratum which is empty of all other relative phenomena, and thus is described as the profound emptiness of other (*gzhan stong*). This is the mode of emptiness for the true nature (*chos nyid*, *dharmatā*) of reality. Absolute truth is uncreated and indestructible, noncomposite and beyond the chain of dependent origination. Relative truth and ordinary phenomena are empty of self-nature (*rang stong*), and completely unestablished in the ontological sense. The relative is the created and destructible phenomena which are composite and dependent upon causes and conditions.

One of the central themes of Dolpopa's work is the importance of correctly distinguishing the meaning of the term *emptiness* when used in reference to the incidental stains which veil the Buddha-nature, and when used in reference to the Buddha-nature itself. Both *are* empty, but not in the same sense. In a text addressed to one of the rulers of Chang, Dolpopa made the following statement:

Because everything which exists in the two modes of emptiness are equal in being emptiness, there are statements

> with the single phrase—"Everything is emptiness." But there are also statements in which there is a distinction between empty of self-nature and empty of other. The intent of those [statements] must also be precisely presented.
>
> In regard to this, because relative and incidental entities are completely nonexistent in their mode of existence, they are empty of individual essence. That is being empty of self-nature.
>
> Because the primordial absolute which is empty of those relative [phenomena] is never nonexistent, it is empty of other.[13]

In brief, Dolpopa considered the Buddha-nature to be naturally luminous radiant light, which is synonymous with the buddha-body of reality (*dharmakāya*), and a primordial, indestructible, and eternal state of great bliss inherently present in all its glory within every living being. On the other hand, the incidental stains or impurities which veil the Buddha-nature are the various states of mind associated with the myriad experiences of mundane existence. Whereas the veils of temporary defilement are empty of self-nature (*rang stong*), the Buddha-nature is empty only of phenomena other than itself (*gzhan stong*).

In discussions of these topics, Dolpopa often employed the three-fold paradigm of the basis or ground, the spiritual path, and the result or fruit of enlightenment. Using this approach, he would first say that the Buddha-nature is the gnosis which is the universal ground or substratum (**ālayajñāna*, *kun gzhi ye shes*) for every phenomenon experienced in saṃsāra and nirvāṇa. He is careful to point out that although this luminous enlightened expanse inherent within the mind-stream of each living being is not the cause of saṃsāra, even saṃsāra would be impossible without it, and from this point of view only is it referred to as the ground of saṃsāra.[14] It is the basis from which all imperfections and faults are cleansed, and the ground in which all spiritual qualities are actualized.

Second, the spiritual path is the process of erasing all imperfections or faults from that ground or substratum, and thereby allowing the spiritual qualities to actualize or become evident. This path is composed of two aspects. The first is the accumulation of gnosis (*jñāna*, *ye shes*) that burns away all the veils that have been obscuring the spiritual qualities of the buddha-body of reality (*dharmakāya*), which is eternal and spontaneously present within each living being. The second aspect of the path is the accumulation of merit (*puṇya*, *bsod nams*), which gradually creates the previously absent spiritual qualities of the buddha-bodies of form (*rupakāya*).

Third, the result of this process is the state of buddhahood, the optimum condition in which the greatest good may be achieved for both oneself and others. This is accomplished by means of what Dolpopa speaks of as the attainment of "the separated result" (*bral 'bras*) of the buddha-body of reality (*dharmakāya*), the absolute state of authentic being which has been separated from obscuration by the emotional and intellectual veils. It is also accomplished by means of the attainment of the buddha-bodies of form (*rupakāya*), referred to by Dolpopa as "the produced result" (*bskyed 'bras*), which is the relative symbolic manifestations of buddhahood.

As pointed out above, the majority of Buddhist teachers in Tibet did not agree with Dolpopa's ideas. Personal statements by Dolpopa about his earlier views before coming to Jonang are almost nonexistent. The following excerpt from his writings is very revealing in regard to the opinions of others, and to what Dolpopa himself had accepted earlier in his career while he was still at Sakya.

> According to the opinions of some scholars in India who were not noble individuals, and some spiritual friends in Tibet as well, other than the emptiness such as that of a pillar or a pot, the emptiness of other does not fit the definition of emptiness. Furthermore, only the emptiness of self-nature, in which all phenomena are each empty of individual essence, fits the definition of emptiness; there is absolutely no definition of emptiness beyond that. That being the case, as with the emptiness of the relative, the absolute is also empty of the absolute. As phenomena are empty of phenomena, the true nature is also empty of true nature. As saṃsāra is empty of saṃsāra, great nirvāṇa is also empty of great nirvāṇa. As the buddha-bodies of form are empty of the buddha-bodies of form, the buddha-body of reality is also empty of the buddha-body of reality, and so forth. In brief, there are many opinions in which everything is accepted as empty of self-nature, but in which it is impossible for anything whatsoever not to be empty of self-nature.

> For a long time my mind was also accustomed to the habitual propensity for that well-known [view]. Even though I did understand a small amount of Dharma, for as long as I had not beheld the great kingdom of the exceptional, profound, uncommon, and sublime Dharma, I also merely relied upon the verbal regurgitation of others, and said, "Only an emptiness of self-nature fits the definition of emptiness; there is no definition of emptiness beyond that," and so forth, as was mentioned above. Therefore, it is not the case that I do not also understand that tradition.
>
> At a later time, due to the kindness of having come into contact with *The Trilogy of Bodhisattva Commentaries*, [I understood] many profound and extremely important points of Dharma which I had not understood well before. . . . Now, if I think about the understanding I had at that time, and the corresponding statements I made, I am simply mortified.[15]

The process of enlightenment according to Dolpopa may be further illuminated by means of some traditional examples. First of all, Dolpopa maintained that there are two types of "universal ground" (*ālaya, kun gzhi*). He considered the Buddha-nature to be the "universal ground gnosis" (**ālayajñāna, kun gzhi ye shes*). While it is still veiled by the temporary emotional and intellectual stains, it is like the sky filled with clouds, or a jewel covered with mud. On the other hand, the "universal ground consciousness" (*ālayavijñāna, kun gzhi rnam shes*) is the impurities or incidental stains which are to be removed, and the deeply imprinted habitual propensities associated with it. They may be likened to the clouds in the sky, or the mud covering the jewel. Second, the spiritual path is composed of the various techniques of practice which bring about the removal of the impurities. This path may be likened to the wind which scatters the clouds, or the stream of water which washes the mud from the jewel. Finally, the result is spoken of as an attainment, but it is really the total integration of bliss and emptiness, a self-arisen gnosis which has been eternally present, but is now manifest or actualized. This is like the appearance of the clear cloudless sky, or the jewel separated from the mud. Therefore, Dolpopa would say, the incidental stains should be understood as empty of self-nature (*rang stong*), and suitable to be removed through spiritual practice, while the Buddha-nature itself is empty only of other extrinsic factors (*gzhan stong*), such as the incidental stains which veil its eternal and indestructible nature.[16]

2. A Redefinition of Cittamātra and Madhyamaka

It is significant that Dolpopa often signs his works with the pseudonym Dönpa Zhiden (Rton pa bzhi ldan), which means "endowed with the four reliances." This clearly summarizes his hermeneutical approach, referring to the four guidelines, or points to be relied upon (*catuḥpratisaraṇa*, *rton pa bzhi*), which the Buddha himself prescribed in several Mahāyāna sūtras, such as the *Catuḥpratisaraṇa sūtra*, and the *Saṃdhinirmocana sūtra*. These four are:

> Rely upon the teaching, not the teacher.
> Rely upon the meaning, not the text.
> Rely upon the definitive meaning, not the provisional meaning.
> Rely upon gnosis, not consciousness.

Dolpopa strongly felt that the Buddhist tradition as it had developed in Tibet emphasized the teachings of provisional meaning at the expense of those of definitive meaning. For centuries scholars had been concerned with resolving apparently conflicting notions about the meaning of emptiness, and in particular its relationship or identity with the Buddha-nature. In the opinion of many Tibetan experts the teachings of emptiness found in the Second Turning of the Dharma Wheel, for example in the *Prajñāpāramitā sūtra*s, are definitive in meaning, while the teachings of the Buddha-nature found in the Third Turning of the Dharma Wheel, for example in the *Uttaratantra* attributed to Maitreya, and a large number of Mahāyāna sūtras, are of provisional meaning. There were, however, other traditions which maintained just the opposite, that the teachings of Buddha-nature were definitive and only by means of them could the true meaning of emptiness be understood.

Mati Panchen, who was one of Dolpopa's chief disciples and successors, gives a succinct definition of the Jonang position in regard to this question:

> The meaning of the Middle Wheel is the manner in which the relative is empty.

The meaning of the Final Wheel is the manner in which the absolute is empty.

Since they teach the nonexistence of what does not exist, and the existence of what does exist, the ultimate intention of both are identical.[17]

According to Dolpopa the first two Turnings of the Dharma Wheel, concerned respectively with the Four Noble Truths and the presentation of emptiness (*śūnyatā*) as a lack of all defining characteristics, do not emphasize the definitive teachings on ultimate truth. Specifically, he stated that the Second Turning primarily presented relative phenomena as empty of self-nature (*rang stong*) and not transcending the chain of dependent origination. On the other hand, the Third Turning of the Dharma Wheel presented the teachings on the Buddha-nature, which are the final definitive statements on the nature of ultimate reality, the primordial ground or substratum beyond the chain of dependent origination, and which is only empty of other relative phenomena (*gzhan stong*).

However, Dolpopa was also very concerned with showing that the nature of absolute reality taught in the *Prajñāpāramitā sūtra*s of the Second Turning, and the teachings of the Buddha-nature found in the scriptures of the Third Turning were fundamentally in agreement, as indeed were the traditions of Nāgārjuna, Asaṇga, and Vasubandhu.[18] In this regard he emphasized that the absolute emptiness taught in the Second Turning of the Dharma Wheel, in the Third Turning, and in all the highest teachings of the tantras, was the profound emptiness of other, and not that of a mere emptiness of self-nature.[19] An integral part of his approach in this regard was to illustrate that the different terminology utilized in a wide variety of Buddhist scripture was actually often used to describe the same thing. For example, in a text devoted primarily to clarifying the nine true or fully established natures (*pariniṣpanna*, *yongs grub*) in the context of the three-nature (*trisvabhāva*) theory, Dolpopa alternately refers to them as the nine fully established natures (*pariniṣpanna*), the nine transcendent knowledges (*prajñāpāramitā*), and the nine Buddha-natures (*tathāgatagarbha*). Elsewhere he further illustrated his point that such Dharma language is interchangeable by also speaking of the nine Great Seals (*mahāmudrā*), the nine Great Madhyamakas, and the nine absolute states that are empty of other (*gzhan stong*), all of which describe the same profound ground of emptiness (*stong gzhi*) or profound mode of reality (*gshis lugs*).[20]

In opposition to the dominant tradition of interpretation in Tibet, Dolpopa maintained that Indian masters such as Asaṅga, Vasubandhu, Dignāga, and Nāgārjuna were all representative of the tradition which he labeled the Great Madhyamaka (**mahāmadhyamaka, dbu ma chen po*). Dolpopa considered one of the essential characteristics of this Great Madhyamaka to be the use of the paradigm of the three-nature theory (*trisvabhāva*), which was almost always considered a hallmark of the Yogācāra or Cittamātra tradition.[21] A significant Tibetan precedent for Dolpopa's point of view was recorded by one of his most important successors, Jonang Kunga Drolchok. He recorded some of the actual teachings of the eleventh-century master Tsen Khawoche, who is often thought to be the first Tibetan to have taught what later came to be known as the Zhentong view.[22] Kunga Drolchok preserved these teachings under the title of *Instructions on the View of the Emptiness of Other* (*Gzhan stong gi lta khrid*), which he states have been condensed from the instruction manual of Tsen Khawoche himself. This short text provides a fascinating glimpse into an early source for the Zhentong tradition in Tibet. There are themes present here which can definitely be identified in the later work of Dolpopa, but there is none of Dolpopa's characteristic terminology, such as the term "empty of other" (*gzhan stong*):

> The attachment to delusory [phenomena] as true is the imagined [nature]. The attachment to the incorrect pervasive conceptualization itself as actual objects and subjects, is like [mistaking] a rope for a snake. As many [subjects] as there are from form to omniscience,[23] there are also that many imagined objects.
>
> If based upon causes and conditions, they are dependent [in nature], and appear in various [guises], but are merely incorrect conceptualization, [like] the rope as the basis which is mistaken for a snake. Due to karma and the afflicting emotions, [there are such] conceptualizations, from form to omniscience.
>
> The self-arisen true nature, pervading the dependent from the beginning like the space pervading the rope, is the unmistaken fully established [nature], the immutable fully established [na-

ture], the two buddha-bodies of form, the components of enlightenment, the Truth of the Path, and [the topics] from the form of true nature to omniscience. In the conventional sense they are empty of the imagined [nature's] characteristics.

Although classified as three [natures] without essence, if investigated, only the dependent phenomena and the fully established true nature have a single true nature which is taintless and spontaneous, because there are no objects and subjects except for the mind. Therefore, the imagined [nature] is an emptiness of self-nature, like the horn of a rabbit. Empty of the imagined [nature], the dependent is like an illusion. Empty of both the imagined and the dependent [natures], the fully established is like the sky. The distinctions of an imagined and a dependent [nature] exist in the relative, but do not exist in the absolute. The fully established true nature exists in the absolute, but it is the Great Madhyamaka free from all extremes, without any essence which is identical or different than relative phenomena.[24]

There are several points of considerable interest in Tsen Khawoche's teachings as presented by Kunga Drolchok. The first thing which strikes the reader is that it is structured according to the three-nature (*trisvabhāva*) doctrine usually associated with the Yogācāra tradition of the Mahāyāna, and not the Madhyamaka. In particular, Tsen Khawoche states that the fully established nature is empty of both the imagined and the dependent. In this he is certainly following the description found in the *Bṛhaṭṭīkā* (*Yum gsum gnod 'joms*), a vast commentary on the *Prajñāpāramitā sūtra*s, and not the orthodox Yogācāra position as found in the works of Vasubandhu. Dolpopa would later do the same, and specifically point to the *Bṛhaṭṭīkā* as the scriptural source for his position. These teachings of the *Bṛhaṭṭīkā* and their relation to Dolpopa's theories will be investigated in some detail below.

Like Tsen Khawoche, Dolpopa would also refer to his teaching as the Great Madhyamaka.[25] He makes his case for this in *The Fourth Council*:

In the flawed traditions of the Tretayuga and later [eons], it is claimed that the immutable fully established nature is only Cittamātra.

They allege that all three natures are also only Cittamātra.

Because the three natures are repeatedly taught in the treatises of the flawless Kṛtayuga Madhyamaka,

Because that language does not occur in the Cittamātra treatises, and because there are many refutations to the contrary,

It emerges from the Kṛtayuga tradition that the three natures are the Dharma tradition of only the Madhyamaka.

Therefore, by not understanding that type of classification, and by mixing it up, the dregs of the view have arisen.

Those Madhyamaka [treatises] which present the three natures of the fully established, and so forth, have been demoted to Cittamātra treatises.[26]

The great experts of the Great Madhyamaka who taught them have also been demoted to Cittamātra adherents.[27]

In his autocommentary Dolpopa explains this section in considerable detail.[28] First he notes that the three-nature (*trisvabhāva*) theory occurs in many of the scriptures which he considers Kṛtayuga Madhyamaka, such as *The Eight Thousand Line Prajñāpāramitā*, *The Twenty-five Thousand Line Prajñāpāramitā*, *The Five Hundred Line Prajñāpāramitā*, the *Laṅkāvatāra*, the *Saṃdhinirmocana sūtra*, and the *Suvarṇaprabhāśa*. Furthermore, he maintains that texts in which the term *three natures* (*trisvabhāva*) occur cannot be considered Cittamātra treatises because the immutable fully established nature (*pariniṣpanna*) and the philosophical system of the Cittamātra are in conflict. Whereas the Cittamātra assert that momentary consciousness is truth in the absolute, Dolpopa contends that the immutable fully established nature (*pariniṣpanna*) is absolute noncomposite space and intrinsic awareness indivisible, which transcends momentary consciousness. Momentary consciousness is a composite, impermanent, fabricated, and incidental limited phenomenon, whereas the immutable fully established nature (*pariniṣpanna*) is a noncomposite, permanent, natural, and primordial middle ground free from extremes. Therefore, momentary consciousness cannot be equated to the immutable fully established nature.

As long as the phenomena of momentary consciousness are not transcended, there can be no nondual gnosis, Great Madhyamaka, or immutable fully established nature (*parinișpanna*). When the phenomena of momentary consciousness have been transcended, the immutable fully established nature is attained. But at this point the doctrine of Cittamātra has also been transcended. The immutable fully established nature is thus Madhyamaka, not Cittamātra. Here Dolpopa mentions that it is also necessary to understand the division of the Cittamātra according to the two truths. He maintains the existence of an absolute Cittamātra which may be considered identical to the Madhyamaka, because both state that in reality there are no phenomenona other than absolute mind, and because absolute mind always exists as the omnipresent indestructible thusness. To say that there are no phenomena other than the expanse of reality (*dharmadhātu*) is equivalent to saying that there are no phenomena other than nondual gnosis. Dolpopa identifies the relative Cittamātra with what was usually referred to as Cittamātra in Tibet during his time. This position should properly be called Vijñānavada.

The three-nature theory as one of the fundamental paradigms associated with the Yogācāra or Cittamātra tradition of Indian Buddhism derives its authority from a number of scriptures, perhaps the most important of which are the *Saṃdhinirmocana sūtra* and the *Laṅkāvatāra sūtra*. It was especially elaborated upon by Asaṅga in works such as the *Bodhisattvabhūmi*, the *Mahāyānasaṃgraha*, and the *Madhyāntavibhaṅga*, as well as in the *Trisvabhāvanirdeśa* and *Triṃśikā* of his brother Vasubandhu. Although the three-nature theory is an integral part of the Yogācāra system, as Dolpopa pointed out it is also found in some of the *Prajñāpāramitā sūtras*. In Tibet this fact had important hermeneutical implications for the understanding of the development of Indian Buddhist doctrine. In particular, what might be called the "orthodox" Tibetan view of the Three Turnings of the Dharma Wheel was challenged by the presence of this theory in the *Prajñāpāramitā sūtras*. This was because it was generally accepted in Tibet that the scriptures and treatises of the Yogācāra or Cittamātra school belonged to what was known as the Third Turning of the Dharma Wheel, while those of the Second Turning of the Dharma Wheel, such as the *Prajñāpāramitā sūtras*, were associated with the Madhyamaka tradition. In this context it is of particular significance that the *Bṛhaṭṭīkā* (*Yum gsum gnod 'joms*), a commentary upon the specific *Prajñāpāramitā sūtras* in which the three-nature theory are presented, has survived in Tibetan translation, and that Tibetan teachers have often attributed this commentary to Vasubandhu. The intense interest in the presence of the three natures in the *Prajñāpāramitā sūtra*s, and in the interpretations found in the *Bṛhaṭṭīkā*, seems to have only arisen in Tibet.

As Dolpopa noted, the presentation of the three-nature theory is found in the twenty-five-thousand-line and the eighteen-thousand-line versions of the *Prajñāpāramitā sūtra*s. In each of these sūtras the theory is taught by the Buddha in response to questions from the bodhisattva Maitreya; in the seventy-second chapter of the twenty-five-thousand-line version and the eighty-third chapter of the eighteen-thousand-line version.[29] It is quite surprising that no modern scholars have examined the section in the Tibetan translation of the *Bṛhaṭṭīkā*, the enormous commentary to the *Prajñāpāramitā* in which the "Maitreya Chapter" in the twenty-five-thousand-line sūtra is specifically explained.[30] The *Bṛhaṭṭīkā* is the only extant text of Indian origin which directly comments upon the controversial chapter. This anonymous commentary, which has often been attributed to Vasubandhu, is the obvious place to look for clarification of the three-nature theory as found in the *Prajñāpāramitā*. The work is best known in Tibet by the short title *The Conquest of Objections in Regard to the Three Mother Scriptures (Yum gsum gnod 'joms)*. It is a commentary upon the versions of the *Prajñāpāramitā* in eighteen-thousand, in twenty-five-thousand, and in one-hundred-thousand lines. Dolpopa emphasized that the *Bṛhaṭṭīkā* was the work of Vasubandhu, and gave it a place of central importance in his interpretation of *Prajñāpāramitā* thought.[31]

In his translation of Budön's *History of Buddhism*, Obermiller first mentioned the existence of a Tibetan controversy concerning the authorship of the *Bṛhaṭṭīkā*. In the Nartang edition of the Tibetan canon, which was edited by Budön, the title page of the work specifically states "composed by the master Vasubandhu." Although Budön rejected the opinion of some scholars that it was the work of the Kashmiri master Daṃṣṭrāsena, Tsongkapa would later state that it had been composed by the Kashmiri scholar.[32] Ngorchen Kunga Zangpo (1382-1456), representing the opinion of the Sakya tradition in Tibet, accepted the commentary as a work by Vasubandhu. Scholars of the ancient tradition of the Nyingma still accept it as an authentic work by Vasubandhu.[33] In short, the only Tibetan scholars who did *not* accept it as a composition of Vasubandhu seem to have been followers of the Geluk tradition.[34] The lineage of sūtra interpretation maintained by Dolpopa's tradition in Tibet was eventually eclipsed by that of the Geluk school in the early fifteenth century. Although this is not yet generally acknowledged, it is clear that much of Tsongkapa's philosophical doctrine was formulated in direct reaction to the teachings of Dolpopa which he had come in contact with during his studies of Mahāyāna treatises under the direction of some of Dolpopa's disciples. It seems quite possible that Tsongkapa's unique attribution of the *Bṛhaṭṭīkā* to Daṃṣṭrāsena, instead of to Vasubandhu as was accepted by both Dolpopa and Budön, was part of his broader refutation of Dolpopa's teachings which had been so influential in the preceding generation.

Although the "Maitreya Chapter" itself is the primary locus for the expression of the three-nature theory in the twenty-five-thousand- and the eighteen-thousand-line *Prajñāpāramitā sūtra*s, there is frequent mention of the three natures throughout the *Bṛhaṭṭīkā*, and not just in the final section which specifically comments upon this chapter as found in the twenty-five-thousand-line sūtra. A very informative example is found in a section of the *Bṛhaṭṭīkā* which is concerned with proving the nature of emptiness to be free from the two extremes (*mtha' gnyis dang bral ba*).[35] In commenting upon the intention of the Buddha in teaching that form is emptiness and emptiness is also form, the *Bṛhaṭṭīkā* makes the following statements:

> In regard to the statement "form is empty of form," [it should be known that] there are three aspects of form—imagined form, discerned form, and the form of the true nature.
>
> The tangible form that is apprehended by childish ordinary persons as a characteristic suitable to be [referred to] as form, is known as "imagined form."
>
> Precisely that, in whatever aspect it becomes an object of consciousness appearing as an external entity, is known as "discerned form."
>
> That which is free from the aspects of both the imagined and the discerned, and which is solely the fully established thusness, is known as "the form of the true nature."

Since that which is the form of the fully established true nature is empty of the characteristics of existence as imagined form, and so forth, and also [empty] of form which appears in the aspect of an object discerned as form, it is known as "empty."

So it has been explained, but these doubtful thoughts about it may arise: "Does that which is the form of the true nature, empty of imagined and discerned form, have some other characteristic of form? Why is it even known as 'form'?"

Therefore it is explained: "That which is the emptiness of form is also not form." That which is empty of imagined and discerned form, and is the form of true nature possessing the characteristic of fully established thusness, is not the nature of form, because it is in every way isolated from the aspect of form.[36]

This section of the *Bṛhaṭṭīkā* is extremely clear in establishing that the true nature, or fully established nature, is referred to as "empty" because it is free from *both* the imagined and discerned natures. Here there are definite grounds for Dolpopa's declaration of absolute reality as empty only of other relative phenomena (*gzhan stong*). In a manner very similar to the above passage from the *Bṛhaṭṭīkā* in which the fully established (*pariniṣpanna*) nature is presented as empty of both the imagined (*parikalpita*) and the discerned (*vikalpita*) natures, Dolpopa stated that ultimate reality was empty of other relative phenomena, but not itself empty. For example, he claimed that "the imagined and the dependent natures are impossible if the fully established true nature does not [really] exist."[37] In one of his earliest major works, *A General Commentary on the Doctrine* (*Bstan pa spyi 'grel*), the theory is touched upon in the following verse:

I bow at the feet of the masters who state that all the imagined and dependent phenomena are nonexistent, but the fully established true nature is never nonexistent,

Thus carefully distinguishing and teaching that which transcends existence and nonexistence, and eternalism and nihilism.[38]

In his commentary to *A General Commentary on the Doctrine*, Nyaön Kunga Bal specifically refers to Dolpopa's opinions several times when explaining this verse.[39] According to Dolpopa, the phenomena of the imagined nature (*parikalpita*) are simply nonexistent. The elements, and so forth, which appear to be external, actually have no existence outside of the consciousness of the beholder, and thus are totally nonexistent, like the horn of a rabbit. This is termed the "authentic imagined nature" (*kun brtags mtshan nyid pa*). The concepts which arise in the mind in the wake of the appearance of apparent phenomena, and which thus identify those phenomena as external, are termed "the imagined nature existing in merely the conventional sense" (*tha snyad tsam du yod pa'i kun brtags*). The dependent nature (*paratantra*) is also twofold. The "impure dependent nature" (*ma dag pa'i gzhan dbang*) is all the ordinary worldly thoughts and mental states. The "pure dependent nature" (*dag pa'i gzhan dbang*) is the composite gnosis which directly realizes selflessness, and the worldly gnosis experienced outside of meditation sessions. These are dependent in nature because they arise from causes and conditions. The fully established nature (*parinişpanna*) is the state of ultimate reality which can withstand rigorous and reasoned examination from the absolute point of view, and is empty of both the imagined and the dependent natures. In this way all the imagined and dependent phenomena are nonexistent in reality, whereas the fully established nature is fully established in reality, is never nonexistent as the true nature of phenomena, and always exists in truth. To say that the first two natures exist in the absolute sense is the extreme view of eternalism, and to say that the third nature does not exist in the absolute sense is the extreme view of nihilism. This fully established nature, or absolute reality, is the ultimate Madhyamaka or middle which transcends those two extremes.

In numerous writings Dolpopa consistently maintained that the three-nature theory belonged to the Madhyamaka tradition, and not to the Cittamātra or Yogācāra. As mentioned above, he was able to make this statement in large part by claiming that Vasubandhu and Asaṅga were upholders of what was known as the Great Madhyamaka tradition, one of the key themes of which was the combination of the three-nature theory with standard Madhyamaka doctrine.[40] Dolpopa wrote more than two thousand pages of annotations and explanations concerning the different

Prajñāpāramitā sūtras. It is especially interesting to note that large portions of his annotations to the twenty-five-thousand- and eighteen-thousand-line versions of the *sūtra* are copied directly from the *Bṛhaṭṭīkā*, although it is not acknowledged as the source. At the end of such glosses he repeatedly adds "thus the Madhyamaka teaches."[41] In his interpretations of the three natures Dolpopa clearly followed the unique interpretation of the *Bṛhaṭṭīkā*.

Dolpopa also mentions the occurrence of the three-nature theory in still other versions of the *Prajñāpāramitā sūtras*. He specifically refers to the versions of the sūtra in five hundred, eight thousand, eighteen thousand, and twenty-five thousand lines as teaching the three natures. The "Maitreya Chapter" is found only in the eighteen-thousand- and twenty-five-thousand-line versions. In citing the other versions Dolpopa is referring to statements in the sūtras which present the three-nature theory without actually using the three specific terms. For example, in the autocommentary to *The Fourth Council* he makes the following statement:

> In the *Five Hundred Line Prajñāpāramitā* it is also stated that since the form, and so forth, which are nonexistent entities, are the imagined [nature], they are to be understood [as totally nonexistent]; since the form, and so forth, which are base entities, are the dependent [nature], they are to be rejected; and since the form, and so forth, which are entities existing in reality, are the fully established [nature], they are precisely what is to be obtained after the removal of impurities. Those which are in the three categories in this way are to be understood, rejected, and actualized after the removal of impurities.
>
> It is also stated that if even the enlightenments of the listeners and solitary buddhas are not achieved if one does not practice in that way, what need is there to mention that the enlightenment of the Mahāyāna [is not achieved]?[42]

This quotation clearly illustrates how Dolpopa would interpret a passage of scripture in order to highlight its significance in the context of his own philosophical agenda. Let us compare his interpretation to what is actually found at the very beginning of the Tibetan translation of the five-hundred-line *Prajñāparamitā sūtra*, which is of course the version Dolpopa was using. The first words of the Buddha are: "Form, Subhūti, is a nonexistent entity, a base entity, and an existent entity."[43] After stating that the same threefold classification applies to the remaining aggregates, bases of sense cognition, and so forth, the Buddha continues:

> Since childish persons do not precisely comprehend form in those three categories, they are addicted to form, cultivate it, and obscure it. If certain renunciation will not come about by means of the vehicle of the listeners or the vehicle of the solitary buddhas for those who are addicted to form, cultivate it, and obscure it, what need is there to mention [that it will not come about] by means of the great vehicle of the Mahāyāna?[44]

Now the extent of Dolpopa's interpretation is obvious. In the original sūtra passage there is only a bare mention of the three categories, although they are clearly of fundamental importance in understanding the intent of the scripture. Dolpopa has elaborated upon them, and seen them to correspond to the three aspects of the three-nature theory. Without examination of the numerous *Prajñāpāramitā* commentaries in the Tibetan canon, it is uncertain whether he based his interpretations on earlier Indian or Tibetan precedent, or whether this is another facet of his still largely unexplored and perhaps original hermeneutical work. Jonang Tāranātha, certainly the most influential heir to Dolpopa's tradition, also emphasized the presence of the three natures in the *Prajñāpāramitā*, and quoted a large portion of the "Maitreya Chapter" when later seeking to establish the canonical sources for the Madhyamaka tradition of "the emptiness of other" (*gzhan stong*) in his school.[45]

Dolpopa not only tried to show the compatibility of different Mahāyāna scriptures and treatises, but to illustrate as well how the same points of doctrine were expressed in the Vajrayāna scriptures. In particular, he often taught the *Kālacakra tantra* according to the *Prajñāpāramitā sūtra*, and vice-versa.[46] For example, he pointed out that Nāgārjuna had presented the infallible teachings of the Madhyamaka by means of refuting the extreme of the nihilistic view of nonexistence through his *Collection of Eulogies* (*Bstod pa'i tshogs*), and refuting the eternalistic view of existence through his *Collection of Reasoning* (*Rigs pa'i tshogs*). Likewise, Asaṅga and Vasubandhu had established the meaning of the *Prajñāpāramitā sūtra*s as Madhyamaka by refuting the extreme view of existence through denying the reality of both the imagined (*parikalpita*) and dependent (*paratantra*) natures, and refuting the extreme view of nonexistence through affirming the reality of the profound and fully established nature (*pariniṣpanna*). In this way, Dolpopa felt, there is no contradiction between the teachings of Nāgārjuna, Asaṅga, and Vasubandhu, nor are any of the flaws of the inferior Cittamātra doctrine to be found. Moreover, all of the categories of pristine form, and so forth, which are taught in the *Prajñāpāramitā sūtras* are actually to be understood as indicating the divine assemblies described in the tantras.[47]

Dolpopa's consistent treatment of doctrinal topics of both sūtra and tantra in the same works, and his insistence that these two traditions of explication and practice are in actuality saying the same thing, albeit with different terminology and style, is another area in which he departed from what was the norm in Tibetan scholarly discourse. Mahāyāna and Vajrayāna theory and practice had for the most part been the subjects of separate works, and were not discussed side by side. But Dolpopa felt that the entire Buddhist tradition as it had been received in Tibet should be utilized when seeking to understand the true intentions of the Buddha and his great successors. As he stated in the autocommentary to *The Fourth Council*:

> Tantras should be understood by means of other tantras.
> Sūtras should be understood by means of other sūtras.
> Sūtras should also be understood by means of the tantras.
> Tantras should also be understood by means of the sūtras.
> Both should be understood by means of both.
> Moreover, [they should be understood] by means of pristine learning, contemplation, meditation, explication, and practice.
> By means of that, the many profound [aspects of] the ground, path, and result of the many profound teachings are realized.
> All the ground and result of definitive meaning are one as the Buddha-nature itself, and the path is its yoga.[48]

3. Two Approaches to Enlightenment

When it came to the question of how enlightenment actually occurs, Dolpopa, like almost all Tibetan masters, taught that the spiritual path described in the Buddhist tantras was the superior way. However, it may be said that there are two basic views of how enlightenment itself comes about. The first view is that enlightenment occurs only when the vital winds (*vāyu*, *rlung*) which normally circulate in the right and left channels (*nadī*, *rtsa*) within the human body are drawn into the central channel (*avadhūti*) through the practice of yoga. The second view is that enlightenment is attained through simply recognizing the nature of one's own mind, which was also often expressed as recognizing the essence of thoughts to be the buddha-body of reality (*dharmakāya*).

Here Dolpopa did not depart from the position of the founders of Sakya, the first of whom, Sachen Kunga Nyingpo (1092–1158), had told his disciple Phagmodrupa Dorje Gyalpo (1110–1170) that birth in saṃsāra occurs because the vital winds have not been drawn into the central channel of the subtle body.[49] Dolpopa stated that absolute truth is accessible only to nonconceptual gnosis, and not to relative consciousness. Moreover, absolute truth is not accessible while the vital winds have not ceased, or else entered the central channel, whereas only the relative is accessible while there is a circulation of the winds.[50] These comments allude to the necessity of the practice of tantric yoga, especially that of the Six-branch Yoga, for the realization of the true nature of reality.

For Dolpopa the practice of the Six-branch Yoga (*ṣaḍaṅgayoga*, *sbyor ba yan lag drug pa*) was the most efficacious method available for the rapid attainment of enlightenment according to the tradition of Buddhist tantra. As referred to many times in the preceding pages, the Six-branch Yoga is the perfection-stage (*rdzogs rim*) practice of the *Kālacakra tantra*. It may be helpful to briefly outline its structure and objectives at this point.

The first of the six branches is Individual Withdrawal (*pratyāhāra*, *so sor sdud pa* or *so sor gcod pa*), which is practiced in order to sever the connection between the ordinary five sense organs and their five objects, and thus withdraw the projected consciousness from those objects. When this is accomplished there is an appearance of certain signs, or "empty forms" (*śūnyabimba*, *stong gzugs*). According to Dolpopa these are actually manifestations of the Buddha-nature. The second branch is Mental Stability (*dhyāna*, *bsam gtan*), during which the mind becomes stable and firmly fixed upon its new points of reference, the "empty forms." The third branch is Breath Control (*prāṇāyāma*, *srog rtsol*). This branch is practiced in order to draw the vital winds (*vāyu*, *rlung*) into the central channel (*avadhūti*, *rtsa dbu ma*) of the subtle body, thus gaining control over the energies of the body and quieting the movements of ordinary consciousness. The fourth branch is Retention (*dhāraṇā*, *'dzin pa*). The main purpose here is to prevent any movement of the vital winds, and thereby perfect the retention of the sexual fluids. During the fifth branch, Subsequent Mindfulness (*anusmṛti*, *rjes dran*), various yogas are practiced together with an actual or visualized sexual partner. The meditations of the "fierce fire" (*caṇḍālī*, *gtum mo*) are also included in this branch. The blazing appearances of "fierce fire" form a basis for the occurance of the special "empty forms" which actually elicit the experience of immutable bliss and emptiness. The sixth and final branch is Meditative Concentration" (*samādhi*, *ting nge 'dzin*). The practice during Meditative Concentration is not different than the one during Subsequent Mindfulness, but there is an increase of immutable bliss, the actual accomplishment of a radical dematerialization of the physical body, and the actualization of the buddha-body of nondual gnosis.

In the practice of tantra, the ordinary "vital karmic winds" (*karmavāyu*, *las rlung*) are drawn into the central channel during the practice of yoga, and are thereby transformed into the "vital gnostic wind" (*jñānavāyu*, *ye shes rlung*). Until this is achieved one remains under the power of ordinary consciousness, which is mounted upon the vital karmic winds. When they have been drawn into the central channel, and are transformed into the vital gnostic wind, this then serves as the support for nonconceptual gnosis. In a series of verses Dolpopa clearly summarized the essential points of this approach to enlightenment:

> Therefore, as long as delusion has not ceased it is impossible for the manifestation of delusion, the cycle of birth and death, to cease.
>
> As long as this circulation of the vital winds has not stopped, it is impossible for this stream of consciousness to stop.
>
> While this stream of mind and mental events has not stopped, it is also impossible for this manifestation of delusion, the three worlds, to stop.
>
> Therefore, with the wish to transcend the three worlds, whose nature is suffering, if you abandon all distractions and meditate upon the profound Vajrayoga, the sublime nectar

from the mouth of the excellent master, this circulation of vital winds and mind together will stop.[51]

Dolpopa took great exception to the view that recognition of the nature of mind, or recognition of thoughts as the buddha-body of reality (*dharmakāya*), would alone bring about enlightenment. As he stated in *The Fourth Council*:

> I cannot defer to those who accept that since buddhahood is reached through self-recognition it is not necessary to accumulate the two assemblies and purify the two obscurations, because through self-recognition the basis is purified without rejection.
>
> Joining my palms together, I offer an appeal: A sentient being without intrinsic self-awareness is impossible, and if there is intrinsic self-awareness there is self-recognition.
>
> If there were no intrinsic awareness of self and others, it would contradict being intrinsically aware, like the gross elements.[52]
>
> Therefore, since all sentient beings have minds, and since all who have minds have intrinsic self-awareness, there is self-recognition from the moment of birth.
>
> This topic is known to those who understand scripture and reasoning.
>
> It is unimaginable that the numerous arrogant fools with little learning who are usurpers, pretenders, and fabricators of Dharma, understand this topic, or have even heard about or seen it.
>
> Therefore, that type of perverse view, in which self-recognition is sufficient, is the secret words of Māra.
>
> Reject that kind of evil view, the work of Māra, which says that the perfect path or the wrong path is determined by that sort of realization or lack of realization, and that therefore liberation[53] is through self-recognition.
>
> Objection: The meaning of self-recognition of the essence refers to just the realization that this consciousness of one's own mind is the buddha-body of reality.

> [Reply:] Since this consciousness is the incompatible opposite of the buddha-body of reality, it is never the buddha-body of reality.[54]

The specific Tibetan controversies surrounding the issue of instantaneous enlightenment through recognition of the nature of the mind have recently been studied in depth by David Jackson.[55] As he has shown, it was mainly members of the Kagyü schools in Tibet who maintained this doctrine, although it was certainly common in Chinese Ch'an Buddhism as well. Dolpopa quotes the position which is the object of his refutation as maintaining, "Through self-recognition the basis is purified without rejection." This may be understood as alluding to both the idea that through recognition of the essence of the thoughts or concepts (*vikalpa*, *rnam rtog*) as being the buddha-body of reality (*dharmakāya*) they are purified or dissolved into the buddha-body of reality, and also to the idea that any afflicting emotion (*kleśa*, *nyon mongs*) which arises is actually a manifestation or self-presencing (*rang snang*) of gnosis itself. Thus there is no need to reject thought or afflicting emotion, the basis or ground which is naturally purified by means of the recognition. This type of viewpoint was very widespread in Tibetan Buddhism.[56]

In marked contrast to these views, Dolpopa claimed that the definition of an ordinary sentient being or a buddha, and of saṃsāra or nirvāṇa, was determined by the presence or absence of the incidental and temporary obscurations which veil the true nature of reality.[57] It was not determined solely by a recognition of the nature of the mind or the thoughts. In a text of spiritual advice which he composed for the physician Tsultrim Ö, Dolpopa wrote at length about these problematic issues:

> Even though deluded appearances are realized to be just deluded appearances, as long as this circulation of the vital winds and mind has not ceased, this appearance of delusion will not cease. Likewise, as long as jaundice is not cured, the appearance of the conch as yellow will not cease. To stop the circulation of the vital winds and mind it is necessary to have the sublime Dharma of Shambhala to the north, the heart advice of the Kalkins on the tenth spiritual level, the uncommon oral instructions of Kālacakra, who is the Buddha-nature; it cannot be stopped by other minor [instructions].

When this circulation of the vital winds and mind has stopped, there is not an insentient state, or a nothingness. The abandoning of all pervasive conceptualization itself [yields] a spontaneous nonconceptual gnosis which transcends the phenomena of consciousness, and is a state of great nondual gnosis. It is like the curing of jaundice and seeing the white conch just as it exists, or the breaking of a vase and seeing the lamp flame that exists within it, or the clearing of clouds in the sky and seeing the planets and stars. Nevertheless, if that kind of realization is rare even among Dharma practitioners, and rare even among serious meditators, what need to even mention that it is so among other people.

The Great Seal of radiant light, the inconceivable expanse of the four buddha-bodies and the five gnoses, is stated in authentic sūtras and tantras to permanently exist in the hearts of all sentient beings. This is the truth, but those who have not penetrated the meaning of those [scriptures] exaggerate by saying that all apparent existence is the Great Seal, the four buddha-bodies, and the five gnoses.[58]

He again picks up the same topic later in the text:

In regard to that, while the buddha-body of the ground-buddhahood and the buddha-body of the result-buddhahood have not the slightest difference in essence, they are distinguished as ground and result by means of the presence or absence of incidental stains. It is like referring to the expanse of the sky in situations when it is free or not free of clouds, and so forth.

Buddhahood is stated to be the buddha-body of gnosis, and the incidental impurities are stated to be the groups of consciousness. In that way gnosis and consciousness are stated to be extremely different, like light and dark, or nectar and poison. Nevertheless, the differentiation of those two is very rare. These days the majority maintains that this very mind-as-such is the buddha-body of reality, self-arisen gnosis, and the Great Seal, and many maintain that concepts are the buddha-body of reality, the afflicting emotions are gnosis, saṃsāra and nirvāṇa are indivisible, these appearances and sounds are the three buddha-bodies or the four buddha-bodies, and so forth.[59]

And he concludes with the following advice:

> Seek out the uncommon esoteric instructions which separate natural radiant light and the incidental stains, like separating clear water and sediment. Without it, this incidental mind and deceptive mental events are taken to be the buddha-bodies, gnosis, and so forth, which is like taking poison to be medicine, or taking brass to be gold. And it will be maintained that if this deceptive impure mind is recognized, it is buddhahood, but if it is not recognized it is saṃsāra, and that if it is recognized it is gnosis, but if it is not recognized it is ignorance, and so forth, which are not in agreement with the words of the Buddha, and also contradict reason. For example, that is like maintaining that if this fire is recognized it is cool, but if it is not recognized it is hot, or maintaining that if this deadly poison is recognized it is nectar, but if it is not recognized it is poison, or maintaining that if this great abyss is recognized it is a pleasant plain, but if it is not recognized it is a great abyss, or maintaining that if this razor is recognized it cannot cut the body, but if it is not recognized it can cut, and so forth.[60]

For Dolpopa appearances cannot be the manifestation or self-presencing of gnosis (*ye shes rang snang*), or the buddha-body of reality, because ordinary appearances are completely fictitious, imaginary (*parikalpita*) and dependent (*paratantra*) phenomena, which are both actually nonexistent. The fully established true nature (*pariniṣpanna*), nondual gnosis, the buddha-body of reality, and so forth, are real and existent. Ordinary sentient beings spend their lives occupied with nonexistent phenomena, asleep to the reality of the true nature within each of them.[61] Enlightenment is achieved only when the incidental obscurations are removed through the practice of the spiritual path, and the eternally present ground of emptiness, the Buddha-nature, is allowed to shine forth as the awakened result.[62]

Dolpopa in these quotations mentions several times that ordinary consciousness is the opposite of the buddha-body of reality (*dharmakāya*), or is extremely different than gnosis. This is because consciousness, in all its varieties, is only relative and empty of self-nature, whereas the buddha-body of reality and nondual gnosis are only empty of other relative phenomena. They are two great and separate kingdoms. And the objects of these two different states of perception are saṃsāra and nirvāṇa, which are indivisible only in the sense that the first, which is actually nonexistent, could not appear without the presence of the second, which is truly existent.[63] For, as Kalkin Puṇḍarīka stated, "Existence and nirvāṇa are not identical, but like a shadow and the sun."[64]

Part Two

Texts in Translation

Introduction to the Translation of *A General Commentary on the Doctrine*

When Dolpopa first began to record his unique reconfiguration of the Buddhist Doctrine, he composed a number of small works to express his views. Although it is not actually dated, the short text entitled *A General Commentary on the Doctrine* (*Bstan pa spyi 'grel*) was certainly among those early efforts, and indeed seems to have been the most significant of them all.[1] There are several reasons for assigning an early date to this work. The commentary to the text, written by Nyaön Kunga Bal, was apparently completed in the summer of 1333 while the great stūpa at Jonang was still under construction.[2] It was during the construction of this monument in the years 1330–1333 that Dolpopa had first openly spoken of the distinction between the relative as empty of self-nature and the absolute as empty of other. Several of the key technical terms Dolpopa first borrowed from certain Mahāyāna scriptures are found in *A General Commentary on the Doctrine*, but not the terms such as *gzhan stong* ("empty of other"), and *kun gzhi ye shes* ("universal ground gnosis"), which seem to have been introduced only somewhat later. Although the full development of his radical innovations in terminology is not yet evident, most of the themes he would emphasize for the rest of his life already dominate this early work.[3] Since the use of the contrasting terms *rang stong* and *gzhan stong* is, of course, found in *The Ocean of Definitive Meaning* (*Nges don rgya mtsho*), as well as in Nyaön's commentary, but not in *A General Commentary on the Doctrine* itself, it seems clear that this brief work must be placed among the earliest of Dolpopa's compositions.

The importance of the text is underscored by the fact that it is mentioned in several sources as one of Dolpopa's three most important works, along with the *Ocean of Definitive Meaning*, which was perhaps also completed before the summer of 1333, and *The Fourth Council*, composed in the last years of his life.[4] *A General Commentary on the Doctrine* was perhaps the first attempt by Dolpopa to present a systematic summary of how his revolutionary vision encompassed the entire scope of the Buddhist tradition, from the earliest teachings of the First Turning of the Dharma Wheel up through those of the tantras. This would help to explain why it was singled out within the Jonang tradition as a significant work despite its brevity.

A General Commentary on the Doctrine is also the only one of Dolpopa's works to itself receive full treatment by another writer in a separate commentary. The fact that Nyaön Kunga Bal, one of Dolpopa's most important disciples, chose to compose a detailed commentary to explain the text is indicative of its important role in the first spread of Dolpopa's teachings.[5] Nyaön's commentary, entitled *Removing Mental Darkness to Illuminate the True Intentions* (*Dgongs pa rnam gsal yid kyi mun sel*), was composed at Jonang itself, and clearly follows Dolpopa's own explanation of his text.[6] *A General Commentary on the Doctrine* may have been widely distributed very early, since Nyaön's commentary on it was requested from afar by a certain Tashi Dorje, identified as the imperial chaplain (*bla'i mchod gnas*) of a Chinese Emperor.[7] An indication of the impact of Dolpopa's text upon another of his main disciples, Tangpoche Kunga Bum (1331–1402), is also recorded. When still young, Kunga Bum saw a copy of *A General Commentary on the Doctrine*, which caused him to feel great devotion to Dolpopa. As a result he the . traveled to Jonang and received extensive teachings and initiations from the master himself.[8]

A General Commentary on the Doctrine is structured as a prayer, and was clearly composed in a state of deep inspiration and faith. When Dolpopa himself recited this text, as well as several others specifically mentioned in his biography, he did so with great feeling:

> At the end of intensely praying according to the exceptional supplications he had composed, such as *A General Commentary on the Doctrine*, which is a supplication to the masters and

> chosen deities indivisible, tears flowed like rain from his eyes as he prayed with deep feeling, "You know! You know!"[9]

This work is one which would have been memorized and recited by members of the Jonang tradition, both as a devotional text and as a summary of Dolpopa's teachings. This was clearly the case during Dolpopa's life. For example, as he departed from Central Tibet in 1360, and was being carried by palanquin to the northern shore of the Tsangpo River, the members of the Sangha were reciting *A General Commentary on the Doctrine* as an incredible mass of hysterically wailing people surrounded him, distraught at his departure, many of them falling senseless to the ground.[10] Two hundred years later *A General Commentary on the Doctrine* was one of the main works of Dolpopa that was still being transmitted and studied at Jonang.[11]

There are many types of commentaries for the purpose of unraveling the words and meaning of a given text. According to Nyaön, the present text by Dolpopa may be considered "a commentary on difficult points" (*dka' 'grel*), because it makes it possible to easily realize the meaning of the scriptures of the Doctrine which are otherwise difficult to understand, or as "a commentary of condensed meaning" (*bsdus don 'grel pa*), because it presents the principle meaning of the Buddha's message in a condensed fashion. It is called *A General Commentary on the Doctrine* (*Bstan pa spyi 'grel*) because it comments upon the essential meaning of all the sūtras and tantras, and not upon the specific meaning of individual sūtras and tantras.[12]

In discussing Dolpopa's motives for composing *A General Commentary on the Doctrine*, Nyaön notes that one purpose of the work was to provide a reliable and easily understood guide to the principal meaning of the immaculate sūtras and tantras. This text was thus specifically intended for those individuals who were intently focused upon the practice of the profound path of meditation, and not inclined towards the extensive study and contemplation of the vast scriptures and commentaries of the Buddhist tradition.[13] Nyaön further characterizes the work as a presentation of the complete definitive meaning of the sūtras and tantras, and as a work which unravels the knots of their "adamantine words" (*rdo rje'i tshig*) in a style that produces a lucid state of mind when it is heard. If the text is contemplated, the ultimate nature of relative and absolute truth will be realized, and if it is meditated upon correctly, the sublime attainment will be achieved. Its phrasing is elegant, and although the words are brief, the meaning is vast.[14]

The following translation of *A General Commentary on the Doctrine* is based upon the Bhutanese edition of the text made from tracings of the original Gyaltse Dzong blocks. The Dzamtang edition has also been consulted, and any important textual variants have been discussed in the notes to the translation. The headings provided in a smaller bold type within parentheses in the translation represent the topical outline found in Nyaön's commentary. The annotations to the translation are all close paraphrases or translations of Nyaön's own comments, and thus perhaps represent Dolpopa's own explanations of the text, or at least its meaning as understood by one of his closest disciples and Dharma heirs. It is strongly recommended that the translation of Dolpopa's text be read together with these notes. Page numbers from the Bhutanese edition of the *Bstan pa spyi 'grel* have been placed in the text within brackets. A few words not found in the Tibetan, but which were thought to be helpful in the translation, have been placed within brackets.

One subject in the following translation requires specific comment. In the Tibetan text there is frequent mention of the three well-known "Turnings of the Dharma Wheel." In the original Tibetan a "Turning of the Dharma Wheel" is always referred to by the abbreviated terms "Dharma Wheel" (*chos 'khor*) or "Wheel" (*'khor lo*). For example, instead of "First Turning of the Dharma Wheel" the text simply reads "First Dharma Wheel." This convention has been followed in the translation, but the full phrases have been used when providing explanations in the notes.

The Supplication Entitled
A General Commentary on the Doctrine

(Opening expressions of homage and offering)

OṂ GURU BUDDHA BODHISATTVEBHYO NAMO NAMAḤ[1]

I respectfully pay homage and take refuge at the immaculate lotus-feet of the Dharma Lords, the excellent masters, the emanation buddha-bodies. Please grace me at all times with your great love.[2]

I bow at the feet of the permanent, stable, and eternal precious Dharma Lords, the masters endowed with the four reliances,
Who spontaneously perform enlightened actions filling space, and clarify the unmistaken definitive secret of the absolute.[3]

(Main Section)

(1 Respectfully bowing to the masters because they correctly realize and teach the individual intended meanings of the three Dharma Wheels in sequence)

(1a Respectfully bowing to the masters because they correctly realize and teach the intended meaning of the First Dharma Wheel)

I bow at the feet of the masters who carefully teach that all composite phenomena are impermanent, unstable, and changeable,

Like a mountain waterfall, like a cloud, like lightning, and like dew {687} on a blade of grass.[4]

I bow at the feet of the masters who teach that the nature of suffering is the same for the entire three realms,
Like being caught in a pit of fire or in a vicious viper's mouth, or like a bee circling inside a pot.[5]

I bow at the feet of the masters who teach that those who cling to the impure body as pure
Are the same as ignorant children who like and desire a vase of vomit beautified with ornaments.[6]

I bow at the feet of the masters who cause sentient beings who delight in saṃsāra itself to feel revulsion and sadness toward the impermanent and the impure,
And then teach them the Four Truths for entering the path of empty and peaceful selflessness.[7]

(1b Respectfully bowing to the masters because they correctly realize and teach the intended meaning of the Second Dharma Wheel)

I bow at the feet of the masters who teach that all phenomena {688} arise just from conditions,
Without any self, sentient beings, soul, or creator, and are like a dream, an illusion, a mirage, or an echo.[8]

I bow at the feet of the masters who clearly teach that objects appear to be external, but are merely the habitual propensities of mind,
And that even mind, intellect, and consciousness are mere names, mere designations, just empty like space.[9]

I bow at the feet of the masters who teach that the aggregates of form, and so forth, are only as substantial as foam, water bubbles, a mirage, and so forth,
And who teach that the bases of sense cognition are the same as an empty town, and the constituents the same as vicious vipers.[10]

I bow at the feet of the masters who teach that all the phenomena of existence and nirvāṇa are birthless and ceaseless,

Free from going, coming, and remaining, and without extreme and middle, each empty by nature.[11]

(1c Respectfully bowing to the masters because they correctly realize and teach the intended meaning of the Third Dharma Wheel)

I bow at the feet of the masters who teach that like a butter lamp inside a vase, the treasure of a pauper, and so forth,

The Buddha-nature of radiant light and the buddha-body of reality exist within the sheath of the relative, incidental aggregates.[12]

I bow at the feet of the masters who state that all the imagined and dependent phenomena are nonexistent, but the fully established true nature is never nonexistent,

Thus carefully distinguishing and teaching that which transcends existence and nonexistence, and eternalism and nihilism.[13]

I bow at the feet of the masters who state that all relative phenomena are merely the dependent origination of cause and result, while the self-arisen absolute transcends dependent origination, {689}

Thus teaching the difference between the gnosis that arises from conditions, and that which is self-arisen.[14]

(2 Respectfully bowing to the masters because they correctly realize and teach the meaning of tantra, and mainly what is expressed in the *Kālacakra tantra*)

I bow at the feet of the masters who state that all outer and inner phenomena are merely the deluded sphere of ignorance, while the other is the true nature, self-arisen gnosis,

Thus teaching the distinction between consciousness and gnosis, saṃsāra and nirvāṇa, and the two truths.[15]

I bow at the feet of the masters who distinguish and teach that the relative threefold universe is a deluded appearance, a mere fiction;

Whereas, the absolute threefold universe, the Buddha-nature, is the indestructible, nonfictional, undeluded appearance.[16]

(3 Respectfully bowing to the masters because they correctly realize and teach the intended meaning of all three Dharma Wheels)

I bow at the feet of the masters who teach the intentions of the Dharma Wheel of the Four Truths,

The Dharma Wheel of no characteristics, and the Dharma Wheel of certainty in the absolute.[17]

I bow at the feet of the masters who cleanse the three coarse, subtle, and extremely subtle stains with the nectar of the three Wheels in sequence,

[Enabling disciples] to obtain the sublime jewel of the buddha-body of reality free from stain.[18]

I bow at the feet of the masters who teach those who maintain [the existence of] external objects that everything is mind, who teach the Madhyamaka of no appearance to those who are attached to mind,

And who teach the Madhyamaka of perfect appearance to those who maintain no appearance.[19]

I bow at the feet of the masters who teach the Dharma of cause and result to the inferior, who teach those who adhere to existence that everything is empty,

And who teach the Buddha-nature of radiant light to those who maintain nothing.[20]

(4 Respectfully bowing to the masters because they correctly realize and teach the intended meaning of both sūtra and tantra)

I bow at the feet of the masters who teach the vehicle of the listeners to those of inferior faculties, the vehicle of the solitary buddhas to those of middling faculties, {690}

And the sūtra and mantra styles of cause and result in the sublime vehicle to the superior.[21]

I bow to you who care for trainees with the three Wheels in sequence, and especially secret mantra,

Just like parents care for infants, adolescents, and young adults according to their development.[22]

I bow to you who also teach the three Wheels in sequence, and especially the tradition of mantra, according to the character of trainees,

Like assigning work to an inferior, middling, or superior child according to character.[23]

I bow to you who teach that the three-storied mansion of the Buddhist Doctrine of the three Wheels in sequence,

And especially of secret mantra, is to be climbed in sequence, like climbing to the top of a three-storied mansion.[24]

I bow to you who teach the cleansing of the Buddha-nature by the three Wheels in sequence, and especially by secret mantra,

Just like three layers of stain upon a jewel are cleansed in sequence by a jeweler.[25]

(5 In particular, respectfully bowing to the masters because they correctly realize and teach the intended meaning of mantra)

(5a Praise by presenting the similes of ultimate bliss and emptiness)

I bow to you who teach that the Buddha-nature has another cause and result.

The other cause is the empty images of radiant light, and the other result is immutable great bliss, similar to the eight prognostic images.[26]

(5b Praise by presenting a number of the names of ultimate emptiness)

I bow to you who teach that many various names, such as Secret, Great Secret, Element of Space, and Viśvamāta,

Source of Phenomena, Lotus, Bhagā, Lion-throne, Nairātmyā, and {691} Varāhī, have the single meaning of emptiness.[27]

(5c Praise by presenting a number of the names of ultimate great bliss)

I bow to you who teach that the many names of that itself, such as Vajra, Drop, Heruka, and Gathering,

Restraint, He, Great Compassion, Primal Buddha, and Enlightenment Mind, have the single meaning of great bliss.[28]

(5d Praise by presenting a number of the names of the total integration of bliss and emptiness)

I bow to you who teach that many names, such as Vajrasattva, Evaṃ, Kālacakra, and Cakrasaṃvara,

Hevajra, Māyājāla, and Guhyasamāja, have the single meaning of total integration.[29]

(6 Respectfully bowing to the masters because they correctly realize and teach the intended meaning of the ground, path, and result)

I bow to you who teach that total integration, indivisible, equal-flavored, and indestructible self-arisen gnosis, the primal Buddha,

Is present in everyone as thusness with stains, is like the sky, and exists as the universal ground.[30]

I bow to you who teach the path of the Vajrayoga, the perfection of transcendent knowledge, the Atiyoga,

And the meditation of the Great Seal, together with its branches, as the method for separating that from the sheath of the stains.[31]

I bow to you who teach that through the sublime method of the path, that which is present as the ground is merely actualized as the result,

An immaculate thusness from which all stains have been purged, like the sky clear of clouds, and so forth.[32]

(7 Respectfully bowing to the masters because they correctly realize and teach the two buddha-bodies, together with their enlightened activities, which are the result of the two assemblies)

I bow to you who teach that the sheath of stains upon self-arisen gnosis is destroyed by the assembly of the nonconceptual gnosis of immutable radiant light,

And the excellent benefit for oneself is achieved through the absolute buddha-body of reality.[33]

I bow to you who teach that the assembly of merit, which accomplishes benefit and happiness, [and which is created] by a special attitude of great love for those who go without understanding, [692]

Fully produces the excellent relative buddha-bodies of form, and accomplishes the excellent benefit of others.[34]

I bow to you who teach that after fully perfecting a sea of prayers, fully maturing a sea of sentient beings,

And fully purifying a sea of pure realms, one dissolves into the perfect culmination.[35]

I bow to you who teach that due to prior impetus, benefit to others will spontaneously occur in all directions and at all times, even without effort and without thought,

Like the fine vase, the sun, the jewel, the heavenly tree, and the divine drum.[36]

(8 Respectfully bowing to the masters because they correctly realize and teach the ultimate intended meaning of everything, such as the three Dharma Wheels in sequence)

I bow to you who teach that the ultimate Dharma Wheel is the Final Wheel, the ultimate vehicle is the Mahāyāna,

The ultimate Mahāyāna is the vehicle of the Buddha-nature, and the ultimate Buddha-nature is great bliss.[37]

I bow to you who teach that the ultimate Doctrine is the Mahāyāna, the ultimate Mahāyāna is the Mantrayāna,
The ultimate mantra is Kālacakra, and the ultimate Kālacakra is bliss and emptiness.[38]

I bow to you who teach that the ultimate philosophical system is the Great Madhyamaka, the ultimate Madhyamaka is birthless and free from extremes,
The ultimate freedom from extremes is natural radiant light, and ultimate radiant light is great bliss.[39]

I bow to you who teach that the ultimate view is emptiness free from extremes, the ultimate emptiness is a referential emptiness, {693}
The ultimate conduct is great compassion, and the ultimate compassion is nonreferential.[40]

I bow to you who teach for the benefit of ultimate disciples that the ultimate initiation is the transcendent initiation,
The ultimate realization is the definitive meaning of the perfection stage, and the ultimate attainment is the great sublime attainment.[41]

I bow to you who teach that the ultimate maṇḍala is sublime natural radiant light, the ultimate deity is the buddha-body of the gnosis of bliss and emptiness,
The ultimate seal is the Great Seal of radiant light, and the ultimate mantra protects the mind.[42]

I bow to you who teach the complete ultimate Dharma of the ultimate ground as thusness with stains,
The ultimate path as the Six-branch Yoga, and the ultimate result as the thusness of the separated result.[43]

(Conclusion)

This supplication, entitled *A General Commentary on the Doctrine*, was composed by Sherab Gyaltsen Balzangpo, a servant of the Dharma Lords, the excellent masters.[44]

By this virtue, may I and all sentient beings actualize the separated result of the absolute buddha-body of reality,

And by means of the produced result of the twofold relative buddha-bodies of form, work for the benefit of others for the duration of saṃsāra.[45]

For as long as that has not been achieved, by means of the three Wheels in sequence, and especially secret mantra, {694}

May I always strive to cleanse in sequence the stains upon my own and other's Buddha-nature.[46]

MAṆGALAṂ BHAVANTU[47]

Introduction to the Translation of *The Fourth Council*

During his long teaching career Dolpopa composed a large number of treatises dealing with what he considered to be the most crucial issues facing scholars and practitioners of the Buddhist teachings in fourteenth-century Tibet. Many of these issues continue to be of great interest to the present day. Among his many compositions, three are most often singled out as major works. These are the brief *A General Commentary on the Doctrine* (*Bstan pa spyi 'grel*) and the massive *The Ocean of Definitive Meaning*: *A Mountain Dharma* (*Ri chos nges don rgya mtsho*), both probably completed before 1333, and *The Fourth Council* (*Bka' bsdu bzhi pa*), along with its autocommentary (*rang 'grel*) and summary (*bsdus don*), composed in the last years of Dolpopa's life.[1] In many ways *The Fourth Council* is the culmination of Dolpopa's literary output. As his last major work, this text may be seen as a final verse summation of Dolpopa's views on the various topics that had concerned him throughout his life.

It is of special interest that Dolpopa composed *The Fourth Council* (*Bka' bsdu bzhi pa*) and its autocommentary at the request of Lama Dampa Sönam Gyaltsen, one of the most respected masters in the history of the Sakya tradition. Lama Dampa's request is significant because of the implication that he was not totally opposed to Dolpopa's controversial theories, which were largely rejected by the Sakya tradition in the following centuries. On an earlier occasion, which can only be dated to between the years 1352 and 1355, Lama Dampa had also come to Jonang and engaged in extensive discussions of Dharma with Dolpopa.[2] The actual circumstances of his request to Dolpopa for the composition of works such as *The Fourth Council* are mentioned in several sources. In the summer of 1358 Dolpopa departed from Jonang at the start of a trip to Central Tibet. Along the way he spent a year teaching at the monasteries of Neysar and Chölung. Lama Dampa met Dolpopa at Chölung, presented lavish offerings of horses and gold, and requested the composition of a number of texts, foremost among which were *The Fourth Council (Bka' bsdu bzhi pa)* and its autocommentary.[3] Almost all the available evidence leads to the conclusion that the text was composed in 1358.[4] Traditionally a text would always be given first to the person who had made the original request. Since it is certain that Lama Dampa himself received the textual transmission of the work from Dolpopa sometime between the ninth month of the Dog year (1358) and the first month of the Pig year (1359), the actual composition was probably made during or shortly before that period as well.[5]

Although *The Fourth Council* was undoubtedly one of Dolpopa's most important and influential works, extant references to it by other Tibetan writers after the time of Dolpopa are almost nonexistent.[6] This is certainly due to the severe repression of the Jonang tradition which was discussed above in chapter 2, section 3. Dolpopa's writings, along with those of the Sakya Zhentong advocate Panchen Shakya Chokden and Jonang Tāranātha, were banned by the Tibetan government, and copies were either destroyed or sealed.

The earliest mention of *The Fourth Council* by another author is probably the quotations found in Lhey Gyaltsen's biography of Dolpopa. The only other known contemporary mention of *The Fourth Council* is by Dolpopa's disciple Barawa Gyaltsen Balzang, who refers to it as "our pure teaching of *The Fourth Council*" (*rang re'i bka' bsdu bzhi pa'i bka' yang dag pa*).[7]

Only two editions of *The Fourth Council* and its autocommentary, and one of the summary, are presently available. Until 1984, when the first edition was published in Bhutan, the text was thought to have been lost. The Bhutanese edition is a tracing of a print originally from the fortress of Gyaltse. This version of *The Fourth Council* and its autocommentary has been followed in the translation below. In 1990 M. Kapstein located a set of the Collected

Works of Dolpopa which had been preserved at the monastery of Dzamtang in Eastern Tibet.[8] The Dzamtang edition also contains copies of *The Fourth Council* and its autocommentary, as well as the otherwise unavailable summary. The Dzamtang edition of these texts is written in a somewhat unusual local cursive script.

The following translation follows the versified root text (*rtsa ba*) of *The Fourth Council* (*Bka' bsdu bzhi pa*) as found in the edition published in Bhutan. The readings in this edition are generally preferable to those of the Dzamtang edition. Whenever a significant reading in the Dzamtang edition has been chosen over that of the Bhutanese edition it has been mentioned in a note. The Bhutanese edition of the autocommentary (*rang 'grel*) has also been used extensively to provide notes to the basic text. In addition, virtually the entire text of Dolpopa's own condensed commentary, *A Commentary on the Condensed Meaning of the Fourth Council* (*Bka' bsdu bzhi pa'i bsdus don 'grel pa*), has been translated and inserted into the basic text in a smaller bold type within parentheses. Page numbers from this summary have been inserted into the text at the appropriate points. The inclusion of the summary makes the structure of the basic text much clearer, and provides further important information from Dolpopa himself on the issues at hand. Page numbers from the Bhutanese edition have been placed in the text within brackets. Words and phrases not found in the Tibetan, but which were thought to be helpful in the translation, have been placed within brackets.

A final word to the reader of *The Fourth Council*. It is perhaps helpful to remember that no one understands everything that is said in a text such as this. Later Tibetan authors mention that even Dolpopa's greatest disciples and Dharma heirs did not precisely grasp the full subtlety and depth of their master's genius.[9] *The Fourth Council* was specifically written at the request of another one of Tibet's most exceptional luminaries, Lama Dampa Sönam Gyaltsen. Dolpopa takes the expertise of the reader for granted. Whereas the earlier *A General Commentary on the Doctrine* was specifically written for individuals who were not inclined towards extensive study and contemplation of Buddhist literature, this final work touches upon many themes, and often combines terminology and lines of thought from several different areas of the Buddhist tradition simultaneously. Whereas these nuances would have been appreciated by the advanced audience for whom the text was originally intended, some are unavoidably lost in the process of providing an understandable translation. Hopefully the notes from the autocommentary and other sources will be useful in this regard.

The Great Calculation of the Doctrine Which Has the Significance of a Fourth Council[1]

(Homage to all the sources of refuge in general [254])

OṂ GURU BUDDHA BODHISATTVEBHYO NAMO NAMAḤ[2]

(Homage to ultimate buddhahood, the thusness of self-arisen gnosis)

I respectfully pay homage to the absolute perfect Buddha, the Blessed One who is thusness, ultimate purity, self,[3] great bliss, and permanence.

(The pledge of composition)

I will thoroughly explain the classification of both [sets] of four eons.[4]

(The general nature of both sets of four eons)

The great four eons concern the quality of the eons of a cosmic age; whereas, the lesser four eons concern the quality of the Doctrine.[5]

(The duration in years of both sets of four eons)

The years of the first [set] are four million three hundred and twenty thousand, a quarter of which is stated to be a "foot."[6]

One foot, two, three, and four, in sequence, are stated to be the Kaliyuga, the Dvāparayuga, the Tretayuga, and the Kṛtayuga. {365}

As for the lesser four eons, concerning the quality of the Doctrine, the duration of each of the four eons is a quarter of twenty-one thousand six hundred human years.[7]

(The specific identification of the lesser four eons)

The flawless, with the entire qualities, is the Kṛtayuga Dharma. When a quarter has degenerated, it is the former Tretayuga. When half has degenerated, it becomes the latter Tretayuga.

The remainder when three quarters has degenerated is the Dvāparayuga. If there is not even one quarter, it is the Kaliyuga, stated to be the negative dharma of the anti-gods and barbarians.[8]

(The Kṛtayuga Dharma as the valid witness {255})

Thoroughly understanding each of those divisions, I wish to purge the Doctrine, {366}

And wishing for myself and others to enter upon a fine path, I honor the sublime Kṛtayuga Dharma as a witness.

(The doubtful reliability of all explanations from the flawed Tretayuga treatises)

The Tretayuga and later [eons] are flawed, and their treatises which have been diluted like milk in the marketplace are in every case unfit to act as witnesses.

The higher refutes the lower, as the higher philosophical systems refute the lower.

(The pure view, meditation, and conduct as stated in the flawless Kṛtayuga Dharma)

The Kṛtayuga Dharma is the immaculate words of the Victor, and those well spoken by the lords on the tenth spiritual level, and by the great originators of systems which are flawless and endowed with sublime qualities.[9]

In that tradition all is not empty of self-nature. Finely distinguishing empty of self-nature and empty of other, whatever is relative is all stated to be empty of self-nature, and whatever is absolute is stated to be precisely empty of other.

(The mode of existence of the two truths)

Why? Because in regard to the two truths there are stated to be two modes of truth, two modes of manifestation, and two modes of emptiness,[10]

And because the many forms of exaggeration and denigration,[11] flawed and flawless contradiction,[12] and so forth, phenomena and true nature, and composite and noncomposite,[13] are stated to be two great kingdoms.[14]

(The reason why the two truths cannot be said to have the same or another essence)

It is impossible for the two truths to have a single essence, but they are also not different in essence, nor are they without any difference, for {367} there is the difference of the exclusion of a single essence.

In regard to precisely this, it is stated that the essence is inexpressible as precisely one or another.[15]

Precisely this procedure also [applies] to phenomena and true nature, and for saṃsāra and nirvāṇa, limit and center, incidental and primordial, fabricated and natural, and husk and essence, the procedure is also precisely this.

(The opinions of those with perverse views)[16]

Those of the Tretayuga and later [eons] say other than that: Except for what is empty of self-nature, that which is empty of other does not fit the definition of emptiness.

Therefore, whatever is stated to be the ultimate profound mode of reality, such as the absolute expanse of reality, thusness, natural radiant light, natural coemergence, and the natural immutable state,

The ultimate buddha-body of reality, the ultimate perfection of transcendent knowledge, the ultimate Madhyamaka,[17] the ultimate nirvāṇa, and the ultimate great enlightenment,

The ultimate Buddha, ultimate Dharma, ultimate Saṅgha, ultimate deities and mantras, and ultimate tantras and maṇḍalas, are all said to be precisely empty of self-nature.

They claim that what is empty of self-nature is the ultimate profound mode of reality, such as absolute truth, the expanse of reality, the true nature, and thusness.

Without dividing the two truths into two kingdoms, they claim that {368} whatever is manifest is relative truth and whatever is empty is absolute truth.

They say that the manifest and the empty are in essence indivisible, so there is a single essence, but with different facets.

Without dividing saṃsāra and nirvāṇa into two kingdoms, they say that the manifest aspect is saṃsāra and the empty aspect is nirvāṇa, and also claim the meaning of the indivisibility of saṃsāra and nirvāṇa to be like that.

It is stated that the flawed contradiction is relative truth and the flawless contradiction is absolute truth.

But without dividing them into two such kingdoms,[18] they say that what is manifest and empty are the two truths.

It is stated that the object of action for a dialectician is saṃsāra and the object of action for a yoga practitioner is nirvāṇa.

But without dividing them into two such kingdoms, they claim the pair of manifest and empty to be the meaning of saṃsāra and nirvāṇa.

(The extreme consequences of maintaining that whatever is manifest is relative truth and whatever is empty is absolute truth)

If everything manifest is relative saṃsāra, the manifestation of the absolute would also be relative saṃsāra.[19]

If everything empty is absolute nirvāṇa, all that is empty of self-nature would be absolute nirvāṇa.

If that is claimed, the consequence would be that all sufferings and their sources would also be absolute nirvāṇa.

If even that is claimed, they would be taintless, and also pure, self, great bliss, and permanent.[20]

All the absolute qualities such as the powers, which are as numerous as the sands of the river Ganges, would also be complete. {369}

Those [sufferings and their sources] would be the ultimate which are to be taken up.

They would be the ultimate source of refuge for living beings.

They would be the ultimate omniscient gnosis.[21]

They would also be the imperishable adamantine buddhabody.

They would also be the adamantine deities, mantras, and tantras.

They would be the five great immutable emptinesses, the six immutable empty drops, and so forth, and all the naturally primordial phenomena, such as the ultimate Evaṃ of the profound mode of reality,[22]

The ultimate I, the ultimate Haṃkṣa, the adamantine lotus, the adamantine spiritual being, the adamantine bhagā, the adamantine summit, the adamantine expanse, the tetrahedron drop, and the adamantine vowels and consonants.[23]

It would be totally incorrect to reject [those sufferings and their sources] with the antidote.

To reject them would mean that the Truth of the Path would really be meaningless.[24]

The attainment of buddhahood would be totally impossible.

Dharma and Saṅgha would also be impossible.

In this [position] there are also infinite other faults and flaws.

(The extreme consequences of maintaining that the two truths are identical in essence, and that saṃsāra and nirvāṇa are identical in essence {256})

If the two truths, and saṃsāra and nirvāṇa, are identical in essence, examine whether it is feasible or not to separate the Buddha-nature and the incidental stains![25]

As it is feasible to destroy the incidental stains, is it also feasible to destroy the Buddha-nature, or what?

As the incidental stains are composite, is the Buddha-nature also {370} composite, or what?

As the incidental stains are relative, is the Buddha-nature also relative, or what?

As the incidental stains are the imagined nature, is the Buddha-nature also the imagined nature, or what?

As the incidental stains are the inner and outer, is the Buddha-nature also inner and outer, or what?[26]

As the Buddha-nature is absolute, are the incidental stains also absolute, or what?

As the Buddha-nature is permanent, are the incidental stains also permanent, or what?

As the Buddha-nature is the fully established nature, are the incidental stains also the fully established nature, or what?

As the Buddha-nature is Buddha, are the incidental stains also Buddha, or what?

As the Buddha-nature is self-arisen, are the incidental stains also self-arisen, or what?

As the Buddha-nature is gnosis, are the incidental stains also gnosis, or what?

As the Buddha-nature is omniscient, are the incidental stains also omniscient, or what?

As the Buddha-nature is the expanse of reality, are the incidental stains also the expanse of reality, or what?

As the Buddha-nature is great bliss, are the incidental stains also great bliss, or what? {371}

As the Buddha-nature is nirvāṇa, are the incidental stains also nirvāṇa, or what?

As the Buddha-nature is the perfection of transcendent knowledge, are the incidental stains also the perfection of transcendent knowledge, or what?

As the Buddha-nature is Madhyamaka, are the incidental stains also Madhyamaka, or what?

As the Buddha-nature is empty of other, are the incidental stains also empty of other, or what?

As the Buddha-nature is the ground of emptiness, are the incidental stains also the ground of emptiness, or what?

As the Buddha-nature is the sublime other, are the incidental stains also the sublime other, or what?

As the Buddha-nature is the Truth of Cessation, are the incidental stains also the Truth of Cessation, or what?

As the Buddha-nature is the ground of cessation, are the incidental stains also the ground of cessation, or what?

As the Buddha-nature is the ground of separation, are the incidental stains also the ground of separation, or what?

As the Buddha-nature is the ground of isolation, are the incidental stains also the ground of isolation, or what?

As the Buddha-nature is the ground of purity, are the incidental stains also the ground of purity, or what?

As the Buddha-nature is the ground of absence, are the incidental {372} stains also the ground of absence, or what?

If they are claimed to be so, there are infinite faults and flaws.

(Our own flawless tradition)

For the Kṛtayuga tradition, those faults and flaws do not exist.

(The flawed opinion)

To claim that everything knowable is included in [the categories of] entity and nonentity is the tradition of the Tretayuga and later [eons].

(With the use of the autocommentary, presenting a refutation of that opinion through scripture and reasoning)

Although the Madhyamaka of the true nature is the most sublime of knowables, to accept it as a third category, never an entity or nonentity, is the Kṛtayuga tradition.

Therefore, everything is not included within entity and nonentity, because there is a third category.[27]

(With the use of the autocommentary, establishing through the scripture and reasoning of the Kṛtayuga that everything knowable is included in the two categories of the inanimate and the aware)

In this Kṛtayuga Dharma tradition everything is determined to be either inanimate or aware, therefore there is no third category in regard to that.[28]

(Proof that the expanse of reality is cognition)

Those of the Tretayuga and later [eons] claim that the true nature, thusness, is a third category which is never inanimate or aware.

If the expanse of reality is not intrinsic awareness, what about the gnosis of indivisible space and intrinsic awareness?

What about the gnosis of the expanse of reality?

What about absolute self-arisen gnosis?[29]

"I bow to you, absolute immobile and discriminating intrinsic self-awareness, absolute total intrinsic awareness of self and intrinsic awareness of others,

"Absolute excellent cognition of all and intrinsic awareness of all, the absolute omnipotent self of the five gnoses, absolute self-arisen buddha-body of gnosis,

"Sea of absolute omniscient gnosis, retainer of the treasury of {373} absolute omniscient gnosis,

"Absolute gnosis, great source of gnosis, endowed with absolute gnosis and awareness of existence and nonexistence,

"Upholder of each and every absolute buddha-body of gnosis, absolute Samantabhadra with fine intelligence, great essence of all absolute buddhahood,

"The great absolute offering of vast passion, the great absolute offering of vast hatred, the great absolute offering of vast ignorance,

"The great absolute offering of vast wrath, and the great absolute offering of vast attachment,

"The vast bliss of great absolute desire, the vast pleasure of great absolute joy, holder of the great magic of absolute expertise,

"The joy beyond joy of the great absolute magic, site of the meditative concentration of absolute great mental stability,

"Holder of the body of great absolute transcendent knowledge, sea of the gnosis of absolute prayer,

"Absolute great love, infinite in nature, absolute great compassion, sublime intellect, absolute great transcendent knowledge, endowed with great intellect,

"Absolute great expertise, great method, the absolute ten gnoses with a pristine quintessence,[30]

"Holder of the ten pristine absolute gnoses, absolute sole cognition, {374} definitely bright,

"Holder of the realization of the eight knowledges,[31] great fire of absolute transcendent knowledge and gnosis, brilliant manifestation of absolute gnosis,

"Flame of absolute gnosis, pellucid light, absolute buddhahood, unsurpassed enlightenment,

"Absolute buddhahood, Mahāvairocana, absolute perfect buddhahood, guide for the world,

"Pure and pristine intrinsic awareness of the three absolutes, the six absolute clairvoyances, and the six subsequent mindfulnesses,[32]

"Absolute sublime perfection of transcendent knowledge, the absolute powerful Sage omnipotent with the ten powers,[33]

"Absolute Mañjuśrī, endowed with splendor sublime, and the absolute buddha-body of gnosis itself."

In many such forms the absolute is presented as being cognition, intrinsic awareness, and gnosis.

(Demonstrating, with the use of the autocommentary, that although the expanse of reality is gnosis it is not impermanent, but ultimate reality)

Therefore, the Victors have stated, "Gnosis transcending the momentary is the ultimate thusness of all phenomena."[34]

(The extreme consequences that would arise if the expanse of reality were not intrinsic awareness)

If the ultimate were not intrinsic awareness, the ultimate buddha-body of reality and the essential buddha-body would not be intrinsic awareness, and there would be no omniscience.

If there were no omniscience there would be no buddhahood. (375)

If there were no buddhahood there would be no buddha-body of reality.

If that is claimed it would contradict even the existence of phenomena.[35]

(Establishing that the expanse of reality, the Buddha-nature, is permanent and stable cognition (257))

If the absolute is intrinsic awareness, it carries the implication of noncomposite intrinsic awareness.

It also carries the implication of permanent and stable intrinsic awareness.

It also carries the implication of eternal and everlasting intrinsic awareness.

It also carries the implication of the intrinsic awareness of the Buddha-nature.

It also carries the implication of the intrinsic awareness of the nine fully established natures.[36]

(The disastrous consequence of maintaining that the expanse of reality is not cognition)

If the absolute were not cognition, it would contradict all profound sūtra and tantra, the Kṛtayuga Dharma which presents the profound mode of reality.

(The accusation that if the absolute is cognition it is impermanent)

Objection: If the absolute is cognition, it is also composite and impermanent.

(The opinion that whatever is cognition is impermanent is a perverse view held by those who have not comprehended the noncomposite cognition taught in the Kṛtayuga, and have not comprehended the most profound and comprehensive points of the scriptures)

[Reply:] That is so in the tradition of the Tretayuga and later [eons], but in the exceptional tradition of sublime Kṛtayuga Dharma there is composite and noncomposite cognition.

For intrinsic awareness there is also composite and noncomposite.

For gnosis there is also composite and noncomposite.

For everything, even the Triple Gem, and so forth, there is a stated division into two truths, and composite and noncomposite.

There is a stated division of impermanent and permanent.

There is a finely stated division of empty of self-nature and empty of {376} other.

There is a finely stated division of consciousness and gnosis.

There is a finely stated division of arisen due to another and self-arisen.[37]

There is a finely stated division of phenomena and true nature, and of limit and center.

There is a finely stated division of fabricated and natural.

There is a finely stated division of incidental and primordial.

There is a finely stated division of the imagined and the fully established.

There is a finely stated division of postattainment and meditative equipoise.

There is a finely stated division of discrimination and determination.

There is a finely stated division of divisible and indivisible.[38]

There is a finely stated division of a mode of delusion and a mode of reality.[39]

There is a finely stated division of a mode of assertion and a mode of being.[40]

There is a finely stated division of an original tradition and an obstructing tradition.[41]

There is a finely stated division of the existence and non-existence of a third category.[42]

There is a finely stated division of the greater and lesser four eons.[43]

And in regard to the lesser, having clearly divided the sublime Kṛtayuga Dharma and that of the inferior Tretayuga and later [eons], there is a stated division of suitability and unsuitability as a witness.

There is a finely stated division of the three natures.[44]

There is a finely stated division of a classification of three selves.[45] {377}

There is a finely stated division of a classification of three emptinesses.[46]

There is a finely stated division of outer, inner, and sublime other.[47]

If one becomes accustomed to the sublime Kṛtayuga Dharma as stated in the Dharma Wheels which finely distinguish the Four Truths, the four topics, five topics, and so forth, one will become a great peerless expert.[48]

All the Victors and their sons will be pleased.

The stage of a Victor will quickly be attained.

(Refutation through scripture and reasoning of the opinion that all maṇḍalas, deities, mantras, tantras, spiritual races, and sources of refuge are previously absent, but later arisen composite phenomena)

While all the classifications of the essential maṇḍalas, deities, tantras, and spiritual races stated in the exceptional, sublime Kṛtayuga Dharma,

Are indivisible space and intrinsic awareness, absolute, noncomposite, partless, omnipresent, and omnipotent, the [treatises] of the flawed Tretayuga and later [eons] allege that they are all composite.

If that were so they would be relative. They would not be the ultimate and durable sublime refuge. They would also be false and deceptive phenomena.

That is refuted by the repeated statements in the five *Sūtras* [*on the Buddha-nature*], the ten *Sūtras on the Buddha-nature*, and so forth,[49] (378)

That the ultimate three sublime refuges are all also permanent, stable, eternal, everlasting, noncomposite absolute truth.

(The absence of proof for the opinion that the ultimate, permanent, and stable buddhahood, and so forth, are provisional in meaning, and the presence of refutations to the contrary)

Objection: Those statements are provisional in meaning.

[Reply]: There is no proof whatsoever that they are provisional in meaning.

There are numerous pristine scriptures and reasons to refute it.

Therefore, abandon that sort of perverse explanation!

(The refutation of the opinion that everything exists in the relative sense, but is never established in the absolute, is presented by means of demonstrating its extreme consequences, such as the fact that if the pervader is negated that which is pervaded is negated, and if there is no absolute there is also no relative)

Objection: Since they are all relative and never established in absolute truth, they are also not the essential maṇḍalas, and so forth.

[Reply]: If the pervader is negated, that which is pervaded is negated, and if the support is negated, the supported is also negated.

Therefore, if the absolute is negated, the relative is negated.
If the true nature is negated, phenomena are negated.
If the center is negated, the extremes are negated.
If the fully established nature is negated, the imagined is negated.
If the natural is negated, the fabricated is negated.
If the primordial is negated, the incidental is negated.
If empty of other is negated, empty of self-nature is negated.
If the essence is negated, the stains are negated.
If the pure is negated, the impure is negated.
If the sublime self is negated, all phenomena are negated.
If great bliss is negated, suffering is negated. {379}
If permanence is negated, impermanence is negated.
If there were no Buddha, there would be no sentient beings.
If there were no gnosis, there would be no consciousness.
If there were no self-arising, there would be no arising due to another.
If there were no sublime other, there would be no outer and inner.
If there were no Truth of Cessation, there would be no truth.
If there were no ground of purification, there would be nothing such as an object of purification, an agent of purification, and a result of purification.
If there were no thusness, all other phenomena, such as names, would also not exist.
There are also numerous others like this.[50]

(The wish that the blessings of the profound and exceptional Dharma enter into all sentient beings {258})

Therefore, may the blessing of the profound sublime Kṛtayuga Dharma enter into all living beings!

(The exceptional Dharma traditions of the Kṛtayuga, such as the general division of knowables and the specific division of cognition and gnosis)

To divide what is knowable into both composite and noncomposite, or inanimate and aware, is the Kṛtayuga tradition.

In the Kṛtayuga tradition there is the fine division of composite and noncomposite in regard to the inanimate, and also composite and noncomposite in regard to the aware.

There is also consciousness and gnosis in regard to cognition, and self-arisen and arisen due to another in regard to gnosis,

Permanent and impermanent gnosis, and composite and noncomposite gnosis. {380}

Therefore, that which is the gnosis of the expanse of reality is a permanent noncomposite gnosis, an absolute gnosis of indivisible space and intrinsic awareness,

A gnosis of flawless contradiction beyond simile, a gnosis of natural coemergence, a gnosis of the natural, immutable, fully established nature, and a gnosis of natural great bliss.

(The intended meaning of scriptural statements that the expanse of reality is the profound perfection of transcendent knowledge)

In the exceptional, sublime Kṛtayuga Dharma, those statements that the expanse of reality, thusness, is the profound ultimate perfection of transcendent knowledge,[51]

Mean that it is permanent noncomposite gnosis, the five great immutable emptinesses, the five permanent noncomposite Victors,[52]

The five permanent, stable, eternal, and everlasting consorts, the self of the five Buddhas, the five buddha-bodies of the Buddha, the self of the omnipotent five gnoses, and the self of the ten pristine gnoses.[53]

(The opinions of those with perverse view, the dregs of the view which are to be discarded)

[The adherents of] the Tretayuga and later [eons] do not speak in that way, and that which is transcendent knowledge is a composite entity.

Therefore they also claim that even the profound ultimate perfection of transcendent knowledge is composite, impermanent, and momentary.

That has also brought up the dregs of the view. {381}

In regard to cause, not knowing to divide it into the two kingdoms of productive and separating, they claim that all causes are only productive.

Also in regard to result, not knowing to divide it into the two kingdoms of produced and separated, they claim that whatever is a result is only a produced result.[54]

Therefore, the flawed and diluted traditions of the Tretayuga and later [eons] do not accept a permanent cause and result,

And not accepting a noncomposite cause and result, they do not accept that the cause and result have a single essence,

And also without accepting that the ground and result have a single essence, they do not accept a transcendent and sublime other cause and result.[55]

(The classifications according to the Kṛtayuga tradition)

The Kṛtayuga has an exceptional Dharma tradition which is the opposite of each of those.

And in regard to the universal ground, the Kṛtayuga tradition has fine classifications, such as dividing consciousness and gnosis, relative and absolute, phenomena and true nature, and composite and noncomposite,

Dividing the object of purification and the ground of purification, dividing the incidental and the primordial,

Dividing the fabricated and the natural, the mode of delusion and the mode of reality,

And dividing the husk and essence, the permanent and the impermanent, and the extremes and the center.[56]

(The flawed opinions)

For the Tretayuga and later [eons] that type of Dharma language has disappeared. {382}

They have come to claim that what is the universal ground is unobscured and neutral, precisely the appropriating consciousness.[57]

That has also brought up the dregs of the view.

(That universal ground gnosis is the ultimate definitive meaning of all sūtras and tantras)

The statements of the universal ground that is the Buddha-nature, the universal ground that is stated to be taintless virtue, the universal ground that is the various spiritual levels, and the universal ground that is natural radiant light,[58]

Are intended to mean the immutable fully established nature of Great Madhyamaka, great nirvāṇa, the Great Seal, great enlightenment, and the ultimate Evaṃ,[59]

All the deities, mantras, and tantras, such as ultimate Kālacakra, ultimate Cakrasaṃvara, Hevajra, and Guhyasamāja,

And everything ultimate, such as the ultimate maṇḍalas, the expanse in which the myriad drawn together from everywhere has a single taste, and the culmination of the ultimate perfection of transcendent knowledge.

Precisely that is the impartial primal Buddha, the primordially free Tathāgata, the Truth of Cessation which is pure, self, bliss, and permanent,

The twelve aspects of truth, sixteenfold thusness,[60] Vajrasattva, absolute enlightenment mind, noncomposite emptiness and compassion,

Permanent and stable, indivisible method and transcendent knowledge, that was Buddha even before all the buddhas. {383}

(The fault of not realizing that to be so)

For the Tretayuga and later [eons] that type of classification has disappeared. That has also brought up the dregs of the view.

(The necessity to carefully divide the two universal grounds, since the universal ground consciousness is not the cause continuum, natural radiant light, and so forth; whereas, the universal ground gnosis is the cause continuum, natural radiant light, and so forth)

In the exceptional, sublime Dharma of the Kṛtayuga, the statements in the tantric scriptures about a "cause continuum" are intended towards the Buddha-nature, the universal ground gnosis, and never intended towards the universal ground consciousness.

This is because in the tantric scriptures what is profound is stated to be the expanse of reality, absolute and noncomposite.

If it is the universal ground consciousness, it is not absolute.

It is also not naturally primordial and noncomposite.

It is also not the sublime state that is pure, self, great bliss, and permanent.

It is also not the natural spiritual races and the essential buddha-body.

It is never the nine or twelve fully established natures.[61]

If it is not those, it is never the deities, mantras, tantras, and maṇḍalas of the profound mode of reality.

It is also not a continuum in which ground and result are indivisible.

If it is not those it is not natural radiant light.

Since it is also not natural coemergent bliss, the primal Buddha, and so forth, it is also not the cause continuum and the result continuum.

I cannot defer to those who accept the universal ground consciousness as natural radiant light, and so I join my palms together and offer an {384} appeal.[62]

Because the universal ground consciousness is unobscured, neutral, and includes incidental stain, because natural radiant light is pure and stain has been primordially purified, and because the universal ground consciousness is composite and natural radiant light is noncomposite,

If it is consciousness, it is not natural radiant light.

If it is consciousness, it is not self-arisen gnosis.

If it is consciousness, it is not permanent, stable, and eternal.

If it is consciousness, it is not the Buddha-nature.

If it is consciousness, it is not the Great Madhyamaka.

If it is consciousness, it is not the Great Seal.

If it is consciousness, it is not great nirvāṇa.

If it is consciousness, it is not the coemergent buddha-body.

If it is consciousness, it is not the profound perfection of transcendent knowledge.

If it is consciousness, it is not the profound emptiness of other.

If it is consciousness, it is not all that is fully established.

If it is not those it is also not the cause continuum.

If it is natural radiant light it is not consciousness.

If it is not consciousness, it is not the universal ground consciousness. Since gnosis and consciousness exist just like light and darkness, and like nectar and poison, it is completely impossible for them to have a common ground, so do not mix them together as one! {385}

(The infinite negative consequences resulting from mixing the two together as one {259})

If they are mixed together it causes the degeneration of the Buddha's Doctrine, not the illumination.

(The ground of purification, and so forth, together with their similes)

In the exceptional, sublime Kṛtayuga Dharma, the ground of purification is the universal ground gnosis which is like the sky, the object of purification is the incidental stains which are like clouds,

The agent of purification is the Truth of the Path which is like an inexorable wind, and the result of purification is the separated result which is like the sky clear of clouds.

(The extreme consequences which would arise if the ground of purification and the object of purification were one)

It has been stated in that way, but many [adherents] of the flawed Tretayuga and later [eons], who are not experts in that,

Claim that the object of purification and the ground of purification are one, which is the same as claiming that the clouds and the sky are one.

Here the ground of purification, thusness with stains, is the noncomposite universal ground gnosis.

The object of purification is the composite stains, so please consider whether those two are one or not.

The ground of purification is permanent and the object of purification is impermanent, so please consider whether those two are one or not.

The ground of purification is taintless and the object of purification is the taints, so please consider whether those two are one or not.

The ground of purification is completely pure and the object of purification is total defilement, so please consider whether those two are one or not.

There are also numerous others like that. (386)

(The identity of the immutable, fully established nature and the Great Madhyamaka)

In the Kṛtayuga tradition the fully established nature and Madhyamaka are different merely in name, but no different in meaning.[63]

(The absence of proof for the opinion that the "three natures" are found only in the Dharma language of the Cittamātra tradition, and the presence of refutations to the contrary)

In the flawed traditions of the Tretayuga and later [eons], it is claimed that the immutable, fully established nature is only Cittamātra.

They allege that all three natures are also only Cittamātra.

Because the three natures are repeatedly taught in the treatises of the flawless Kṛtayuga Madhyamaka,

Because that language does not occur in the Cittamātra treatises, and because there are many refutations to the contrary,

It emerges from the Kṛtayuga tradition that the three natures are the Dharma tradition of only the Madhyamaka.[64]

(As a result of not having correctly understood the classifications of philosophical systems, perverse views have arisen which maintain that every text teaching the three natures is a Cittamātra text, and all their authors are thus adherents of the Cittamātra. Maintaining that in the absolute sense nothing whatsoever is established, those with perverse view say that Madhyamaka is also completely unestablished, and that everyone who teaches this is an adherent of the Great Madhyamaka)

Therefore, by not understanding that type of classification, and by mixing it up, the dregs of the view have arisen.

Those Madhyamaka [treatises] which present the three natures of the fully established, and so forth, have been demoted to Cittamātra treatises.[65]

The great experts of the Great Madhyamaka who taught them have also been demoted to Cittamātra adherents.[66]

Those perverse treatises[67] which teach that the absolute Madhyamaka is totally unestablished, and which thus fall into the extreme of denigration,

And fall into the nihilistic position of nonexistence, are complimented and praised as the Madhyamaka.

They are not, yet the words of Māra which take them to be so have arisen in the Tretayuga and later [eons].

But for the Kṛtayuga that kind of perverse view is the same as the {387} horn of a rabbit.

(Without a support there can be nothing supported, and so forth, which leads to the extreme consequence that without an absolute there would also be no relative)

Those of the Tretayuga and later [eons] may object: "Absolute truth is totally unestablished, but since relative action and result are infallible, there is freedom from the extremes of exaggeration and denigration of existence and nonexistence."

[Reply]: Is a relative possible without an absolute?

Is that which is pervaded possible without a pervader?

Is the supported possible without a supporting ground?

Is the incidental possible without the primordial?

Are phenomena possible without a true nature?[68]

If they are possible, don't *they* become an omnipresent true nature?

If it is impossible that there is no absolute, doesn't that contradict a totally unestablished absolute?

(Rejecting both "independent inference" and "logical consequence" as valid divisions of Madhyamaka, and then establishing by means of scripture and reasoning that all the absolute deities and mantras which are thusness, and so forth, are the divisions of Madhyamaka)

The division of Madhyamaka according to independent inference and logical consequence is an improper division of Madhyamaka, because it is an improper division of thusness.[69]

Although it is not stated in that way in the treatises of the Kṛtayuga, it occurs in the treatises of the flawed Tretayuga and later [eons].

That also has brought up the dregs of the view.

As for the division of Madhyamaka in the Kṛtayuga tradition, the divisions such as the nine fully established natures,[70] the divisions of the spiritual races stated in the tantric scriptures,

And also the entire presentation by means of the divisions of the names finely stated in *The Tantra of the Recitation of the Names of the Absolute*,[71] are the divisions of the Great Madhyamaka beyond extremes. [388]

Likewise, all the stated divisions of the profound and ultimate mode of reality are also the divisions of the Great Madhyamaka beyond extremes.

Here there is no mixing with even one composite [factor]. They are the divisions of the noncomposite expanse of reality.

Here there is not the slightest mixing with the impermanent. They are the divisions of a permanent, stable, and eternal expanse.

Here there is no mixing with even one relative [factor].

In the division of the absolute fully established nature alone, there is not even the slightest division of essence.

There are numerous divisions of name and aspect.

Why? Because the meaning of the expanse of reality in which the myriad has a single taste is that the names are myriad but the meaning has a single taste, and that the aspects are myriad but the essence has a single taste.

Therefore these are the divisions of all that is profound and ultimate, such as the ultimate perfection of transcendent knowledge, great nirvāṇa, the Great Seal, the Atiyoga, the Vajrayoga,[72] the coemergent yoga, Kālacakra, Cakrasaṃvara, and Hevajra.

If understood in that way, everything is understood by understanding one thing.

One will become a great expert without confusion about the entire profound and ultimate mode of reality.

(Demonstrating that since both "independent inference" and "logical consequence" fall into the extreme of existence they are incorrect divisions of Madhyamaka [260])

Both independent inference and logical consequence are composite. [389] Therefore, they fall into the material extreme, and since they fit into the category of existence, they are not Madhyamaka.[73]

That which is not Madhyamaka is never fit to be the ground for the divisions of Madhyamaka, and to be one of the divisions.

That which is not authentic is never fit to be the ground for the divisions of authenticity, and to be one of the divisions.

That which is not true is never fit to be the ground for the divisions of truth, and to be one of the divisions.

That is certainly the way of the Kṛtayuga tradition.

(The opinion of others)

But those of the flawed Tretayuga and later [eons] allege that mere freedom from extremes is just labeled "Madhyamaka," while there is no Madhyamaka in the absolute sense, because even Madhyamaka is empty of Madhyamaka.[74]

(The reasons why such an opinion is an evil view)

If that were the case, it would be a great evil view denigrating[75] the absolute buddha-body of reality, the essential buddha-body, the coemergent buddha-body,

And all the permanent, stable, eternal, everlasting, and omnipresent Buddha, Dharma, and Saṅgha.

Why? Because it is stated that they are the profound [truth] that is empty of other, but not empty of self-nature.

(That ultimate profound emptiness is a ground empty of all extremes, but is not an absolute negation empty of self-nature and merely a freedom from extremes)

All the statements about profound emptiness in all the pure and profound sūtras and tantras refer to a ground that is empty of both exaggeration and denigration.

Likewise, they refer to a ground that is empty of both existence and nonexistence, {390}

A ground that is empty of both entities and nonentities, and a ground that is empty of everything relative.

(That profound expanse of reality, which is the ground of emptiness, is never these relative phenomena, but is instead the gnosis of great bliss, the profound emptiness of other that is the mode of existence and is all of the ultimate profound deities, tantras, and so forth. Thus all of the scriptures and treatises which teach that to be so are the scriptures of the Great Madhyamaka)

Precisely that ground of emptiness is the Buddha-nature, the natural spiritual races, the natural Buddha, the natural Dharma, and the natural Saṅgha,

The natural spontaneous maṇḍalas, natural deities, natural tantras and mantras, natural nirvāṇa, natural radiant light, natural purity, primordial purity, pristine form up through omniscience,

Form up through the phenomena of the buddhahood of the immutable fully established true nature, and so forth,

The ten noncomposite powers,[76] and so forth, thusness with infinite qualities complete, the ground buddhahood, and the primal Buddha.

It is the originally free Tathāgata, initially liberated enlightened mind with the nature of space, Buddha even before all the buddhas.

Therefore, the ultimate [reality] in all profound sūtras and tantras which finely present thusness, and so forth, is empty of other, never empty of self-nature.

It is absolute, never relative. {391}

It is the true nature, never the phenomena.[77]

It is the middle, never the extreme.

It is nirvāṇa, never saṃsāra.

It is gnosis, never consciousness.

It is pure, never impure.

It is a sublime self, never a nothingness.

It is great bliss, never suffering.

It is permanent and stable, never impermanent.

It is self-arisen, never arisen due to another.

It is the fully established, never the imagined.

It is natural, never fabricated.
It is primordial, never incidental.
It is Buddha, never a sentient being.
It is the essence, never the husk.
It is definitive in meaning, never provisional in meaning.
It is ultimate, never transient.
It is the ground and result, never the Truth of the Path.
It is the ground of purification, never the object of purification.
It is the mode of reality, never the mode of delusion.
It is the sublime other, never the outer and inner.
It is true, never false.
It is perfect, never perverse. {392}
It is the ground of emptiness, never just empty.
It is the ground of separation, never just a separation.
It is the ground of absence, never just an absence.
It is an established phenomenon, never an absolute negation.
It is virtue, never nonvirtue.
It is authentic, never inauthentic.
It is correct, never incorrect.
It is immaculate, never stain.
Therefore, they are the same as the Great Madhyamaka.

All the sublime sūtras of the Third Dharma Wheel, and all the treatises of Maitreya are the same as the Great Madhyamaka.[78]

The pristine tantric scriptures are also likewise.

(Maintaining that dependent origination is Madhyamaka and Madhyamaka is dependent origination leads to the extreme consequence that all composite phenomena would be Madhyamaka)

The majority of experts in the Tretayuga and later [eons] allege that relative dependent origination is the Great Madhyamaka, and that whatever is Madhyamaka is dependent origination.[79]

If that were the case, since composite and impermanent [phenomena] are also dependent origination, they would be Madhyamaka.

If that were accepted, they would be the absolute expanse of reality.

If even that were accepted, they would be noncomposite.

If that were accepted, it would contradict even [the existence of] phenomena.[80]

(The necessity to also understand the division of the two truths in regard to dependent origination {261})

Therefore, in regard to statements about dependent origination, a division of the two truths is stated in the Kṛtayuga Dharma.[81]

(The realization of relative dependent origination is the path of Madhyamaka, but that dependent origination is not all the ultimate profound modes of reality, such as Madhyamaka)

The correct realization of relative dependent origination is the path {393} of entry into the city of Great Madhyamaka.[82]

(The absolute dependent origination is stated in all sūtras and tantras to be the twelve aspects of truth, and so forth, that are the ground in which the twelve aspects of relative dependent origination, and the vital karmic winds of the twelve zodiac signs, have ceased from the beginning)

The absolute dependent origination, the profound expanse of reality, is not this dependent origination, but a sublime other dependent origination.[83]

The twelve limbs illustrate the root of existence.[84]

They hold the twelve pure aspects.[85]

They are the twelve aspects of truth,[86] and the twelve such as the places.[87]

They are the cessation of the vital winds of the signs of the zodiac and the sun.[88]

[This] is stated in the *Prajñāpāramitā* [*sūtra*s],[89] the *Avataṃsaka*, and the Mantra[yāna].

It is stated by the sublime experts of the Kṛtayuga.[90]

It is not a sphere of activity for most of those in the Tretayuga and later [eons].

(The pure ground of absolute thusness, the immutable fully established nature empty and barren of all relative phenomena from the beginning, is far beyond the Cittamātra, and thus those who teach and accept this are far beyond being adherents of the Cittamātra)

The reason they are not Cittamātra is because they are a third category, the ground of emptiness beyond extremes, and because if they were Cittamātra there would be acceptance of an entity.

Since those grounds of emptiness transcend the phenomena of consciousness and uphold a nondual gnosis, and since they are beyond single and multiple moments, how could they be phenomena accepted as entities?

(The main subject of the Middle Wheel of the Teaching is also the thusness of the profound emptiness of other, which is never like the completely unestablished emptiness of self-nature, a reduction into nihilistic emptiness, an inanimate emptiness of total negation, but is instead an emptiness in which infinite qualities are complete, which is endowed with all sublime aspects, and is everything profound and ultimate, such as the absolute Evaṃ, the buddha-body of gnosis, the natural radiant light, the Great Mother, Vajrasattva, Vajradhara, and the profound perfection of transcendent knowledge)[91]

Because the meaning of the Second Dharma Wheel is also thusness in which infinite qualities are complete, it is not an absolute negation, an emptiness of absolute nothingness, or a nihilistic emptiness. {394}

It is the ground of emptiness endowed with all sublime qualities, and it is the immutable sublime great bliss.

It is the Great Seal equivalent to the eight prognostic images,[92] and it is the absolute letter Evaṃ.[93]

It is the buddha-body of gnosis equivalent to the eight prognostic images, and it is the absolute tetrahedron drop.

It is the adamantine buddha-body equivalent to the eight prognostic images, and it is the absolute adamantine bhagā.[94]

It is the buddha-body of mantra equivalent to the eight prognostic images, and it is the absolute vowels and consonants.

It is the everlasting buddha-body equivalent to the eight prognostic images, and it is the absolute vajra and lotus.

It is the eternal buddha-body equivalent to the eight prognostic images, and it is the absolute adamantine moon and sun.

It is the buddha-body of the true nature equivalent to the eight prognostic images, and it is the absolute adamantine sperm and ovum.[95]

It is the adamantine expanse equivalent to the eight prognostic images, and it is the absolute partless and omnipresent state.

It is the expanse of mantra equivalent to the eight prognostic images, and it is the absolute powerful tenfold anagram.[96]

It is the expanse of bliss equivalent to the eight prognostic images, and it is the absolute incorporeal adamantine state.

It is the Great Madhyamaka equivalent to the eight prognostic images, and it is the absolute adamantine nature. (395)

It is Vajradhara equivalent to the eight prognostic images, and it is all that is profound and ultimate, such as absolute Vajrasattva, and such as the absolute perfection of trancendent knowledge, which is the Mother of the Victors.

(The main subject of the last two Wheels of the Teaching, and of the four sets of the tantric scriptures, is the same profound emptiness that cannot be any relative phenomenon, such as consciousness, emptiness of self-nature, and so forth. It is all that is ultimate and profound, such as self-arisen gnosis, the absolute authentic state of the total awareness of self and others, and of the aggregates, constituents, and so forth, and which is the partless, omnipresent, immutable, and fully established nature (262))

Therefore, the profound emptiness of the Second Dharma Wheel, such as in the extensive, medium, and condensed *Prajñāpāramitā* [*sūtra*s],

The profound emptiness of the Third Dharma Wheel, such as in the five *Sūtras* [*on the Buddha-nature*] and the ten *Sūtras on the Buddha-nature*,[97]

And the profound emptiness of the four sets of the tantric scriptures,[98] all the profound emptiness of the profound sūtras and tantras, is not the relative, but the absolute truth.

It is not composite, it is a noncomposite expanse.

It is not unstable, it is permanent, stable, and eternal.

It is not false, it is perfect truth.

It is not fallible, it is the sublime infallible refuge.

It is not changeable, it is the immutable, fully established nature.

It is not this authenticity, it is the absolute authenticity.

It is not this reasoning,. it is the reasoning of the true nature.

It is not this Cittamātra, it is a sublime other Cittamātra.

It is not this intrinsic self-awareness, it is a sublime other intrinsic self-awareness.

It is not this self-luminosity, it is a sublime other self-luminosity.

It is not this pure awareness, it is a sublime other pure awareness.

It is not consciousness, it is self-arisen gnosis.

It is not the imagined nature, it is the fully established gnosis. **[396]**

It is not acceptance of an entity, it is the Great Madhyamaka.

It is not inanimate, it is cognition of everything and intrinsic awareness of everything.

It is not a concept, it is a nonconceptual gnosis.

It is not for a dialectician, it is the object of the actions of a yoga practitioner.

It is not this aggregate, it is a sublime other aggregate.[99]

It is also not this constituent, it is a sublime other constituent.

It is not this base of sense cognition, it is a sublime other base of sense cognition.

It is not this action faculty, it is a sublime other action faculty.

And its functions are likewise.

It is not this three realms, it is a sublime other three realms.[100]

It is not this threefold universe, it is a sublime other threefold universe.

It is not this three times, it is a sublime other three times.[101]

It is not this three vehicles, it is a sublime other three vehicles.[102]

It is not this stable and mobile [world], it is a sublime other stable and mobile [world].

It is not this cause and result, it is a sublime other cause and result.

It is not this birth and cessation, it is a sublime other birth and cessation.

It is not this manifest and empty, it is a sublime other manifest and empty.

It is not this central figure and entourage, it is a sublime other central figure and entourage.[103]

It is not this Father and Mother, it is a sublime other Father and Mother.[104]

It is not this male and female, it is a sublime other male and female.

It is not this androgyny, it is a sublime other androgyny.

It is not this dependent origination, it is a sublime other dependent origination. {397}

It is not this perfection, it is a sublime other perfection.

It is not this emptiness, it is a sublime other emptiness.

(Applying the division of the two truths to all the factors conducive to enlightenment, from phenomena up through the eighteen exclusive qualities, in order to demonstrate that all the absolute factors conducive to enlightenment are never relative, but instead are the profound Truth of Cessation)

All the factors conducive to enlightenment are also not this Truth of the Path, they are the absolute Truth of Cessation.[105]

The noble truths, the measureless meditations, the formless absorptions, the nine absorptions of liberation,[106]

The three doors of liberation,[107] the dhāraṇī door of meditative concentration,

And a tathāgata's ten powers, four intrepid factors, four specific awarenesses, great love and great compassion, eighteen exclusive qualities, and three noble knowledges,[108]

Are also not this relative, composite Truth of the Path, but a sublime transcendent Truth of Cessation other than this.

(The intended meaning of the Dharma as expressed by the simile of the sky)

Being without causes, without change, partless, omnipresent, all-pervasive, and so forth, were stated by means of the simile of the noncomposite sky.

(The intended meaning of similes for the mode of emptiness which are applicable to the emptiness of the expanse of reality)

Not empty of self-nature, but empty of other, was stated by means of similes such as an empty village and an empty vase.

(The use of a simile to indicate something that is sometimes manifest, but sometimes unmanifest)

Unmanifest to concept, but directly manifest to nonconceptual gnosis, was stated by means of the simile of the prognostic image.[109]

(The use of a simile to indicate the great bliss of the expanse of reality)

The discriminating intrinsic self-awareness of natural great bliss was stated by means of the simile of the bliss born during sexual union.[110]

(The meaning indicated by the simile of a great roll of cloth)

The equal extent of the two truths, their similar aspects, multiple [398] aspects, many qualities, difficulty to contain within the sheath of the stains, and so forth, were clearly stated by means of the simile of a great roll of cloth.[111]

(The meaning indicated by the simile of not seeing because of eye diseases such as cataracts, and by the simile of digging a well, and so forth)

Omnipresent and always existing before one, but unseen by all the consciousnesses, was spoken of by means of many similes, such as those of digging a well, and those of eye diseases, such as cataracts.

(The intended meaning of statements that the expanse of reality transcends similes (263))

By means of similes that present many flawless contradictions, such as the fine formless form, and the sublime incorporeal body,

It was finely stated that since it does not exist in this world it transcends worldly simile, and transcends all conceivable similes.

(The intended meaning of similes such as a lamp within a vase, and the great treasure of a pauper)

That it is present in everyone, but obscured by the afflicting emotions of sentient beings, was stated by means of many similes, such as a lamp within a vase, and a great treasure [beneath the home] of a pauper.[112]

(The intended meaning of similes such as the element water, gold, and the sky)

That it will become evident if the stains are removed was stated by means of similes such as the element water, gold, and the sky.

(The intended meaning of similes such as the unending sky)

That even though the stains end the essence does not end, was also stated by means of many similes, such as the sky.

(The intended meaning of the simile of the sky with clouds and without clouds, which is the same sky)

Although the ultimate ground and result are indivisible in essence, and no different in pure nature,

By means of the similes of the sky with clouds and the sky without clouds, they were stated to be the ground with stain and the result (399) separated from stain.

(The intended meaning of the simile of the cloudy sky becoming clear of clouds)

In the transformation of the ultimate and profound definitive meaning, the essence does not change, but the stained becomes stainless,

And the result separated from stain is obtained, as stated by means of the simile of the sky clear of clouds.

(The intended meaning of the use of similes)

Although no simile completely presents it exactly, there are many similes which partially present it.

(Although the pure teachings present the mode of reality and the mode of delusion, what is to be rejected and the antidote, and so forth, without mixing them up, those of the flawed Tretayuga and later {eons} apply their own flawed understanding to the meaning, and thus cause the deterioration of the pure view and meditation)

With numerous perfect reasons the Kṛtayuga Dharma clearly states the condensed meaning of the mode of reality, the mode of delusion, the rejection of delusion, and the removal of delusion,

The ground, path, result, and accompanying factors in regard to the ground of purification, the object of purification, the agent of purification, and the result of purification, as well as the condensed meaning of the pure view, meditation, and conduct.

But that kind of classification has deteriorated among those of the Tretayuga and later [eons].

(The pure view and meditation)

The view is realizing the mode of reality just as it is, and meditation is seeing the mode of existence just as it is.

(Rejoicing in the pure conduct of those who preserve moral discipline, and so forth, even though they lack the view and meditation of the profound definitive meaning, and also rejoicing with faith and respect for those who engage without error in all the view, meditation, and conduct {264})

Although most of that has deteriorated, among those sublime individuals who have greatly accumulated merit, many have also appeared who are endowed with good experience and good conduct.

I also join my palms together and happily rejoice for all those who have accomplished virtues such as generosity, moral discipline, patience, and diligence, [400]

Meditation, transcendent knowledge, power of method, and prayer, and bow with the crown of my head in faithful and respectful homage.

I also have faith in those who serve, honor, and revere the Triple Gem with faith and respect, as well as the three representations with faith and respect, thus enriching themselves and others.

I pay homage with pure thoughts to those who have realized with certainty that all sentient beings are [our] kind parents who possess the essence of buddhahood,

And exchange self for others with love and compassion, while respectfully teaching it to all.

With the crown of my head I take the dust from the feet of all those who have realized the total integration of appearances and emptiness indivisible,

Who have realized that all this which is manifest and audible is like the horn of a rabbit, never established in the real mode of existence, but like a dream or an illusion on the level of conventional delusion,

And who with the realization that cause and result are infallible, reject evil actions and carefully cultivate good actions, thus fulfilling sublime prayers in order to liberate all living beings.

I respectfully pay homage to those sublime individuals who have realized that all relative phenomena are each empty of self-nature, [401]

And who do not act with attachment, having realized well that all this stable and mobile [world] that appears while nonexistent is only an appearance of delusion.

I also have faith in those who have realized that all the concepts and afflicting emotions which have arisen from clinging to a self are like an enemy, and utterly subduing them, live in peace and quiet.

I respectfully pay homage to those sublime individuals who are victorious over the enemy of the concepts and afflicting emotions, having thoroughly cultivated the individual antidotes for what is to be rejected,

Such as ugliness as the antidote for passionate desire, meditation upon love as the antidote for hatred, dependent origination as the antidote for ignorance, the divisions of the constituents as the antidote for pride, and the exhalation and inhalation of breath as the antidote for conceptualization.

I pay homage to those who have transformed the circulating vital karmic winds, upon which the consciousness is mounted, into the vital gnostic wind within the central channel,[113] and who practice the yoga of nonconceptual nondual gnosis.

I have faith in those who have correctly realized that the appearances of the outer and inner relative and incidental stains are only the appearances {402} of delusion,

And have then actualized the appearances of a transcendent and absolute sublime other than this.[114]

I also have faith in those who have utterly abandoned all the things towards which attachment and anger are born, such as a homeland, relatives, and valuable possessions,

And who [uphold] the Doctrine by increasing the practice of Dharma in places without distinction, without bias, and toward which they have no attachment.

I also have faith in those who have utterly abandoned financial occupations and affairs, and fully applying body, speech, and mind in areas of virtue, have fulfilled sublime prayers by means of the three pure spheres,[115] and raised a great wealth of virtue.

I also have faith in those who, by carefully giving them away to higher recipients and lower recipients, effortlessly extract an essence from naturally apparent but deceptive riches which have no essence.

I also have faith in those who correctly accomplish, cause to be accomplished, and urge others toward accomplishing the ten kinds of Dharma practice,[116] such as copying the exceptional, sublime Kṛtayuga Dharma.

I also have faith in those who do not think and talk about the faults of everyone who practices the Dharma,

Such as the abbots, disciples, masters, spiritual friends, and close companions, and who act with faith and respect without jealousy. {403}

I also have faith in those who, with great beneficial intentions, make careful appeals to evil and nonreligious persons who have entered a wrong path,

And who happily rejoice for those who have entered a good path and are accomplishing virtue.

I also have faith in those who teach that, not to mention what is not Dharma, even Dharma is to be abandoned in the context of determination during profound meditative equipoise,[117]

And who carefully distinguish existence, nonexistence, and so forth in the context of discrimination during postattainment.[118]

I also have faith in those who correctly realize, correctly practice, and correctly teach that the changeable melting bliss is to be rejected, the immutable melting bliss is to be relied upon,[119] and what is immutable by nature is to be obtained.

In brief, I also respectfully pay homage to all those who correctly realize, correctly practice, and correctly teach the ground, path, result, view, meditation, and conduct in agreement with the Kṛtayuga Dharma.

(Motivated by the enlightenment thought, an appeal is made for those who have entered into wrong views and meditation to renounce those wrong views and meditation)

I cannot defer to those who, in reliance upon the flawed [treatises of] the Tretayuga and later [eons], accept that everything is merely empty of self-nature, and accept that an emptiness of self-nature is the absolute,

Accept that the absolute is empty of self-nature, and accept that concepts are the buddha-body of reality,[120] {404}

Accept that the five poisons are gnosis, and accept that consciousness is the Buddha,[121]

Accept that karmic appearances are the Buddha, and accept that Buddha is just an empty name,

Accept that buddhahood never exists, and accept that there is no absolute buddhahood,

Accept that the two truths have a single essence, and accept that saṃsāra and nirvāṇa have a single essence,

Accept that what is to be rejected and the antidote have a single essence, and accept that the object of purification and the ground of purification are one,

And accept that this saṃsāra of suffering arisen from its origins is buddhahood if it is realized, but is saṃsāra if it is not realized.

Like sending out an appeal, I here send forth these fine words.

(Since it is taught in the scriptures of definitive meaning that the nine and twelve immutable and fully established natures permanently exist as thusness, it must not be said that the absolute is nothing)

Please consider a statement from the Kṛtayuga Dharma: "Whether the tathāgatas appear or do not appear, the nine fully established natures permanently exist as immutable thusness itself."[122]

(Particularly, since no pure scriptures and reasoning teach that precisely these afflicting emotions are the ultimate gnosis, here is an instruction to reject the perverse view in which these afflicting emotions and concepts are accepted as gnosis)

I cannot defer to those who accept that even these afflicting emotions, concepts, and groups of consciousness are the buddha-body of reality if realized, but are the stains if not realized,

And so I join together my palms and send out an appeal with the words, "Be in agreement with the Kṛtayuga Dharma!" {405}

What difference do you see in claiming, "If realized it is gold, if not realized it is brass,

"If realized it is a horse, if not realized it is a bull,

"If realized it is light, if not realized it is darkness,

"If realized it is medicine, if not realized it is poison?"

If there are pure scriptures, reasoning, and esoteric instructions which state that to be so, please show them to me also.

(Since the pure scriptures of definitive meaning state that the expanse of reality is the basis, support, and ground of all phenomena, it must not be said that everything is groundless and rootless)

I cannot defer to those who accept that everything is groundless and rootless, so I join together my palms and send out an appeal.

Please consider that it is also stated in the Kṛtayuga Dharma that the universal ground gnosis, the expanse of thusness, is the partless, omnipresent, all-pervasive ground, basis, and support of all phenomena.[123]

(Since everything that is the ultimate absolute is a third category which is never an entity or a nonentity, all knowables must not be determined to be either entities or nonentities)

To all who accept that everything knowable is determined to be an entity or a nonentity, and accept that anything inanimate or aware is an entity, I also join my palms together and make an appeal.[124]

It is stated that the ultimate mode of reality is a third category, a sublime central, middle, and androgynous state.

The noncomposite bliss, cognition, gnosis, intrinsic awareness, {406} aggregates, constituents, and so forth, from form up through the exclusive qualities,

Are all the phenomena of permanent, stable, eternal, everlasting, and immutable form up through omniscience,[125]

Which are form up through the phenomena of the buddhahood of the immutable and fully established true nature, and which are also the ultimate knowable and the absolute truth.

They are noncomposite, not composite entities.

Please look at the sublime scriptures which state that to be so.

Please also look at the sublime scriptures which state that the thirty-six aspects of taste, the constituents, and so forth, the thirty-six aspects of the aggregates, and the thirty-six such as the aggregates and constituents,[126] are the ultimate knowable, thusness, but are never entities or nonentities.

(Although all phenomena are untrue, it is stated in many scriptures of definitive meaning that the thusness of the true nature is the most sublime truth, and so it must not be said that what is true is not {265}**)**

I cannot defer to those who accept that there is no perfect truth, and so I send forth an appeal.

It is stated in the Kṛtayuga Dharma that great nirvāṇa is true, it is stated that the Truth of Cessation is the sublime truth,

It is stated that thusness is true but others are false, and that the {407} twelve aspects of truth,[127] and so forth, are the ultimate truth of the mode of reality.

Please carefully look at those [scriptures] also.

(Motivated by thoughts to benefit them, those who maintain that this is the view of eternalism or nihilism are urged not to hold such opinions)

I also cannot defer to those who accept that every realization of permanence is the flawed view of eternalism, every realization of nothingness is the flawed view of nihilism,

Every realization of existence is the flawed view of existence, and every realization of nonexistence is the flawed view of nonexistence, so I join my palms together and send forth a message of appeal.

(It is not a flaw to realize what is actually permanent, and so forth, to be so, and it is not a flaw to realize what is actually nothing, and so forth, to be nothing, but it is a flaw to reverse each of those realizations)

Please look at the statements in the Kṛtayuga Dharma that in realizing permanence there is both a flaw and a quality,

In realizing impermanence there is also both a flaw and a quality,

In realizing purity there is also both a flaw and a quality,

In realizing impurity there is also both a flaw and a quality,

In realizing bliss there is also both a flaw and a quality,

In realizing suffering there is also both a flaw and a quality,

In realizing there is a self there is also both a flaw and a quality,

In realizing there is no self there is also both a flaw and a quality,
In realizing existence there is also both a flaw and a quality,
In realizing nonexistence there is also both a flaw and a quality,
And in realizing nothingness there is also both a flaw and a {408} quality.[128]

(In the absolute sense buddhahood *is* established, because the primal Buddha is established, and therefore it must not be said that in the absolute sense there is no buddhahood)

I cannot defer to those who accept that in reality there is no buddhahood, who do not accept a noncomposite buddhahood, and who do not accept a permanent, stable, and eternal buddhahood, and so I join my palms together and offer an appeal.

Please also look at those statements in the Kṛtayuga [Dharma] which say that absolute truth, indivisible space and intrinsic awareness,
Is the primal Buddha, the ground buddhahood, permanent, stable, eternal, everlasting, all-pervasive thusness, and the enlightenment of the Buddha.

(Since a permanent and stable gnosis beyond the momentary is taught in many of the scriptures of definitive meaning, it must not be said that there is actually no gnosis)

I also offer a request to those who claim that in reality there is no gnosis, and who do not accept self-arisen gnosis as permanent.
Since the sublime Victors have stated in the Kṛtayuga Dharma that gnosis beyond single and multiple moments is thusness, please look at those [scriptures].

(The extreme negative consequences that would result if the Buddha-nature were provisional in meaning)

I also cannot defer to those who accept that the Buddha-nature is provisional in meaning, and joining together my palms I offer an appeal.[129]

The Buddha-nature is thusness, and thusness is also the Buddha-nature, so if the Buddha-nature were provisional in meaning, thusness would {409} also be provisional in meaning.

The absolute buddha-body of reality would also be provisional in meaning.

The essential buddha-body would also be provisional in meaning.

The natural spiritual races would also be provisional in meaning.

The profound perfection of transcendent knowledge would also be provisional in meaning.

The Great Madhyamaka would also be provisional in meaning.

Great nirvāṇa would also be provisional in meaning.

The Great Seal would also be provisional in meaning.

The great radiant light would also be provisional in meaning.

Since all the ultimate deities, mantras, maṇḍalas, tantras, and mudrās of the profound mode of reality,

Such as Cakrasaṃvara, Hevajra, Kālacakra, and Guhyasamāja, would also be provisional in meaning, [that opinion] is refuted by extreme consequences.

(The absence of valid proof that the Buddha-nature is provisional in meaning {266})

If there is scripture and reasoning which presents the Buddha-nature to be provisional in meaning, please show them.

(Since valid scripture and reasoning establish that it is definitive in meaning, there is no proof that it is not definitive in meaning)

There are numerous profound scriptures, reasoning, and esoteric instructions which present it as definitive in meaning.

(Demonstrating the absence of proof and the presence of refutations of the opinion that statements in the scriptures of definitive meaning that the Buddha-nature is endowed with infinite qualities should be interpreted as meaning that the Buddha-nature is definitive in meaning but its qualities are provisional)

Some with perverse ideas may make this objection: "Although the Buddha-nature is not provisional in meaning, all of its qualities are {410} provisional in meaning. Therefore, there is really no Buddha-nature in which the multiple qualities are complete."

[Reply:] Since it is correctly stated in the *Prajñāpāramitā* [*sūtras*] of the Victor that "The qualities of each of the nine fully established natures are also measureless,"

And it is also stated in other [scriptures] of the Kṛtayuga Dharma, such as the ten *Sūtras on the Buddha-nature* and the ten *Sūtras on Definitive Meaning*, that the absolute permanent qualities are countless,[130] please look [at those].

(If permanent buddhahood were impossible, there would also be no noncomposite buddhahood, which is its equivalent. Since relative buddhahood exists, absolute buddhahood also exists. No valid scripture and reasoning teach that absolute buddhahood does not exist)

Objection: Since permanent buddhahood is impossible, the statements that it is permanent are provisional in meaning.

[Reply:] Well then, I would ask you, "Are statements that it is noncomposite provisional in meaning or not?"

Noncomposite and permanent are equivalent in meaning.
Impermanent and composite are equivalent in meaning.
Therefore, if one is negated, both are negated.

If permanence is negated, noncomposite is negated, and even the absolute expanse of reality is thus negated, so that, alas, all phenomena are negated.

This is because if the pervader is negated, that which is pervaded is negated; and if the support is negated, the supported is negated.[131]

There are numerous [examples] of the support and the supported, and the pervader and that which is pervaded, such as center and limit, the absolute as the support and the relative as the supported,

The true nature as the support and phenomena as the supported, and the absolute as the pervader and the relative as that which is pervaded. {411}

Please consider them all in detail.

The many statements about the pervader and that which is pervaded, and the many about the support and the supported, such as, "All beings are pervaded by the Buddha-nature,"

Also indicate that if the pervader is negated that which is pervaded is negated, and if the support does not exist, the supported does not exist.

If permanent buddhahood is impossible, please present scripture and reasoning as proof of that.

There is infinite scripture and reasoning regarding its possibility.

(The negative consequence of the claim that buddhahood is reached merely through self-recognition, even though the two assemblies have not been accumulated, is that all sentient beings, who are endowed with self-recognition since they have cognition, would have already reached buddhahood)

I cannot defer to those who accept that since buddhahood is reached through self-recognition it is not necessary to accumulate the two assemblies and purify the two obscurations, because through self-recognition the basis is purified without rejection.

Joining my palms together, I offer an appeal: A sentient being without intrinsic self-awareness is impossible, and if there is intrinsic self-awareness there is self-recognition.

If there were no intrinsic awareness of self and others, it would contradict being intrinsically aware, like the gross elements.[132]

Therefore, since all sentient beings have minds, and since all who have minds have intrinsic self-awareness, there is self-recognition from the {412} moment of birth.

This topic is known to those who understand scripture and reasoning.

It is unimaginable that the numerous arrogant fools with little learning who are usurpers, pretenders, and fabricators of Dharma, understand this topic, or have even heard about or seen it.

Therefore, that type of perverse view, in which self-recognition is sufficient, is the secret words of Māra.

Reject that kind of evil view, the work of Māra, which says that the perfect path or the wrong path is determined by that sort of realization or lack of realization, and that therefore liberation[133] is through self-recognition.

(The extreme negative consequences, such as all light being darkness, that would result from maintaining that buddhahood is reached by realizing this consciousness of one's own mind to be the buddha-body of reality)

Objection: The meaning of self-recognition of the essence refers to just the realization that this consciousness of one's own mind is the buddha-body of reality.

[Reply:] Since this consciousness is the incompatible opposite of the buddha-body of reality, it is never the buddha-body of reality.

If it is, is poison also nectar, or pitch-black darkness also light, or what?

Are negative factors also positive factors, or what?

Are what are to be rejected also the antidotes, or what?

Are executioners also sublime friends, or what?

Are the types of Māra also the spiritual masters, or what?[134] {413}

Are sins also virtues, or what?

Are all the lower realms also the higher realms, or what?

Is everything composite permanent, or what?

Is all saṃsāra bliss, or what?

Is all consciousness gnosis, or what?

Is all emission nonemission, or what?

Is all fabrication natural, or what?

Is all the incidental the primordial, or what?

Are all the stains the essence, or what?

Is all the relative the absolute, or what?

Are all phenomena the true nature, or what?

Are all the karmically determined forms the radiant light, or what?

Are all the faults the qualities, or what?

Are all the ominous signs the splendorous, or what?

Is all wrong right, or what?

Is all low high, or what?

Is all bad good, or what?

Is all far close, or what?

Is all the tainted the taintless, or what?

Is all the hindered the unhindered, or what?

Is all that has form the formless, or what?

Is all the tangible the intangible, or what? {414}

Is all the provisional meaning the definitive meaning, or what?

Is all the perverse dharma the sublime Dharma, or what?

Are all the wrong paths the sublime paths, or what?

Are all the frightening places the pleasant places, or what?

Is all black white, or what?

Are all squares round, or what?

This also applies in the same way to other colors and shapes.

This also applies to all such knowables.

Why? Because if [consciousness] were the buddha-body of reality even though it is the incompatible opposite of the buddha-body of reality, they would be identical in type.

Experts are aware of this procedure and this sort of reasoning in regard to all composite and noncomposite phenomena.

It is not a sphere of activity for foolish fabricators.

(A careful division of the true nature and emptiness, showing that the buddha-body of reality and emptiness are no different, and yet not identical, because there are endless examples of emptiness which are not the buddha-body of reality (267)**)**

If it is claimed that if one's own mind, these groups of consciousness, were not the buddha-body of reality, they would not be emptiness,

And if they were not the expanse of reality, they would not be emptiness, and if they were not the true nature, they would not be emptiness, that is a doctrine of foolish pretense.

Why? Because emptiness and the buddha-body of reality are two alternatives, and are not at all synonymous.

It is merely the ravings of those who lack the profound esoteric instructions about the two alternatives in regard to emptiness and all that is fully established, such as the expanse of reality, and who are intoxicated {415} by the poisonous drink of perverse explanations.

Therefore, one must never separate in any way from the Kṛtayuga [Dharma], which classifies all phenomena by means of the two alternatives, the three alternatives, and the four alternatives.[135]

(Refuting with beneficial intentions the claim that since everything is empty of self-nature, tangible virtues such as the construction of the three representations should not be performed, while intangible virtues such as tantric feasts should be performed)

Those of the flawed Tretayuga and later [eons] say, "Buddhahood, enlightenment, and gnosis are merely names. The statements about the many qualities are also provisional in meaning. Therefore, the construction of the three representations is meaningless.[136]

"As a side-effect sentient beings die, and the sin of their ruin is even greater than the merit of their construction. The earth is sinless, while a stūpa is sinful.[137]

"Therefore, without performing tangible virtues, fully offer up all offerings, and make all virtues intangible!"

I also cannot defer to those statements, and joining together my palms, I offer an appeal.

(Establishing through scripture and reasoning that since all the sources of refuge which are subsumed under the two truths have incredible blessing and power, the construction of their three representations will result in incredible merit)

The Victor has stated that the absolute Buddha exists as absolute truth, and even the relative Buddha who is born from his blessings and accumulated virtue exists in just the relative sense.

It is stated in the Kṛtayuga Dharma that even though the relative Buddha is indeed empty of self-nature, benefit for others occurs like from a {416} [wish-fulfilling] jewel and a heavenly tree,

And that for infinite sublime bodhisattvas and arhats the infinite qualities of the absolute buddha-body of reality act for the benefit of others.[138]

Fabricators and pretenders who have not heard about or seen anything like that, denigrate the Victor, and denigrating also his three representations,[139] completely shut many great doors of virtue.

May they also quickly see the sublime Kṛtayuga Dharma, completely reject the evil views, and open many great doors of virtue!

(Great merit is gained by the construction of the three representations of the Buddha, because he perfected the two goals. If such constructions are destroyed on purpose it is a great sin, but there is no sin in their natural ruin. Thus those who desire merit should construct the three representations)

The Victor has perfected all the flawless qualities, and therefore it is stated that the results of any benefit or harm done to him are much greater than others.

Therefore, if the destruction [of a stūpa, etc.] were on purpose, it would be a great sin, but I have not seen it stated that natural ruin is a great sin.[140]

(The wish to be able to perform in all lifetimes what is to be done for the precious Doctrine)

May I clarify the Doctrine in all lifetimes!

Even if unable to clarify the Doctrine, may I carry the great load of the Doctrine!

Even if unable to carry a great load, may I at least stand watch with concern for the Doctrine, and fear for the decline of the Doctrine! {417}

May I remove all the suffering of all the pervasive sentient beings who have been my parents!

Even if unable to remove all suffering, may I at least be their companion in suffering![141]

(An instruction and prayer for the rejection of the perverse explanations maintained by others who have not realized the profound essential points of the scriptures {268})

May I and all others always reject the perverse explanations that contradict the Kṛtayuga Dharma,

Such as the perverse explanation of Cittamātra and Madhyamaka [based upon] whether the three natures are accepted or not accepted,[142]

The perverse explanation of Cittamātra and Madhyamaka [based upon] whether the universal ground consciousness is accepted or not accepted,[143]

The perverse explanation of Cittamātra and Madhyamaka [based upon] whether the eight groups of consciousness are accepted or not accepted,[144]

And the perverse explanation of Cittamātra and Madhyamaka [based upon] whether no spiritual race is accepted or not accepted.[145]

This impartial and unbiased treatise is known as The Great Calculation of the Doctrine Which Has the Significance of a Fourth Council. As a result of the glorious Lama Dampa Sönam Gyaltsen Balzangpo bestowing many fine gifts and stating: "Compose many treatises like this," it was composed by the one endowed with the four reliances, and is complete.[146]

May it benefit the Doctrine and sentient beings!

MAṄGALAM

Notes

Introduction

1. For interesting comments on this point see Ruegg (1989), 8.

2. See Schaeffer (1995), for the translation and study of an important text by Rang byung rdo rje on the Buddha-nature (*tathāgatagarbha*). See Ruegg (1966), (1969), and (1973), for studies and translations of Bu ston's biography and his writings on the *tathāgatagarbha*. Also see Ruegg (1963) for some information on both Dol po pa's life and the *gzhan stong* teachings, but from the viewpoint of a Dge lugs pa critic. Kapstein (1992) provides a translation of a synopsis of Dol po pa's life, a brief discussion of his views, and the translation of a short text. Hookham (1991) uses Dol po pa's *Nges doṇ rgya mtsho* in her discussion of the *gzhan stong* approach to the interpretation of the *Ratnagotravibhaga*. In Stearns (1995) I already presented some of the material found in chapter 1, sections 3–5, and chapter 2, section 2. Germano (1992) is a translation and study of a section of one of Klong chen pa's major works. H. Guenther has translated a number of Klong chen pa's writings over the last twenty years. The life and thought of Bla ma dam pa Bsod nams rgyal mtshan remains largely unexplored. Van der Kuijp (1993) provides a list of works by Bla ma Dam pa which are preserved in Beijing. 'Ba' ra ba Rgyal mtshan dpal bzang, who studied with both Dol po pa and Bu ston, left a huge corpus of work on the *tathāgatagarbha* and related issues. No modern scholars have published any research on 'Ba' ra ba.

3. See especially Thurman (1984) and Ruegg (1963).

4. As noted by Ruegg (1989), 5–6, the teachings of Hva shang Mahāyāna suffered a similar fate in Tibet.

5. For instance, see the important comments in Ruegg (1995), 168.

6. See Dol po pa, *Kun mkhyen*.

7. This summary of the orthodox Sa skya position is based upon private conversations with the late Sde gzhung Rin po che, Kun dga' bstan pa'i nyi ma (1906–1987).

8. For example, see Dol po pa, *Bka' bsdu bzhi pa*, 387. Unless otherwise noted, all references to the *Bka' bsdu bzhi pa* and the *Bka' bsdu bzhi pa'i rang 'grel* are to the 1984 Bhutanese reproductions from original Rgyal rtse rdzong blocks.

9. Dol po pa, *Bka' bsdu bzhi pa'i rang 'grel*, 663: *thams cad rang stong du rtogs pa/ma rtogs pa dang cis ma mnyam/thams cad rang stong du bshad pa/ma bshad pa dang cis ma mnyam/thams cad rang stong du bris pa/ma bris pa dang cis ma mnyam/*.

10. For instance, Dol po pa specified that the distinction between an emptiness of self-nature and an emptiness of other was clearly presented in the *Angulimālaya sūtra*. Dol po pa, *Gsung*, 348: *rang stong gzhan stong dbye ba te/sor mo phreng ba'i mdo na gsal/*.

11. For example, see Dol po pa, *Lha*, 678–79, and Dol po pa, *Lo*, 774. Although the extant Sanskrit manuscripts have the spelling Sambhala, the more familiar spelling of Shambhala, as found in all Tibetan sources, has been followed in this work.

12. Martin Buber and Franz Rosenzweig, in their translation of the Hebrew Bible into German (1925–1962), also strove to remove what Buber referred to as the "palimpsest," or the accumulated theological, historical, and psychological ideas that they felt had often obscured the true meaning of the scripture. See Edward Hirsch (1995), 5.

13. See especially Ruegg (1963), (1968), (1969), (1973), and (1989); Kapstein (1992); Hookham (1991), as well as the critical reviews of Hookham's work by Griffiths (1993), Need (1993), and Ehrhard (1994); and Broido (1989).

14. See Dol po pa, *Bstan*. All references to this text are from the Bhutanese edition prepared from tracings of the original Rgyal rtse rdzong blocks.

15. See Nya dbon, *Bstan*. I am grateful to Prof. Leonard van der Kuijp for a copy of this rare manuscript.

16. See Dol po pa, *Bka' bsdu bzhi pa*. Unless otherwise noted, all references to this text are to the Bhutanese edition.

Chapter 1. The Life of the Buddha from Dolpo

1. Lamotte, trans. Sara Webb-Boin (1988), XXIV.

2. For brief summaries of Dol po pa's life see Kapstein (1992), 7–21, Roerich (1976), 775–77, and Ruegg (1963), 80–81.

3. See Lha'i rgyal mtshan, *Chos*, and Kun spangs, *Chos*. Kun spangs pa's work was the earlier of the two, apparently written in 1362 or 1363, whereas Lha'i rgyal mtshan's can only be dated to between 1380, when Lo chen Byang chub rtse mo died (mentioned on 55b), and 1401, the year of the author's death. Nevertheless, Lha'i rgyal mtshan's work is the more reliable, being based on information given by Dol po pa himself, and notes set down by his chosen heir, Jo nang Lo tsā ba Blo gros dpal (1299–1353), as well as a biography composed by Dus 'khor ba 'Jam sgeg only one month after Dol po pa's death. Lha'i rgyal mtshan's work also includes what the author himself had seen, heard, or remembered. For these reasons, in the following treatment of the major phases of Dol po pa's career, the chronology set forth in Lha'i rgyal mtshan's work will be followed, with reference to variances found in the other sources. As will be noted below, there are also serious chronological problems in Kun spangs pa's work, and certain later additions by an unknown editor. I should like to thank Prof. Leonard van der Kuijp for a copy of Lha'i rgyal mtshan's rare work.

Ngag dbang blo gros grags pa, *Dpal*, 35–36, gives a sketch of the life of Gha rung ba Lha'i rgyal mtshan, whom other sources refer to as 'Ga' rong ba. For example, Tāranātha received the textual transmission for the *rnam thar* by 'Ga' rong ba in 1588. See Tāranātha, *Rgyal*, 89. See also Dkon mchog bstan pa rab rgyas, *Yul*, 11. For a sketch of the life of Kun spangs Chos grags dpal bzang, see Ngag dbang blo gros grags pa, *Dpal*, 32–33. The two later sources that deal with Dol po pa's life are Tāranātha, *Dpal*, and Mang thos Klu sgrub rgya mtsho, *Bstan*.

Other than the two full-length biographies of Dol po pa by Lha'i rgyal mtshan and Kun spangs pa, it is known that another was written by Zhwa lu Lo tsā ba Chos skyong bzang po (1441–1528). See Dkon mchog bstan pa rab rgyas, *Yul*, 11. For an extremely abbreviated version of Lha'i rgyal mtshan's work, see Lha'i rgyal mtshan, *Kun*. In modern times, the Jo nang scholar Ngag dbang blo gros grags pa has written a lengthy verse *rnam thar* of Dol po pa, but no copy of this work is presently available. See the editor's preface to Ngag dbang blo gros grags pa, *Dpal*, 2.

4. Lha'i rgyal mtshan, *Chos*, 2a–4a, and Kun spangs, *Chos*, 297. Also see Kapstein (1992), 8–9.

5. Kun spangs, *Chos*, 296.

6. Lha'i rgyal mtshan, *Chos*, 5a.

7. Ibid. Mang thos klu sgrub, *Bstan*, 178, mentions that Skyi ston Shāk 'bum and Skyi ston Grags pa rgyal mtshan were uncle and nephew (*khu dbon*).

8. Kapstein (1992), 10–11, understandably mistook this event for Dol po pa's own later departure for Sa skya. The original source for the condensed text translated and reproduced by Kapstein can now be identified as Lha'i rgyal mtshan, *Chos*, which was not available to Kapstein.

9. See Lha'i rgyal mtshan, *Chos*, 6a, Kun spangs, *Chos*, 298, and Tāranātha, *Dpal*, 25.

10. See Roerich, trans., (1976), 756, 785, and Stearns (1996), 163, note 117, for information on Rong pa Shes rab seng ge. Lo tsā ba Mchog ldan was a disciple of Shong ston Rdo rje rgyal mtshan and his brother, and became the teacher of Dpang Blo gros brtan pa. See Dgra' dul dbang po, *Tha*, 299.

11. The trilogy of texts known as the *Sems 'grel skor gsum* are: (1) the *Vimalaprabhā* (Peking #2064), an immense commentary upon the *Kālacakra tantra* by Kalkin Puṇḍarīka, (2) the *Hevajrapiṇḍārtha ṭīkā* (Peking #2310), a commentary upon the *Hevajra tantra* by Bodhisattva Vajragarbha, and (3) the *Lakṣābhidhanād uddhṛta laghutantra piṇḍārthavivaraṇa* (Peking #2317), a commentary upon the *Cakrasaṃvara tantra* by Bodhisattva Vajrapāṇi. The first section of the *Vimalaprabhā* has now been translated and studied in Newman (1987).

12. According to Dol po pa, *Zhu*, 344–45, the ten *Snying po'i mdo* are (1) *De bshin gshegs pa'i snying po'i mdo*, (2) *Rnam par mi rtog pa la 'jug pa'i gzungs*, (3) *Lha mo dpal phreng seng ge sgra'i mdo*, (4) *Rnga bo che chen po'i mdo*, (5) *Sor mo'i phreng ba la phan pa'i mdo*, (6) *Stong nyid chen po'i mdo*, (7) *De bzhin gshegs pa'i thugs rje chen po bstan pa'i mdo*, (8) *De bzhin gshegs pa'i yon tan dang ye shes bsam gyis mi khyab pa'i bstan pa'i mdo*, (9) *Sprin chen po'i mdo rgyas pa*, and (10) the condensed and extensive *Myang 'das chen po'i mdo* both counted together as one. The first five texts in this list are also referred to as "The Five Sūtras on the Buddha-Nature." Lha'i rgyal mtshan, *Chos*, 10b, has simply copied the same list from Dol po pa's work.

13. The five *Nges don mdo* are (1) *Sher phyin lnga brgya pa*, (2) *Byang chub sems pa'i bslab pa rab tu dbye ba'i le'u cha gnyis gcig tu byas pa byams zhus su'ang grags pa*, (3) *Rgyan btug po'i mdo*, (4) *Rab tu zhi ba rnam par nges pa'i cho 'phrul gyi ting nge 'dzin kyi mdo*, (5) *Dkon mchog sprin gyi mdo*. A set of ten "Sūtras on the Definitive Meaning" is made by adding the following texts to this list: (1) *Gser 'od dam chen,* (2) *Dgongs pa nges par 'grel pa,* (3) *Lang kar gshegs pa,* (4) *Ye shes snang ba rgyan gyi mdo,* and (5) *Sangs rgyas phal po che.* See Dol po pa, ibid., and Lha'i rgyal mtshan, ibid., 11a. The two versions of the *Byams zhus*, or "Maitreya's

Questions," mentioned in #2 are those found in the eighteen-thousand- and the twenty-five-thousand-line *Prajñāpāramitā sūtra*.

14. The five *Byams chos*, or "Treatises of Maitreya" are (1) *Ratnagotravibhāga*, (2) *Abhisamayālaṇkāra*, (3) *Dharmadharmatāvibhāga*, (4) *Mahāyānasūtrālaṅkāra*, and (5) *Madhyāntavibhāga*. Dol po pa also received from Skyi ston a number of texts by Nāgārjuna. The teachings Dol po pa received from Skyi ston are said to all be listed in his *Gsan yig*, which does not seem to have survived. See Lha'i rgyal mtshan, ibid., 6a.

15. A brief discussion of the nature of the six branches is given below in chapter 3, section 3. See Grönbold (1982) and (1983) for further information.

16. Lha'i rgyal mtshan, *Chos*, 8b.

17. Tāranātha, *Dpal*, 25.

18. Kun spangs, *Chos*, 301, places Dol po pa's studies with Grags pa rgyal mtshan at a later time, after he returned to Sa skya from a tour of the teaching institutes of Gtsang and Dbus. Lha'i rgyal mtshan, *Chos*, 6a, mentions these studies before his departure from Sa skya. See Mang thos klu sgrub, *Bstan*, 170, for Grags pa rgyal mtshan's possible dates. Van der Kuijp (1994), 143–45, has gathered considerable information about Kun spangs Grags pa rgyal mtshan, also known as Bla ma mnyam med pa, from whom Ta'i Si tu Byang chub rgyal mtshan (1302–1364) received the Lam 'bras teachings.

19. Lha'i rgyal mtshan, *Chos*, 6a–b. Kun dga' rdo rje, *Deb*, 51, mentions that Seng ge dpal died in China at the age of thirty, while his brother Kun dga' bsod nams held the Shar pa throne (*gdan sa*) for thirty-four years and died at the age of sixty-two in a *me pho khyi* year (1346). Dpal 'byor bzang po, *Rgya*, 353, relates the same information in a somewhat clearer fashion.

20. Dol po pa's studies with Rin chen ye shes are mentioned in Tāranātha, *Dpal*, 25, and Lha'i rgyal mtshan, ibid., 6b. Also see Kun dga' grol mchog, *Khrid*, 326: *thams cad mkhyen pa bu ston gyi dris lan zhig na'ang/sngon rta nag pa rin chen ye shes pa'i grub mtha' zhig yod pa phyis dol bu pas rtsal 'don du skyong bar snang gsungs pa la yang zhib dpyod mdzad 'tshal/*. Kun dga' grol mchog's text is translated below in chapter 2, section 1.

21. See Lha'i rgyal mtshan, ibid., 6b, and Kun spangs, *Chos*, 299–300.

22. Lha'i rgyal mtshan, ibid. Kun spangs, ibid., 302, lists many of the places Dol po pa visited.

23. Tāranātha, *Dpal*, 25.

24. Lha'i rgyal mtshan, *Chos*, 7b. Kun spangs, *Chos*, 300, places Dol po pa's ordination ceremony at Zhwa lu when Dol po pa was twenty-one years

old. It is interesting to note that Dol po pa wrote a short verse text on the Madhyamaka view at the order of this Mkhan chen Bsod nams grags pa. See Dol po pa, *Dbu*. This text, which does not contain the special Dharma language Dol po pa later developed, is obviously one of his earlier works, and could conceivably have been composed at the time of his ordination in 1314, although there is no way to be certain. The death of Bsod nams grags pa is mentioned in Byang chub rtse mo, *Chos*, 31a. See Ruegg (1966), 77–78, for the ordination of Bu ston, and Byang chub rtse mo, ibid., 9b–10a, for the ordinations of Bla ma Dam pa and his brother.

25. For example, he received the *Phyag rgya chen po ga'u ma* of the Shangs pa tradition from Mkhas grub (Gzhon nu grub, d. 1319) at Bsam sdings, and many Gcod, Zhi byed, Phyag rgya chen po, and Rdzogs chen teachings from a yogin called Nag 'bum, and from a Mkhan chen 'Dzims pa. See Lha'i rgyal mtshan, ibid., 7b–8a. Teachings from those traditions were also received from a Bla ma Rdo rje rgyal mtshan. See Kun spangs, *Chos*, 302.

26. Lha'i rgyal mtshan, ibid., 8b, describes the texts written at this time as a *Sems bskyed cho ga* and a *Jo bo rin po che la bstod pa'i tshigs bcad*. Neither is found in the presently available works of Dol po pa.

27. Lha'i rgyal mtshan, ibid. Kun spangs, *Chos*, 300, places this event earlier, before Dol po pa received full ordination.

28. See Tāranātha, *Dpal*, 25–26, and Kun spangs, *Chos*, 302–303.

29. Tāranātha, ibid., 26.

30. Lha'i rgyal mtshan, *Chos*, 9a: *mkhas pa mang po ji tsam 'tshogs kyin yang nga zhums nas mi 'gro'i stengs su spobs pa je bzang je bzang la 'gro ba gcig yod pa yin pa la/jo nang du phyin dus sgom chen pho mo re re'i sgom gyi gnas lugs rtogs tsa na nga yang shin tu zhum par gyur cing/ khong tso la dad pa dang dag snang dbang med du skye ba byung/*. Tāranātha, ibid., 26, also refers to this event.

31. See Tāranātha, ibid., 26, for the meeting with Rang byung rdo rje. The significance of this meeting is discussed below in chapter 2, section 2. For the now available *rnam thar* of Yon tan rgya mtsho, see Dol po pa, *Bla*. The first meeting with Yon tan rgya mtsho is described in Lha'i rgyal mtshan, ibid., and Kun spangs, *Chos*, 304.

32. See Kun spangs, ibid., 304–306. Two of the monks accompanying Dol po pa were named Rin chen dpal and Blo gros dpal. Dol po pa himself would later be considered an emanation of Kalkin Puṇḍarīka, who in turn was believed to have been an emanation of Avalokiteśvara. Kun spangs pa provides a long list of the many *ṣaḍaṅgayoga* transmissions which Dol po pa received: *kha che pan chen gyi sbyor drug, a bha ya'i sbyor drug, rga*

lo'i sbyor drug, na ro pa'i sbyor drug, sha ba ri pa'i sbyor drug, bram ze bsod snyoms pa'i sbyor drug, dpal gsang ba 'dus pa'i sbyor drug, kye'i rdo rje'i sbyor drug, gnyos khong pa'i sbyor drug, zhang g.yu brag pa'i sbyor drug, etc. He also received many Tibetan treatises on the *ṣaḍaṅgayoga*, such as the *tsa mi lo tsā ba'i sbyor drug, kyi jo lo tsā ba'i sbyor drug, 'bro lo tsā ba'i sbyor drug, rwa lo tsā ba'i sbyor drug, 'jam dbyang gsar ma'i sbyor drug*, etc. He is said to have achieved precise experience and realization according to each, and mastered all the words and meanings.

33. Kun spangs, ibid., 306–308, and Lha'i rgyal mtshan, *Chos*, 9a–9b.

34. Kun spangs, ibid., 308.

35. Ibid., 308: *sor bsam gnyis la brten nas sangs rgyas kyi sku dang zhing khams dpag du med pa gzigs so/srog rtsol dang 'dzin* [309] *pa la brten nas bde drod 'bar bas nyams rtogs khyad par can 'khrungs so/.*

36. Tāranātha, *'Khyog*, 2a: *chos rje kun mkhyen chen pos kyang lo gnyis ngo gsum bzhugs/sor sdud bsam gtan srog rtsol gsum mthar phyin pa'i tshul ston sa yang 'di lags/.* I would like to thank Dr. Franz-Karl Ehrhard for a copy of this text.

37. Tāranātha, *Dpal*, 26: *sbyor drug la nyams 'khrid mdzad/dmigs pa zhu ba'i skabs ma gtogs su dang yang mi 'phrad par mkha'spyod bde ldan du bzhugs/sor bsdud bsam gtan gyi nyams rtogs mthar phyin pas/bla ma'i gsung nas mgyogs khrid bya gsung pa la/gol le skyong bar zhu zhus te sgom par mdzad pas/srog rtsol mthar phyin pa'i rtags rgyud nas bshad pa bzhin mnga'/.*

38. Ibid., 27: *gzhan stong gi lta sgom khyad par can ni/mkha' spyod bde ldan du bzhugs pa'i tshe thugs la 'khrungs pa yin kyang/lo shas shig gzhan la ma gsungs/.*

39. Ibid.

40. Lha'i rgyal mtshan, *Chos*, 10a, mentions that the request was made about two years before the death of Yon tan rgya mtsho in 1327. Dol po pa's own words are quoted in describing these events and his feelings about them.

41. Kun spangs, *Chos*, 309–11, Lha'i rgyal mtshan, ibid., 10a–b.

42. See notes 11–14 in the present chapter for an identification of these texts. Also see Lha'i rgyal mtshan, ibid., 10b–11a.

43. Kun spangs, *Chos*, 312.

44. Ibid., 310: *nga'i ri khrod 'dir bu bas tsha bo bzang/tsha bo bas kyang yang tsha bzang bar 'ong/ma 'ongs pa na bzang ldan gong mar chos 'chad/bzang ldan 'og mar mchod rten chen po bzhengs/.* This prophecy is

also found, in less detail, in Lha'i rgyal mtshan, *Chos*, 12a, and also on 23b, where it is quoted from a letter sent to Dol po pa by a Rin po che Sher 'bum pa, who was a disciple of Kun spangs Thugs rje brtson 'grus. Sher 'bum pa expressed his certainty that Dol po pa was the one Kun spangs pa had prophesied. Kun spangs pa's spiritual son, or successor, was Rgyal ba ye shes (1257–1320), the grandson was Yon tan rgya mtsho, and the heralded great-grandson was, of course, Dol po pa.

45. Lha'i rgyal mtshan, ibid., 12a. Khro phu Lo tsā ba's stūpa was probably the model upon which Dol po pa based his own monument. Khro phu Lo tsā ba began his stūpa when he was fifty-eight years old (1230), and completed the shrines on the third floor in 1234. It was constructed to serve as a reliquary shrine for some of the remains and *ring bsrel* of his master Śākyaśrībhadra (d. 1225?), which were brought from Kashmir to Tibet by two *paṇḍita* disciples of Śākyaśrībhadra. See Byams pa dpal, *Khro*, 86a–87a. My thanks to Prof. Leonard van der Kuijp for a copy of this text. The only other available description is the brief mention in Chos kyi rgya mtsho, *Gangs*, 481, where the Khro phu structure is said to have been built of stone, with three stories (*bang rim*) of five temples on each of the four sides, totaling sixty.

46. Lha'i rgyal mtshan, ibid., 12a–b. Kun spangs, *Chos*, 312, gives the date for this event. He also supplies a fantastic story about how the central poles (*srog shing*) were put in place in upper Bzang ldan, but were hurled down to the sandy plain of lower Bzang ldan through the supernatural intervention of the Rgyal chen bzhi, or Protectors of the Four Directions, and the stūpa therefore had to be constructed there. See Kun spangs, ibid., 313. Based on the tone and contents of both sources, it would seem that the first attempt to build at upper Bzang ldan was unsuccessful, and construction was delayed until the next spring, when it was moved to the more favorable site of lower Bzang ldan.

47. Kun spangs, ibid., 316–19, and Lha'i rgyal mtshan, ibid., 12b.

48. Kun spangs, ibid., 318–19. The actual construction of the Jo nang stūpa, which was known by many names, such as Dpal yon can, Sku 'bum chen po, Dpal sgo mangs, and so forth, is detailed in Kun spangs, ibid., 313–28, and Lha'i rgyal mtshan, ibid., 12a–20a. Dol po pa also wrote two short texts in praise of the stūpa. See Dol po pa, *Mchod rten dpal*, and *Mchod rten bzhengs*. Lha'i rgyal mtshan, ibid., 23a, mentions that Dol po pa wrote five texts concerning the Sku bum chen po, the most important of which was the *Chos sgo mang du 'byed pa'i thabs mchog*, which is now available. See Dol po pa, *Chos kyi sgo*. The stūpa at Jo nang was visited and its interior art work described by Tucci (1980), 190–96. Photographs of it are found in Tucci (1973), pls. 78 and 79, although incorrectly captioned as the stūpa at Rgyang. See Vitali (1990), 128, pl. 82, for a photo-

graph of the ruined remains following the Cultural Revolution, and 129 for a reproduction of Tucci's old photograph, but with the correct caption. Another photograph of a largely reconstructed stūpa is found on the inside cover of the Tibetan periodical *Gangs ljongs rig gnas* (1991.4).

49. It is extremely interesting that four long iron chains (*lcags thag*) were salvaged from an iron suspension bridge (*lcags zam*) in the Ngam ring district, and used for structural support in the Jo nang stūpa. Kun spangs, ibid., 326–28. This is barely mentioned in Lha'i rgyal mtshan, *Chos*, 13a. The existence of an iron bridge is noteworthy because the received tradition is that iron suspension bridges were not introduced in Tibet until Grub chen Thang stong rgyal po (1361–1485) built the first one over the Skyi chu river in 1430, exactly one hundred years after Dol po pa began the construction of his stūpa. See Stearns (1980), especially 111--18. What is even more incredible is that Tāranātha, *Dpal*, 30, states that the iron bridge (from which the chains were salvaged) was at Rin chen sding. This is the birthplace of Thang stong rgyal po, who would later claim to be the rebirth of Dol po pa!

50. See Lha'i rgyal mtshan, ibid., 13a and 15b. One of those who sent offerings was the Sa skya Ti shri Kun dga' rgyal mtshan, who was a disciple of Dol po pa. On 20a, this same Sa skya master is also stated to have offered materials for the construction of a large silk maṇḍala of Kālacakra after the completion of the stūpa.

51. The participation of these teachers in the construction work is mentioned by Lha'i rgyal mtshan, ibid., 12b. The date and location of Nya dbon's composition is found in Nya dbon, *Bstan pa*, 53a.

52. See Kun spangs, *Chos*, 323: *chos rje'i thugs dgyes nas/kun rdzob rang stong dang don dam gzhan stong gi phye bsal chen mo dang . . . /*. In Stearns (1995), 833, note 17, Bzang ldan gong was identified as Bzang ldan chos sde, near Byang Ngam ring, which was founded by Dol po pa's disciple and biographer, Kun spangs Chos grags dpal bzang. This is incorrect. As seen above, upper (*gong*) Bzang ldan and lower (*'og*) Bzang ldan were apparently names of areas within the monastic environs of Jo nang itself. Tāranātha's comments are found in Tāranātha, *Dpal*, 27.

53. See Lha'i rgyal mtshan, *Chos*, 15a–b.

54. Ibid., 21a: *sngar bod du ma grags pa don dam gzhan stong dang . . . /*. This is the first in a long and significant list of topics that Dol po pa felt he had been the first in Tibet to realize and explicate correctly.

55. Both Dol po pa's own comments and the opinions of Lha'i rgyal mtshan are found in Lha'i rgyal mtshan, ibid., 22a.

56. The three-fold knowledge is that arisen from study (*thos pa*), contemplation (*bsam pa*), and meditation (*sgom pa*). This single couplet is also

quoted in Roerich (1976), 776. Lha'i rgyal mtshan's work is the earliest available source for it.

57. Lha'i rgyal mtshan, *Chos*, 22a: *kye ma bdag gi skal ba rab dman yang/'di 'dra snyed pas skal ba bzang snyam byed/le lo can gyi blun pos 'di rnyed pa/rigs ldan rgyal pos byin gyis brlabs yin nam/lus kyis ka lā pa ru ma sleb kyang/dad pa'i sems la rigs ldan zhugs sam ci/shes rab gsum la blo 'gros sbyangs min yang/lhun po bzhengs pas rgya mtsho rdol ba snyam/ 'phags rnams kyis kyang rtogs par dka' ba'i gnas/gang gis drin gyis ji bzhin rtogs mdzad pa/bla ma sangs rgyas rigs ldan thams cad dang/de yi mchod rten che la phyag 'tshal 'dud/.*

58. See Broido (1989), for a very brief sketch of Dol po pa's views according to the *Ri chos nges don rgya mtsho*. Several examples of the *Ri chos* have now been published. See especially the edition cited in the bibliography as Dol po pa, *Ri*, which has many useful annotations. Lha'i rgyal mtshan, ibid., 17a, gives the date of the stūpa consecration as *dpal ldong gyi lo smin drug gi zla ba'i dkar phyogs kyi tshes bcu*, which corresponds to Friday, October 30, 1333. The date of the composition of Nya dbon's commentary is given in Nya dbon, *Bstan pa*, 53a: *chu mo bya'i lo dbyar zla 'bring po'i tshes bco lnga*, but there is some uncertainty about its accuracy. This problem is discussed in detail below in note 2 of the Introduction to the Translation of *A General Commentary on the Doctrine*. Both of the preceding dates have been calculated based upon Schuh (1973).

59. See Tāranātha, *Dpal*, 27. The very appropriate term *hermeneutical shock* has been borrowed from Nathan Katz (1983), 110.

60. Tāranātha, *Zab don*, 793–94.

61. 'Jam mgon A myes zhabs, *Dpal*, vol. 2, 285: . . . *kun mkhyen dol bu yis/sngon med gzhan stong lta ba'i srol btod pas/'di la mkhas mchog rnams kyis mgrin gcig tu/khyed* [286] *nyid sa skya'i grub mtha'i rjes 'jug tu/khas lan bzhin du rje btsun gong ma yi/gsung dang 'gal ba'i lta ba 'di 'dod pa/ 'thad pa min zhes rtsod ngag mang du bsgrags/*. A myes zhabs's following declaration that Dol po pa repented of the *gzhan stong* view as a result of a visit to Sa skya during which he touched a robe of Sa skya Paṇ ḍi ta's to his lips, and then again upheld the *rang stong* position for the rest of his life, must be regarded as nothing more than wishful thinking on the part of the Sa skya hierarch. A similar polemic claim that Paṇ chen Shākya mchog ldan (1428–1507) repented of the *gzhan stong* view at the time of his death, and suffered greatly in his later rebirths because of the vile views he had held, is found in Ruegg (1963), 90.

62. Lha'i rgyal mtshan, *Chos*, 45b, mentions all of these Sa skya masters, with the exception of Don yod rgyal mtshan, in a list of Dol po pa's disciples. In regard to Chos kyi rgyal mtshan and Blo gros rgyal mtshan,

see van der Kuijp (1988), 300, note 24. For Tāranātha's remarks, see Tāranātha, *Dpal*, 25.

63. The monastery of Chu bzang had been offered by the Lam 'bras master Ston pa Ye shes dpal (1281–1365) to Dol po pa's disciple Kun spangs Chos grags dpal bzang, from whom he had received the *ṣaḍaṅgayoga*. Kun spangs pa then taught there. See Ngag dbang blo gros grags pa, *Dpal*, 33, and Dgra 'dul dbang po, *Tha*, 174.

64. 'Ba' ra ba, *Skyes mchog chen*, 637–39. See especially 639, where he quotes from Dol po pa's letter to him: *'di skad ces byung ste kun gzhi la dbye na/ye shes yin pa'i kun gzhi dang/rnam shes yin pa'i kun gzhi gnyis lung rigs rnam dag gi legs par grub kyang/de gnyis rang bzhin tha dad du de ni mi 'dod cing/gzhan 'dod pa 'dug na'ang/'di skad byung ste/lung rigs rnam dag gi dgag pa byed do gsungs pas/slob mas chos rje'i dgongs pa mtha' ma longs pa'i bab chol smras par zad/*. Dol po pa's statements in this letter directly contradict the opinions of his disciples quoted by 'Ba' ra ba on 638. Therefore, there would seem to be some truth to 'Ba' ra ba's final comment that the so-called great disciples did not really comprehend the depth of Dol po pa's thought. The same point about the chief disciples not truly mastering Dol po pa's intentions was later made by Byams gling Paṇ chen Bsod nams rnam rgyal (1400–1475), specifically when discussing the master's works concerning the *Kālacakra tantra*. See Kun dga' grol mchog, who quotes Byams gling Paṇ chen in *Rigs*, 22b: *kun mkhyen chen po nyid kyi mkhyen rab zab cing gting dpag dka' pa'i cha rnams slob ma'i gtso bor grags pa kun gyis kyang/ji bzhin du ma rtogs pa 'dra/*. Tucci (1980), 164, mistakenly attributed this work to Tāranātha.

65. Tāranātha, *Dpal*, 27.

66. For sketches of the lives of Ma ti Paṇ chen and Jo nang Lo tsā ba Blo gros dpal, see Ngag dbang blo gros grags pa, *Dpal*, 33. According to Tāranātha, *Dpal*, 30, Blo gros dpal was also known as Klubs Lo tsā ba. These two scholars were among the greatest Sanskrit grammarians in Tibetan history. Their translation of Sanskrit grammatical texts is reviewed in Verhagen (1994), 142–44. See also Ruegg (1963), 81, notes 36 and 37. Prof. Ruegg's conjecture that the attribution of a revised translation of the *Kālacakra* to Ma ti Paṇ chen and Lo tsā ba Blo gros dpal referred to their translation of the *Garudasādhana* is no longer tenable. The colophon to this work clearly states that it is an extract from the *Kālacakra tantra*, and that it has been written out precisely according to the new translation (*'gyur gsar*) of Jo nang Lo tsā Blo gros dpal and Sa bzang Blo gros rgyal mtshan. See the *Mkha' lding gi sgrub thabs* (*Garudasādhana*), Peking Tripitaka, #5167, vol. 87, 253–5–8: *'di'i rgya skad dus kyi 'khor lo'i rgyud tshig las bkol ba kho na yin pa ste/jo nang lo tsa blo gros dpal dang/sa bzang blo gros rgyal mtshan gyi 'gyur gsar ji lta bar bris so/*.

67. See Kun spangs, *Chos*, 331, concerning Dol po pa's orders for the new translation, as well as his own composition of the outline and annotations: *de nas khyi lor bde ba can du bzhugs nas/lo tsa blo gros rnam gnyis la dus kyi 'khor lo'i 'gyur gyi dag pa'i gzhi gyis gsungs nas/chos rje dang kho bo gnyis dpang por bzhag nas/slar legs pa'i nang nas legs pa yang dag par mdzad do/de nas bdag gis bskul nas sa bcad dang mchan pu mdzad do/*. Also see Roerich, trans., (1976), 776. Here and elsewhere, the terms *condensed meaning* (*bsdus don*) and *topical outline* (*sa bcad*) are used to refer to the same work by Dol po pa. It is doubtful that these important works by Dol po pa have survived to the present day. Sde srid Sangs rgyas rgya mtsho (1653–1705) used and quoted Dol po pa's annotations when composing his own *Bai ḍurya g.ya' sel* in 1668, but no clear reference to their existence after that time has been located. See Sangs rgyas rgya mtsho, *Bstan*, vol. 1, 94: *kun mkhyen do bu pa'i 'grel chen gyi mchan du/'dzam gling chung ngu'i lho nas byang gangs ldan chen po'i bar la sa'i dum bu drug du byas pa'i byang gi dum bu lnga pa'i sa la shambha la'i yul 'yod de zhes stong phrag nyer lnga'i phyed rang la 'dzam gling chung ngur bzhed pa dang/*. Dol po pa's two works are also referred to with effusive praise by the modern writer Ngag dbang blo gros grags pa, but it is not clear whether he actually had access to the texts. See Ngag dbang blo gros grags pa, *Dpal*, 541–42.

68. The Jo nang translation of the *Kālacakra tantra* has apparently been preserved only in the Peking edition of the Tibetan Tripitaka. All other available editions of the *Kālacakra tantra* in Tibetan are copies of the translation by Shong ston Rdo rje rgyal mtshan. The translation of the *Vimalaprabhā* in the Peking edition is also by Shong ston. Three-fifths of the Jo nang translation of the *Vimalaprabhā* has also survived in a single unique copy, but only in the Sde dge edition of the Tibetan Bstan 'gyur. In this example the Jo nang translation of the *Vimalaprabhā* is preserved in a strange hybrid version, consisting of Shong ston's translation of the first two sections of the work, and the revised Jo nang translation of the last three sections. See Kalkin Puṇḍarīka, *Bsdus*. The same colophon translated below is found both at the end of the tantra in the Peking edition and at the end of the commentary in the Sde dge edition. That the Sde dge edition of the *Vimalaprabhā* is in fact a hybrid, despite the colophon identifying it as the revised Jo nang translation, is specified by Zhu chen Tshul khrims rin chen (1697–1774), the editor of the collection. See Tshul khrims rin chen, *Kun*, 624. Si tu Paṇ chen Chos kyi 'byung gnas (1700–1774) also expressed a desire to have the new Jo nang translations cut into woodblocks for printing at Sde dge. See Chos kyi 'byung gnas, *Ta'i*, 151: *jo nang pa'i gsar 'gyur rnams kyang par du dgod par 'dod do/*. It is curious that the Sde dge edition of the *Bka' 'gyur*, for which Si tu wrote the descriptive catalogue, contains the Shong ston translation, and not that of the Jo nang pa scholars.

69. The Omniscient Dharma Lord is Dol po pa himself, and Dharmakīrtiśrībhadra is the Sanskrit form of the name of his great disciple and biographer, Kun spangs Chos grags dpal bzang, who was also a skilled translator of Sanskrit texts. Sthiramati is the Sanskrit translation of Blo gros brtan pa, the personal name of the great master Dpang Lo tsā ba (1276–1342), who was the early teacher of both Ma ti Paṇ chen Blo gros rgyal mtshan and Jo nang Lo tsā ba Blo gros dpal bzang po. See Ngag dbang blo gros grags pa, *Dpal*, 33, and Roerich, trans. (1976), 837. Dgra' 'dul dbang po, *Tha*, 299–303, provides the most information about Dpang Lo.

70. Kalkin Yaśas (P), *Mchog*, 174.5: *slar yang dpal ldan bla ma dam pa chos kyi rje thams cad mkhyen pa dang/dpal dus kyi 'khor lo pa chen po dharma kīrti shrī bhadras/'di'i don rnams legs par dgongs shing bka' yis bskul nas de dag gi gsung bzhin du/paṇ ḍi ta chen po sthi ra ma ti'i bka' drin las/legs par sgyur ba'i tshul rig pa lo tsā ba shākya'i dge slong blo gros rgyal mtshan dang/blo gros dpal bzang pos/rgyud dang 'grel pa'i rgya dpe mang po la gtugs nas dag pa rnams dang mthun par bsgyur cing zhus te gtan la phab ba'o/*. Part of this colophon is also quoted in the Fifth Dalai Lama's "record of teachings recieved" (*thob yig*), where the Jo nang translation would seem to have been the version of the *Kālacakra* that he received. But an unidentified note in the Tibetan text mentions that although this version was very famous "nowadays," the best scholars preferred the Shong translation itself. See the annotation to Ngag dbang blo bzang rgya mtsho, *Zab*, vol. 4, 610: *deng sang grags che'ang ha cang skye ba mi dgos par ma nges pas shong 'gyur rang bzang zhes mkhas pa rnams gsung/*.

71. Dol po pa, *Lo*, 773. Kun spangs, *Chos*, 358, mentions the visit of Lo tsā ba Shes rab rin chen some time after 1336, and that he offered about fifty rolls of silk to Dol po pa, prayed to be reborn at his feet, and requested a practical meditation instruction (*dmar khrid*).

72. Rnam rgyal grags bzang, who viewed Dol po pa as the final authority in the *Kālacakra*, wrote a great many works on the *Kālacakra* system, none of which are presently available. See Kun dga' grol mchog, *Rigs*, 28a–29b, for a list of his works related to the *Kālacakra*. Byams gling Paṇ chen was also one of the greatest Tibetan masters of the *Kālacakra*. His seven-volume explication of the *Vimalaprabhā*, also not presently available, was the most extensive in Tibet. See Padma dkar po, *Mchog*, 57.

73. The Tibetan translation made in the thirteenth century by Shong ston Rdo rje rgyal mtshan was widely accepted as the definitive version.

74. The points Bu ston felt were in need of correction were in the translations of both the *Kālacakra tantra* and the *Vimalaprabhā*. By comparing the Peking edition of the Shong ston translation of some of the

phrases Bu ston singled out for correction in the *Vimalaprabhā* against those in the Sde dge edition, it does become clear that the first two sections in the Sde dge example contain no revisions as suggested by Bu ston, whereas the last three sections do contain Bu ston's suggested changes. This in large part verifies Zhu chen Tshul khrims rin chen's assertion that the last three sections are the revised work of the Jo nang translators, while the first two are the original work of Shong ston. See note 68 immediately above.

75. Roerich, trans. (1976), 794, translated the second sentence referring to this event in *The Blue Annals* as follows: "While he [Bu ston] was writing down notes on the *Vimalaprabhā*, he revised the translation by Shong. He wrote it out properly, after it had been translated by two translators at Jo nang." A more correct translation of the passage would read: "When [Bu ston] made annotations to the [*Kālacakra*] *tantra* commentary, he made many revisions to the Shong translation. When the two translators translated it at Jo nang, they wrote down [Bu ston's revisions] just as they were." See 'Gos lo Gzhon nu dpal, *Deb*, vol. 2, 929: *rgyud 'grel la mchan bu mdzad pa na/shong 'gyur la 'gyur bcos mang du mdzad de/de jo nang du lo* [930] *tsa ba gnyis kyis 'gyur mdzad pa na ji lta ba bzhin du bris/.*

76. The Tibetan phrase *don la brton pa*, refers to one of the "four reliances" (*rton pa bzhi*), which is to rely upon the meaning (*don*), not the words (*tshig*). See chapter 3, section 2 below for a discussion of the meaning of the phrase *rton pa bzhi ldan*, "endowed with the four reliances," which was Dol po pa's favorite pseudonym.

77. As briefly discussed in the introductions to the translations in part 2 below, these are often mentioned as Dol po pa's three most important works.

78. Kun dga' grol mchog, *Rigs*, 22a–b: *thams cad mkhyen pa bu ston pas kyang shong 'gyur nyid 'chad dpe'i mthil du mdzad nas/'dir mi bcos su mi rung ba sum bcu so bgrangs tsam yod ces bka' stsal pa ltar/kun mkhyen chen po dol bu sangs rgyas kyis lo tsa ba rnam gnyis la bka' bsgo nas 'gyur sar mdzad skabs sngar gyi bu ston gyis mchan bur btab pa'i 'gyur bcos kun thad sor bzhag/~~de las~~ don la rton pa'i dbang gis nges pa'i mthar thug rnams rang skad zur phyin par mdzad de/dol mchan nyid kyi gzer bur bsdams nas/gnas don rgyas 'grel nges* [22b] *don rgya mtsho bstan pa spyi 'grel bka' bsdu bzhi pa sogs kyis gsal zhing gsal ba'i shing rta'i srol phye ba 'di las gung pa'i byang shambha la na yang dpal ldan rgyud la 'grel mdzad med nges snyam pa'i yid ches yod cing/bstan pa spyi'i sgo mtha' dag la 'chad rtsom gyi khur bu ston che ba tsam 'dug kyang/dus 'khor nyag gcig gi nges gsang 'doms pa'i skabs dol bu ba'i char mi bskrun nges/.*

79. The new translation made at Jo nang did not receive universal approval. For example, Ngor chen Kun dga' bzang po later criticized the Jo nang translation in a written reply to questions from Sa bzangs Bsod nams dpal, one of the successors to Ma ti Paṇ chen at Sa bzangs monastery. See Kun dga' bzang po, *Sa*, especially 380, where he compares a passage from the two translations.

80. Ngag dbang blo gros grags pa, *Dpal*, 33. Dpang Lo tsā ba's statement was made to Dol po pa's future disciple, Jo nang Lo tsā ba Blo gros dpal, who then proceeded to Jo nang to request all the teachings from Dol po pa.

81. Ruegg (1966), 110–11.

82. Lha'i rgyal mtshan, *Chos*, 20b: *chos rje'i zhal nas/nges don zab mo'i gnad thams cad dus kyi 'khor lo'i rgyud 'grel chen po nas rnyed pas khong shin tu bka' drin che/ngas kyang gzhung la 'khrul pa 'gog pa la bsdus don dang chan bu khyad 'phags dang/gzhan yang yig cha du ma byas/.*

83. Ibid., 22a: *rgyud 'grel chen po'i chan bu la sogs pa dus 'khor gyi phyogs la yig cha sum bcu so brgyad/nges don rgya mtsho la sogs pa grub mtha'i bskor bcu drug/yum gsum gyi chan bu la sogs pa sher phyin kyi phyogs* [22b] *la bdun/.*

84. Ibid., 34b: *chos rje nyid kyi zhal nas/rgyud 'grel chen po'i chan la gzigs nas/a la la 'di 'dra kho kun su'i mdzad dam ngo mtshar che gsung nas yang yang thal mo sbyar/nges don zab mo go lugs 'di 'dra la bltas tsa na nga rang yang su yin nam snyam pa yong gin 'dug gsung/.*

85. See for example Kun spangs, *Chos*, 327; Tāranātha, *Myang*, 90; Nya dbon, *Bstan pa*, 53a; and Lha'i rgyal mtshan, ibid., 35b. Specifically, the anonymous series of verses at the end of Dol po pa, *Lta*, 810, refers to him as the emanation buddha-body (*nirmāṇakāya*) of Kalkin Puṇḍarīka. The modern Jo nang scholar Ngag dbang blo gros grags pa, when discussing the significance of Dol po pa's exclamation in regard to his composition of the annotations, also arrives at the conclusion that Dol po pa himself was stating his own belief that he was an actual emanation of the Kalkin emperor. See Ngag dbang blo gros grags pa, *Dpal*, 542.

86. See Lha'i rgyal mtshan, ibid., 24a, and especially Kun spangs, ibid., 333–48.

87. Kun spangs, ibid., 333 and 348. His visionary trip to Shambhala seems to have occurred in 1335. Also see Stearns (1995), 838–39. During a visit to the monastery of Gsang phu he also directly beheld the pure land of Sukhāvatī, and composed a praise of it, which is recorded in Kun spangs, ibid., 337–43. This praise is different than both *Bde ba can smon lams* found in Dol po pa's collected works.

88. Kun spangs, ibid., 343. In this instance, and many others, Kun spangs pa cannot be relied upon to provide accurate chronological information. The texts mentioned by name are the *Dbang chog ye shes rgya mtsho*, *Dbang gi legs bshad lung sbyor*, *Dbang gi cho ga bsdus pa rdo rje 'pheng ba*, *Gar kyi brjed byang*, *Dbang mdor gyi sa bcad*, *Shag 'byed che chung*, and *Thig rtsa*. He also mentions that Dol po pa wrote praises to Rdo rje 'jigs byed, Mkha' 'gro rgya mtsho, and Bde mchog, as well as many texts on astrology, such as the *Rtsis kyi rgyu mtshan*, *Gza' lnga*, and *Gza' zin*. These texts are all found in the *Collected Works*, but there are many indications that some of them were not written during this period. For example, the three texts on astrology are found in a collection of similar works in Dol po pa's *Collected Works*, vol. 6, 76–129. Although not mentioned by name, one of this group of texts on astrology, the *Gza' bcu stong par 'jug tshul*, 109–14, was written in the *shing mo glang* year of 1325, ten years before the period being discussed here. This work—and the *Sha chang bkag pa'i lung 'dren rnams*, vol. 5, 757–78—are the earliest *dated* texts written by Dol po pa. The *Dbang chog ye shes rgya mtsho*, which Kun spangs pa does list among the texts composed at Skyid phug, was actually written at Sa skya. See *Collected Works*, vol. 6, 734. Finally, the *Gar kyi brjed byang*, also mentioned by Kun spangs, was actually written at the request of Yon tan rgya mtsho, who passed away in 1327. See *Collected Works*, vol. 7, pt. 1, 25.

89. See Lha'i rgyal mtshan, *Chos*, 23b. The series of letters between Dol po pa and Don yod rgyal mtshan can be dated 1333–1334, and is preserved in Dol po pa's Collected Works, vol. 7, Pt. 2, 739–58. For the mention of offerings from Kun dga' rgyal mtshan and Rang byung rdo rje, see Kun spangs, *Chos*, 347. Other offerings were also made by Nya dbon Ghu na shri, Ston pa Nam mkha' seng ge, and the brothers Rtse'i dbon Rdo rje dpal and Shang rdo'i dpon Chos grags gsar ma.

90. Kun spangs, ibid., 349–50. Some of the renowned scholars in attendance were Mkhan chen Gtogs rgyal, Gnas drug pa, 'Jam ston, and 'Jam sgegs. The last of these may possibly be identified as the Dus 'khor ba 'Jam sgag (*sic*) who wrote a biography of Dol po pa about one month after his death. This text was later used by Lha'i rgyal mtshan as the basis for his biography of Dol po pa. See Lha'i rgyal mtshan, ibid., 56b.

91. Lha'i rgyal mtshan, ibid., 24a.

92. Lha'i rgyal mtshan, ibid., 24b. For the invitation to Bu ston, see Ruegg (1966), 122. For information on Dzam bha la, and the significance of his title Tu shri (Ch. *tuanshi*, "judge, legal officer") and Bha the's title Tshe dben (Ch. *qian yuan*, "department secretary"), see van der Kuijp (1993b). Emperor Toghon Temür (Shun Di Emperor, reigned July 19, 1333—September 10, 1368) would have first heard of Dol po pa soon after the

completion of the great stūpa at Jo nang on October 30, 1333, when Dol po pa's disciple Slob dpon Zla ba bzang po was sent to the imperial court to solicit offerings for the monument. Lavish offerings were received at Jo nang. See Lha'i rgyal mtshan, ibid., 17b.

93. Lha'i rgyal mtshan, ibid., 24b.

94. Tāranātha, *Dpal*, 29. While in retreat Dol po pa composed a prayer for no obstacles such as the Mongolian envoys to come his way: *da lta rtse gcig bsgrub pa 'phel ba'i rkyen/gnas 'khor la sogs mthun rkyen phun tshogs shing/hor kyi 'bod mi gtong ba la sogs pa'i/'gal rkyen bar chad gang yang med par shog/*. He sent this prayer to Jo nang, and it was recited by all the men and women in meditation there. See Lha'i rgyal mtshan, ibid., 24b–25a.

95. Lha'i rgyal mtshan, ibid., 25a, and Tāranātha, ibid., 29. It is interesting that one modern source mentions that Kun spangs pa went to China as Dol po pa's representative (*sku tshab*). See Ngag dbang blo gros grags pa, *Dpal*, 33.

96. It is known that Toghon Temür later invited Bu ston to the imperial court again in 1355. See Bkra shis dbang 'dus, ed. *Bod*, 213–14, for the text of this imperial edict.

97. The following narrative is summarized from Kun spangs, *Chos*, 400–21. As is often the case in this work, these events seem to be entirely out of place chronologically. In Kun spangs pa's text they are the last events described before the narration of Dol po pa's final days.

98. Byang rtse Lo tsa ba may be identified as Lo chen Byang chub rtse mo (1302–1380), who is known to have studied with Dol po pa. Ma ṇi ka shri, the 'Bri gung Lo tsā ba, is counted as one of Dol po pa's thirteen great disciples. See Ngag dbang blo gros grags pa, *Dpal*, 33–34.

99. Since Blo gros dpal is known to have passed away in 1354, this statement is the main reason the previously mentioned *sprel* year should be understood as 1344 and not 1356.

100. See Kun spangs, *Chos*, 405, and 420–21, for the events surrounding the making of this image. See Ngag dbang blo gros grags pa, *Dpal*, 35, for information on the life of Mkhan chen Rin tshul ba. The construction of this image more probably occurred in 1359 when Dol po pa was in the Lha sa area, partly at the invitation of Rin tshul ba. Ngag dbang blo gros grags pa, *Dpal*, 35, who was probably following the information in Kun spangs pa's work, also states that Rin tshul ba made the image when Dol po pa was on his way to China, and that it was kept in the Jo khang temple in Lha sa. Lha'i rgyal mtshan, *Chos*, 54b, mentions that after Dol po pa's death Rin tshul ba made two more images, of the buddha Amitabha

and the bodhisattva Avalokiteśvara, which were placed to the right and left of the clay image (*sku lder*) of Dol po pa in the Lha sa 'phrul snang temple, which is more commonly known as the Jo khang. All three images are mentioned by the great Fifth Tā la'i bla ma Ngag dbang blo bzang rgya mtsho in his guide to the Jo khang temple, written in 1645, and they were still present in the temple when it was visited by Si tu Chos kyi rgya mtsho in 1918. See Ngag dbang blo bzang rgya mtsho, *Lha*, 24, and Chos kyi rgya mtsho, *Gangs*, 126.

101. This teaching, which seems quite authentic, is found in Kun spangs, *Chos*, 411–19.

102. See Kapstein (1992c) on the *Ma ṇi bka' 'bum*.

103. Lha'i rgyal mtshan, *Chos*, 37b–38a. Both classical Tibetan and modern Western scholars have consistently confused this Jo nang Phyogs las rnam rgyal with Bo dong Phyogs las rnam rgyal (1376–1451), who never met Dol po pa. The best available sources for information about Jo nang Phyogs las rnam rgyal, who was also born in the Dol po area of present day Nepal, are Ngag dbang blo gros grags pa, *Dpal*, 37–38, and Mang thos klu sgrub, *Bstan*, 181. Lha'i rgyal mtshan, ibid., 38a, mentions that Phyogs las rnam rgyal held the throne for four years, but Ngag dbang blo gros grags pa, ibid., 37, says he held the position for six years, and Mang thos klu sgrub, ibid., 181, says for five years.

104. Ngag dbang blo gros grags pa, ibid., 37, states that Phyogs las rnam rgyal was already at Ngam ring when Lo tsā ba Blo gros dpal passed away. The founding of this institute is mentioned in a number of sources, but dated only in Mang thos klu sgrub, *Bstan*, 181, where it is mentioned that it was enlarged by Phyogs las rnam rgyal in 1338, and in the *Re'u mig* of Sum pa mkhan po, which according to Ruegg (1963), 81, note 39, gives the date 1354. Lha'i rgyal mtshan, *Chos*, 25a, says that while Dol po pa was at Ngam ring he cured the Dpon chen pa of an illness. Tāranātha, *Dpal*, 30, connects this event with the time at which Dol po pa founded the institute at Ngam ring. If that is the case, the Dpon chen pa may be identified as Ta'i dben Nam mkha' brtan pa. See Dpal ldan chos kyi bzang po, *Sde*, 176, for information on Nam mkha' brtan pa, who received the title Ta'i dben Gu shri in 1345. For more details about his career, see Petech (1990), 120–21, 132. Nam mkha' brtan pa's demand that Phyogs las rnam rgyal continue to hold both the Ngam ring and Jo nang thrones simultaneously is mentioned in Lha'i rgyal mtshan, ibid., 38b.

105. Kun spangs, *Chos*, 352. This is probably Ta dben Kun dga' rin chen (1339–1399).

106. Ibid. This master, who was so instrumental in the power struggle between the Sa skya pa and the Phag mo gru pa, has been identified by

Petech (1990), 103, note 75, etc., as Dol po pa's disciple Kun spangs Chos grags dpal. This is a very complicated problem which cannot be completely solved here. First of all, the present mention of a Kun spangs pa at the teachings by Dol po pa is recorded by Kun spangs Chos grags dpal himself. He cannot here be referring to himself as "Kun spangs pa," because throughout the biography he refers to himself in the first person if he is involved in events. In general, none of the many instances in which Kun spangs Chos grags dpal appears in the biographies of Dol po pa, and elsewhere in the literature of the Jo nang pa tradition, indicate that he was in any way active in the political intrigues of the time. There is only mention of him as a great yogin, scholar, and translator of Sanskrit texts. Nevertheless, he could certainly have been brought into negotiations as a mediator, as were Bla ma dam pa Bsod nams rgyal mtshan, Bla ma Mnyam med pa (also called Kun spangs pa!), and others. The problem is that the personal name of the politically involved Kun spangs pa is never given.

Kun spangs Chos grags dpal, the senior disciple of Dol po pa, is said to have died in 1363, murdered by one Byang pa Sid dhi. See Ngag dbang blo gros grags pa, *Dpal*, 33. The Sa skya bla ma Kun spangs pa certainly died in 1357, also murdered, and with the Byang Dpon chen perhaps under suspicion. See Byang chub rgyal mtshan, *Rlangs*, 298. In the year 1352 the Sa skya Patriarch Bla ma dam pa Bsod nams rgyal mtshan visited Jo nang and had extensive discussions with Dol po pa about points of Buddhist doctrine. At that time a Bla ma Kun dpangs pa invited Bla ma dam pa to Bzang ldan monastery, and together with the Byang ruler Ta dben Nam mkha' (brtan pa), requested the Hevajra initiation. See Byang chub rtse mo, *Chos*, 31a–b. As noted above, Kun spangs Chos grags dpal founded the monastery of Bzang ldan, so it is certain that he is indicated here.

There is also a full treatment of Dol po pa's death in 1361, and the following ceremonies, in the biography by Kun spangs Chos grags dpal, which is not possible if he is the same as the political figure who died in 1357. On the other hand, there is considerable evidence that material was inserted into this work as late as the fifteenth to sixteenth centuries; most notably Dol po pa's long versified last testament (*kha chems*), in which Kun spangs Chos grags dpal's own murder by Byang pa Sid dhi is predicted (426), and many religious and political figures long after Dol po pa's time are mentioned. See Kuṇ spangs, ibid., 425–37. It is also very suspicious that the biography of Dol po pa by Lha'i rgyal mtshan does not mention Kun spangs Chos grags dpal at the funereal of Dol po pa, when all the other senior disciples gather. And to top matters off, when Dol po pa's disciple Sman chu kha ba Blo gros rgyal mtshan (1314–1389) was sixty-seven years old (1381), he is said to have received many teachings from Chos grags dpal! See Ngag dbang blo gros grags pa, ibid., 35. These problems will have to be solved by future research.

107. Kun spangs pa, ibid., 352. Rgyal bzang is the famous Sa skya Dpon chen, or Grand Governor, Rgyal ba bzang po. See Petech (1990) and van der Kuijp (1988) about these figures and the political situation in Tibet at this time. Byang pa Sid dhi has yet to be definitely identified. As mentioned above, he is said to have murdered Kun spangs Chos grags dpal. G.yag sde Paṇ chen was an eclectic master who studied under Dol po pa, Bu ston, Karma pa Rang 'byung rdo rje, and other great teachers of the fourteenth century. See Roerich, trans. (1976), 532–36. Dol po pa's reply to some of his questions is found in Dol po pa's *Collected Works,* vol. 7, pt. 2, 758–63. G.yag sde Paṇ chen should not be confused with the famous Sa skya master G.yag phrug Sangs rgyas dpal (1350–1414). See Mang thos klu sgrub, *Bstan,* 193–94.

108. Lha'i rgyal mtshan, *Chos*, 38a.

109. This master from the House of Shar at Sa skya was the youngest brother of Seng ge dpal and Kun dga' bsod nams, who had been teachers of Dol po pa when he had studied as a young man in Sa skya. Kun dga' rdo rje, *Deb*, 51, states that Rin chen rgyal mtshan was born on a *rta* year, and lived for fifty years.

110. Lha'i rgyal mtshan, *Chos*, 38a. An instruction by Dol po pa to his disciple Dus 'khor ba Rdo rje snying po is found in the *Collected Works*, vol. 7, pt. 1, 658–61.

111. Lha'i rgyal mtshan, ibid., 38b.

112. Kun spangs, *Chos*, 352.

113. Lha'i rgyal mtshan, *Chos*, 38b and 40a. Phyogs las rnam rgyal then retired to the hermitage of Se mkhar chung, which had been home centuries before to the renowned Lam 'bras master Se ston Kun rig (1025?–1122?). Later, after the death of Dol po pa, he would once again occupy the teaching throne at Jo nang, and also hold the leadership position at Ngam ring a second time. See Ngag dbang blo gros grags pa, *Dpal*, 37–38, and Dpal ldan chos kyi bzang po, *Sde*, 200–01.

114. Kun spangs, *Chos*, 363, says that Dol po pa's disciple, the abbot Rin tshul ba had sent an invitation, and came to escort him to Lha sa.

115. See Lha'i rgyal mtshan, *Chos*, 26b and 39a, for descriptions of Dol po pa's weight and size, and 39b for his departure for Central Tibet and his early route along the way.

116. Lha'i rgyal mtshan, ibid., 40a, does not mention the *Bka' bsdu bzhi pa*, which is mentioned by Byang chub rtse mo, *Chos*, 36b, and Kun spangs, *Chos*, 363. Mang thos klu sgrub, *Bstan*, 178, also mentions the *Bka' bsdu bzhi pa*, but dates its composition to 1361. The *Bka' bsdu bzhi*

pa is translated and studied in part 2 below, where the circumstances of its composition will be fully discussed.

117. Lha'i rgyal mtshan, ibid., 40a. Thang po che Kun dga' 'bum (1331–1402) was one of Dol po pa's major disciples. He later became the head of Rta nag monastery in 1378, and in 1387 Slob dpon Ye dpal offered him a monastery in Yar lung. See Ngag dgang blo gros grags pa, *Dpal*, 34. Kun spangs, ibid., 363, also mentions that Dol po pa taught the *Sekoddeśa* (*Dbang mdor bstan pa*) at Thang po che's request.

118. Lha'i rgyal mtshan, ibid., 40a–b. Information on the life of Mkhan chen Rin tshul ba is found in Ngag dbang blo gros grags pa, *Dpal*, 35. The "Commander in Chief" (*du dben sha*) Gzhon nu rgyal mtshan was at this time probably the highest ranking official of the Yüan imperial organization in Tibet. See Petech (1990), 122, note 144.

119. Lha'i rgyal mtshan, ibid., 41a. Kun spangs, *Chos*, 364, states that Dol po pa taught the one-hundred-thousand-line *Prajñāpāramitā sūtra* according to the *Kālacakra* (*'bum 'dus 'khor ltar bshad pa*) at Brag lha klu phugs.

120. Lha'i rgyal mtshan, ibid. Tāranātha, *Dpal*, 31, states that Dol po pa gave the instructions of the Six-branch Yoga (*ṣaḍaṅgayoga*) seven times in Lha sa. At first he gave it to fifty, one hundred, or two hundred people, as the situation required. The last time he gave it was known as the "vast instruction" (*'khrid mo che*), to which more than eighteen hundred people came. He gave the great initiation of the Kālacakra to many thousands of people. Lha'i rgyal mtshan, ibid., 42a, describes the scenes.

121. Lha'i rgyal mtshan, ibid, 42a. The great leader (*chen po*) Dge ba'i blo gros is also mentioned in Byang chub rtse mo, *Chos*, 35b, where Bla ma dam pa Bsod ṇams rgyal mtshan is stated to have bestowed initiations upon him at Gung thang in 1357. On 42a his death is mentioned in the tenth month of the *'brug* year (1364).

122. This text is translated below in part 2.

123. Lha'i rgyal mtshan, *Chos*, 43a–b.

124. Ibid., 43b. Slob dpon Si tu pa is Ta'i si tu Byang chub rgyal mtshan (1302–1364), the supreme political power in Tibet at this time, and Dpal rin was one of his close assistants. See van der Kuijp (1988) and Petech (1990). An important meeting had occurred at Rab btsun between the leaders of the Sa skya faction and that of the Phag mo gru in 1350. Petech (1990), 110.

125. See Tāranātha, *Myang*, 48, 90–91, and 93. Also see Lha'i rgyal mtshan, ibid., 43b–44a. Ricca and Lo Bue (1993), 11–17, provide convenient

biographical information on the Nyang ruler Nang chen 'Phags pa dpal bzang and his younger brother Du dben sha ("Commander in Chief") 'Phags pa rin chen. 'Phags pa Dpal bzang was a very important political figure in fourteenth-century Tibet, and founded the great castle palace of Rgyal rtse in 1365. In fulfillment of Dol po pa's prophecy, he also laid the foundations for the monastery of Rtse chen, which was founded by Dol po pa's disciple Nya dbon Kun dga' dpal in 1366.

126. Lha'i rgyal mtshan, ibid., 44a.

127. Padma dkar po, *Chos*, 311–12. Ri phug is the hermitage near Zha lu, which was Bu ston's residence.

128. Tāranātha, *Dpal*, 31. Tāranātha also states that there is an account that the great Bu ston had earlier wished to see the Jo nang stūpa, and in order to do so had taken conscious control of a dream, as may be done in some tantric yoga practices, and traveled towards Jo nang. But when he reached the lower Jo nang valley, Dol po pa exclaimed "*Phet*," and Bu ston woke up. He was thus unable to see the monument. See ibid., 31–32. This indeed seems like the sort of story that could have originated in the meditative experiences of practitioners in retreat at Jo nang.

129. The following information is summarized from Kun spangs, *Chos*, 365–66. As discussed in note 106 in the present chapter, the death date of Kun spangs pa is in some doubt. If he is to be identified with the Kun spangs pa who mediated in the political discussions of the time, and certainly died in 1357, this event involving Bu ston would have occurred after the purported author's death. Thus it may be a later addition to the original work.

130. The *'Grel chung padma can* (*Padmani nāma pañjikā*) is an important commentary on difficult points in the *Kālacakra tantra*. Translated into Tibetan in the eleventh century by the Kashmiri master Somanātha, it is found in the Peking edition of *The Tibetan Tripitaka*, vol. 47, 36.5.1–105.4.3.

131. Lha'i rgyal mtshan, *Chos*, 44a–b. The abbot of Snar thang was 'Chims Blo bzang grags pa, who had previously requested teachings from Dol po pa on several occasions. He was an important teacher of the time, and his devotion to Dol po pa is significant because of the implication that the ancient Bka' gdams pa monastery of Snar thang was probably strongly influenced by Dol po pa's teachings during this period. The Bla ma Gdan sa pa, or "throne holder," who came to escort Dol po pa back to Jo nang was Dkon mchog rgyal mtshan, whom Dol po pa had installed upon the Jo nang teaching throne in 1359, before leaving for Dbus.

132. Lha'i rgyal mtshan, ibid. The autobiography of Khro phu Lo tsā ba is the *'Phags bsam khri shing*, which has survived. Lha'i rgyal mtshan,

ibid., 28b, mentions it by name as a text that particularly moved Dol po pa. The emotional procession back to Jo nang is vividly described by Lha'i rgyal mtshan, who was present at the time. See Lha'i rgyal mtshan, ibid., 44b.

133. Dol po pa's arrival at Jo nang is described in Lha'i rgyal mtshan, ibid., 45a, and Kun spangs, *Chos*, 367, where the *bya* year should be corrected to *byi* year. Drung Bzhi thog pa is probably the Sa skya master Ta dben Kun dga' rin chen (1339–1399). Bla ma Paṇ chen pa is Ma ti Paṇ chen. Bla ma Mkhan chen pa is Phyogs las rnam rgyal, who had been abbot of Jo nang and would later hold the post for a second time. Mkhan chen Nam mkha' ye shes has not been identified. The Dpon chen pa is probably the Byang ruler Nam mkha' brtan pa.

134. This is only found in Kun spangs, *Chos*, 371 and 378. Kun spangs pa states that he received from Dol po pa this "extremely direct transmission of the path of profound esoteric instructions" (*man ngag zab mo'i lam shin tu nye rbyud*), which came directly from Śavaripa. From the context and terminology it is clear that these instructions were on the *ṣaḍaṅgayoga*. See Kun spangs, ibid., 377. Once again, if our author Kun spangs pa were to be identified with the politically involved Kun spangs pa who died in 1357, this episode would have to have occurred earlier in Dol po pa's life. This may be considered additional evidence for the existence of two different teachers known as Kun spangs pa.

135. The throne-holder (*gdan sa pa*) was Dkon mchog rgyal mtshan. The following description of Dol po pa's last days is mostly based upon Lha'i rgyal mtshan, *Chos*, 47b–48b, but some is taken from Kun spangs, ibid., 423–25, and 437–38. Once again, either our author is not the same as the Kun spangs pa who died in 1357, or this section was added at a later time by an unknown hand.

136. This is only in Kun spangs, ibid., 423.

137. In ibid., 424, Dol po pa is asked what he saw at this time. He laughed and spoke a series of verses about his visions of deities and great teachers in the sky.

138. Lha'i rgyal mtshan, *Chos*, 50b, mentions that Dol po pa had often said, "I will make the stūpa my place to die" (*'chi sa sku 'bum du byed do*). At this point he knew he was going to die soon.

139. This is only in Kun spangs, *Chos*, 425. The "powerful tenfold anagram" (*rnam bcu dbang ldan*) is the term for the famous anagram in Lañtsa script of the ten syllables of the Kālacakra mantra. The entire system of the Kālacakra may be explained using this single symbol. See note 96 in the translation of *The Fourth Council* below.

140. Drung Bzhi thog pa is probably the Sa skya master Ta dben Kun dga' rin chen.

141. Lha'i rgyal mtshan, *Chos*, 51a–b. Kun spangs, *Chos*, 439, gives somewhat different information. He says that on the eighth day the body was placed into a casket of white and red eaglewood, and white and red sandalwood. It was then taken onto the roof of the residence, and everyone was allowed to pay their respects.

142. Lha'i rgyal mtshan, ibid., 51b. Bla ma Paṇ chen pa is Ma ti Paṇ chen, Bla ma Mkhan chen pa is Phyogs las rnam rgyal, and Bla ma Gdan sa pa is Dkon mchog rgyal mtshan. Also mentioned at this ceremony are Bla ma Rgyal 'byung ba, Mkhan chen Brag ram pa (Dkon mchog bzang po), Mkhan chen Nags phug pa, and Mkhan chen Gha rong pa.

143. Ibid., 52a–b. As explained in note 109 of the present chapter, Bla ma Shar pa is Shar pa Rin chen rgyal mtshan, who is later listed among Dol po pa's chief disciples. See ibid., 45b and 46a, where it is stated that most of the teachers and Saṅgha members at Sa skya were disciples of Dol po pa.

144. Kun spangs, *Chos*, 450.

145. Lha'i rgyal mtshan, *Chos*, 27b.

146. Ibid, 28a: *'u cag jo mo nang pa ni/gang gi yang phyogs su lhung ba med/phyogs ris kyi chos kyis sangs rgyas mi thob pas/don med sdig pa'i sgo skal ma len/'u cag ni nam mkha'i sprin dang 'dra bar gang gi'ang phyogs su lhung ba med do/.*

147. Ibid: *phyogs med ris med pa rton pa bzhi ldan gyis sbyar ba'o/.* The significance of the "four reliances" is touched on below in chapter 3, section 2. *The Fourth Council*, translated in part 2 below, is also described as an "impartial and unbiased" treatise.

Chapter 2. A Historical Survey of the Zhentong Tradition in Tibet

1. 'Jam mgon Kong sprul, *Gzhan*, 609: *kun mkhyen dol po pas/bde gshegs snying po'i mtshan thos pa tsam gyis kyang sangs rgyas thob par 'gyur na/dad cing gus pa dang mngon tu byas nas bsgoms pa lta ci smos/ mkhas pa snying rje dang ldan pa rnams kyis rang gi srog la sogs pa dor nas kyang bstan par bya ba dang/thar pa don du gnyer ba rnams kyis me'i 'obs chen po las 'bogs nas kyang btsal cing mnyan par bya'o/zhes gdams par* [610] *mdzad pa nyid snying gi thig ler bcang bar bya'o/.*

2. See Lha'i rgyal mtshan, *Chos*, 54b: *sngar bod du nges don phyogs re tsam nas dgongs pa'i gang zag ni mang du byon zhing/khyad par sgom*

chen pa rnams shas che na'ang bka' bstan chos man ngag rnams kyi nges don mtha' dag thugs su chud pas grub mtha' khyad par can myur du sangs rgya ba'i lam mchog ston pa ni / chos rje rin po che 'ba' zhig las sgnar bod du ma byon no /.

3. Tāranātha, *Zab mo*, and Tāranātha, *untitled*.

4. Tāranātha, *Zab mo*, 488–89. It is of particular interest that Dol po pa's teacher Skyi ston 'Jam pa'i dbyangs is listed here before Dol po pa, and that Bcom ldan Ral gri is listed before Skyi ston, as though he were the latter's teacher.

5. Tāranātha, *Zab mo*, 485, lists the Tibetan translator Dga' ba'i rdo rje, who translated for Btsan Kha bo che, as the first Tibetan in the lineage of the *gzhan stong* approach to Madhyamaka realization. He states that this translator was a great expert who beheld the face of the deity Cakrasaṃvara, taught the *gzhan stong* in Tibet (*phyogs 'dir*), and achieved the adamantine buddha-body (*vajrakāya*) in the Kashimir city of Dpe med. Tāranātha provides the personal name of Btsan Kha bo che, and mentions that he was a monk and that Btsan was his family name. For some very brief information on Btsan Kha bo che's life, see Roerich (1976), 347–48.

6. A translation of the only extant passages from the work of Btsan Kha bo che, which was also preserved by Kun dga' grol mchog, is found below in chapter 3, section 2.

7. Kun dga' grol mchog, *Khrid*, 325–26. The text actually has the spelling Dol bu pa, an alternate form for Dol po pa, which has been standardized in the translations.

8. There is indeed a reply to a Bla ma Rin chen ye shes included in Bu ston's collected works, but there is no passage corresponding to that indicated by Kun dga' grol mchog. See Bu ston, *Thams*, 185–216.

9. Tāranātha, *Dpal*, 25, also mentions that these teachings were received while Dol po pa was performing certain fasting austerities that involved subsisting on the ingestion of small pebbles. Lha'i rgyal mtshan, *Chos*, 6b, only mentions that Dol po pa received this fasting practice, and that of the physical yogic exercises (*'khrul 'khor*) from Rin chen ye shes.

10. See Yu mo ba Mi bskyod rdo rje, *Gsal*. Published as a set under the title *Gsal sgron skor bzhi*, the four texts are *Zung 'jug gsal sgron*, 1–14, *Phyag rgya chen po'i gsal sgron*, 14–26, *'Od gsal gsal sgron*, 27–50, and *Stong nyid gsal ba'i sgron me*, 51–105. The modern publisher has mistakenly attributed them to an A wa dhū ti pa Bsod nams. Ngag dbang blo gros grags pa, *Dpal*, 18, states that Yu mo ba was born in the first Tibetan calendrical cycle, which began in 1027. The most information on Yu mo ba is found in Anonymous, *Bcom*, 36b–39a. I am grateful to Dr. Dan Martin

for a copy of this incomplete history of the Kālacakra tradition, which was written in the year 1360. Although the author has not yet been identified, he speaks of himself as a personal disciple of Dol po pa, from whom he received all of the most important transmissions of the Kālacakra scriptures and practices. On fol. 16b this author mentions another of his compositions entitled *Bstan rtsis rin chen sgron me*. The most published information on Yu mo ba's life, which is very meager, is found in Tāranātha, *Dpal*, 16, where the statement about Yu mo ba as the originator of the tantric *gzhan stong* system is found: *sngags kyi gzhan stong grub mtha'i srol ka phye/*.

11. It should be noted that Thu'u bkwan seems to attribute the use of the terms *rtag* ("permanent"), *brtan* ("stable"), and *ther zug* ("eternal") to Yu mo ba, but they are not found in his available writings. See Thu'u bkwan, *Thu'u*, 217, and Ruegg (1963), 82–83. In a eulogy written at the time of Dol po pa's death, his disciple Ma ti paṇ chen 'Jam dbyangs blo gros rgyal mtshan refers to him as one who taught the *Gsal sgron rnam bzhi* of Grub thob Yu mo. See Ma ti paṇ chen, *Chos*, 1087/2.

12. Yu mo ba, *Gsal*, 12–14. The mention of "the Precious Omniscient One" (Kun mkhyen rin po che) as the recipient of the direct transmission from Śavaripa (Sha wa ra dbang phyug) refers to an event mentioned in Dol po pa's biography. See Kun spangs, *Chos*, 377–78.

13. See Yu mo ba, ibid., 57–59, and 100–101.

14. See note 11 in chapter 1 for a full identification of the three commentaries. See Dol po pa, *Dpon*, 487, for his comments to the ruler of Byang, which are translated and discussed below in chapter 3, section 1.

15. Lha'i rgyal mtshan, *Chos*, 20b: *chos rje'i zhal nas/nges don zab mo'i gnad thams cad dus kyi 'khor lo'i rgyud 'grel chen po nas rnyed pas khong shin tu bka' drin che/*.

16. Tanabe (1992), 1.

17. See Kun spangs, *Chos*, 348, for a description of the Shambhala experience. For the claims of a unique knowledge of the nature of Shambhala and Kailash, see Dol po pa, *Zhing*, 860: *rgya bod mkhas pas sngon chad ma rnyed pa'i/sham bha la dang dpal ldan ke la sha'i/gnas tshul ci bzhin bdag gi skal bas rnyed/*. Kun spangs, *Chos*, 333–37, records a praise of Shambhala which Dol po pa composed after directly perceiving (*nye bar gzigs*) that pure land.

18. Dol po pa, *Nye gnas dad*, 634: *lar drang por smras na gzhan mi dga'/gzhan gang zer byas na slob ma bslu/*[635] *dus da lta'i slob dpon bya bar dka'/de yin yang khyed la drang por smra/byang sham bha la na rigs ldan bzhugs/ka la pa chos kyi pho brang na/nyams 'di 'dra mkhyen pa*

mang du bzhugs/bod kha ba can gyi rgyal khams na/nyams 'di 'dra shes pa kho bo tsam/.

19. Dol po pa, *Shes*, 628: *tshul 'di deng sang mkhas par grags rnams dang/ bsgom bzang rtogs pa mtho bar 'dod rnams dang/grub thob chen po rlom pa phal cher gyis/ma tshor ba de rigs ldan drin gyis rnyed/.* Also see Dol po pa, *Nye gnas sang*, 638: *sham bha la chos kyi pho brang na/nyams 'di 'dra mkhyen pa mang du bzhugs/yul gangs can khrod na kho bo tsam/de kha po ma lags drang gtam yin/pha chos rje'i snying gtam sems la babs/.* Another example is found in Kun spangs, *Chos*, 385: *lta ngan med pa'i dpal ldan sham bha lar/ sems nyid mkhyen pa'i skye bo mang du bzhugs/yul gangs can khrod na kho bo tsam/bu khyod yang dag chos la 'jug par 'tshal/.*

20. The only surviving example of a teaching by Btsan Kha bo che is translated below in chapter 3, section 2.

21. No evidence has been found in the writings of Rang byung rdo rje, or any other early Tibetan source, that would support the assertion in Hookam (1991), 173, that Rang byung rdo rje "was very much influenced by Dol po pa and his Shentong doctrine." At the time of their meeting, it seems clear that the young Dol po pa was encouraged by the Karma pa, and not the other way around. Nor do the biographies of Dol po pa or Rang byung rdo rje provide any information to justify Hookam's certainty that the Karma pa visited Jo nang. Furthermore, her hypothesis that Rang byung rdo rje was actually the author of Dol po pa's commentary on the *Uttaratantra* is totally without basis. The text is signed by "the one endowed with the four reliances" (*rton pa bzhi ldan*), which was the most common pseudonym used by Dol po pa in his works.

22. Mang thos Klu sgrub rgya mtsho, *Bstan*, 179: *des na rje 'di karma rang byung rdo rje dang mjal te rang stong pa'i grub mtha' bzung bas/ karma pas phyis gzhan stong par 'gyur bar lung bstan zer/spyir gzhan stong pa'i lugs thog mar karma rang byung rdo rjes bzung bar sems/jo nang du ni kun mkhyen chen po man chad gzhan stong par song ba yin no/.*

23. Tāranātha, *Dpal*, 26: *de nas lha sa dang 'tshur phu sogs su phebs/ chos rje rang byung pa dang chos kyi gsung gleng mang du mdzad/rang byung pas rje 'di'i lung rig gi zhal ya ma thegs kyang/mngon shes bzang po mnga' bas/khyed la lta grub dang chos skad da lta'i 'di bas kyang ches bzang ba cig myur du 'ong/ces lung bstan/.*

24. There is a mere mention of gifts sent (?) by Chos rje Rang byung rdo rje to Dol po pa at Jo nang around 1335. Kun spangs, *Chos*, 347.

25. Chos kyi 'byung gnas, *Bsgrub*, 208: *kun mkhyen dol po pa chen pos kyang 'di skabs mjal bar 'dug cing khyed kyis da lta'i 'di ma yin pa'i lta*

ba khyad 'phags zhig rtogs par 'dug gsungs pa/khong de skabs dbu ma rang stong gi grub mthar dgyes kyang/mi ring bar gzhan stong dbu ma chen po'i gnad ji bzhin du mkhyen pa la dgongs par 'dug/.

26. Tāranātha, *Dpal*, 27.

27. See Ruegg (1995), 158–60, for a discussion of source/author-familiar and source/author-alien terminology.

28. See especially Ruegg (1989), 19, 26–35, etc.

29. Rgyal ba ye shes, *Kun*, 2a, quotes the *Laṅkāvatāra sūtra* in regard to the status of the *tathāgathagarbha* as: *rtag pa dang/brtan pa ther zug . . . /*. Dol po pa, *Bde*, 426, quotes the *Gaṇḍavyūha*: *de bzhin gshegs pa ni rtag pa/brtan pa ther zug mi 'jig pa ste/*. On ibid., 432, he quotes the *Rab tu zhi ba rnam par nges pa'i cho 'phrul gyi mdo*: *bde bzhin bshegs pa ni rtag pa'o/ de bzhin bshegs pa ni g.yung drung ngo/*. On ibid., 433, he quotes the *Aṅgulīmālīya*: *bde bzhin bshegs pa rtag pa dang yang dag pa nyid du bsngags par bya'o/*. For the occurrence of these terms in the *Śrīmālādevī*, *Mahāparinirvāṇa*, and the *Uttaratantra* itself, see Takasaki (1966), especially 38–40, and 256–57. Also see Ruegg (1969), 360–71, etc.

30. For Bu ston's refutations, see Ruegg (1973), especially 122–40. Very rarely Karma pa Rang byung rdo rje also uses at least one of these terms, *bdag* ("self"), in a similar context. See Rang byung rdo rje, *Zab*, 1b.

31. For example, see Dol po pa, *Bstan*, 686; Dol po pa, *Dbu*, 1172, 1174, 1177, and 1178; and Dol po pa, *Bka' bdu bzhi pa*, 364, 375, 394, etc.

32. Cf. Kapstein (1992), 23–24.

33. Dol po pa, *Bden*, 814–15: *rje po ri pas/kun rdzob bden pa rang gis stong pa dang/don dam bden pa gzhan gyi stong pa ste/bden gnyis stong* [815] *tshul de ltar ma shes na/rdzogs sangs rgyas la bskur pa btab nyen gda'o/*.

34. A few lines about Po ri ba Dkon cog rgyal mtshan are found in Tshe dbang rgyal, *Dam*, 751. He was a disciple of the Bka' brgyud master Rgod tshang pa Mgon po rdo rje (1189–1258). In Roerich, trans. (1976), 687, his name is given as Phu ri ba.

35. Rwa Ye shes Seng ge, *Mthu*, 178: *'di [i.e. rig pa ye shes] rang stong min te bdag 'dzin yul las 'das/'di gzhan stong min te shes 'dzin dri ma med/*. My thanks to Mr. Hubert Decleer for a copy of his unpublished paper in which he investigates the evidence for a later revision of Rwa Lo tsā ba's biography. See Decleer (n.d.).

36. See Klong chen Rab 'byams pa, *Rdzogs*, 220–21, and Padmasambhava, *'Bras*, 64: *gzhaṇ la ma ltos pas gzhan stong pa/*. I am

grateful to Prof. David Germano for providing me with this information, as well as the other references from Klong chen pa and Padmasambhava cited below.

37. Lha'i rgyal mtshan, *Chos*, 21a.

38. 'Jam mgon Kong sprul, *Rnal*, 17b: *'dir rang 'grel las/'khor 'das thams cad kyi gzhir gyur pa'i chos nyid de bzhin nyid la kun gzhi'i sgrar gsungs nas de'i nang gses dag pa dang bcas pa la kun gzhi'i ye shes dang sa bon thams cad pa'i cha nas kun gzhi'i rnam shes su gsungs te sems la dag ma dag gnyis su dbye/kun gzhi'i rnam shes las 'khor ba snang ba'i tshul dang kun gzhi'i ye shes las myang 'das snang ba'i tshul sgrub byed theg pa* [18a] *gong 'og gi khyad par dang bcas pa gsungs so/*. I am indebted to Mr. Kurtis Schaeffer for directing me to this reference.

39. 'Jam mgon Kong sprul, ibid., 188b, quotes the colophon of an edition of the *Zab mo nang don* in which the year Water-male-Dog (*chu pho khyi*, 1322) is given. The available published edition of the *Zab mo nang don* gives the year of composition with only the single element "Dog" (*khyi*). See Rang byung rdo rje, *Zab*, 32a. See Roerich, (1976), 492, for the dating of the autocommentary, and Rang byung rdo rje, *Rang*, 97–98, for the spiritual song.

40. See Klong chen rab 'byaṃs pa, *Rgyab*, 263–70, and Germano (1992), 231–61.

41. See Sa skya Paṇḍi ta, *Sdom*, 87: *mig mangs rgya dang ma 'brel na/ rde'u mang yang shi ro yin/de bzhin khungs dang ma 'brel ba'i/chos lugs mang yang ro dang 'dra/*. Cf. Dol po pa, *Bka' bsdu bzhi pa'i rang 'grel*, 661: *mig mang rgya dang ma brel na/rde'u mang yang shi ro yin/lha chos brgya dang ma 'brel na/mi chos mang yang shi ro yin/*. Dol po pa then continues with similar verses for the next two pages.

42. For the special significance of the terms *Tretayuga* and *Kṛtayuga* in the works of Dol po pa, see the beginning of chapter 3 below, and the translation of *The Fourth Council* in part 2.

43. Dol po pa, *Bka' bsdu bzhi pa'i rang 'grel*, 661–63. Some of these same verses are also found in Dol po pa, *'Phags*, vol. 3, pt. 1, 602; *'Phags*, vol. 3, pt. 2, 1005; and *'Phags*, vol. 4, pt. 1, 39.

44. Although no name is given for this ruler, who is only referred to as "the Byang Ruler" (Dpon Byang pa), he may be tentatively identified as Ta'i Situ Slob dpon Rdo rje dpal, the father of Ta'i dben Nam mkha' brtan pa (b. 1316), or perhaps even as Nam mkha' brtan pa himself. See Chos skyong bzang po, *Sde*, 173–77, and Petech (1990), 84, 121. It must be taken into account that the Byang ruler in question had written doctrinal tracts Dol po pa disagreed with and was responding to in this text.

45. These three are Avalokiteśvara, Mañjuśrī, and Vajrapāṇi.

46. Kalāpa is the name of the court of the Kalkin emperors of the legendary land of Shambhala, which is the stronghold of the Kālacakra teachings.

47. And so he apparantly did, for there survives the 230-page *Dpon byang pa'i phyag tu phul ba'i chos kyi shan 'byed*, which deals with the same points as the briefer *Gshag 'byed bsdus pa*, but with exhaustive scriptural quotations and extensive explanations. See Dol po pa, *Dpon*. Kun spangs, *Chos*, 343, also places the composition of this text between 1334 and 1336, although his chronology is often unreliable.

48. Dol po pa, *Kun*, 468–71. According to the sometimes questionable chronology of Dol po pa's life as found in Kun spangs, ibid., 343, this text was composed between 1334 and 1336.

49. See Ma ṭi paṇ chen, *Byang*, and Nya dbon, *Bstan pa* and *Bstan bcos*. Nya dbon's explanations of Dol po pa's teachings are provided in some detail in the annotations to the translation of *A General Commentary on the Doctrine*, found below in part 2. Jackson (1989b), of which only an early unpublished version was available, catalogues a very important example of an early refutation of the Jo nang pa theories, addressing chiefly some works by Nya dbon, but also mentioning the author's refutation of Phyogs las rnam rgyal, which he sent to him. The author, Bka' bzhi pa Rin chen rdo rje, praises Tsong kha pa (1357–1419) as one of the great teachers of that time. This text, which is kept in the collection of the Bihar Research Society and is thus not available, is the earliest known extensive refutation of the Jo nang pa doctrine. It was probably written before the end of the fourteenth century. A refutation of the Jo nang pa by this same Bka' bzhi pa Rin chen rdo rje is mentioned in the translation by Ruegg (1963), 88.

50. For example, see Mang thos klu sgrub, *Bstan*, 194.

51. Kun spangs, *Chos*, 427: . . . *kha ba can gyi rgyal khams 'dir/med par lta ba'i rigs can kha rgyal che/bsam yas chos 'bar snying la zhugs pa yi/ dge slong gzugs can mda' yi ming can 'byung/kye ma kyi hud bdud rigs nag po des/gzhi yi mthar thug bder gshegs snying po bkag/lam gyi mthar thug rdo rje rnal 'byor smod/'bras bu'i mthar thug dri bral med par sgrog/rtsa rgyud 'di skad bdag thos med do skad/bsdus pa'i rgyud la gshe ba sna tshogs byed/rgyud 'grel dpe cha bsdus nas chu la bskur/bstan pa'i snying po rin chen nyams chung byed/bkra mi shes pa de ni shi nas zung* . . . /.

52. That there was a great deal of angry reaction to his criticisms of the *Kālacakra* is referred to by Red mda' ba himself in Sangs rgyas rtse mo, *Dpal*, 70b, and in the annotations to Red mda' ba, *Dus*, 303.

53. Red mda' ba, *Dus*, 302: *'on kyang 'phags pas mdzad dam min kyang bla / legs par bshad pa'ang mang du mthong bas na / thar 'dod rnams kyi 'jug ngogs ma yin zhes / kho bo 'di la gcig tu skur mi 'debs /*. See Sangs rgyas rtse mo, *Dpal*, 54b–55a, where these verses are also cited, and for the clarification of Red mda' ba's position in regard to the *Kālacakra*.

54. Red mda' ba, *'Phrin*, 304: *deng sang gangs ri'i khrod kyi mkhas rlom rnams / ldem po'i ngag gis zab mo'i tshul ston pa / dus kyi 'khor lo 'grel pa dang bcas pa'i / tshig la ji bzhin sgra ru mngon zhen nas / rnam dag mdo rgyud tshogs dang 'gal ba yi / log pa'i tha snyad mang du spel mthong nas / 'khyog po'i shing la srong ba'i tshul bzhin du / rgal zhing brtag pa'i sgo nas bdag gis dris /*. These verses are also quoted in Sangs rgyas rtse mo, ibid., 54b.

55. For example, see Dpa' bo, *Chos*, vol. 2, 1482–85, for a refutation of Red mda' ba's criticisms. Dpa' bo also mentions Bcom ldan Rig pa'i ral gri's doubts about the Kālacakra.

56. These events are described in the greatest detail in Red mda' ba's biography written by his disciple Sangs rgyas rtse mo. See Sangs rgyas rtse mo, *Dpal*, 53a–55b. Mang thos klu sgrub, *Bstan*, 195, has summarized the account of Red mda' ba's threefold examination of the scriptures from this source.

57. Sangs rgyas rtse mo, ibid, 53a.

58. Ibid., 54b. While still at Sa skya, Red mda' ba also composed the *Nor bu'i phreng ba'i rang lan*, his own reply to the *Nor bu'i phreng ba*.

59. Ibid., 53b–54b. The master Drung Bzhi thog pa can be identified as the Sa skya master of the Bzhi thog Palace, Ta dben Kun dga' rin chen (1339–1399), who was an important disciple of Dol po pa.

60. The sequence of events related in Sangs rgyas rtse mo, *Dpal*, 63b, 72b, etc., clearly indicates that Red mda' ba spent much of the latter part of his life at Gangs bu le, where he was in retreat for five years and taught for another seven. It thus seems certain that his third work on the *Kālacakra* was a product of this later time.

61. Red mda' ba, *Dpal*, 412–413: *rgyud 'di'i lugs kyis bden pa gnyis kyi rnam gzhag 'di ltar ma rig pa'i 'khrul rkyen las byung ba'i glo bur dri ma'i chos ji snyed pa rnams de kho na nyid mthong ba la sgrib pa dang / kun nas nyon mongs pa'i dmigs pa yin pa'i phyir kun rdzob kyi bden pa yin la / de yang yang dag pa'i ye shes kyi yul du ma grub pa'i phyir / rang stong dang / chad stong dang / bems po'i stong pa nyid do / gnyug ma sems kyi chos nyid rang bzhin 'od gsal gyi chos ji snyed pa rnams ni don dam pa'i bden pa ste / de yang rigs pas dpyad bzod du grub pa'i sgo nas min gyi /* . . . [a single quotation omitted] *rnam par mi rtog pa'i spyod yul yin pa'i*

phyir don dam pa yin la/glo bur dri mas dben pa'i phyir gzhan stong dang/so so rang rig pa'i tshul gyis nyams su myong ba'i phyir chad stong dang bems stong min no/ . . . [a single quotation ommited] *de la rang stong ni chad pa'i mthar ltung ba'i phyir/de rtogs pa ni thar pa'i lam yang dag pa ma yin gyi/gzhan stong sems kyi chos nyid 'od gsal bsgoms pa'i stobs kyis so so rang rig pa'i tshul gyis myong ba'i nang rig 'gyur med kho na yang dag pa'i lam du gzhed de/.*

62. Ibid., 404–405: *gang dag rdo rje'i sku brtan g.yo kun la khyab pa'i rtag brtan du 'dod pa ni/mu stegs pa gang dag rig byed kyi gzhung las/tshangs pa dang dbang po la sogs pa lha chen po gsum gyi chos sku rtag pa rang byung gi thams cad mkhyen pa brtan g.yo kun la khyab cing byed pa por 'dod pa dang khyad par ci yang med pa'i phyir/ches shin tu 'khrul pa kho na yin no/.* On 406–407 he further refutes the notion of a permanent reality always present as both the ground of purification (*sbyang gzhi*) and the result of purification (*sbyang 'bras*). On 443, and elsewhere, he repeats his opposition to any notion of a permanent and true reality.

63. See for example Dpa' bo, *Chos*, vol. 2, 1482–1485.

64. This sūtra quote is given by Kun spangs, *Chos*, 365.

65. Tāranātha, *Dpal*, 34.

66. Ibid.

67. Except, of course, the brief passage translated above, which focused on the work of Btsan Kha bo che.

68. See Tāranātha, *Zab don*. In response to questions from Lha mthongs Lo tsā ba Bshes gnyen rnam rgyal (b.1512), who had just returned from Nepal, the 'Brug pa Bka' brgyud heirarch Padma dkar po (1527–1592) also expressed his opinion as to the differences between the views of Dol po pa and Shākya mchog ldan: *paṇ chen shāk mchog pa dang/jo nang pa'i gzhan stong la khyad yod med dri ba la/paṇ chen gyi bzhed pa/sems tsam rnam rdzun pa'i lugs gtsang ma yin tshul/jo nang pa sngags dang bsres nas 'chad kyi 'dug pa'i khyad par zhib gsed cig byas pas . . . /.* See Padma dkar po, *Sems*, 451. Lha mthongs Lo tsā ba's own strong preference for the *gzhan stong* view is evident in his versified travel journal of the trip to Nepal. For example, see Lha mthongs Lo tsā ba, *Lha*, 13b: *mtha' bral dbu ma'i blta ba gzhan gyi stong/brtag brtan g.yung drung zhi ba chen po'i lam/mngon sum gangs can yul 'dir 'dom pa'i rje/'jam dbyangs grags pa mchog de slar byon nam/de bas lta ngan mun pa yi/tshangs skud 'dzin pa'i u lu ka/smongs pa'i phug ring da dor las/lhag bsam dad spro'i gar byos shig/.* These are among his comments when visiting Jo nang on the way to Nepal. I am grateful to Mr. Hubert Decleer for a copy of this text.

69. For the Dge lugs pa critic's comments, see the translation in Ruegg (1963), 89–90. Whereas Shākya mchog ldan's views did not survive in the Sa skya tradition, Go rams pa's treatises have become accepted as canonical. His *Lta ba'i shan 'byed* in particular is to the present day referred to as the ultimate reference for understanding the orthodox Sa skya pa doctrinal position. In this work Go rams pa refutes the views of Dol po pa as eternalistic (*rtag mtha'*), those of Tsong kha pa as nihilistic (*chad mtha'*), and establishes the true Sa skya view as the real Middle Way beyond all extremes (*mtha' bral*). Dol po pa's views are first summarized in Go rams pa, *Lta*, 1.4–2.3.

70. For information on Rong ston, see Jackson (1989). Gdong thog Rin po che's opinion is found in Gdong thog, *Paṇḍi*, 21: *paṇ chen 'di pas kun mkhyen rong ston chen po'i rjes su 'brangs nas gzhan stong dbu ma'i legs bshad kyi sgra dbyangs gsang por bsgrags pa dang/rje rin po che tsong kha pa'i gzhung lugs la rigs pas dgag pa mdzad pa sogs . . . /*. These remarks also highlight one of the weaknesses of the methodology in Hookam (1991), where the views of Rong ston are lumped together with the views of Tsong kha pa's disciple Rgyal tshab Dar ma rin chen as representative of a *rang stong* tradition.

71. This is found in Rong ston, *Rong*, 28a: *kun mkhyen chen po dol po pa shes rab rgyal mtshan la bstod pa/zab don rin chen phreng ba zhes bya ba/bla ma dang lhag pa'i lha la phyag 'tshal lo/blo gros zab mo rtogs pa'i brlabs phreng can/kun rtog mi g.yo ting 'dzin brtan pa'i sku/zab mo'i legs bshad snang ba rab rgyas te/ma rig mun sel rtogs pa klong du gyur/grub pa'i nye lam rgyud la sbyor mdzad pa/gsung rab kun gyi snying po'i don bsdus nas/'chad rtsod rtsom pa'i bya bas gzhan dag la/brtse bas rjes su 'dzin pa'i 'phrin las can/snyan pas sa gsum khyab mdzad la bstod pa'i/dge bas bshes gnyen dam pa mnyes gyur cig/ces rong ston chen pos shrī nā lentra'i dgon par sbyar ba'o/*. I thank Prof. Leonard van der Kuijp for a copy of this work.

72. Karma phrin las, *Dri lan yid*, 91–92, explains how his teacher, the seventh Karma pa, Chos grags rgya mtsho, interpreted the nature of the *gzhan stong* accepted by the third Karma pa, Rang byung rdo rje.

73. See Kun dga' grol mchog, *Paṇḍi*, 203 and 206, for a description of the two meetings, and Dpa' bo, *Chos*, vol. 2, 1103, for the arrival of the Karma pa in Rin spungs. Kun dga' grol mchog, *Paṇḍi*, 206, mentions the length of Shākya mchog ldan's stay at the court. Dpa' bo, ibid., 1104, says that Shākya mchog ldan accepted the Karma pa as his main spiritual master at this point. For the Karma pa's declaration that their minds had blended together, see 'Be lo, *Bsgrub*, vol. 1, 584, and for the statement of both of their views as *gzhan stong*, see the same text, 646.

74. The late Sde gzhung sprul sku, Kun dga' bstan pa'i nyi ma told me this in a private conversation in Seattle, Washington, in the late 1970s. Rinpoche was probably basing his opinion on the information found in 'Be lo, *Bsgrub*, vol. 1, 582–84.

75. Gdong thog, *Paṇḍi*, 22–23. As will be mentioned below, the works of Jo nang Tāranātha were also banned at this time.

76. See Jackson (1994), 128–33, for a discussion of the stratagies Shākya mchog ldan employed in trying to bring the views of the Sa skya pa and the Bka' brgyud pa into harmony. Ruegg (1989), 105–108, is excellent in regard to this topic. In regard to the views of Shākya mchog ldan and Dol po pa, see in particular Tāranātha, *Zab don*, a text entirely devoted to the differences between the views of these two masters. On 792 Tāranātha points out that the single basis for their minor differences was that Shākya mchog ldan maintained that nondual gnosis (*gnyis med ye shes*) is momentary and impermanent, whereas Dol po pa asserted that it is permanent, partless, and omnipresent. Dreyfus (1997), 28–29, briefly discusses Shākya mchog ldan and the *gzhan stong* view.

77. See Shākya mchog ldan, *Untitled*. It is interesting to see that Shākya mchog ldan was not alone in this opinion. His younger contemporary Gung ru ba Shes rab bzang po (1411–1475), a Sa skya master who opposed the *gzhan stong*, also stated that both Dol po pa and Bu ston proclaimed that the *gzhan stong* was the supreme view and denigrated the older traditions of tantric exegesis, by which he probably intended that of the earlier Sa skya pa. See Gung ru ba, *Lam*, 122.3. As will be mentioned below, the Sa skya master 'Jam dbyangs mkhyen brtse'i dbang phyug (1524–1568) also felt that Dol po pa and Bu ston were essentially in agreement.

78. For 'Be lo's comments, see 'Be lo, *Bsgrub*, vol. 1, 651, and for Karma 'phrin las pa's record of the Karma pa's teachings, see Karma 'phin las pa, *Dri lan yid*, 88–92. The text by the eighth Karma pa is Mi bskyod rdo rje, *Dbu*. For Mi bskyod rdo rje's refutations of the *gzhan stong*, see Ruegg (1988), 1267–69, and Williams (1983), especially 140, note 17, and 143, note 39.

79. See Bstan pa'i rgyal mtshan, *Rje*.

80. 'Jam dbyangs Mkhyen brtse'i dbang phyug, *Rje*, 278, describes the teachings Sgo rum pa received from the Jo nang abbot Nam mkha' chos skyong in about 1495. Writing in 1561, the author also refers to the present-day, unadulterated Jo nang tradition of the Kālacakra initiation and teachings. Ibid., 333 and 341, mention the years of Sgo rum pa's tenure, and on 341–42, those of his successor.

81. Up until the present day a strong link has remained between the Shangs pa Bka' brgyud lineages and those of Jo nang. This is in large part

due to Tāranātha's writings on the Six Teachings of Ni gu ma (*ni gu chos drug*) and other fundamental doctrines of the Shangs pa lineage, which are now considered to be the definitive texts for the practice of those teachings.

82. As mentioned in note 69 in the present chapter, Go rams pa had already clearly defined the authentic Sa skya position as a middle path between the two extremes of the Jo nang pa and Dge lugs pa. See Jackson (1989) for an example of the strong influence of the Dge lugs pa at a great Sa skya monastery.

83. For example, in Shākya mchog ldan, *Bshes*, 367, he first cites the opinions of some latter-day adherents to the Lam 'bras teachings (*lam 'bras pa phyi ma dag*), and then, in regard to certain terminology he is criticizing, says "This is the Dharma language of Tsong kha pa, which doesn't exist in the Sa skya pa [tradition]" (*'di tsong kha pa'i chos skad yin gyi/sa skya pa la med do/.*).

84. Kun dga' grol mchog, *Lta*, 8b: *khyed bstan las log tsong kha pa'i/ bsang chos yid la gnags pa 'gas/sa skya'i bstan pa spel tshul gyis/bu ru rdzus nas khyod rabs bcad/*. In this text Kun dga' grol mchog is solely concerned with establishing the authentic view of the original masters of the Sa skya Lam 'bras teachings, which he defends against two threats. The first threat is the views of Tsong kha pa, and the description of the second seems to match what is known of the teachings of La stod Dbang rgyal, a disciple of the founder of Jo nang monastery, Kun spangs Thugs rje brtson 'grus, although it is uncertain whether La stod pa's lineage of the Lam 'bras had survived into the sixteenth century. I am grateful to Prof. Leonard van der Kuijp for a copy of Kun dga' grol mchog's text. See Stearns (1996), 149, note 78, for details on La stod Dbang rgyal's view, which had earlier been criticized by Ngor chen Kun dga' bzang po.

85. For example, as mentioned in the previous note, Kun dga' grol mchog defended the authentic view of the Lam 'bras against that of what would seem to be a version of the *gzhan stong*, although considerably different than that maintained by Dol po pa. See Kun dga' grol mchog, *Lta*, 9a–10a.

86. This is most obvious in Kun dga' grol mchog, *Zab lam*.

87. Ibid., 26b–27a: *rje bla ma rnams gsum 'dus pa'i sku/ma khams gsum 'gro ba'i skyabs gcig pu/dpal dus gsum kyi sangs rgyas dol bu pa/mtshan shes rab rgyal mtshan ma lags sam/rje khong gi chos kyi khrir 'khod nas/ rje khong gi ring lugs skyongs ba la/rje do bu sangs rgyas slar logs pa/nga rnal 'byor rang grol ma yin nam/*. The "three regal masters" is a reference to Dol po pa's predecessors at Jo nang: Kun spangs Thugs rje brtson 'grus, Byang sems Rgyal ba ye shes, and Mkhas btsun Yon tan rgya mtsho.

88. For example, ibid., 28a: "the great kingdom of natural radiant light, the permanent and stable stone mountain of the expanse of reality" (*rang bzhin gyi 'od gsal rgyal khams che / chos dbyings kyi brag ri rtag cing brtan*), and in a short untitled instruction in Kun dga' grol mchog, *Gsung*, 44a: "the immutable and permanent buddha-body of gnosis" (*dus 'gyur med rtag pa'i ye shes sku*).

89. Ngag dbang blo bzang rgya mtsho, *Rigs*, 65a, quotes Tshar chen himself as saying: *ri khrod la rgyang bltas byas pas blo 'gro zhing yid 'phrog pa/sngon gyi dam pa rnams kyis 'di lta bu'i gnas su sgrub grwa'i rgyun btsugs/skye bo mang po thar pa'i lam la 'god par mdzad pa ches cher ngo mtshar zhing rmad du byung ba'i rnam thar du 'dug/kho bo cag kyang 'di lta bu'i dben gnas zhig tu byang chub sgrub pa zhig nam 'ong snyam pa snying gi dkyil du lhang lhang ba'i dag snang byung ngo/*.

> When I gazed upon the hermitage from afar my mind went out to it and I was awestruck. A distinct pure vision arose in the center of my heart, and I thought, "A continuous tradition of meditation was established by the early excellent beings at a site such as this. Placing many people on the path of liberation, their lifestyles were so amazing and so incredible. When will I also practice for the sake of enlightenment in an isolated site like this?"

During his second visit a model of the great stūpa of Svayaṃbhunāth, in the Kathmandu valley of Nepal, was being erected in the center of the Jo nang teaching arena. See ibid., 84a–84b.

90. 'Jam dbyangs Mkhyen brtse'i dbang phyug, *Bla*, 29b.

91. See ibid., 66a–66b. Mkhyen brtse's concluding verses sum up the event and his view of Dol po pa nicely: *rgyal bas lung bstan kun mkhyen jo nang pa/'gal 'du skyon med grub mtha' bzhed lags mod/gtsang dag bde dang rtag pa'i mthar thug pa'i/bde gshegs snying po dngos por bzhed re skan/*.

> While the Omniscient Jo nang pa, who was prophecied by the Victor, accepted a philosophical system of flawless contradiction,
> It is impossible that he accepted the ultimately pure, pristine, blissful, and permanent Buddha-nature to be an entity.

What is meant by "flawless contradiction" (*'gal 'du skyon med*) is elaborated on by Dol po pa in *The Fourth Council*, translated in part 2 below. And see Dol po pa, *Dpon*, 511, where he does in fact discuss the use of the term *dngos po* ("entity") as applied to the absolute true nature (*don dam chos nyid, paramārthadharmatā*). In this case it is clarified to be "a nonsubstantial entity" (*dngos po med pa'i dngos po*). There is also mention of the eight "noncomposite entities" (*'dus ma byas kyi dngos po*). This is in the context of a continuing discussion of the doctrine taught in texts such as the *Madhyāntavibhaṅga*.

92. As mentioned above, Shākya mchog ldan and Gung ru ba Shes rab bzang po also maintained that Dol po pa and Bu ston both taught the *gzhan stong*.

93. A number of Tāranātha's translations are found in the Tibetan canon. His translation of the *Kalāpāvatāra*, a guide to Shambhala, was made in the year 1615 from a Newar Sanskrit manuscript found among the ten volumes of Sanskrit texts Tāranātha received from Gcung Ri bo che, the monastery of the great adept Thang stong rgyal po. Because of its title, the *Kalāpāvatāra* had been misplaced among many Sanskrit grammatical texts. See Tāranātha, *Rgyal*, 489, 499–500. The *Kalāpāvatāra* has been translated and studied in Bernbaum (1985), 44–80, but see Newman (1987), 193–206, for a critical discussion of Bernbaum's conclusions.

94. Tāranātha, *Rgyal*, 329b–330a, is very forthright about his eclectic nature. He is also extremely outspoken about not having the brainless and emptyheaded naive view (*klad med mgo stong pa'i dag snang*) that sees faults as qualities. He rejoices at the good qualites of others, but does not hesitate to point out their faults. By being honest he admits to having made many enemies of those who cannot accept unbiased criticism.

95. Ibid., 74a–b.

96. Ibid., 140b–141a. Tāranātha received numerous visions during his life. For instance, he mentions that on many occasions during the years 1618–1619 he had repeatedly experienced visions of the Kalāpa court of the Shambhala emperors, and also had visions of them and heard their teachings. These visions were a result of his belief that all sūtras and tantras were *gzhan stong* Madhyamaka. See ibid., 280a.

97. Ibid., 141b. See Tāranātha, *Gzhan stong dbu ma'i rgyan* and *Gzhan stong dbu ma'i rgyan gyi lung sbyor*. The colophon of the former states that he was thirty years old when he wrote it.

98. Tāranātha, *Gsang*, 680: *da lta kun mkhyen chen po dol po pa'i lta ba la mkhas shing dgongs pa skyong ba'i rgyu mtshan* [681] *yang de lags/*.

99. Tāranātha, *Rgyal*, 154b, mentions a discussion of *rang stong* versus *gzhan stong* with an otherwise unidentified Slob dpon Grub thob pa who had studied many works which refuted the *gzhan stong*, by authors such as Rje Go ram pa, Rtse thang Sang lhun, and Dngos grub dpal 'bar. The meeting and discussions at Grom pa Lha rtse are described in ibid., 200a–201b.

100. Ibid., 298b. The sixth Zhwa dmar sprul sku was Chos kyi dbang phyug (1584–1635). He was under the impression that the Jo nang pa philosophical system of a permanent, stable and eternal absolute entailed the acceptance that the First Turning of the Dharma Wheel taught the existence of a veridically established absolute, the Second the nonexistence, and the Third the existence. Tāranātha answered that the Jo nang pa accepted that all three Turnings had a single intention (*dgong pa gcig*), not that the later ones found fault in the earlier ones.

101. Ngag dbang blo gros grags pa, *Dpal*, 60.

102. This was first noted by Vostrikov (1970), 228, based on a note in the *Bai ḍūrya ser po* of Sde srid Sangs rgyas rgya mtsho. See also Ruegg (1963), 77–78, and 82, for information on the Dge lugs conversion of Jo nang monastery.

103. See Smith (1970), 17.

104. Ngag dbang blo bzang rgya mtsho, *Za*, vol. 1, 521. As commented on by Smith (1968), 16–17, Situ Paṇ chen Chos kyi 'byung gnas (1700–1774) visited Rtag brtan and Jo nang in 1723, and his account places the blame for the Dge lugs conversion of Jo nang upon the Fifth Dalai Lama's teacher Smon 'gro Paṇ chen, who had earlier received Jo nang pa teachings and then later spread slander about them to the Fifth Dalai Lama. The Dalai Lama took his teacher's advice, ordered the change of the Jo nang pa philosophical system to that of the Dge lugs pa (*grub mtha' sgyur*), and had the silver reliquary containing Tāranātha's remains destroyed. See Chos kyi 'byung gnas, *Tā'i*, 104–105.

105. Ngag dbang blo bzang rgya mtsho, *Za*, vol. 1, 521. See also Byams pa thub bstan, *Dga'*, x, who dates both the conversion of the Jo nang pa and the change of the name of Tāranātha's monastery to the year 1650, not 1658. He is certainly correct about the initial conversion but not about the name change, which did not take place for another eight years.

106. Ngag dbang blo gros grags pa, *Dpal*, 60–61

107. Ngag dbang blo bzang rgya mtsho, *Za*, vol. 1, 309.

108. Ngag gi dbang po, *Khyab*, 286. I am grateful to Mr. Hubert Decleer for directing my attention to this source. Also see Smith (1969), 12, and Byams pa thub bstan, *Dga'*, 330–34. The Khalka Rje btsun dam pa incarnations have continued as the leaders of Buddhism in Mongolia up into modern times.

109. 'Jam dbyangs bkra shis founded the monastery of 'Bras spungs in 1417, and was an important disciple of Rje Tsong kha pa. Also see Ngag gi dbang po, *Khyab*, 277–78.

110. *Ibid.*, 278: *nged kyi jo nang pa'i bstan pa spel ba de tsam gyis chog pa bgyis/da ni dga' ldan pa'i bsrung ma rnams kyis gsol ba btab pa dang/ sngon gyi smon lam gyi mthus mtha' 'khob tu rje tsong kha pa'i bstan pa spel bar byed do/*. The source of this account is identified only as *skyabs mgon sku gong ma'i rnam thar*, "the biography of the previous refuge lord."

111. Cf. Ngag dbang blo gros grags pa, *Dpal*, 59.

112. Quoted in Ngag gi dbang po, *Khyab*, 279. The event was originally recorded in Tāranātha, *Gsang*, 662, from which it has been translated.

113. See Kun spangs, *Chos*, 386, where Dol po pa sends a yellow hat he had worn himself (*nga rang gyon pa'i zhwa ser*) to a disciple. Also see Jackson (1996), 188, for the reproduction of a beautiful seventeenth-century (?) painting of Tāranātha wearing a yellow hat.

114. See note 61 in chapter 1.

115. Byams pa thub bstan, *Dga'*, 331, mentions the vows and teachings from the Paṇ chen bla ma.

116. Blo bzang chos kyi rgyal mtshan, *Chos*, 249. The Paṇ chen bla ma notes that at this time there were about eight hundred monks at Rtag brtan.

117. Ngag dbang blo bzang rgya mtsho, *Za*, 521.

118. There is much evidence in Ngag dbang blo gros grags pa, *Dpal*, that shows that the Jo nang pa teachings continued to be taught to a surprising extent in Gtsang after the suppression. For information on the state of the Jo nang pa tradition today in Amdo, see Kapstein (1991).

119. Tshe dbang nor bu, *Ma*, 605.

120. Chos kyi dbang phyug, *Dpal*, 139. On this occasion Tshe dbang nor bu also remembered his earlier life as a certain 'Jam dbyangs ye shes rgya mtsho, the son of the Gting skyes rgyal po, which is also stated as a reason why he was so attracted to the view and philosophical system of the Jo nang pa, and why he understood it without much effort.

121. For a study of Tshe dbang nor bu's restoration activities in Kathmandu, see Ehrhard (1989). Tshe dbang nor bu, *Lha*, 224, and Chos kyi dbang phyug, *Dpal*, 122, describe Tshe dbang nor bu's first attempts to receive teachings from Kun bzang dbang po. For a short biographical note on Kun bzang dbang po, often known as Samantabhadrendra, the Sanskrit form of his name, see Ngag dbang blo gros grags pa, *Dpal*, 534–35.

122. Tshe dbang nor bu's final success in receiving teachings from Kun bzang dbang po are described in Chos kyi dbang phyug, ibid., 138–39, and Tshe dbang nor bu, *Ma*, 604–605. His teaching at Jo nang in 1734 is described in Chos kyi dbang phyug, ibid., 164.

123. Ngag dbang blo gros grags pa, *Dpal*, 536.

124. See note 104 in the present chapter, and Chos kyi 'byung gnas, *Tā'i*, 104–105.

125. Smith (1968), 8, mentions that this ban was not lifted until 1874, when the Zhwa lu master Blo gsal bstan skyong (b.1804) finally gained permission to reopen the printery at Dga' ldan phun tshogs gling and reprint some of the Jo nang texts. The original sealing of the books probably occurred at the same time as the banning of Shākya mchog ldan's works in the mid–seventeenth century, as was mentioned above.

126. Chos kyi 'byung gnas, *Tā'i*, 105.

127. In Si tu's own autobiography, ibid., 267, it seems that the event occurred at Bodhnāth, but Ngag dbang blo gros grags pa, *Dpal*, 536–37, locates it at the self–arisen stūpa (*rang byung mchod rten*), which would signify Svayaṃbhunāth.

128. Chos kyi 'byung gnas, *Tā'i*, 267: *nged la zab mo gzhan stong gi lta ba 'dzin dgos tshul dang/de ltar na sku tshe mdzad phrin rgyas pa'i rten 'brel yod tshul dang/lta ba'i skor gsung 'phros mang po byung/*. I first heard about this event in a private conversation in the 1970s with the late Sde gzhung sprul sku Kun dga' bstan pa'i nyi ma, who also believed that adherence to the *gzhan stong* view would bring longevity.

129. Ibid., 267: *bdag gis ni gzhan stong rang la'ang bzhed tshul cung zad mi 'dra ba 'ga' re yod pa'i nang nas/dol po'i bzhed pa las thal rang gnyis po'ang rig tshogs kyi dgongs pa rma med du 'dod pa ni khyad par dang/rje bdun pa dang zi lung pa'i bzhed pa dang ches nye ba zhig 'dod pa yin no/*. The Seventh Lord is the seventh Karma pa, Chos grags rgya mtsho, and Zi lung pa is Paṇ chen Shākya mchog ldan.

130. Smith (1970), 34.

131. The best treatment of the *ris med* movement is still Smith (1970).

132. At least one brief work by Mkhyen brtse is concerned with the *gzhan stong*. See 'Jam dbyang Mkhyen brtse'i dbang po, *Gzhan*.

133. Mi pham, *Gzhan*, presents the version of *gzhan stong* that this master accepted.

134. For example, see 'Jam mgon Kong sprul, *Gzhan*, a text devoted solely to the instructions of the *gzhan stong* view, which he wrote at 'Dzam thang monastery. For information about Kong sprul's life and works, see Smith (1970).

135. 'Jam mgon Kong sprul's treatment of the Six-branch Yoga (*ṣaḍaṅgayoga*) instructions in his *Theg*, vol. 3, 429–57, is drawn almost verbatim from Tāranātha, *Zab lam*, and his historical survey of these

instructions in *Theg*, vol. 1., 549–51, is copied directly from Tāranātha, *Rdo*, 476–78. See 'Jam mgon Kong sprul, *Theg*, vol. 1, 552, for his opinion of the Jo nang tradition of Dol po pa and Tāranātha as the most exceptional of all the *ṣaḍaṅgayoga* lineages.

136. On several occasions, the late Sde gzhung Rin po che, Kun dga' bstan pa'i nyi ma, told me that Chos kyi blo gros, who was his teacher, was pleased (*thugs brnyes*) with the *gzhan stong*. In his own secret autobiography, Chos kyi blo gros records a marvelous dream-vision of Tāranātha, who bestows upon him the Kālacakra initiation. This experience in 1943 caused him to have the greatest faith in Tāranātha. See 'Jam dbyangs chos kyi blo gros, *Khyab*, 96–98.

137. See especially Dudjom (1991), 169–216, concerning the *rang stong* and *gzhan stong* contrasts and the teachings of the Great Madhyamaka. According to Kapstein (n.d.), this section of Bdud 'joms' text is largely derived from the earlier work of the Kaḥ thog master Dge rtse Paṇḍi ta 'Gyur med tshe dbang mchog sgrub (b. 1764), who was regarded as an emanation of Dol po pa, and actively taught the *gzhan stong*.

138. In the late 1970s I once asked the late Sde gzhung Rin po che, Kun dga' bstan pa'i nyi ma, about the view of the *gzhan stong* teachings in the different Tibetan traditions. Rin po che replied that members of the Rnying ma and Bka' brgyud traditions had to accept (*khas len dgos red*) the *gzhan stong* because it was the view of Bdud 'joms Rin po che, Dil mgo mkhyen brtse Rin po che, and Ka lu Riṅ po che. When I asked about followers of the Sa skya tradition, Rin po che laughed and said they had to keep an open mind about the topic (*dag snang dgos red*). When I asked about the Dge lugs pa position, Rin po che exclaimed that they viewed the *gzhan stong* teachings as "the enemy of the Doctrine" (*bstan pa'i dgra bo red*).

139. In a private conversation in Bodhnāth, Nepal, in 1989, Mkhan po Tshul 'khrims rgya mtsho told me that he had not received even the reading transmission of any texts by Dol po pa.

140. The actual differences between the teachings of Dol po pa and the many later adherents to the *gzhan stong*, such as Shākya mchog ldan, Karma pa Chos grags rgya mtsho, Tshe dbang nor bu, Si tu Paṇ chen, and most recently, 'Jam mgon Kong sprul and Mi pham rgya mtsho, remains a subject for future research. One of the most obvious points of Dol po pa's doctrine, which has been dropped by later Bka' brgyud and Rnying ma teachers, is the radical separation of the thoughts or concepts (*rnam rtog*) from the buddha-body of reality (*chos sku*). This will be discussed below in chapter 3, section 2, and in note 120 in the translation of *The Fourth Council*. For a brief note on some other differences between Dol po pa and modern followers of the *gzhan stong*, see Broido (1989), 89–90.

Chapter 3. The Doctrine of the Buddha from Dolpo

1. This simple statement could well serve as a slogan expressing the crux of Dol po pa's message. Bhagavān Avalokiteśvara is the pseudonym of Kalkin Puṇḍarīka, and this quotation is found in the first chapter of his *Vimalaprabhā*. My thanks to Prof. John Newman for locating this quote for me. See Newman (1987), 373. It is cited in Dol po pa, *Jo*, 731: *bcom ldan 'das spyan ras gzigs dbang phyug gi zhal snga nas kyang/srid pa dang mya ngan las 'das pa ni gcig pa nyid ma yin te/grib ma dang nyi ma bzhin no/*. For the original Sanskrit see Kalkin Puṇḍarīka, *Vimalaprabhāṭīkā*, 44, *bhavanirvāṇayonaikṣyam(-rnaikyaṃ)/chāyātapayoryathā/*.

2. See for example the detailed descriptions in Bu ston's *History of Buddhism*, translated in Obermiller (1932), pt. 2, 73–101. A great deal has been written about the three councils. Two of the more important studies are Hofinger (1946) and Bareau (1958). Prebish (1974) reviews and evaluates the results of previous research.

3. The term *bstan rtsis* ("calculation of the doctrine") generally denotes a genre of Tibetan literature concerned with calculating important historical events in the development of Buddhism, usually by means of calculating the number of years that have passed since the final nirvāṇa of Śākyamuni Buddha. Dol po pa uses the term more in the sense of an analysis of the Buddhist Doctrine itself, in this case on the basis of the historical degeneracy through the eons of the Kṛtayuga, Tretayuga, and so forth, as will be discussed below. The most detailed treatment of the genre of *bstan rtsis* in Tibet is found in Vostrikov (1970), 101–37, who translates the term as "chronological treatise."

4. *Bka' bsdu bzhi pa'i rang 'grel*, 664–65.

5. See the opening section of the translation of *The Fourth Council* in part 2 below. On the theme of the four eons in Dol po pa's writings, see the brief treatment in Kapstein (1992), 24–25. Dol po pa, *Bka' bsdu bzhi pa'i rang 'grel*, 614, specifies the *Vimalaprabhā* as the source of these ideas.

6. Kapstein (1994).

7. Dol po pa, *Bka' bsdu bzhi pa'i rang 'grel*, 614–15.

8. Kapstein (1994), briefly discusses this aspect of Dol po pa's doctrine.

9. See Kalkin Puṇḍarīka, *'Jig*, 470–71, for the Tibetan translation of verses 22 and 23 of the *Lokadhātupaṭala* of the *Kālacakra tantra* with Bu ston's annotations. For an English translation of these verses, with the annotations by Bu ston, see Newman (1987), 514–19.

10. See notes 11–13 in chapter 1 for complete lists of these texts.

11. Kapstein (1992), 25.

12. Dol po pa, *Bka' bsdu bzhi pa*, 365–66.

13. Dol po pa, *Dpon*, 489.

14. Dol po pa, *Dbu*, 1174: *dbyings de 'khor ba'i rgyu ni min mod kyang/ de med na ni de yang mi srid pas/mkha' la rlung gi dkyil 'khor brten pa ltar/'khor ba'i gzhi gyur zhes pa'i rnam bzhag byas/*. The *dbyings*, "expanse," in this quotation refers to *don dam dbyings*, which in turn is equivalent to *tathāgatagarbha* or Buddha-nature.

15. Dol po pa, *Dpon*, 486–88. A long list of important points of Dharma that Dol po pa felt he realized as a result of the teachings in *The Trilogy of Bodhisattva Commentaries* has been omitted in the translation. See note 11 in chapter 1 for information on *The Trilogy of Bodhisattva Commentaries*.

16. See Dol po pa, *Kun mkhyen*, 443–52.

17. Ma ti Paṇ chen, *Chos*, 1082: *kun rdzob stong tshul 'khor lo bar pa'i don/don dam stong tshul 'khor lo tha ma'i don/med la med dang yod la yod ces par/ston pas gnyis ka'ang mthar thug dgongs pa gcig/*.

18. For a recent work concerned with showing the continuity of Madhyamaka and Yogācāra in India, see Harris (1991).

19. Dol po pa's position on the relation between the teachings of the Three Turnings of the Dharma Wheel is clear in the translation below of *A General Commentary on the Doctrine* and in the accompanying annotations based upon the commentary of his disciple Nya dbon Kun dga' dpal, as well as in the translation of *The Fourth Council*.

20. See Dol po pa, *Dpal*, 116, and *Gzhon*, 682–83.

21. The Buddhist "three-nature theory" is a very difficult and complex issue. No attempt is made in this book to explain it outside the context of a discussion of Dol po pa's theories. For more information on the theory in general the reader should consult the works by Anacher, Harris, Kochumuttom, Nagao, and Williams listed in the bibliography.

22. See also 'Jam mgon Kong sprul, *Theg*, vol. 1, 460–61, who mentions Kun mkhyen Dharmākara as saying that in Btsan Kha bo che's manuals (*yig cha*) there were statements that nondual empty and pristine self-luminous cognition, which is veridically established (*bden grub*), is the vital cause of buddhahood. Kun mkhyen Dharmākara is Si tu paṇ chen Chos kyi 'byung gnas.

23. The phrase "from form to omniscience" (*gzugs nas rnam mkhyen gyi bar*) is a standard phrase referring to all the phenomena that make up the universe. In full form there are 108 categories, beginning with form, the first of the five aggregates, and ending with a Buddha's omniscience. See Lopez (1996), 224, note 6.

24. Kun dga' grol mchog, *Zab khrid,* 412–413.

25. For a recent translation of instructions on the Great Middle Way, taken from the same collection by Kun dga' grol mchog, see Kapstein (1996), 282–83.

26. Dol po pa, *Bka' bsdu bzhi pa'i rang 'grel*, 632, mentions the *Mahāyānasūtrālaṃkara* and the *Madhyantavibhaṅga* as examples of texts that he considers to be Great Madhyamaka but that are usually classified as Cittamātra.

27. Dol po pa, *Bka' bsdu bzhi pa*, 386. Dol po pa, *Bka' bsdu bzhi pa'i rang 'grel*, 632, mentions Vasubandhu and Dignāga as great teachers of the Great Madhyamaka who have been incorrectly called representatives of Cittamātra.

28. Dol po pa, *Bka' bsdu bzhi pa'i rang 'grel*, 629–32.

29. Among European scholars, this "Maitreya Chapter" first attracted the attention of Obermiller, who noted the Tibetan controversy about its origins and teachings in his translation of Bu ston's *History of Buddhism*. See Obermiller (1932), pt. 2, 50, note 335. But it was not until 1968 that Edward Conze, the foremost modern scholar of the *Prajñāpāramitā sūtra* literature, published an edited Sanskrit text of the chapter with Iida Shotaro. See Conze and Iida (1968). This Sanskrit text corresponds almost literally to the Tibetan translation of the "Maitreya Chapter" found in the eighteen-thousand-line scripture, but only approximately to that found in the translation of the twenty-five-thousand-line sūtra. It is not found in other versions of the *Prajñāpāramitā*. Conze published a translation of the Sanskrit text of the chapter in his *The Large Sutra of Perfect Wisdom*. See Conze (1975), 644–52. More recently Thurman has translated an important text of Rje Tsong kha pa, one chapter of which deals with apparent contradictions between the presentation of the three natures as found in the *Saṃdhinirmocana sūtra* and the "Maitreya Chapter." See Thurman (1984), 355–63. Several years earlier some of Tsong kha pa's treatment of the "Maitreya Chapter" had also been translated in Iida (1980), 259–69. Finally, Ian Harris has also recently dealt with the significance of the views expressed in the "Maitreya Chapter," and compared them to other Yogācāra sources. See Harris (1991), 102–31.

30. The section of the *Bṛhaṭṭīkā* that comments on the "Maitreya Chapter" is found in Anonymous (Vasubandhu?), *'Phags*, 334.2.1–339.3.6. It was

translated from Sanskrit into Tibetan by the Indian abbot Surendrabodhi and the Tibetan translator Ye shes sde, who were active in the late eighth century. Ruegg (1969), 61, 325–26, 343, utilizes the *Bṛhaṭṭīkā*, and sometimes quotes from it via Tsong kha pa's critique, but does not seem to have consulted the section devoted to the "Maitreya Chapter."

31. See in particular Dol po pa, *Bka' mdo*, 332–33, and Dol po pa, *Gzhon*, 679–83, which is a very interesting instruction addressed to a man who disliked the *gzhan stong* presentation of emptiness.

32. See Obermiller (1988), 4, note 7, and 146, note 1038. Also see Thurman (1984), 244–48. In his catalogue to the Sde dge edition of the Tibetan Bstan 'gyur, the enormous collection of translated exegetical literature, Zhu chen Tshul khrims rin chen quotes Bu ston's comments verbatim. See Tshul khrims rin chen, *Kun*, 625. Dol po pa, *Dpal*, 137, listed Daṃṣṭrāsena in the transmission line of the extensive version of the *Prajñāpāramitā sūtra*, but long after Vasubandhu.

33. See Kun dga' bzang po, *Bstan*, 359: *shes rab kyi pha rol tu phyin pa 'bum pa dang/nyi khri lnga stong pa dang/khri brgyad stong pa rnams kyi bshad pa/slob dpon chen po dbyig gnyen gyis mdzad pa ye shes sde'i 'gyur/*. The text is also mentioned in Dudjom (1991), vol.1, 944.

34. Bu ston had stated that the *Bṛhaṭṭīkā* was actually the *Paddhati* of Vasubandhu mentioned by Haribhadra in the opening verses of his *Abhisamayālaṃkārālokā*. But Tsong kha pa later pointed out that the *Bṛhaṭṭīkā* contains an opinion of Śāntarakṣita in relation to the epochs of the Buddhist teachings. See Obermiller (1988), 4, note 7. The original statement in the *Bṛhaṭṭīkā* about the duration of the Doctrine is found in Anonymous (Vasubandhu?), *'Phags*, 300.4.3. If this Śāntarakṣita is the same as the Indian master who was active in Tibet in the late eighth century, this alone would be sufficient to prove that the text was not by Vasubandhu. Ruegg (1992), 269, note 22, has also noted that the *Bṛhaṭṭīkā* gives five thousand years as the total duration of the Buddhist teachings, whereas Vasubandhu's *Abhidharmakośabhāṣya* (viii. 39) gives one thousand years for the duration of the *adhigama* section alone. One Tibetan source seems to have considered the *Bṛhaṭṭīkā* to have been written by the Tibetan translator of the text, Ye shes sde, who was also active in the later eighth century. Finally, it should be mentioned that a massive, although apparently incomplete, commentary to the one-hundred-thousand-line version of the *Prajñāpāramitāsūtra* is also generally attributed to the master Daṃṣṭrāsena. See Tshul khrims rin chen, *Kun*, 779, where it is also mentioned that the earlier 'Phang khang catalogue to the Tibetan canon attributed this text to the Tibetan king Khri srong lde'u btsan. This text (P #5205) immediately precedes the *Bṛhaṭṭīkā* in the Tibetan canon. As will be discussed below, the three-nature paradigm is frequently utilized

in the *Bṛhaṭṭīkā*. If it were actually authored by Daṃṣṭrāsena, it would seem reasonable to expect occurrences of the three natures in his commentary to the one-hundred-thousand-line version as well. But such is not the case. This fact argues for the conclusion that the two texts were written by different authors.

35. See especially Anonymous (Vasubandhu?), *'Phags*, 250.4. ff. There is no clear indication in the text as to which version of the sūtra is being commented upon in this chapter, and no attempt has been made to trace the quotations elsewhere.

36. Anonymous (Vasubandhu?), *'Phags*, 250.3–4.

37. Dol po pa, *Bka' bsdu bzhi pa'i rang 'grel*, 599.

38. Dol po pa, *Bstan*, 688. This entire text is translated and studied in part 2 below.

39. See Nya dbon Kun dga' dpal, *Bstan pa*, 34b–36a. The following paragraph is closely based upon Nya dbon's commentary.

40. Also see Kapstein (1992), 24–25, and 35–43. Among the great Tibetan scholars of the fourteenth century, Dol po pa was not alone in feeling that the attribution of idealism to Asaṅga and Vasubandhu was inaccurate. The Rnying ma master Klong chen rab 'byams-pa also made this point. See Kapstein (1992), 23, note 1.

41. For example, Dol po pa, *'Phags*, 1006–22, is a collection of annotations to the "Maitreya Chapter" from the twenty-five-thousand-line version. Almost all of it seems to have been drawn directly from the *Bṛhaṭṭīkā*. See Anonymous (Vasubandhu?), *'Phags*, 334.1.1.–339.3.4.

42. Dol po pa, *Bka' bsdu bzhi pa'i rang 'grel*, 616. Dol po pa, *Ngo*, 607–608, is also excellent on the *trisvabhāva* in the *Pañcaśatikāprajñāparamitā*.

43. Anonymous, *Pañcaśatika*, 243.3. The text is preserved only in Tibetan translation. Conze (1973b), 108, translates this passage as "Form, Subhūti, is non-existence, it has a poorish kind of existence, it is existence."

44. Anonymous, *Pañcaśatika*, 243.3–4. Cf. Conze (1973), 108. The Tibetan term translated here as "addicted" is *mngon par zhen pa*, which literally means to be directly or obviously attached to or obsessed with something. Dol po pa's connection of this with the *parikalpita* is also intriguing in light of Nagao's statement that a suggestion of attachment is conveyed by the Sanskrit participle form, and that the Chinese translation of *parikalpita* conveys this as well. See Nagao (1991), "The Buddhist World View," 62. The translation as "cultivate" (*mngon par bsgrub*) is problematic. Conze reconstructs the Sanskrit as *abhinirharanti*, which he translates as "aspire for."

45. Tāranātha, *Gzhan stong dbu ma'i rgyan kyi lung sbyor*, 534–37, and 538–39.

46. See Dol po pa, *Dpal*, 116, 126, and 137. In this he was following the lead of the *Vimalaprabhā*, in which the *Prajñāpāramitā* is also discussed.

47. Dol po pa, ibid., 127.

48. Dol po pa, *Bka' bsdu bzhi pa'i rang 'grel*, 642.

49. Bsod nams dpal, *Bde*, 151. Phag mo gru pa was in the habit of asking each teacher he met about the cause for birth in saṃsāra. He was not impressed with Sa chen's answer, nor that of Byang sems Zla ba rgyal mtshan, who said that the cause was ignorance, nor the replies of others who said that it was not having accumulated the assemblies of merit and gnosis, or not having purified the obscurations. But then he met the Bka' brgyud master Rje Sgam po pa (1079–1153), who told him that the cause for birth in saṃsāra was not resting the mind in "ordinary awareness" (*tha mal gyi shes pa*). Just hearing this from Sgam po pa caused Phag mo gru pa to experience that awareness, and he gained an instant and total certainty in Sgam po pa's words. See ibid., 154. See Jackson (1994), 40–41, for some information on what Sgam po pa meant by "ordinary awareness."

50. Dol po pa, *Bka' bsdu bzhi pa'i rang 'grel*, 588.

51. Dol po pa, *Untitled*, 851. *Vajrayoga* is another term for the *ṣaḍaṅgayoga*, or Six-branch Yoga.

52. Dol po pa's point here is that if sentient beings had no intrinsic awareness at all they would be no different than the inanimate gross elements (*mahābhūta*, *'byung chen*) of earth, water, and so forth.

53. Translation according to the 'Dzam thang, 248, reading of *grol*, "liberation," instead of the Bhutanese reading of *gol*, which is an obvious scribal error.

54. Dol po pa, *Bka' bsdu bzhi pa*, 411–12.

55. See Jackson (1994).

56. See note 120 below in the translation of *The Fourth Council* for examples of prominant Bka' brgyud and Rnying ma masters who taught in this manner.

57. Dol po pa, *Ston*, 652: *glo bur dri ma bral dang ma bral ba'i/de bzhin nyid la sangs rgyas sems can dang/mya ngan 'das dang 'khor ba pa zhes brjod/.*

58. Dol po pa, *Lha*, 670–71.

59. Ibid., 672.

60. Ibid., 677–78.

61. The early Tibetan Rnying ma pa master Rong zom Chos kyi bzang po gives a quotation from the *Ye shes snang ba rgyan gyi mdo* (*Jñānālokālaṃkāra sūtra*, Derge 100, GA, 276a–305a), which could well be used to illustrate Dol po pa's viewpoint: "Those with childish minds, who grasp at conceptual characteristics, engage in phenomena which do not exist in the world." See Rong zom, *Gsang*, 345: *byis pa'i blo can mtshan mar 'dzin pa dag/'jig rten dag na med pa'i chos la spyod/.*

62. An eloquent verse discussion of all these points is found in Dol po pa, *Untitled*.

63. In another context, Dol po pa states that in the ultimate sense there is no saṃsāra and nirvāṇa; such designations are only made on the level of relative perception. See Dol po pa, *Ston*, 652: *dam pa'i don du 'khor 'das gang yang med/kun rdzob snang ngor brjod pa de ltar lags/.*

64. See note 1 in the present chapter.

Introduction to the Translation of *A General Commentary on the Doctrine*

1. The correct translation of the title of this text is *A General Commentary on the Doctrine*, not *A Commentary on the General Doctrine*, as found in Roerich, trans. (1976), 777. This is made clear in Nya dbon, *Bstan pa*, 52a, and Lha'i rgyal mtshan, *Chos*, 28b, both of whom expand the title to *Bstan pa'i spyi 'grel*. It is possible that Dol po pa named his text in recognition of an earlier work by Kun spangs Thugs rje brtson 'grus, the founder of Jo nang monastery. Kun spangs pa's text, entitled *Bstan pa spyi'i 'grel*, is listed in a 43 fol. edition in the catalogue of the Phun tshogs gling printery compiled by Zhwa lu Blo gsal bstan skyong. See Blo gsal bstan skyong, *Rje*, 301.

2. The date of composition is given on Nya dbon, *Bstan pa*, 53a: *chu mo bya'i lo dbyar zla 'bring po'i tshes bco lnga*. This corresponds to May or June 30, 1333. However, there is clearly a problem in the text. In what is perhaps an anachronistic error, Nya dbon, *Bstan pa*, 52b, states that the text was composed at the request of a Bkra' shis rdo rje, who is identified as the imperial chaplain (*bla'i mchod gnas*) of a Chinese emperor. The Chinese ruler is referred to as *Ta'i mi[ng] rgyal po*, which is the Tibetan title for a Ming dynasty emperor. The Ming dynasty did not begin until 1368. Therefore, either the *chu mo bya* (Water female Bird) year of composition, corresponding to 1333, or the reference to the Chinese ruler as a Ming dynasty emperor must be mistaken.

3. For a discussion of the circumstances of Dol po pa's first public explanations of the *gzhan stong* view, see chapter 1, section 4–5 above, and for information on the development of his special terminology, see chapter 3, section 2.

4. See Kun dga' grol mchog, *Rigs*, 22b (passage translated in chapter 1, section 6 above), and Roerich, trans. (1976), 777.

5. See chapter 2, section 3 above for more information about Nya dbon as the most influential of Dol po pa's disciples in the last decades of the fourteenth century. When Nya dbon was still a young man he lost the use of his arms and legs and was a paraplegic. Some of his friends carried him to Sa skya to meet Dol po pa, who instantly cured him with a blessing. He studied extensively with both Dol po pa and Jo nang Phyogs las rnam rgyal, and became extremely learned and realized. He also taught for many years at Sa skya monastery itself. Later he founded the monastery of Rtse chen, which became an important center for the teachings of definitive meaning. Nya dbon also became one of the main teachers of both Red mda' ba and Rje Tsong kha pa. See Ngag dbang blo gros grags pa, *Dpal*, 38. Information about Nya dbon is also found in Tāranātha, *Myang*, 93–94, where he is described as one of the main Dharma heirs of Bla ma dam pa Bsod nams rgyal mtshan. According to this source he was the foremost of Bla ma dam pa's eight great disciples who upheld his tradition of the Sa skya Lam 'bras teachings (*lam 'bras srol 'dzin mkhas pa mi brgyad*). In his prayer to the masters of the Lam 'bras the great Tshar chen Blo gsal rgya mtsho also composed a verse in praise of Nya dbon as the treasury of the profound teachings of definitive meaning. See Tshar chen, *Gsung*, 239. A photograph of an old Rgyal rtse image of Dol po pa flanked by Nya dbon and Phyogs las rnam rgyal is reproduced in Ricca and Lo Bue (1993), 295.

6. See Nya dbon, *Bstan pa*, 35a, for specific mention of Dol po pa's opinions.

7. Also see note 2 immediately above.

8. Ngag dbang blo gros grags pa, *Dpal*, 34.

9. Lha'i rgyal mtshan, *Chos*, 28b: *bla ma yi dam dbyer med la gsol ba 'debs pa bstan pa'i spyi 'grel . . . la sogs pa'i gsol 'debs khyad par can mdzad pa ltar gsol ba drag tu btab pa'i mthar spyan chab char bzhin du 'bab cing/ khyed mkhyen khyed mkhyen zhes phur tshugs su gsol ba 'debs pa/.*

10. Ibid., 48a. See chapter 1, section 10 above for a full description of this event.

11. Writing in 1561, 'Jam dbyangs mkhyen brtse'i dbang phyug, *Rje*, 278, describes the teachings Sgo rum pa received from the Jo nang abbot

Nam mkha' chos skyong in about 1495, among which he singles out the *Nges don rgya mtsho*, the *Bka' bsdu bzhi pa'i rtsa 'grel*, and the *Bstan pa spyi 'grel*. He also refers to the present day unadulterated Jo nang tradition of the Kālacakra initiation and teachings.

12. Nya dbon, *Bstan pa*, 2a–b, gives several examples. A commentary that explains both the words and the meaning in detail is termed "a vast commentary" (*rgya chen 'grel pa*); one which clearly explains every word of the basic text is "a word-by-word commentary" (*tshig 'grel*); one which presents the principle meaning of the text in a condensed fashion is "a commentary of condensed meaning" (*bsdus don 'grel pa*); one which explains the meaning without citing every word is "a commentary on just the meaning" (*don tsam gyi 'grel pa*); and one which is easy to understand is "an easily understood commentary" (*go sla'i 'grel pa*).

13. Ibid., 1b.

14. Ibid., 52b.

The Supplication Entitled *A General Commentary on the Doctrine*

1. Nya dbon, *Bstan pa*, 2b–3a: This Sanskrit invocation is the first part of Dol po pa's expression of homage and offering. *OṂ* is an opening expression of homage. In the context of definitive meaning *OṂ* is the Buddha-nature, and its position at the beginning of all mantras is to indicate that the Buddha-nature pervades all sentient beings. *GURU* in Sanskrit means "heavy," in the sense of being full of spiritual qualities. The main cause for liberation from saṃsāra is the practice of the Dharma, and the main reason the Buddha appeared in the world was to teach the Dharma. A guru is considered "heavy" with kindness by virtue of the fact that such a person teaches the Dharma and thus carries out the enlightened activity of the Buddha. *BUDDHA* has the meaning of both awakening from the sleep of ignorance and the expansion of the mind to encompass everything knowable. Since it is explained in many scriptures that a buddha is the quintessence of gnosis (*ye shes kyi bdag nyid can*), the view that there is no gnosis at the point of buddhahood is simply a nihilistic view (*chad lta*). *BODHISATTVA* has the meaning of a being (*sattva*) who is intently focused upon the ultimate buddha-body of reality (*dharmakāya*), or enlightenment (*bodhi*). *BYHO* is merely the Sanskrit dative plural indicator. Here Dol po pa intends the first *NAMO* as an expression of homage, and the second *NAMAḤ* as an expression of offering.

2. Ibid., 3b: The term Dharma Lord (*chos kyi rje*) actually applies to the Buddha himself, since he is the Lord of all the Dharma teachings, and

the master of all who accept the Doctrine and teach the Dharma. But here the masters who carry out the Buddha's activities and act in a manner similar to that of the Buddha himself are referred to as Dharma Lords. In all the verses of this text Dol po pa is bowing at the feet of Buddha Śākyamuni, the master of the three realms, and in particular at the feet of his own masters, Mkhas btsun Yon tan rgya mtsho and Skyi ston 'Jam pa'i dbyangs grags pa rgyal mtshan (ibid., 9b). This homage is offered to those excellent masters who are embodiments of the buddhas and bodhisattvas, and are thus regarded as *nirmāṇakāyas*, or emanations appearing in this world for the benefit of others. This homage is humbly offered to the lowest portion of those teachers, which is their feet, poetically rendered in the form of lotus flowers (*padma'i gzugs su bkod pa*). Not only does he pay homage to his masters, but further prays for their protection in all the terrifying circumstances encountered in saṃsāra. Finally he asks, on behalf of himself and all sentient beings, to be graced by their great love, saved from the abyss of saṃsāra into which everyone has fallen, and led on to the pleasant plain of liberation.

3. Curiously, Nya dbon does not touch upon this verse in his commentary. The significance of Dol po pa's use of the terms *permanent* (*rtag*), *stable* (*brtan*), and *eternal* (*g.yung drung*) in this early text has been mentioned above in chapter 2, section 2. The "four reliances" (*rton pa bzhi*) have also been mentioned above in chapter 3, section 2, where it was pointed out as well that Dol po pa's favorite pseudonym was "the one endowed with the four reliances" (*rton pa bzhi ldan*), which alludes to his own hermeneutical approach. He also signs *The Fourth Council*, translated below, with this name.

4. Nya dbon, *Bstan pa*, 8b–9b: Basically, all composite entities (*'dus byas kyi dngos po*) are considered impermanent simply because they are present for a certain length of time and then are no longer present. There are two ways to consider the impermanence of phenomena, both of which are illustrated here by way of traditional examples. First of all, any composite inanimate entity does not remain the same from one moment to the next, in the same way that a waterfall cascading down a mountain cliff is rapidly moving downward, and is composed of different molecules of water from one moment to the next. It is thus unstable and constantly changing. Secondly, a phenomenon may be considered impermanent in the sense that it appears and disappears in a moment, like a cloud that appears in the sky and then immediately vanishes, or like a flash of lightning, or the dew on a blade of grass.

5. Ibid., 9b–11a: The realization that all composite phenomena are impermanent by nature leads to the realization that they are tainted and produce suffering. This verse points out that suffering is the nature of the

desire realm, the form realm, and the formless realm. There is attachment to the objects of the senses in the desire realm. In the absence of those, there is still attachment to form in the form realm. And even without both of those there is still attachment to self-identity in the formless realm. Thus the nature or state of all three realms is suffering. The examples of falling into a pit of fire or being caught by a poisonous viper directly illustrate the suffering of suffering, and allude to the suffering of change. The example of a bee flying in circles inside a pot, and not knowing how to escape from the only opening, illustrates the suffering of conditioning. These examples, and those in the previous verse, are drawn from scriptures such as the *Lalitavistara sūtra*.

6. Ibid., 11a–b: Having demonstrated that all tainted phenomena produce suffering, Dol po pa now points out that they are not worthy of attachment. In particular, he illustrates why human beings in the desire realm should not be attached to their own or other's bodies. For many people the greatest delusion is in thinking that their own bodies, and those of persons to whom they are attached—bodies that are actually composed of various impure substances—become pure when they are cleaned, perfumed, dressed, and adorned. Attachment and desire for a body which is in reality impure is the same as attachment or desire for a vase filled with vomit, urine, or feces. If a vase is cleaned on the outside, smeared with perfume, wrapped in silk, adorned with many beautiful jewels, and then filled with vomit, urine, or feces, and shown to some children who are ignorant of what is inside the vase, they will be delighted by it, and want it. Desire for the body of another attractive person is much the same, and should be understood as a cause for many of the sufferings in saṃsāra's lower realms.

7. Ibid., 13a–14a: After describing the nature of the three realms of saṃsāra, and so forth, Dol po pa presents the method for liberation from saṃsāra. Karma and the afflicting emotions are the causes of repeated birth and death in saṃsāra. Sentient beings who delight in the inferior and tainted happiness of saṃsāra, and have no thoughts of practicing the Dharma, should be taught that everything in the three realms of saṃsāra in general is impermanent, and that in particular the lives of human beings are impermanent and unstable. As explained before, since the desired body is composed only of impure substances, it should not be an object of attachment. All the attractive objects of the senses, such as physical form, wealth, pleasant sensations, and so forth, are by nature impermanent and unstable, and are actually deceptive and false phenomena with no true essence, like a plantain tree. Teaching this produces a revulsion, disgust, and sadness towards those objects. When disillusionment has thus arisen in the mental stream, the individual can study and contemplate selflessness, or the fact that oneself and others are empty of self

or substantial nature, and then through meditation actually realize it. This will result in a total or partial cessation of suffering. The Four Truths are taught as the path for achieving this result. Briefly, the Truth of Suffering is the teaching that all the three realms are by nature suffering. The Truth of Origination is that all tainted karma and afflicting emotions produce suffering. Therefore all the causes of saṃsāra are what must be abandoned. The Truth of Cessation, which is the cessation of all suffering, is what must be achieved. The Truth of the Path is the method by which that goal is reached.

8. Ibid., 17a–18b: The First Turning of the Dharma Wheel taught that all internal phenomena, such as the aggregates (*skandha*), are empty of an individual self, and that coarse external entities, such as forms, are merely phenomena that appear as a result of a combination of elements, atoms, and so forth. Now Dol po pa begins to describe the teachings of the Second Turning of the Dharma Wheel, which demonstrate not only the absence of a self or substantial nature in individual living beings, but also that there is no substantial nature to phenomena that are apprehended as external objects. Nya dbon specifies that although Dol po pa simply says "all phenomena" (*chos rnams thams cad*), it should be understood that he is referring only to "composite phenomena" (*'dus byas kyi chos*), all of which do indeed arise from a conjunction of causes and conditions, and never appear without a cause. However, it must be understood that there is no permanent self (*ātman*), no truly existing sentient beings, and no eternal soul (*srog*), in contrast to what the different non-Buddhist schools in India maintained. Nor is there any creator (*byed pa po*) of the animate and inanimate universe, such as the gods Śiva or Viṣṇu. In the absence of any permanent creator, phenomena appear only due to a combination of causes and conditions. For example, like a dream, which appears as a result of a combination of sleep and habitual propensities; or like the horses and cattle, which may appear in an illusion created by an illusionist using certain spells, drugs, and substances; or like seeing a shimmering mirage as a result of a combination of vapor from the earth being moved by subtle winds and struck by sunlight; or like an echo, which occurs due to the conditions of sound in conjunction with stone or other substances.

9. Ibid., 21a–23b: Having illustrated that all entities lack any substantial and absolute nature, Dol po pa now shows that both the dependent apprehending mind and the apprehended objects that appear to be external lack any such absolute nature. Although mountains, houses, human bodies, and so forth, appear to the five sense faculties to exist externally, there is no external entity that can withstand a rigorous examination in search of an absolute nature. Both the apprehension of the external appearance of the objects and the objects that so appear are merely the appearances of a deluded mind or consciousness contaminated by the

habitual propensities for dualistic appearances. It is a situation similar to that of a person with an eye disease who sees everything permeated with fine hairlike lines. There are no real external entities to be apprehended, but an apprehension of their external presence appears clearly in the mind, and thus it can be said that there is also no internal apprehending mind, intellect, or consciousness which is not deluded. The apparently external objects and the internal mind, intellect, and consciousness that perceive them to be so are merely affixed names or designations, empty of any true internal or external existence. They are empty like noncomposite space.

10. Ibid., 24b–26a: After demonstrating in the previous verse that both the apprehending mind and the apprehended objects that depend on the existence of external phenomena are not entities existing in absolute truth, Dol po pa now proceeds to show that the aggregates, constituents, and bases of sense cognition are also not entities existing in absolute truth. The ephemeral nature of the first three of the five aggregates of form, feeling, perception, conditioning factors, and consciousness are respectively compared to foam, water bubbles, and a mirage. The last two are traditionally compared to a plantain tree and an illusion. There is no truly existing self to be found in the twelve bases of sense cognition, the six pairs such as the eyes and form, and so forth, and so they are said to be like an empty town in which there are no residents and property owners. This example is from the *Dpal byin gyis zhus pa'i mdo*. The eighteen constituents, which are comprised of the six pairs of the twelve bases of sense cognition plus the six consciousnesses of sight, and so forth, are considered to be the causes or sources of suffering produced through interaction with entities. Since they cause a variety of harm, they are compared to vicious vipers.

11. Ibid., 26b–32a: In this verse Dol po pa indicates that among all the phenomena included in saṃsāra and nirvāṇa, there is not one truly existing entity. None of these phenomena have a true essence that can withstand a rigorous and reasoned examination. Therefore, in the ultimate sense, they are birthless. Since they have never been born, they cannot cease, and thus in the ultimate sense they are ceaseless. They are originally at peace and unestablished, and thus by nature nirvāṇa, empty and selfless. When reasonably examined from the absolute point of view, they do not go from here to anywhere else, they have not come here from anywhere else, and they do not remain like the noncomposite sky. Another way to interpret these terms is to say that the nature of all phenomena never goes out of existence or is destroyed, never comes into existence or is born, and does not permanently remain. Since extreme and middle are established in relation to each other, in the ultimate sense there is no first and last extreme, and thus no true phenomena in the middle between the two extremes. In brief, each and every one of these phenomena is in reality empty of any true essence.

12. Ibid., 32a–34a: With this verse Dol po pa begins to describe the Third Turning of the Dharma Wheel, the most distinctive feature of which is the teachings on the *tathāgatagarbha*, or Buddha-nature. The term *sugata*, "one gone to bliss," is used to describe a perfect buddha. The nature, heart, or essence (*garbha*) of such a buddha is radiant light, which is the essence of mind. While one is still an individual bound by all the various restrictions of the afflicting emotions, and so forth, this essence of mind, or radiant light, is referred to as *tathāgatagarbha*, Buddha-nature, but when one has become free from all the incidental impurities, it is referred to as the absolute buddha-body of reality (*don dam chos sku*). This definition is based on statements found in the *Śrīmālādevī*. This essence of buddhahood (*sangs rgyas kyi snying po*), the absolute buddha-body of reality, exists as noncomposite radiant light, which is the nature of all sentient beings, like the immutable sky. However, this is not directly perceived because it is obscured and covered by relative phenomena that do not exist by nature, because unlike the Buddha-nature, which is originally unproduced by causes and conditions, these relative factors are newly arisen and thus incidental accumulations or aggregates of various phenomena. The Buddha-nature exists within the mental stream of all emotionally afflicted sentient beings as their true nature (*dharmatā*) but is concealed within the incidental heaps or aggregates, the sheath or envelope of the incidental impurities. In a number of scriptures, such as the *Tathāgatagarbha sūtra* and the *Avataṃsaka sūtra*, nine similes are used for the Buddha-nature concealed within the impurities. The simile of the expanse of reality (*dharmadhātu*), which is considered synonymous with the Buddha-nature, being like a lamp inside a vase, is perhaps most widely cited from the *Dharmadhātu stotra* of Ārya Nāgārjuna. The simile of the Buddha-nature being like an unrecognized treasure in the earth beneath the home of a pauper, is found in the *Tathāgatagarbha sūtra*, and elsewhere.

13. Ibid., 34b–36a: Having established the existence of the Buddha-nature in the previous verse, Dol po pa now notes the importance of carefully distinguishing between what actually exists and what does not. This analysis is based on the paradigm of the *trisvabhāva*, or "three natures," common to the Cittamātra school of Indian Mahāyāna Buddhism. Dol po pa's opinions about this theory have already been discussed in some detail in chapter 3, section 2 of the present study. Nya dbon specifically refers to Dol po pa's opinions several times when commenting on this verse. According to Dol po pa, the phenomena of *parikalpita*, the "imagined nature," are nonexistent. The elements, and so forth, which appear to be external, actually have no existence outside of the consciousness of the beholder and thus are totally nonexistent, like the horn of a rabbit. This is termed the "authentic *parikalpita*" (*kun brtags mtshan nyid pa*). The concepts that

arise in the mind in the wake of the appearance of apparent phenomena, and thus identify those phenomena as external, are termed "the *parikalpita* existing in merely the conventional sense" (*tha snyad tsam du yod pa'i kun brtags*). The *paratantra*, the "dependent nature," is also twofold. The "impure *paratantra*" (*ma dag pa'i gzhan dbang*) is all the ordinary worldly thoughts and mental states. The "pure *paratantra*" (*dag pa'i gzhan dbang*) is the composite gnosis which directly realizes selflessness and the worldly gnosis experienced outside of meditation sessions. These are the "dependent nature" because they arise from causes and conditions. The *parinispanna*, the "fully established nature," is the state of ultimate reality, which can withstand rigorous and reasoned examination from the absolute point of view and is empty of both *parikalpita* and *paratantra*. In this way all the imagined and dependent phenomena of *parikalpita* and *paratantra* are nonexistent in reality, whereas the *parinispanna* is fully established in reality, is never nonexistent as the true nature of phenomena, and always exists in truth. To say that the first two natures exist in the absolute sense is the extreme view of eternalism, and to say that the third nature does not exist in the absolute sense is the extreme view of nihilism. This *parinispanna*, or absolute reality, is the ultimate Madhyamaka, or middle, which transcends those two extremes. Here Nya dbon pointedly observes that those who maintain that the absolute buddha-body of reality, and so forth, do not exist in the absolute sense, but do exist in the relative sense, are maintaining a very unreasonable position. He says this is not different from saying "there is no horse in this horse, but there is in a donkey" (*rta 'di rta du med kyi bong bu du yod*).

14. Ibid., 36a–b: Now Dol po pa points out the necessity to distinguish between what arises in dependent origination (*pratītyasamutpāda*, *rten cing 'brel bar byung ba*) and what does not. All composite and relative phenomena are the results of specific causes and conditions, and thus are said to merely arise in a process of dependent origination. On the other hand, the absolute noncomposite buddha-body of reality is self-arisen, and not produced by causes and conditions. The gnosis of the expanse of reality (*dharmadhātu*), which is naturally established from the beginning, transcends dependent origination. A distinction must be made between gnosis that is newly arisen from causes and conditions and self-arisen gnosis, which is different from that. In his explanatory comments on this verse Nya dbon specifically notes that Nāgārjuna's famous statement that there are no phenomena whatsoever that do not arise in dependent origination is intended to apply to composite phenomena. Furthermore, Nya dbon mentions that Avalokiteśvara, by whom he means the Shambhala emperor Kalkin Puṇḍarīka, stated that absolute truth, such as the essential buddha-body (*svābhāvikakāya*), is not subject to dependent origination. It is also taught in the *Saṃdhinirmocana sūtra* that noncomposite phenomena transcend dependent origination.

15. Ibid., 36b–37b: In this verse Dol po pa first begins to speak of tantra, and especially the teachings of the *Kālacakra tantra*. In the particular terminology of the *Kālacakra*, the "outer" is the inanimate world, the "inner" is the bodies of sentient beings, and the "other" is chiefly the *svābhāvikakāya*, the "essential buddha-body," or the *sahajakāya*, the "coemergent buddha-body." All of the outer and inner, or inanimate and animate phenomena included in saṃsāra are the deluded appearances of consciousness projected (*sprul pa*) by a beginningless ignorance. Thus they are merely the deluded sphere of this ignorance, and if examined carefully can be seen to lack any truth whatsoever. Self-arisen gnosis, which is the true nature of reality, is other than, or superior to, that deluded sphere of outer and inner phenomena, because it has not been produced by causes and conditions, and is a primal buddhahood (*ādibuddha*, *dang po'i sangs rgyas*). Furthermore, the eight groups of consciousness, and so forth, are characterized by imperfect conceptualization, and thus deluded and lacking in awareness. The dominance of this state of consciousness keeps sentient beings circling in saṃsāra. On the other hand, the gnosis of a bodhisattva of the tenth spiritual level during meditation, as well as the composite gnosis of a buddha, directly perceives the perfect nature of reality and is not included in the categories of outer and inner. It is the authentic other, as referred to above. Consciousness is blind to perfect reality, whereas even the composite self-arisen gnosis of highly realized bodhisattvas and buddhas directly perceives reality. It is also important to clearly distinguish between saṃsāra, which is composed of all the outer and inner inanimate and animate phenomena that are projections of ignorance, and the varieties of gnosis mentioned above, which are the phenomena of nirvāṇa. There are many different ways to describe relative and absolute truth. For example, they may be distinguished by speaking of the creation stage meditations as the relative and the profound perfection stage as the absolute. In this context, the process of an ordinary person mentally conceiving of a deity in meditation—which is not actually the perfect deity—is the relative, whereas the emptiness endowed with all sublime aspects which arises as the actual object of meditation during the cultivation of the profound perfection stage practices, such as *pratyāhara*, Individual Withdrawal, the first branch of the Six-branch Yoga, is the absolute truth. The gnosis arisen due to another (*gzhan byung ye shes*) directly perceives sublime emptiness due to the force of meditation, and is absolute truth, but not actually the ultimate absolute truth (*mthar thug don dam bden pa dngos*).

16. Ibid., 37b–38a: After distinguishing between the two truths, and so forth, in relation to the triad of outer, inner, and other, Dol po pa again defines the two truths, but now in relation to the threefold universe (*srid gsum*). This verse continues to focus on the specific view of the *Kālacakra*

tantra as explained in the *Vimalaprabhā*. The relative threefold universe is the three realms included in saṃsāra. These are deluded appearances projected by ignorance, and as such they are in reality a mere fiction, and may be destroyed by perfect gnosis. The empty forms (*śūnyabimba*, *stong gzugs*) which clearly arise in the form of the threefold universe that appears during direct yogic perception are the absolute threefold universe. Since precisely that is the radiant light of the nature of mind, it is the Buddha-nature. It is indestructible, and since it is the ultimate perfect nature, it is not fictionalized by concepts of the yoga practitioner, and is the appearance of an undeluded cognition.

17. Ibid., 38a–b: Previously Dol po pa presented the individual teachings of each of the Three Turnings of the Dharma Wheel, and now he deals with the teachings of all three together. The teachings of the First Turning of the Dharma Wheel focus primarily on the Four Truths, and stress that all composite phenomena are impermanent, that everything tainted produces suffering, that all phenomena lack substantial nature, that individual beings are empty of self-nature, and so forth. The Second Turning of the Dharma Wheel teaches that in the absolute sense all phenomena are without essence, are birthless, ceaseless, and so forth, and in reality have no true specific or general characteristics. In the Third Turning of the Dharma Wheel it is taught that everything relative does not exist in absolute reality, but it is also taught that the ultimate nature of phenomena certainly and truly does exist in absolute reality.

18. Ibid., 38b: After the three stains of the mental continua of fortunate disciples have been cleansed by the nectar stream of the Three Turnings of the Dharma Wheel in sequence, which cures the illnesses of the afflicting emotions, the sublime jewel of the buddha-body of reality (*dharmakāya*) free from stain may be obtained. The stains of ignorance due to which the existence of a self in individuals is accepted are removed by the teachings of the First Turning of the Dharma Wheel. The stains of ignorance due to which composite entities such as the apprehending mind and apprehended objects are believed to actually exist are removed by the teachings of the Second Turning of the Dharma Wheel. The stains of ignorance due to which it is believed that nothing exists in the absolute are removed by the teachings of the Third Turning of the Dharma Wheel, which carefully distinguish between what really exists and what does not.

In this verse there are significant variants among the two editions of the *Bstan pa spyi 'grel* and its commentary. Following the 'Dzam thang edition of the basic text, 496, and Nya dbon, *Bstan pa*, 38b, which both read *rin chen*, instead of the *rang bzhin* found in the Bhutanese edition, 689, I have translated "jewel" instead of "nature." Both the Bhutanese edition, 689, and Nya dbon, *Bstan pa*, 38b, have *thob*, instead of the *ston* found in the 'Dzam thang edition, 496. Thus I have translated "obtained" instead of "teach." It should be noticed, however, that *ston*, "teach," is found at the end of most of the other verses in both editions of the text.

19. Ibid., 38b–39a: Those individuals who maintain the truth of external phenomena, such as atoms, learn through reasoned examination, study, and contemplation, that the three realms are not externally existent, and are actually just mind. They are taught that everything is just mind, consciousness, or the appearance of consciousness. But then some individuals who accept the nonexistence of external phenomena become attached to the internal mind that appears as external phenomena, and believe it to be true or real. They must be taught that all external and internal entities are in the absolute sense empty. Therefore, in the absolute sense nothing is established as real, and nothing appears or is seen during meditative equipoise. This is the Madhyamaka of no appearance (*snang med dbu ma*), in which it is taught that seeing nothing is seeing reality. Statements to this effect, found in certain sūtras, and in some of the works of Ārya Nāgārjuna, are intentional (*dgongs pa can*) and provisional in meaning. But some individuals become attached to these teachings, and maintain that absolutely nothing is established in the absolute sense, and that even in the meditative equipoise of highly advanced bodhisattvas of the Mahāyāna nothing whatever appears, and there is merely an absence of conceptual elaboration (*spros bral tsam*). These persons must be taught that perfect reality directly appears and is seen in the meditative equipoise of the Mahāyāna, and that this is the authentic Madhyamaka of perfect appearance (*yang dag snang ba'i dbu ma*), or the profound referential emptiness (*dmigs bcas stong nyid*).

20. Ibid., 39b–40a: Individuals with inferior faculties who believe that pleasant and painful results are caused by a permanent self in individuals, or by a supreme creator god, or by chance, are taught the infallible truth of cause and result, in which it is understood that good results come from good causes, bad results come from bad causes, and mixed results come from mixed causes. In this way they learn to cultivate virtuous actions and avoid nonvirtue. But those who adhere to the true and absolute existence of all phenomena, such as cause and result, must be taught that all such phenomena are in reality empty of any true essence. Such teachings as these in the scriptures are intended to show that all relative phenomena have no absolutely true nature. But those individuals who have not fully comprehended the significance of these teachings, and have come to believe that the nature of reality is a simple freedom from conceptual elaboration (*spros bral*), and that nothing whatsoever is established, must be taught that the immutable Buddha-nature of radiant light, the absolute buddha-body of reality, is always present (*rtag du gnas*).

21. Ibid., 40a–41a: In this verse Dol po pa refers to the necessity of giving teachings that correspond to the abilities of the recipients. Individuals who are striving for liberation may be classified according to their naturally dull, middling, or acute faculties. Those disciples who have naturally inferior and dull faculties are taught the "vehicle of the listeners" (*śrāvakayāna*), and thus escape from saṃsāra. The śrāvaka, or "listener," listens to and practices the teachings of a buddha, or other spiritual master, throughout all stages of the path. When this individual finally becomes an arhat, which is the goal of the śrāvaka vehicle, he then orally explains the Dharma to others based upon the degree of his own realization. Those disciples with naturally middling faculties are taught the "vehicle of the solitary buddhas" (*pratyekabuddhayāna*), and thus escape from saṃsāra. The pratyekabuddha, or "solitary buddha," strives to become an arhat only for his own benefit, and at the point of achieving the goal he does not teach the Dharma of the Buddha to others. Those disciples with naturally superior and acute faculties are taught the sublime vehicle, the Mahāyāna. From among them, those with dull faculties are taught the vehicle of the perfections (*pāramitāyāna*) in which the cause, emptiness, is taken as the path. Those with acute faculties are taught the mantra vehicle (*mantrayāna*), in which the result, bliss, is taken as the path.

22. Ibid., 41b: After mentioning the importance of teaching the three vehicles according to the natural faculties of disciples, Dol po pa now focuses upon the need to care for disciples according to their stages of development. Loving fathers and mothers care for their children from when they are infants up until they are young adults, providing them with food and drink, clothing and shoes, and so forth, according to the development of their bodies and minds. Likewise, a spiritual master cares for disciples according to their states of mind, inclinations, faculties, and so forth, by means of the teachings of the Three Turnings of the Dharma Wheel in sequence, and especially by means of the Vajrayāna teachings of secret mantra.

23. Ibid., 41b–42a: Now Dol po pa speaks of guiding disciples according to the mental abilities (*blo nus*) that will enable them to achieve either the results of the higher realms or of liberation. This verse presents an alternative approach to that of the previous verse. It is customary to assign worldly work to children of inferior, middling, and superior faculties or intelligence, according to each one's character (*rgyud*) or mental ability. Likewise, the classifications of the view, meditation, conduct, result, and so forth, of the Three Turnings of the Dharma Wheel, and especially of the tradition of secret mantra, should be taught according to the individual character, mental ability, and good fortune of the disciples.

24. Ibid., 42a–43a: With this verse Dol po pa makes clear the necessity to progress through the teachings of the Three Turnings of the Dharma

Wheel in sequence, and then proceed to those of the mantra vehicle, in that way moving from the lower teachings up to the highest. For example, in the three-storied mansion of a royal minister one climbs up to the top floor and there enjoys oneself. Likewise, one should climb up in the three-storied Dharma mansion of scripture and realization, the Doctrine of the Buddha which is arranged sequentially according to the teachings of the Three Turnings of the Dharma Wheel, and especially the Turning of the Dharma Wheel of secret mantra. Then one should enjoy the teachings of the Mahāyāna, which are like the top floor, and from among them, those of the Vajrayāna. In this way the sublime result may quickly be reached. Furthermore, Nya dbon declares that those who claim that the mantra vehicle follows the Cittamātra tradition, and that the view and meditation of the Madhyamaka is higher than that of the tantras, are extremely deluded. They hold a nihilistic emptiness (*chad stong*) to be supreme, and are lacking the practical experience of the profound Dharma.

25. Ibid., 43a--b: There are numerous statements of definitive meaning in many sūtras and tantras which specify that all sentient beings possess the Buddha-nature, which is synonymous with the nature of mind, radiant light, and emptiness endowed with all sublime aspects. This is also the absolute buddha-body of reality, which is thus present in all sentient beings. This is not something achieved or obtained, but the innate true nature of all living beings. It is always present, but while it is obscured or veiled by the incidental stains, such as attachment, it is not seen or heard about, and living beings continue to circle in saṃsāra. To gain liberation from saṃsāra it is necessary to remove those stains. The method of their removal is mentioned by Dol po pa in this verse. For example, a skillful jeweler cleanses in sequence the coarse, subtle, and extremely subtle stains which may cover a large piece of beryl, or any other jewel. Likewise, the Buddha-nature, the absolute buddha-body of reality, exists in the mental continua of all sentient beings, but is obscured by the veils of the incidental stains. Therefore, the three coarse, subtle, and extremely subtle incidental stains that veil the existence of the Buddha-nature within each living being must be cleansed by means of training in the meaning of the Three Turnings of the Dharma Wheel in sequence, and especially the Turning of the Dharma Wheel of secret mantra. This is the most important message of all the Turnings of the Dharma Wheel. Dol po pa's use of the example of the jeweler cleaning the beryl, and the teachings of the Three Turnings of the Dharma Wheel cleansing the three stains of the Buddha-nature, is based upon a detailed passage found in the *Bde bzhin gshegs pa'i thugs rje chen po bstan pa'i mdo*.

26. Ibid., 43b–44b: Dol po pa begins this series of verses on mantra by mentioning the cause and result of the Buddha-nature that are taught in numerous sūtras and tantras. This cause and result is not a productive

cause, like a seed, or a produced result, like a sprout. As stated in the *Vimalaprabhā*, there is another cause and another result, a noncomposite cause and result. The other cause of the Buddha-nature is the natural radiant light of emptiness endowed with all sublime qualities. This is the other forms of emptiness (*stong nyid gzugs gżhan*), the empty forms (*stong gzugs*) that are directly seen by means of the yogic practices of the *ṣaḍaṅgayoga*, or Six-branch Yoga. These forms are also referred to in the *Prajñāpāramitā sūtra*s, and elsewhere, as "the forms of the true nature" (*chos nyid kyi gzugs*). The other result of the Buddha-nature is naturally immutable great bliss (*rang bzhin 'gyur med kyi bde ba chen po*), which is not merely the bliss of immutable melting bliss (*zhu bde 'gyur med kyi bde ba*). This noncomposite bliss and emptiness is the Buddha-nature, the absolute buddha-body of reality, the ultimate true nature of phenomena. It is not just the absence of conceptual elaboration (*spros bral*), which is so well known in the ordinary vehicles as an emptiness of negation established through analytical refutation. This other result is similar to the prognostic images (*pratisenā*, *pra phab*) or other forms that may directly appear to a young girl during a traditional ceremony of divination. The simile of the eight prognostic images has an important role in the teachings of the *Kālacakra tantra* and the *Vimalaprabhā*. (See note 92 in the translation of *The Fourth Council* for a full explanation of the eight types of prognostic images.) Likewise, the other result, other forms, or empty forms arise clearly and directly to the specifically self-aware gnosis (*so so rang rig ye shes*) of a yogin. If this were only the emptiness that is an absence of conceptual elaboration, an emptiness of negation established through analytical refutation, it would be impossible for it to ever appear directly to anyone. In this way, those who pride themselves in maintaining that sublime emptiness is only an emptiness of self-nature (*rang stong*) are left with a problem—the impossibility of a direct realization, or appearance as a knowable, of absolute reality, the true nature of phenomena.

27. Ibid., 44b–45a: Ultimate emptiness, the emptiness endowed with all sublime aspects, is referred to by many different names in the profound tantras. Dol po pa has drawn his examples from a number of sources. In both the *Saṃvara mūla tantra* and the *Saṃvara laghu tantra*, the "secret" (*gsang*) and the "great secret" (*gsang chen*) are spoken of as the ever-present quintessence (*bdag nyid*) of everything, or of all sentient beings. In the *Vajrapañjāra tantra*, and elsewhere, the "element of space" (*mkha' khams*) is referred to as being not inanimate (*bems min*), and also described as awareness or cognition (*shes pa*). And in the *Prajñāpāramitā sūtra*s it is said that meditation on the perfection of transcendent knowledge is meditation upon space. In the *Kālacakra tantra* emptiness is called by the name Viśvamāta (Sna tshogs yum), who is actually the consort of

Kālacakra. She bears this name, meaning "Variegated Mother," because she is both emptiness endowed with all sublime aspects and the Great Seal (*mahāmudrā, phyag rgya chen mo*). In the *Hevajra tantra*, and elsewhere, emptiness is spoken of as *dharmākara*, "source of phenomena," and as *bhagā*, "vagina, womb." This is because the qualities such as the ten powers of an enlightened being, which arise due to other factors (*gzhan byung yon tan*), are newly born in the continuum of an individual who has perfected the meditation and actualized the realization of emptiness; whereas, the infinite qualities of the noncomposite buddha-body of reality are naturally present. In other scriptures, such as the *Vajrabhairava tantra* known in Tibetan as the *Rnal 'byor rjes su rig pa'i rgyud*, emptiness is referred to as *padma*, "lotus." In the *Kālacakra tantra* emptiness is also given the name "lion-throne" (*seng ge'i khri*). It is like a lion because all the packs of the wild beasts of the two emotional and intellectual obscurations have been naturally vanquished from the beginning, and like a throne because it naturally supports the great bliss from which it is indivisible. Likewise, emptiness is Vajra Nairātmyā, "the Adamantine Selfless One," the consort of Hevajra, because it is empty of both types of self. It is Vajra Varāhī, "the Adamantine Sow," the consort of Cakrasaṃvara, because it is free from all concepts of pure and impure, and so forth. Almost all of the names cited in this verse are also found mentioned together in quotes from the *Kālacakra mūla tantra*.

28. Ibid., 45a–b: Now Dol po pa notes that this same emptiness itself is also absolute, ultimate, and immutable great bliss, and as such is referred to by many different names. This great bliss is *vajra*, "adamantine," because it cannot be cut or destroyed by the weapons of conceptualization, but in fact vanquishes them. It is called *bindu* (*thig le*), "drop," because it is by nature great bliss. *He* means emptiness of cause, and so forth; *ru* means apart from groups; and *ka* means not dwelling anywhere. It is *samāja*, "gathering," because it gathers the great bliss of all the buddhas. It is *saṃvara* (*sdom pa*), "restraint," because the habitual propensity for the emission of sexual fluids has been abandoned. *He* and *mahākaruṇā* both mean great compassion. Great bliss is referred to as the primal Buddha (*ādibuddha*) because all obscurations have been absent from the beginning, not just removed by the force of meditating upon the path. According to the *Vimalaprabhā*, the term *ādi* (*dang po*) means without beginning and without end. In a number of scriptural sources great bliss is also referred to as absolute *bodhicitta*, "enlightenment mind."

29. Ibid., 45b–46a: Dol po pa now makes the important point that ultimate great bliss is cognition (*shes pa*), because it is a complete intrinsic awareness of both self and others (*bdag rig gzhan rig thams cad pa*). And it is the profound emptiness which is the most sublime of all that can be known or cognized, and is what must be directly realized. Both great bliss

and emptiness, the cognition and that which is to be cognized, appear in enlightened divine forms known by many names, such as Vajrasattva, Evaṃ, Kālacakra, Cakrasaṃvara, Hevajra, Māyājāla, Guhyasamāja, and so forth. All of these names have the single meaning of the total integration of bliss and emptiness.

30. Ibid., 46a–b: In general the Buddhist teachings speak of a triad of spiritual ground, path, and result. Here Dol po pa focuses upon the absolute and ultimate "universal ground" (*ālaya*, *kun gzhi*). This he identifies with the total integration of ultimate bliss and emptiness described in the previous verse. Bliss and emptiness in total integration are indivisible, and thus equal-flavored. This indestructible state cannot be destroyed by conceptualization, and so forth, and is known as self-arisen gnosis because it is an intrinsic awareness of self and others that has not been produced by causes and conditions. Since it is also an originally primal or natural buddhahood, it is called *ādibuddha*, "primal Buddha." These different names all signify the absolute buddha-body of reality that is present as the true nature of the mental continua of all individuals. This exists in impure circumstances and also in circumstances when the impurities have been purified. Since the absolute buddha-body of reality is present as the true nature of a mental continuum in which the incidental stains exist, it is referred to as thusness with stains (*dri bcas de bzhin nyid*). Furthermore, like the sky upon which the wind is dependent, this absolute buddha-body of reality, the total integration of bliss and emptiness, is known as the universal ground because in dependence upon it liberation is achieved through energetic practice of the path to liberation, or the lower realms are experienced because of an accumulation of nonvirtuous acts. This universal ground, the true nature described in scripture as the natural radiant light of mind, must not be confused with the "universal ground consciousness" (*ālayavijñāna*, *kun gzhi rnam shes*), which is one of the eight groups of consciousness.

31. Ibid., 46b: After describing the universal spiritual ground, Dol po pa now briefly mentions the ultimate path for actualizing the reality of the primal Buddha (*ādibuddha*) with stains. Precisely that primal Buddha is in essence itself primordially separate from the sheath of the incidental stains, but there is a special method for separating it from the incidental stains that bind the mental continua of sentient beings in which it is present. This method is known as the path of the Vajrayoga, or "adamantine yoga," which is another name for the Six-branch Yoga (*ṣaḍaṅgayoga*), the path of the perfection of transcendent knowledge (*prajñāpāramitā*), the path of the Atiyoga, and the path of the meditation of the Great Seal. This is felt to be the direct path to the ultimate result. Although Nya dbon does not comment on these terms, it is probable that in this context Dol po pa intends for the term *Atiyoga* (*shin tu rnal 'byor*) to be understood as

the perfection stage practices of the *Guhyasamāja tantra* and not the practices of the Great Perfection, which also go under that name. This seems probable because the Six-branch Yoga is also explicitly taught in the *Guhyasamāja*.

32. Ibid., 46b–47a: The primal Buddha (*ādibuddha*) is present throughout beginningless time as the spiritual ground that is itself naturally separate from all stains. Through the practice of the sublime method of the nonconceptual path, the path of the meditation of the Great Seal, and the force of the cultivation of nonconceptual calm and insight, all of the incidental stains in the mental continuum of an individual who has perfected this meditation are purged, or removed, and the ultimate result of immaculate thusness, or reality, remains. It is essential to understand that this was not previously absent and now newly arisen, but is referred to as the result which is merely actualized or obtained due to the force of having perfected the meditation of the path. For example, when the clouds, dust, and so forth, in the sky are swept away by the force of a strong wind, the noncomposite sky itself remains. The composite clouds, and so forth, do not benefit or harm the essence of the sky in any way. Likewise, the composite incidental stains do not benefit or harm the essence of the absolute buddha-body of reality that is always present as the spiritual ground. The incidental stains merely prevent what is known as the gnosis arisen due to another (*gzhan byung ye shes*) from directly perceiving this reality, and prevent the appearance of the ultimate produced results (*bskyed 'bras*) of the emanation buddha-body (*nirmāṇakāya*) and the buddha-body of rapture (*sambhogakāya*).

33. Ibid., 47a: The excellent benefit of oneself and others is the result to be achieved through the perfection of meditation on the path. In this verse Dol po pa describes the result that is beneficial for oneself. That which is to be cultivated, or meditated upon, is the Great Seal (*mahāṁudrā*) of naturally immutable radiant light. The force of the perfect cultivation of the assembly of nonconceptual gnosis arisen due to another (*gzhan byung ye shes*) destroys the sheath of stains that obscure or veil the self-arisen gnosis (*rang byung ye shes*). This reveals or actualizes the absolute buddha-body of reality endowed with infinite noncomposite qualities, and thus the excellent benefit for oneself is achieved.

34. Ibid., 47a–b: Now Dol po pa describes what it takes to achieve real benefit for others. The radiant light of the absolute buddha-body of reality is present in all sentient beings as the nature of their minds, but it is obscured by ignorance. Without seeing it, and without understanding that it is there, sentient beings go through the three realms of saṃsāra by virtue of their tainted acts and afflicting emotions. Acting with a special attitude of great love for all sentient beings suffering in saṃsāra, and with

a wish to free them from their suffering and its causes, accumulates the assembly of merit which creates benefit in this life and happiness in the next, or the temporary benefit of rebirth in the higher realms and the lasting benefit of the great bliss of liberation. As a result of this accumulation of merit, the two excellent relative buddha-bodies of form (*rūpakāya*) are produced, and with them the ultimate excellent benefit of others is accomplished.

Following the reading in both the 'Dzam thang edition of the basic text, 499, and the commentary, I have in this verse translated "without understanding" (*ma rtogs*), instead of the "maternal" (*ma gyur*), which is found only in the Bhutanese edition of the basic text, 691.

35. Ibid., 47b–48a: In this verse Dol po pa answers a hypothetical objection to his teachings. Some might object that if the noncomposite absolute buddha-body of reality is present within us there is no need for any perfection, maturation, or purification. Dol po pa answers by specifying what must still be perfected, matured, and purified. An infinite sea of prayers for the liberation of sentient beings who have not yet been liberated must be fully perfected or realized. If it is accepted that saṃsāra has an end, the perfection of infinite prayers means actually establishing all sentient beings in buddhahood. If it is accepted that saṃsāra is endless, the perfection of the prayers means becoming endowed with the complete causes necessary for establishing all sentient beings in nirvāṇa. This sea of infinite sentient beings must be spiritually matured, and thus become able to abandon whatever is to be abandoned, able to employ the appropriate antidotes to the afflicting emotions, and so forth, and able to proceed upon the perfect path to liberation. According to the *Vimalakīrti upadésa sūtra*, the purification of pure realms, or buddha fields, actually means the purification of one's own mind. Furthermore, whatever realm one achieves buddhahood in becomes the realm from which one must establish an infinite number of sentient beings in the higher realms or in liberation. Each bodhisattva who achieves buddhahood in the buddha-body of rapture (*sambhogakāya*) in an infinite number of realms throughout the universe then manifests an infinite number of emanation buddha-bodies (*nirmāṇakāya*) for the purpose of benefiting the infinite sentient beings in those infinite realms for whose benefit previous prayers have been made. After perfection, maturation, and purification have been accomplished in this way, one dissolves into, or actualizes, the enlightened form of the absolute true nature (*don dam chos nyid kyi sku*), a culmination which is perfectly true, stable, and infallible, unlike the false and fallible relative phenomena.

36. Ibid., 48a–b: In this verse Dol po pa again addresses a potential objection to his view of enlightenment. Some may say that if one dissolves into the perfect culmination (*yang dag pa'i mtha'*) at the point of attaining

buddhahood, there will then be no gnosis (*ye shes med par 'gyur*), and that in fact this is an excellent view because it is the opinion of the Madhyamaka masters such as Nāgārjuna, Candrakīrti, and Śāntideva. Dol po pa uses traditional examples to illustrate his response. The fine magical vase provides whatever food, clothing, wealth, and so forth are necessary. And the orb of the sun, the wish-fulfilling jewel, the heavenly tree, and the great divine drum of the gods in the thirty-third heaven all benefit sentient beings without effort and without thought. Likewise, without exerting any effort and without any thought of performing a specific action to bring about any specific benefit, what is beneficial to others will spontaneously occur in all directions and at all times due to the fully perfected force of the impetus of previous prayers in which one has prayed for the ability to provide sentient beings with whatever they need. Furthermore, the use of these examples to illustrate the spontaneous occurrence of a buddha's enlightened activities is actually in agreement with the teachings of Nāgārjuna, Candrakīrti, and Śāntideva. The intention of their statements is not that the enlightened actions occur in the absence of gnosis, but that actions beneficial to others still occur in the absence of conscious thought.

37. Ibid., 48b–49a: In keeping with the teachings of the *Saṃdhinirmocana sūtra*, Dol po pa maintains that the Third Turning of the Dharma Wheel clearly presents the ultimate definitive meaning without concealing it in any way, and that this Final or Third Turning of the Dharma Wheel is thus the Ultimate Turning of the Dharma Wheel. From among the three vehicles (*yāna*, *theg pa*), the ultimate or consummate vehicle is the Mahāyāna, the "great vehicle." The ultimate pinnacle of the Mahāyāna teachings are the teachings that actually and clearly present the Buddha-nature that is pure, self (*ātman*), blissful, and permanent (*gtsang bdag bde dang rtag pa*). Thus the ultimate Buddha-nature is pure and permanent great bliss. Here Dol po pa specifies that the ultimate Buddha-nature is great bliss in order to refute the mistaken opinions of those who identify it with a true nature that is a mere freedom from conceptual elaborations (*chos nyid spros bras tsam*), or a nihilistic emptiness (*chad stong*); those who identify it with the mere awareness and clarity of the present state of mind (*da lta'i sems rig cing gsal tsam*); those who identify it with the universal ground consciousness (*ālayavijñāna*, *kun gzhi rnam shes*); and those who maintain that it is the mere seed of buddhahood (*sangs rgyas kyi sa bon tsam*) that is present on the surface of the universal ground consciousness, but which cannot be identified as anything composite or noncomposite, tainted or untainted.

38. Ibid., 49a–b: In general, the ultimate scriptures and realization of the Buddhist Doctrine are the teachings of the scriptures and realization of the Mahāyāna, and the ultimate scriptures and realization of the Mahāyāna are the scriptures and realization of the Mantrayāna. Likewise,

the ultimate scriptures and realization of the Mantrayāna are the teachings of the scriptures and realization of Kālacakra. The ultimate scriptures and realization of Kālacakra are those passages of scripture which present naturally immutable great bliss and emptiness endowed with all sublime aspects, as well as the actual realization of the great bliss and profound emptiness they express. Here Dol po pa has specified the ultimate Kālacakra as a total integration of bliss and emptiness in order to refute those who maintain that the ultimate Kālacakra is only composite, and so forth.

39. Ibid., 49b–50a: From among the four great philosophical systems in Buddhism, Dol po pa maintains that the ultimate philosophical system is that of the Great Madhyamaka (**mahāmadhyamaka*, *dbu ma chen po*), the "Great Middle Way." The ultimate Madhyamaka is free from all extremes, as stated by Ārya Nāgārjuna. Reality may be said to be free from the four extremes of existence, nonexistence, both, and neither. And although it is birthless and ceaseless, it must be free from the extremes of eternalism and nihilism. The ultimate freedom from extremes is not just a separation or absence, but a radiant light which is the nature of mind. And the ultimate radiant light is a naturally immutable great bliss. There is no radiant light that is the true nature of mind and not a naturally immutable great bliss, but some upholders of the tantric teachings identified the true nature as completely unestablished, and merely a nonreferential absence of subject and object. Here Dol po pa makes a point of stating that ultimate radiant light is great bliss in order to refute such mistaken opinions.

40. Ibid., 50a: In general there are both mistaken views, such as those of eternalism and nihilism, and correct views. There are also both the correct mundane view that pleasant and unpleasant results come from virtuous and sinful actions, and the correct views of the Buddhist philosophical systems which are primarily concerned with the nature of the absolute and the relative. In this verse Dol po pa states that the ultimate object of such a view is emptiness free from all extremes, which was dealt with in the previous verse. And the ultimate emptiness free from extremes is the profound emptiness that is referential (*dmigs bcas*), or clearly and directly perceived by a perfectly discriminating self-aware gnosis (*yang dag pa'i so so rang rig ye shes*). The ultimate conduct which serves as a method for achieving enlightenment is a great compassion intent upon liberating all sentient beings from suffering and its causes. And this ultimate compassion has a quintessence of nonconceptual gnosis that is nonreferential (*dmigs med*), and in which there is no thought or concept of object, agent, and so forth.

41. Ibid., 50a–51a: In a majority of the tantric scriptures a fourfold scheme of initiation is taught, beginning with the Vase Initiation. In the *Kālacakra mūla tantra*, the *Vajrapañjāra tantra*, and others, eleven initia-

tions are taught. Moreover, there is a classification of both a mundane and a transcendent Vase Initiation. These are all termed "initiation, empowerment" (*abhiṣeka, dbang bskur ba*), because they initiate the disciple into the practice, or empower the disciple to perform the practice of the yoga of the two stages of meditation which lead either directly or eventually to liberation. From among these initiations, the ultimate initiation is the transcendent initiation, which is the Fourth Initiation. In most of the *laghu tantras* (*bsdus rgyud*), "condensed tantras," and most of the commentaries composed by Indian masters, the third initiation of the Gnosis Dependent on an Embodiment of Transcendent Knowledge (*shes rab ye shes kyi dbang*) is itself explained to be the Fourth Initiation, which is why the Fourth Initiation does not have a separate descriptive name, as do the first three. This explanation is followed in the *Hevajra tantra* and *The Trilogy of Bodhisattva Commentaries*. The ultimate method for the realization and achievement of enlightenment as the result of practice is the nonconceptual yoga of the profound perfection stage, which is taught to be the sole path of perfect enlightenment. The perfection stage is the practice of the definitive meaning made into the path for the attainment of buddhahood in this very lifetime, or in seven lifetimes, or within sixteen lifetimes, depending upon the skill of the practitioner. The paths of conceptual meditation, such as the creation stage, are not direct paths to the attainment of perfect enlightenment, and presentations of them as being so are intended to be understood as provisional in meaning (*drang don dgongs pa can*). The basic intention of such statements is that the creation stage paths act as antidotes to the many erroneous concepts which act as causes of suffering, and thus these paths are merely causes for eventual buddhahood. Initiation is basically granted for the purpose of achieving attainments (*siddhi, dngos grub*). There are two general classifications of attainments. The mundane attainments are just temporary, but the ultimate attainment is the sublime attainment of enlightenment. The ultimate initiation, perfection stage, and great attainment are taught for the benefit of ultimate disciples, who are not attached to the mundane attainments, and who are engaged in the single-minded practice of the nonconceptual yoga of the profound perfection stage.

42. Ibid., 51a–b: In general, many different topics are in the tantric scriptures, such as the nature of the maṇḍalas, deities, mantras, and mudrās. There are maṇḍalas drawn or painted on cloth, constructed of colored powders, and made from bunches of flowers. There is also the naturally created maṇḍala or body-maṇḍala. In some tantras there is a classification of seven maṇḍalas. But the sublime or ultimate maṇḍala is the natural radiant light of emptiness endowed with all sublime aspects. In the tantric scriptures this is what is being referred to when it is said that *maṇḍa* (*la*) is (*tathāgata*) *garbha*, or when the maṇḍala of absolute

enlightenment mind (*bodhicitta*) is mentioned. The ultimate deity is the buddha-body of gnosis (*ye shes sku*), the total integration of naturally immutable bliss and emptiness endowed with all sublime aspects. This is how Kālacakra himself is described in the *Vimalaprabhā*, and likewise his consort Viśvamāta is there described as the ultimate seal (*mudrā*), the Great Seal (*mahāmudrā*) of the natural radiant light of emptiness endowed with all sublime aspects. The term mantra is usually understood as a verbally recited formula, or a mentally conceptualized formula. But here the sublime or ultimate secret mantra is the gnosis of great nonreferential compassion and profound emptiness that directly perceives reality and thus protects the mind from afflicting emotions and conceptual marks. This interpretation corresponds to the etymology of the term *mantra* that is provided in the tantras, where it is stated that *man* means mind and *tra* means to protect.

43. Ibid., 51b–52a: In the sūtras and tantras there is discussion of the spiritual ground, path, and result. In particular there are many different descriptions of the ground, such as the universal ground consciousness (*ālayavijñāna*, *kun gzhi rnam shes*). But the ultimate ground is thusness, or reality, with stains, which has already been explained above. Although there are many descriptions of the paths to the higher realms and to liberation, the sublime ultimate path is the Six-branch Yoga (*ṣaḍaṅgayoga*), which is taught in many tantras and commentaries. There are also many different results mentioned in the scriptures and commentaries, but the sublime ultimate result is the thusness of the separated result (*bral 'bras*) of the absolute buddha-body of reality separate from all incidental stains. In this way, from the opening line of this eighth part of the main section of *A General Commentary on the Doctrine*, which stated "the ultimate Dharma Wheel is the Final Wheel," down through the last line of this final verse, which states "the ultimate result as the thusness of the separated result," the complete ultimate Dharma has been taught.

44. Shes rab rgyal mtshan dpal bzang po is the name Dol po pa received when taking full ordination.

45. As explained above, the separated result (*bral 'bras*) is the absolute buddha-body of reality (*dharmakāya*) separate from all incidental and relative stains; whereas, the produced result (*bskyed 'bras*) is the relative buddha-bodies of form (*rūpakāya*), composed of the emanation buddha-body (*nirmāṇakāya*) and the buddha-body of rapture (*sambhogakāya*), which are produced as a result of the accumulation of the assemblies of merit and gnosis.

46. The cleansing of the coarse, subtle, and extremely subtle stains upon the Buddha-nature, like a jeweler cleansing the three types of stains on a jewel, were mentioned in an earlier verse and explained in note 25 above.

47. This final exclamation, "may it be auspicious," is found in the 'Dzam thang edition, 501, and in Nya dbon, *Bstan pa*, 52b, but not in the Bhutanese edition.

Introduction to the Translation of *The Fourth Council*

1. The *Deb ther sngon po* of 'Gos Lo tsā ba lists these three, along with commentaries on the *Uttaratantra* and the *Abhisamayālaṇkāra*. See Roerich, trans. (1976), 777. Roerich's informant, the Tibetan scholar Dge 'dun chos 'phel, added the comment that monks of the Dge lugs pa sect were specifically forbidden to keep copies of the *Nges don rgya mtsho* and the *Bka' bsdu bzhi pa* within their monasteries. One of Dol po pa's successors, Jo nang Kun dga' grol mchog, quotes Byams gling Paṇ chen Bsod nams rnam rgyal's mention of the *Nges don rgya mtsho*, *Bstan pa spyi 'grel*, and *Bka' bsdu bzhi pa* as Dol po pa's major works. See Kun dga' grol mchog, *Rigs*, 22a–b. For a translation of this passage, see chapter 1, section 6.

2. Byang chub rtse mo, *Chos*, 31b.

3. See Lha'i rgyal mtshan, *Chos*, 39b, and Kun spangs, *Chos*, 363, for descriptions of the beginning of Dol po pa's trip to Central Tibet. The specific mention of horses and gold among the offerings made by Bla ma Dam pa is found only in the colophon of Dol po pa, *Bka' bsdu bzhi pa'i rang 'grel*, 665. The meeting between Dol po pa and Bla ma dam pa is mentioned in Lha'i rgyal mtshan, *Chos*, 39b; Kun spangs, *Chos*, 363; and Byang chub rtse mo, *Chos*, 36b. Mang thos klu grub, *Bstan*, 178, states that Dol po pa gave the *Bka' bsdu bzhi pa* to Bla ma dam pa at Chos lung in 1361, when Dol po pa was sixty-nine years old, which conflicts with the contemporary reports of Kun spangs pa and Byang chub rtse mo. Lha'i rgyal mtshan mentions the meeting in 1358, but not the composition of texts.

4. One troubling exception is a mention by Dol po pa himself of *The Fourth Council*. See Dol po pa, *Dpal*, 122. On 116 in this text Dol po pa mentions teaching the one-hundred-thousand-line *Prajñāpāramitā* according to the *Kālacakra* to a large gathering of scholars and practitioners in a Sheep year, which can only correspond to 1355. After a detailed list of the names of dozens of the recipients of this teaching, he mentions that it was given according to *The Great Calculation of the Doctrine*: *A Fourth Council* (*Bstan rtsis chen po bka' bsdus bzhi pa*), and some other canonical texts. This reference is somewhat problematic because the text in which it is found could well have been written some years after the event, which occurred at Brag lha Klu phug in the Lha sa area in 1355. See Kun spangs, *Chos*, 364.

5. These dates are mentioned in Byang chub rtse mo, *Chos*, 36a and 37a, and the textual transmission is mentioned on 36b.

6. The only known reference is by 'Jam mgon Kong sprul, in his commentary to the *Uttaratantra*. He refers to *The Fourth Council* as expressing the essence of the definitive meaning (*nītārtha*). See Hookam (1991), 277.

7. Lha'i rgyal mtshan, *Chos*, 29b–30a, quotes verses which are found in *Bka' bsdu bzhi pa*, 399–400, and 403. 'Ba' ra ba's comments are found in 'Ba' ra ba, *Skyes mchog 'ba'*, 602.

8. See Kapstein (1992) for a catalogue of the texts in both available editions of Dol po pa's writings. Kapstein (1991) is a description of his trip to Sichuan in search of texts.

9. See note 64 in chapter 1.

The Great Calculation of the Doctrine Which Has the Significance of a Fourth Council

1. In the translation of this title I have followed the spelling *bstan rtsis*, "calculation," found in the colophon of the Bhutanese edition, and in all other titles and colophons of the available editions of the text, its autocommentary, and its summary, instead of the near-homophone *gtan tshigs*, "decree, reasoning," etc., found only in the title of the Bhutanese edition. *Bstan rtsis* is also the spelling found in an independent reference to the text by Dol po pa himself, as mentioned above, and in his own explanation of the meaning of the title. See Dol po pa, *Bka' bsdu bzhi pa'i rang 'grel*, 665. It should also be noted that Dol po pa sometimes referred to himself as a "great calculator of the Doctrine" (*bstan rtsis chen po*). See Dol po pa, *Chos dbyings*, 755.

2. See note 1 in the translation of *A General Commentary on the Doctrine* for a full explanation of this Sanskrit expression of homage and offering with which Dol po pa also began that text.

3. See Ruegg (1989), especially 19–26, 40–44, and 50–55, for discussion of the equation of "self" (*ātman*, *bdag*) with the Buddha-nature (*tathāgatagrabha*) in a number of Mahāyāna scriptures.

4. On the theory of the four *yuga* (*caturyuga*, *dus bzhi*), and the four "feet" of the Dharma referred to below, see Newman (1987), 518, note 47; de La Vallée Poussin (1908), 189; and Jacobi (1908), 200.

5. The division of two sets of the four *yuga*, a greater concerning the duration of an eon and a lesser concerning the degeneration of the Buddhist Doctrine, is found in the *Vimalaprabhā*'s commentary on vs. 22 and

23 of the *Lokadhātupaṭala* of the *Kālacakra tantra*. See Kalkin Puṇḍarīka, *'Jig*, 469–71, and Newman (1987), 514–19. Bu ston's annotations, included in the edition of the Tibetan text, entirely agree with Dol po pa's presentation here. As mentioned in the following verse, the four *yuga* are known as Kṛtayuga, Dvāparayuga, Tretayuga, and Kaliyuga. According to the *Vimalaprabhā* the four *yuga* concerning the duration of the Doctrine are each 4,500 human years in length. The four great *yuga* which make a *kalpa* are each 1,080,000 human years in length. The *Vimalaprabhā* is chiefly concerned with the lesser *yuga*, and provides no further information about the nature of the great *yuga*.

6. The same exact number of years is given by Bu ston in his annotations to the *Vimalaprabhā*. See Kalkin Puṇḍarīka, *'Jig*, 470, and Newman (1987), 516. In the translation I have followed the reading in the 'Dzam thang edition, 208, which has *bzhi cha*, "a quarter," whereas the Bhutanese edition has *bcu cha*, "a tenth," which is clearly a scribal error.

7. This is precisely according to the *Vimalaprabhā*'s commentary on vs. 23 of the *Lokadhātupaṭala* of the *Kālacakra tantra*. See Kalkin Puṇḍarīka, *'Jig*, 471, and Newman (1987), 518. On 519, note 49, Newman mentions that the equal duration of the *yuga*s presented here in the *Vimalaprabhā* is unusual. The more common arrangement, which he mentions as being the case in the *Manusmṛti* and the *Mahābhārata*, is one of unequal *yuga*s, with the Kṛtayuga lasting 4,800 years, the Tretayuga 3,600 years, the Dvāparayuga 2,400 years, and the Kaliyuga 1,200 years. The years of the *yuga*s are more often calculated by divine years consisting of 360 human years. See Jacobi (1908), 200–201. According to Pingree (1981), 14, Āryadeva's *Āryabhaṭīya* has a system of equal *yuga*s, each of which lasts 1,080,000 human years. This agrees with Dol po pa's figure in the previous verse, as well as the annotations of Bu ston mentioned in note 6 immediately above.

8. This description of the degeneration of the Buddhist Doctrine is also based upon the *Vimalaprabhā*'s commentary to vs. 23 of the *Lokadhātupaṭala* of the *Kālacakra tantra*. See Kalkin Puṇḍarīka, *'Jig*, 471, and Newman (1987), 517–19. More of the same is also found in the *Vimalaprabhā*'s commentary to vs. 169, translated in Newman (1987), 650–52.

9. As mentioned at the beginning of chapter 3 above, Dol po pa certainly considered the Kṛtayuga Dharma to include many, if not all of the anuttarayoga tantras, as well as *The Trilogy of Bodhisattva Commentaries*, *The Ten Sūtras on the Buddha-nature*, *The Ten Sūtras of Definitive Meaning*, and the works of Maitreya, Nāgārjuna, Vasubandhu, Asaṅga, Nāropa, Saraha, and other Indian masters. See notes 11–14 in chapter 1 for a list of these commentaries and sūtras.

10. The two truths are, of course, the absolute (*don dam*) and the relative (*kun rdzob*). Dol po pa, *Bka' bsdu bzhi pa'i rang 'grel*, 587, states that absolute truth is only apparent to nonconceptual gnosis, and cannot be apparent to relative consciousness. Moreover, absolute truth does not manifest while the vital winds have not ceased, or else entered the central channel (*avadhūtī*), whereas the relative manifests while there is a circulation of the winds. These comments allude to the necessity of the practice of tantric yoga, especially that of the *ṣaḍaṅgayoga*, for the realization of the true nature of reality. This goal cannot be accomplished merely through passive meditation. In regard to the two modes of emptiness, Dol po pa, ibid., 587–88, states that since the absolute is really not empty of itself, and is the ground that is empty of all relative phenomena, it is the profound emptiness of other, which is the mode of emptiness of the true nature of reality (*dharmatā*). On the other hand, since the relative is really itself empty of self-nature, it is like the horn of a rabbit, the child of a barren woman, or a sky-flower, utterly unestablished and completely nonexistent. He also mentions that these types of distinctions are particularly clear in the teachings that have come from Shambhala.

11. Dol po pa, ibid., 589–601, presents a very detailed analysis of exaggeration (*sgro 'dogs*) and denigration (*skur 'debs*). On 589–90, he says:

> One falls into the extreme of exaggeration if one maintains, "These relative manifest and audible phenomena are established in the mode of reality," or, "They are the true nature, the buddha-body of reality, the Great Seal, and self-arisen gnosis." One falls into the extreme of denigration if one claims, "Since the buddha-body of reality, the Great Seal, self-arisen gnosis, and so forth, are also empty of self-nature, they are not established in reality." If free from those two extremes, one realizes the middle, the center, the third category, the androgynous stage, Vajrasattva, similar to the eight prognostic images. Because of precisely that, the realization of the Great Madhyamaka must be free of all extremes of exaggeration and denigration, or extremes of existence and nonexistence.

One must never deny the existence of absolute reality, nor maintain the true existence of relative phenomena. Dol po pa again mentions that this is most clear in the teachings that have come from Shambhala, and further refers the reader to his own composition on distinguishing what is possible and impossible, the *Srid mi srid kyi rab tu dbye ba*. See Dol po pa, *Srid*.

12. Paradoxical terms of description found in the scriptures, such as *formless form, incorporeal body*, and *mindless mind*, which include contra-

diction (*'gal 'dus*), would have to be considered flawed if applied to relative truth, but are flawless when considered as descriptive of absolute truth. Such statements must be interpreted as only applicable to absolute truth. See Dol po pa, *Bka' bsdu bzhi pa'i rang 'grel*, 601–602.

13. According to Dol po pa, ibid., 602–605, phenomena (*dharma*) and true nature (*dharmatā*) are the relative and the absolute. Everything knowable may be divided into the two categories of the composite and the noncomposite. If the composite is divided, there is the inanimate (*bem po*) and the aware (*rig pa*). If the noncomposite is divided, there is also the inanimate and the aware. He gives stone mountains, and so forth, as examples of inanimate composite phenomena. Examples of composite phenomena which are aware are the eight groups of consciousness, with associating factors, and gnosis arisen due to another (*gzhan byung ye shes*). An inanimate noncomposite phenomena is the noncomposite sky, because it is a particular knowable which is not aware of itself. A phenomena which is noncomposite and aware is the indivisible space and intrinsic awareness of the true nature (*dharmatā*), the essence of which is the five or the ten self-arisen gnoses, which are free of single or multiple moments, and are partless, omnipotent, permanent, stable, eternal, immutable, and transcending all simile. Moreover, the sky is labeled and enumerated as noncomposite merely because it is not produced by anything. The real noncomposite is self-arisen gnosis (*rang byung ye shes*).

Furthermore, everything knowable may be divided into the categories of inanimate and aware, or knowables which are not aware of themselves and knowables which are aware of themselves. Each of those may also be divided into both composite and noncomposite. Dol po pa states that this method comes from the Kṛtayuga tradition.

On the other hand, the traditions of the Tretayuga and later eons claim that if knowables are divided, there are only entities and nonentities, and if entities are divided, there are both the inanimate and the aware. They do not accept the possibility of any noncomposite phenomena which are inanimate or aware. As a consequence, Dol po pa says, if whatever is aware is composite and impermanent, the expanse of reality (*dharmadhātu*) would also be impermanent, because it is the most sublime knowable which is aware. If that were accepted, the expanse of reality would be composite. If so, it could not then be equivalent to the reality of the perfection of transcendent knowledge (*prajñāpāramitā*), the fully established nature (*pariṇispanna*), and so forth. Such a position is unacceptable, because the exact opposite is taught in many scriptures of the Kṛtayuga.

14. The two great kingdoms are the great kingdom of the absolute and the great kingdom of the relative. Dol po pa, ibid., 605.

15. Translated following the 'Dzam thang, 210, reading of *gcig nyid*, "one," instead of the Bhutanese reading of *de nyid*, "precisely that."

16. For both this and the following section Dol po pa provides no explanation in the *Bka' bsdu bzhi pa'i rang 'grel*, 605–606, merely stating that "the meaning of the words is easily understood." This dreaded phrase, *tshig gi don ni go sla*, which seems to so often be found in Tibetan commentaries just when a clear explanation would be greatly appreciated, brings to mind the comment of Michel de Montaigne: "I normally find matter for doubt in what the gloss has not condescended to touch upon. Like certain horses I know which miss their footing on a level path, I stumble more easily on the flat." See de Montaigne (1993), 1210.

17. Here, and elsewhere throughout his writings, Dol po pa uses the term *Madhyamaka*, and especially the *Great Madhyamaka*, as a synonym for ultimate reality, and not just in the sense of the philosophical system known as Madhyamaka.

18. See note 14 immediately above.

19. An example of what Dol po pa regarded as manifestations of the absolute would be the empty forms (*śūnyabimba, stong gzugs*) which manifest to the practitioner during the meditations of the Six-branch Yoga (*ṣaḍaṅgayoga*). In what was a controversial position, Dol po pa considered these to actually be the Buddha-nature (*tathāgatagarbha*), or perfect buddhahood. The later Bka' brgyud pa master Karma 'phrin las pa commented: "Accepting the empty forms endowed with all sublime aspects to be perfect buddhahood is the tradition of the Omniscient Jo nang pa." The Bka' brgyud pa position on this point was different. See Karma 'phrin las pa, *Dri lan drang*, 121: *rnam kun mchog ldan gyi/stong gzugs rdzogs sangs rgyas su khas len pa/de ni kun mkhyen jo nang pa yi lugs*.

20. This is because absolute reality and nirvāṇa are often described by these terms in certain sūtras and tantras.

21. This line is found only in the 'Dzam thang edition, 212: *rnam mkhyen ye shes mthar thug yin par 'gyur/*.

22. The five great immutable emptinesses (*stong pa chen po 'gyur med lnga*) are the five aggregates free from all obscuration. This is from the Kālacakra tradition. See Kalkin Puṇḍarīka, *Bsdus*, vol. 11, 590–91. The six immutable empty drops or *bindu* (*thig le stong pa 'gyur med drug*) are the three realms and the three times. This is also from the Kālacakra tradition. See Kalkin Puṇḍarīka, ibid., 591. The Sanskrit term *Evaṃ* symbolizes the total integration of emptiness and great bliss.

23. These are all terms used in the tantras to indicate the indivisibility, nonduality, and total integration of method (*upāya, thabs*) and transcendent knowledge (*prajñā, shes rab*), as well as the identical essence of the ground and result of the spiritual path. It is interesting that Dol po pa

uses the Sanskrit word *ahaṃ*, "I." For some discussion of these terms see Dol po pa, *Jo*, 728–29, and *Kun mkhyen*, 459–60.

24. This line is translated following the 'Dzam thang edition (212) reading of *de spang*, "to reject them," instead of the Bhutanese reading of *de yang*, "furthermore," which would seem to be a scribal mistake in copying from an *dbu med* original.

25. Dol po pa, *Bka' bsdu bzhi pa'i rang 'grel*, 606, notes that if it were the case that the two truths, and saṃsāra and nirvāṇa, were identical in essence, it would logically follow that the Buddha-nature (*tathāgatagarbha*) and the incidental stains (i.e. the temporary emotional and intellectual obscurations) would also need to be indivisible and identical. But if they were identical it would contradict the existence of two aspects which are suitable and unsuitable to become the result. Therefore, when the incidental stains were removed by the Truth of the Path, the Buddha-nature would also have to be removed, which is impossible.

26. As explained in note 15 to the translation of *A General Commentary on the Doctrine*, the terminology of "outer," "inner," and "other" is from the Kālacakra literature.

27. Dol po pa, *Bka' bsdu bzhi pa'i rang 'grel*, 607, quotes the *Ye shes snying po kun las btus pa* (*Jñānasārasamuccaya*) of Āryadeva as commented upon by the eleventhth-century Indian master Bhadrabodhi in his *Ye shes snying po kun las btus pa zhes bya ba'i bshad sbyar* (*Jñānasārasamuccayanāmabandhana*): "It states, 'Neither existent nor non-existent,' because it is a third category" (*yod med min zhes smos te/phung po gsum par 'gyur pa'i phyir/*). See Āryadeva, *Ye*, 144.3.2, and Bhadrabodhi, *Ye*, 152.5.1–2. Dol po pa discusses a variety of third categories, from among which he says this is the gnosis which is absolute, noncomposite, and permanent. This absolute third category is indicated by paradoxical statements in the scriptures which sometimes refer to absolute reality as beyond the categories of entity and nonentity, and sometimes refer to it as being both an entity and a nonentity. It is significant that another series of verses from Āryadeva's text are embedded in the *Vimalaprabhā* itself. See Newman (1992) for a study of the verses found in the *Vimalaprabhā*.

28. Dol po pa, *Bka' bsdu bzhi pa'i rang 'grel*, 608, explains that everything knowable is either inanimate or aware, and also that a knowable thing must be either self-aware or not aware. Being self-aware contradicts being not aware, and being not self-aware contradicts being aware, so there can be no possible third category in this regard.

29. In response to a hypothetical claim that these types of gnosis are of something which is composite and impermanent, Dol po pa provides the following list of names for absolute reality which he has culled from the

Mañjuśrī jñānasattva paramārtha nāma saṃgīti (*'Jam dpal ye shes sems dpa'i don dam pa'i mtshan yang dag par brjod pa*), the *Perfect Expression of the Absolute Names of the Gnostic Being Mañjuśrī*. See Davidson (1981), for a study and full translation of this text. Since this tantric scripture is accepted in the Tibetan tradition as perhaps *the* most authoritative scripture of definitive meaning, the terms used in it to describe ultimate reality are not open to interpretation. These names from the scripture describe absolute truth in terms of cognition, intrinsic awareness, and gnosis, and do not apply to anything that is composite, impermanent, and ordinary consciousness. Since this tantra is concerned with expressing the names of the absolute, and not those of the relative, other explanations which attempt to portray the meaning to be composite, impermanent, dependent origination, and momentary consciousness are merely perverse explanations. See Dol po pa, *Bka' bsdu bzhi pa'i rang 'grel*, 608–609.

30. The Tibetan text has "ten knowledges" (*shes bcu*), which have been taken to be identical to the ten knowledges or gnoses (*daśajñāna*, *ye shes bcu*) listed in Davidson (1981), 24, note 68. They are gnosis of phenomena, successive gnosis, gnosis of worldly usage, of other's minds, of suffering, of its arising, of its extinction, of the path, of final destruction, and of no future arising.

31. The eight knowledges (*shes brgyad*) are the eight knowledges mentioned in Davidson (1981), 34, note 110. They are the knowledges of the elements of the four noble truths and the knowledges of the succeeding moments of the four noble truths. The first four are the realization of the four noble truths in the desire realm, and the second four are the realization of the same four noble truths in the form and formless realms.

32. The six clairvoyances are listed in Davidson (1981), 37, note 125. They are: realization of the knowledge of the object of concentration, of the knowledge of divine hearing, of the knowledge of the gradations of other's minds, of the knowledge of the memory of previous existences, of the knowledge of the arising and passing away (of beings), and of the knowledge of the utter destruction of impurities. The six subsequent mindfulnesses are also listed in Davidson, ibid., note 126. They are: subsequent mindfulness of the Buddha, the Dharma, the Saṅgha, one's own discipline, one's own renunciation, and one's own chosen deity.

33. The ten powers of an enlightened being are listed in Davidson (1981), 24, note 70. The ten powers are: the power consisting in the knowledge of what is possible and impossible, of the results of actions, of the meditations, emancipations, concentrations, and meditative attainments, of the degree of the faculties of other beings, of the diverse interests of beings, of the diverse dispositions of beings, of the ways of passing into every sort

of circumstance, of previous lives, of the deaths and rebirths of beings, and of the final destruction of the impurities. See also the *Uttaratantra*, translated in Takasaki (1966), 338–39.

34. According to Dol po pa, *Bka' bsdu bzhi pa'i rang 'grel*, 609–10, this is a paraphrase of a statement in the *Vimalaprabhā* that says, "The Victors have stated that thusness is gnosis free from single and multiple moments."

35. As Dol po pa frequently emphasizes in his writings, relative phenomena would be impossible without the existence of a fully established and real absolute, or buddha-body of reality (*dharmakāya*).

36. According to Dol po pa the nine fully established natures (*pariniṣpanna*) are the true nature of phenomena, the expanse of reality, the very place of phenomena, flawless phenomena, thusness, unmistaken thusness, thusness which is not another, the limit of perfection, and inconceivable space. See Dol po pa, *Bka' bsdu bzhi pa'i rang 'grel*, 644–45: *yongs grub dgu ni/chos rnams kyi chos nyid dang/chos kyi dbyings dang/chos kyi gnas nyid dang/chos skyon med pa nyid dang/de bzhin nyid dang ma nor ba de bzhin nyid dang/gzhan ma yin pa de bzhin nyid dang/yang dag pa'i mtha' dang/bsam gyis mi khyab pa'i dbyings rnams so/*. Most of these are also listed among the 108 names of the perfection of transcendent knowledge (*prajñāpāramitā*). See Conze (1973b), 196, and also Dol po pa, ibid., 621.

37. The Bhutanese edition has recorded this line twice with a minor error in the repeated line. The repetition is not found in the 'Dzam thang edition, and has not been translated here.

38. According to Dol po pa, *Bka' bsdu bzhi pa'i rang 'grel*, 611, there are basically two categories, one in which there are divisions and one in which there are not. In the first there are the authentic two truths, the authentic saṃsāra and nirvāṇa, the authentic four truths, the authentic three natures (*trisvabhāva*), and so forth. The second category, in which there are no divisions, refers to all the deities and maṇḍalas of the four sets of the tantras of the true nature (*dharmatā*), such as Kālacakra, Cakrasaṃvara, Hevajra, and Guhyasamāja. Although there are divisions of name and form, their true essence is indivisible. The numerous terms such as Great Seal, Great Madhyamaka, great nirvāṇa, great radiant light, great soul, great offering, great passion, great form, as well as those such as Atiyoga, extreme lack of elaboration, the profound perfection of transcendent knowledge (*prajñāpāramitā*), and the twelve fully established natures (*pariniṣpanna*), are indivisible in true essence. It is only in the flawed explanations of the Tretayuga that these are each explained as different individual topics.

39. The mode of delusion is all the delusion of ordinary consciousness, whereas the mode of reality is the way in which the true nature (*dharmatā*) actually exists, which is as omnipresent self-arisen gnosis. See Dol po pa, ibid., 612.

40. The mode of being is the absolute mode of existence, whereas the mode of assertion is the various opinions of individuals, in which there is no certainty of correspondence to the truth. See Dol po pa, ibid., 612.

41. According to Dol po pa, ibid., 612–14, the original tradition is the teachings of the Kṛtayuga, in which the pairs empty of self-nature and empty of other, consciousness and gnosis, the imagined nature (*parikalpita*) and the fully established nature (*pariniṣpanna*), and so forth, and the triads of outer, inner, and other, and so forth, are presented as mutually exclusive. The obstructing tradition is that of the Tretayuga, whose teachings make such assertions as the following (613):

> Since everything is empty of self-nature, all the profound modes of reality, such as the nine and the twelve fully established natures, are empty of self-nature. Whatever is empty of self-nature, even though claimed to be the ultimate profound mode of reality, such as the absolute buddha-body of reality, is not at all established as an absolute. In reality the enlightenment of the Buddha, bodhicitta, bodhisattvas, deities, mantras, tantras, maṇḍalas, mudrās, Dharma, Saṅgha, and so forth, are not at all established, and are thus all only mere names.

Having caused the depreciation and decline of that earlier fine system, the tradition of the Treyayuga spread and increased this perverse later system.

42. This has been discussed in note 27 immediately above. Briefly, there is a third category in regard to entities and nonentities, because of the permanent existence of thusness, which is not either of those two. This third category is everything that is the fully established nature (*pariniṣpanna*), or absolute reality. There is no third category in regard to the inanimate and the aware, because there is nothing knowable which is not either inanimate or aware. See Dol po pa, ibid., 614.

43. See the section at the beginning of this translation of *The Fourth Council*.

44. These are the triad of the imagined (*parikalpita*, *kun brtags*), the dependent (*paratantra*, *gzhan dbang*), and the fully established (*pariniṣpanna*, *yongs grub*) natures, which are usually considered to be one of the fundamental paradigms employed in the Yogācāra or Cittamātra tradition. Dol po pa challenges this doxographical ascription, and main-

tains that the three natures (*trisvabhāva*) are an integral part of the Great Madhyamaka tradition. As scriptural authority for his opinion, he cites the eighty-third chapter of the eighteen-thousand-line *Prajñāpāramitā sūtra*, and the seventy-second chapter of the version in twenty-five thousand lines. These chapters are usually known as the "Maitreya Chapter." See Conze and Iida (1968) for a discussion and translation of this chapter. See chapter 3, section 2 above for a more detailed discussion of these topics.

45. The three "selves" (*ātman*) are the *ātman* of the individual, the *ātman* of phenomena, and the pure *ātman*. They are the essence of the imagined nature (*parikalpita*), the essence of the dependent nature (*paratantra*), and the essence of thusness or the fully established nature (*parinispanna*), which are respectively to be known, to be rejected, and to be attained. See Dol po pa, *Bka' bsdu bzhi pa'i rang 'grel*, 617.

46. According to the *Mahāyānasūtralaṃkāra*, the three emptinesses are of nonexistence (*med pa'i stong nyid*), existence (*yod pa'i stong nyid*), and natural emptiness (*rang bzhin stong nyid*). This is also mentioned in the *Pañcaśatikāprajñāparamitā*. The first two emptinesses are empty of self-nature, and thus not profound, while the third is the profound emptiness of other. See Dol po pa, ibid., 617.

47. The terminology of a triad of outer, inner, and other is from the Kālacakra tradition. Dol po pa, ibid., 617–18, states that there is this inferior and relative outer and inner, which is the inanimate world and its animate contents, and the transcendent excellent primal Buddha (*ādibuddha*), which is a sublime other than this. These are stated to be like the outer portion of a husk of grain, the inner portion, and the kernel of grain, which are similar in form although not identical in essence. As for that, this outer and inner, static and mobile world, is empty of self–nature, which is not profound, and the transcendent excellent primal Buddha (*ādibuddha*), a sublime other than this, is empty of other, which is profound.

48. The Four Truths are, of course, the Truth of Suffering, the Truth of the Origin of Suffering, the Truth of the Path, and the Truth of Cessation. The first three are empty of self–nature, while the fourth is empty of other. See Dol po pa, ibid., 618.

The four topics (*dharma*, *chos*) are the ground of purification (*sbyang gzhi*), the object of purification (*sbyang bya*), the agent of purification (*sbyong byed*), and the result of purification (*sbyong 'bras*). These may be understood through the similes of the sky, the clouds existing in it, the wind which scatters them, and the sky clear of clouds. The ultimate ground of purification and result of purification are empty of other, which is profound, and the remaining ones are empty of self–nature, which is not profound. See Dol po pa, ibid., 618.

The five topics (*dharma*, *chos*) are name, reason, discursive thought, thusness, and perfect gnosis. Thusness is the profound emptiness of other, but the remaining four are emptiness of self–nature. See Dol po pa, ibid., 618. These five are taught in many different Mahāyāna scriptures and treatises. See Suganuma (1967) for a study of their occurrence in the *Laṅkāvatārasūtra*.

49. See note 12 in chapter 1 for a list of these texts.

50. Dol po pa, *Bka' bsdu bzhi pa'i rang 'grel*, 619, summarizes this section by reiterating that if absolute truth is not at all established in reality, absolute truth would be a total negation, like the horn of a rabbit. But if it were negated, the support for the relative would be negated, so that the relative itself would also be negated. In general, if the support and the pervader are negated, the supported and that which is pervaded are also negated.

51. Dol po pa, ibid., 620–26, provides a number of quotations from Mahāyāna scriptures to prove this point. Two of these are especially clear. On 620–21 he quotes the *Suvikrāntavikramiparipṛcchā prajñāpāramitā nirdeśa* (*Rab kyi rtsal gyis rnam par gnon pas zhus pa*):

> All phenomena, such as the aggregates, constituents, bases of sense cognition, and dependent origination, are not the perfection of trancendent knowledge [*prajñāpāramitā*],
> But the thusness, the thusness without error, the thusness which is not other, and the thusness just as it is of those phenomena is the perfection of transcendent knowledge.

On 624 he quotes the *Gaṇḍavyūha* (*Rgyan stug po*):

> The Tathāgata who is permanent, stable, eternal, and indestructible is the object of those practicing the yoga of cultivating the subsequent mindfulness of the Buddha. That which is known as "the Buddha-nature" [*tathāgatagarbha*] is nirvāṇa indestructible like space and the sky. The past, present, and future blessed buddhas present it with the term nirvāṇa and the phrase "expanse of reality" [*dharmadhātu*]. In this way, whether the tathāgatas appear or do not appear, this true nature of phenomena, the expanse of reality, the flawless phenomena itself, is the Tathāgata.

52. See note 22 immediately above for the five great immutable emptinesses. The five Victors are the five Buddhas known as Akṣobhya, Vairocana, Ratnasambhava, Amitābha, and Amoghasiddhi.

53. The five consorts (*vidyā*, *rig ma*), are the female counterparts to the five Victors or Buddhas. They are Māmakī, Vajradhātvīśvarī, Locanī,

Pāṇḍara Vāsinī, and Samaya Tārā. The five Buddhas are the same as the five Victors listed in the previous note. The five buddha-bodies (*pañcakāya*, *sku lnga*) of the Buddha are usually given as the emanation buddha-body (*nirmāṇakāya*), the buddha-body of rapture (*saṃbhogakāya*), the buddha-body of reality (*dharmakāya*), the essential buddha-body (*svābhāvikakāya*), and the buddha-body of gnosis (*jñānakāya*). The five gnoses are mirrorlike gnosis, gnosis of equality, discriminating gnosis, all-accomplishing gnosis, and gnosis of the expanse of reality (*dharmadhātu*). The text here reads *shes bcu*, "ten knowledges," which are taken to be a short form for *ye shes bcu*, "ten gnoses." The ten gnoses (*daśajñāna*, *ye shes bcu*) are gnosis of phenomena, successive gnosis, gnosis of worldly usage, of others' minds, of suffering, of its arising, of its extinction, of the path, of final destruction, and of no future arising. They are listed in Davidson (1981), 24, note 68.

54. In the Kṛtayuga tradition there are both productive (*skyed byed*) and separating (*bral byed*) causes, which yield produced results (*skyed 'bras*) and separated results (*bral 'bras*). Buddhahood is a separated result, in the sense that the true nature is separated from the various veils that have previously concealed the eternally present Buddha-nature (*tathāgatagarbha*), which is in no way produced.

55. According to the Kṛtayuga, the permanent, noncomposite cause and result, which have a single essence, are not mixed with anything composite and impermanent, or any phenomenon that is empty of self-nature and dependently originated. They are the immutable fully established (*pariniṣpanna*) ground free from all imagined phenomena (*parikalpita*), the naturally primordial ground free from all incidental fabrication, which is indivisible from the absolute result. See Dol po pa, *Bka' bsdu bzhi pa'i rang 'grel*, 627.

56. Dol po pa does not elaborate upon this subject here, but refers the reader to his own *Kun gzhi rab tu dbye ba* for details. See Dol po pa, *Kun gzhi*.

57. That is to say, those of the Tretayuga tradition only accept a universal ground consciousness (*ālayavijñāna*, *kun gzhi rnam shes*), but not a universal ground gnosis (**ālayajñāna*, *kun gzhi ye shes*).

58. Dol po pa, *Bka' bsdu bzhi pa'i rang 'grel*, 629, specifies that this universal ground gnosis is not the same as any state of consciousness, and so is not to be identified with the appropriating consciousness (*len pa'i rnam shes*), the consciousness containing all seeds (*sa bon thams cad pa'i rnam shes*), or the root consciousness (*rtsa ba'i rnam shes*).

59. The Sanskrit term *Evaṃ* symbolizes the total integration of great bliss and emptiness.

60. See Davidson (1981), 34, notes 109 and 111, for an explanation of the twelve aspects of truth, which seem to be the twelve purified senses

and sense-fields. See Davidson ibid., note 112, for information on the sixteen aspects of reality or thusness, which are equated with the sixteen kinds of emptiness.

61. See note 36 immediately above for a list of the nine fully established natures (*pariniṣpanna*). The twelve *pariniṣpanna*s are those nine plus the addition of the true nature (*dharmatā*) which never deteriorates, constantly abiding equanimity, and the gnosis of total knowledge. See Dol po pa, *Bka' bsdu bzhi pa'i rang 'grel*, 645.

62. The position of the Sa skya pa school in regard to the universal ground, as expressed by Sa skya Paṇḍi ta in his famous *Sdom gsum rab dbye*, may well be the object of Dol po pa's objection here. Sa skya Paṇḍi ta stated:

> The statements in some [sūtras] concerning a "taintless mental continuum" is in reference to precisely the radiant aspect of the universal ground consciousness. Since that is unobscured and neutral,. it is not designated as virtue.
>
> If there were a "taintless mental continuum" outside of the eight groups [of consciousness], there would then be nine groups of consciousness. Therefore a taintless mental continuum outside of the eight groups is incorrect.

See Sa skya Paṇḍi ta, *Sdom*, 14: *'ga' las zag med sems rgyud ces/gsungs pa kun gzhi'i rnam shes kyi/gsal cha nyid la dgongs pa yin/de ni ma bsgribs lung ma bstan/yin phyir dge ba'i tha snyad med/'on te zag med sems rgyud ces/tshogs brgyad las gzhan yod na ni/de tshe rnam shes tshogs dgur 'gyur/des na tshogs brgyad las gzhan pa'i/zag med sems rgyud mi 'thad do/*. Dol po pa would perhaps respond by saying that what he is concerned with is the universal ground gnosis, which is not consciousness.

63. As noted above, Dol po pa often uses the term Madhyamaka as a synonym for absolute reality.

64. Dol po pa, *Bka' bsdu bzhi pa'i rang 'grel*, 629–32, explains this section in considerable detail. See chapter 3, section 2 above for a discussion of his explanation.

65. Dol po pa, ibid., 632, mentions the *Mahāyānasūtrālaṃkara* and the *Madhyantavibhaṅga* as examples of texts he considers representative of the Great Madhyamaka but that are usually felt to be Cittamātra.

66. Dol po pa, ibid., 632, mentions Vasubandhu and Dignāga as great teachers of the Great Madhyamaka who have been incorrectly called representatives of Cittamātra.

67. Translation following the 'Dzam thang, 227, reading of *gzhung ngan*, "perverse treatises," instead of the Bhutanese reading of *gzhung don*, "meaning of the treatises."

68. In this context it is very interesting to read the following statement by Bla ma Dam pa Bsod nams rgyal mtshan, the Sa skya master who requested Dol po pa to compose the *Bka' bsdu bzhi pa* and its autocommentary:

> [Bla ma Dam pa] stated, "In general, a true nature would be impossible without phenomena. Phenomena would also be impossible without a true nature. Therefore, the true nature is not realized without realizing [the nature] of phenomena. Although there is no increase or reduction of the essence of the true nature, the obscurations become increasingly thinner during the path, by virtue of which the realization of the true nature becomes increasingly greater."

These comments were recorded by Bla ma Dam pa's direct disciple, Rgyal lha khang pa Blo gros seng ge. See 'Jam mgon A myes zhabs, *Chos*, 3b: *spyir chos can med pa'i chos nyid mi srid/chos nyid med pa'i chos can yang mi srid/des na chos can ma rtogs par chos nyid mi rtogs/chos nyid kyi ngo bo rgya che chung med kyang/lam gyi skabs su sgrib pa je srab la song ba'i dbang gi[s] chos nyid rtog[s] pa rgya cher 'gro ba yin gsungs/*.

69. In this section it is clear that Dol po pa is using the term *Madhyamaka* as a synonym for ultimate reality itself, and not just the philosophical system that goes by that name. Dol po pa, *Bka' bsdu bzhi pa'i rang 'grel*, 635, states that although the division of Madhyamaka into the pair of "establishment by independent inference (*svātantra*) and elimination through logical consequence (*prasaṅga*)" is thoroughly known to the tradition of the flawed Tretayuga and later eons, it is an inappropriate division of Madhyamaka because it is inappropriate as a way to divide reality, because it is inappropriate as a division of the natural spiritual races (*gotra*, *rigs*) and the essential buddha-body (*svābhāvikakāya*) of the true nature (*dharmatā*), and because it is inappropriate as a division of all the profound modes of reality, such as the absolute deities, mantras, tantras, maṇḍalas, and mudrās. The divisions of the Madhyamaka tradition of philosophy into the schools of Svātantrika and Prāsaṅgika may be a Tibetan invention, as Dol po pa seems to be arguing, since these terms are not found in any extant Sanskrit sources. See Ruegg (1981), 58. See Onada (1992), 71–91, for a description of some of the various opinions about *svātantra* and *prasaṅga* in Tibet.

70. See note 36 immediately above.

71. *Don dam mtshan brjod rgyud*. This is the *Mañjuśrī jñānasattva paramārtha nāma saṃgīti* (*'Jam dpal ye shes sems dpa'i don dam pa'i mtshan yang dag par brjod pa*). Dol po pa has already repeated above many names of the absolute drawn from this text. See Davidson (1981), for a study and full translation of this work.

72. *Atiyoga* is a term used for both the perfection stage practices of the *Guhyasamāja tantra* and the highest practices of the Great Perfection tradition. *Vajrayoga* is a synonym for the Six-branch Yoga taught in many tantras, especially the *Kālacakra* and the *Guhyasamāja*.

73. Hence they are not the central third category, and are not appropriate as classifications of Madhyamaka, any more than are other pairs of opposites, such as the colors black and white. See Dol po pa, *Bka' bsdu bzhi pa'i rang 'grel*, 635–36.

74. Dol po pa, ibid., 632, expresses how this opinion makes him experience nausea, revulsion, melancholy, and great compassion for those who make such a serious mistake. The translation follows the 'Dzam thang, 229, spelling of *dbu ma*, instead of *dbus ma*, which is found in the Bhutanese edition.

75. Translation following the 'Dzam thang edition, 229, genitive reading *pa'i*, instead of the Bhutanese instrumental reading *pas*.

76. See note 33 immediately above.

77. Translation following the Bhutanese reading of *chos rnams*, "*dharmas*," instead of the 'Dzam thang, 230, reading of *chos can*, "*dharmin*."

78. The *Five Treatises of Maitreya* are identified in chapter 1, note 14.

79. Dol po pa, *Bka' bsdu bzhi pa'i rang 'grel*, 637, mentions that if it is maintained that Madhyamaka and dependent origination have equal connotation and identical essence, the twelve fully established natures (*pariniṣpanna*), which are noncomposite, would also be dependent origination, because they are synonymous with Madhyamaka. If that is maintained, it would also be composite and impermanent, because it would be the relative dependent origination. If even that is maintained, it would also be a false and deceptive phenomenon, which is an unacceptable conclusion.

80. By definition, ordinary phenomena are composite and impermanent.

81. For example, a division into a relative and an absolute dependent origination is also made by Kamalaśīla in his commentary to the *Śālistamba sūtra*. See Schoening (1995), 95–104, and 243–328. In the translation on 245–64, Kamalaśīla glosses a series of fifteen adjectives used in the sūtra to describe ultimate dependent origination, such as *permanent, noncomposite*, and so forth.

82. Dol po pa, *Bka' bsdu bzhi pa'i rang 'grel*, 638, notes that the essential point to realize is that the ground and the separated result are noncomposite and transcend dependent origination, whereas the phenomena of the path are composite and do not transcend dependent origination.

83. In regard to the absolute dependent origination, Dol po pa, ibid., 638, says: "It is not this external and internal relative dependent origination, but the dependent origination of the transcendent excellent primal Buddha [*ādibuddha*], a sublime other than this, a dependent origination of flawless contradiction which transcends mundane similes."

84. The well-known twelve links of dependent origination (*pratītya-samutpāda*, *rten cing 'brel bar byung ba*) are ignorance, mental formations, consciousness, name and form, the six sense organs, contact between sense organ and sense object, sensations, desire, grasping, coming into existence, birth, and old age and death. See, for example, Hirakawa (1990), 51–54. Dol po pa, *Bka' bsdu bzhi pa'i rang 'grel*, 638, describes the absolute dependent origination as follows: "[It is] the ground from which the twelve links that are the root of existence have been naturally excluded from the beginning. It also bears the absolute twelve [links] indivisible from the ground which is naturally purified of those stains from the beginning."

85. See Davidson (1981), 34, note 109. The twelve pure aspects (*dag pa rnam pa bcu gnyis*) are the result obtained after the eradication of the twelve links of dependent origination. Some sources say that they are the twelve purified senses and sense-fields.

86. Dol po pa, *Bka' bsdu bzhi pa'i rang 'grel*, 638–639, describes the absolute twelve links as follows: "[They are] are the aspects of truth in the absolute, the twelve faces of the four vajras, another ignorance down through another old age and death, and also a primordial and naturally pure, pristine, and extremely pristine ignorance down through old age and death." According to Davidson (1981), 34, note 111, one source states that these twelve aspects of truth (*bden don bcu gnyis*) are also apparently associated with the senses and sense-fields.

87. These twelve are sites in the spiritual topography of the tantras, which are to be understood in both an external and an internal sense. Dol po pa, ibid., 639, speaks of the absolute twelve links as follows: "[They are] also the twelve absolute places, and so forth: the absolute places and nearby places, fields and nearby fields, areas and nearby areas for discussion, areas and nearby areas for congregation, charnel grounds and nearby charnel grounds, and Chandoha and nearby Chandoha."

88. This terminology is from the Kālacakra system, which applies astrological terminology to both the external movements of the heavenly

bodies, and the internal processes within living beings. Here the reference is to the process of the dissolution of the vital winds (*vāyu*) in the central channel (*avadhūtī*) of the subtle body as a result of the practice of the the Six-branch Yoga (*ṣaḍaṅgayoga*). Dol po pa, ibid., 639, also says of the absolute twelve links: "[They are] also the ground in which the twenty-one thousand six hundred winds of the twelve, the zodiac signs (*dus sbyor*) and the sun, are naturally blocked from the beginning."

89. The Tibetan term is *yum*, "mother." Obermiller (1988), 7, notes that the term *yum* is used in the Tibetan tradition to refer to six versions of the *Prajñāpāramitā sūtra*: those in 100,000 lines, 25,000, 18,000, 10,000, 8,000, and the condensed sūtra.

90. Here Dol po pa specifically mentions these topics as having been taught in a lineage beginning with Saraha and continuing down to Nāropa and others. See Dol po pa, *Bka' bsdu bzhi pa'i rang 'grel*, 643.

91. For all the material in the next five folios of Tibetan text (394–403) Dol po pa provides no explanation in the autocommentary, simply remarking at the end, as he often does, "That is easily understood."

92. The simile of the prognostic image (*pratisenā*, *pra phab*) is peculiar to the Kālacakra tradition. Newman (1988), 133, notes the term *pratisenā* as a rare Sanskrit term found only in the Kālacakra literature. He translates a passage from the *Vimalaprabhā* to illustrate the usage of this term: "Like a maiden's prognostic image in a mirror and so forth, the radiant light of the yogis' own minds appears manifest in the sky." He adds that the "sky" here refers to the void. In another passage, the *Vimalaprabhā* states that the Great Seal (*mahāmudrā*) is similar to the eight prognostic images. Furthermore, Newman quotes a reference from Nāropa, who cites the *Pratisenāvatāra tantra* in regard to the manifestation of eight kinds of prognostic images in a mirror, a sword, a thumbnail, a lamp, the moon, the sun, a water well, and the eye. Only these eight specific objects may serve as supports on the basis of which the prognostication can be performed. Orofino (1994), 613, summarizes the topic well:

> In all the texts concerning the *ṣaḍaṅgayoga*, as it is transmitted in the Kālacakra system, the *pratisenā* divination is the main metaphor used to describe the intrinsic nature of the visions that appear in the sky to the yogin once the *pratyāhāra* and the *dhyāna*, the first two stages of this yoga, have been accomplished.
>
> The images that appear to the young girl in the mirror are devoid of any materiality; in the same way one must consider the nature of the images that appear to the yogin

who because of the power of his own mind, sees in the ether immaterial visions that transcend the three realms.

93. As mentioned above the Sanskrit term *evaṃ* symbolizes the total integration of emptiness (*e*) and great bliss (*vaṃ*).

94. In the tantras emptiness is sometimes spoken of as *bhagā*, "vagina, womb." This is because the qualities such as the ten powers of an enlightened being, which arise due to other factors, are newly born in the continuum of an individual who has perfected the meditation and actualized the realization of emptiness, whereas the infinite qualities of the noncomposite buddha-body of reality are naturally present.

95. The Tibetan term is *rdo rje'i khu rdul.*

96. The "powerful tenfold anagram" (*rnam bcu dbang ldan*) is the name used for the well-known anagram of the ten-syllable Kālacakra mantra written in Lañtsa script. The entire teachings of the *Kālacakra tantra* are encoded in this one symbol. The outer teachings concerning the inanimate world may be taught by means of this image. The inner teachings about the nature of the animate beings in the world may also be taught with it. The other teachings of the creation stage meditation may be taught by utilizing it, and the other teachings of the perfection stage of meditation may also be presented on the basis of this single anagram.

97. See note 12 in chapter 1 for a list of these sūtras.

98. The four sets of tantra, according to the categories applied in Tibet to those tantras translated during the second major influx of Buddhism beginning in the tenth century, are highest yogatantra (*anuttarayogatantra*, *bla med rgyud*), yogatantra (*rnal 'byor rgyud*), performance tantra (*caryātantra*, *spyod rgyud*), and action tantra (*kriyātantra*, *bya rgyud*).

99. Generally speaking, Dol po pa's contrasting of "this" and "other" is in reference to a level of absolute reality which is "other" than "this" relative reality. See especially Dol po pa, *Kun mkhyen*, 459–60. He is also certainly alluding to the meaning of "other" in the triad of outer, inner, and other characteristic of the Kālacakra literature. It this context the "other" refers to the level of absolute reality as it is perceived through the gnostic vision of the practitioner who has achieved unity with the deity, which is "other" than "this" relative perception. For example, during the practice of the first branch of the *ṣaḍaṅgayoga* the link between the ordinary five sense organs and their objects is broken, and the consciousness previously projected outward upon those objects is withdrawn, so that five "other" sense organs with the nature of gnosis may engage five "other" objects which have the nature of radiant light. Also see Broido (1989), 88, who notes that "the same *skandha*s, *dhātu*s and *āyatana*s

normally said to be *paratantra* have an *asaṃskṛta*, *parinispanna* and *gzhan stong* aspect."

100. The three realms (*tridhātu*, *khams gsum*) are the desire realm (*kāmaloka*, *'dod khams*), form realm (*rūpadhātu*, *gzugs khams*), and formless realm (*arūpadhātu*, *gzugs med khams*).

101. The three times are the past, present, and future.

102. The three vehicles are the "vehicle of the listeners" (*śrāvakayāna*), the "vehicle of the solitary buddhas" (*pratyekabuddhayāna*), and the "vehicle of the bodhisattvas" (*bodhisattvayāna*).

103. This is in reference to the central figure in a maṇḍala and those in the entourage of surrounding deities.

104. Father (*yab*) and Mother (*yum*) are terms commonly used to designate a pair of male and female deities.

105. The thirty-seven factors conducive to enlightenment (*bodhipakṣadharma*, *byang chub phyogs chos*) are conveniently placed in a chart in Kapstein (1992b), 204–205. As noted earlier, Dol po pa classifies the first three Truths as relative and empty of self-nature, and only the Truth of Cessation as absolute and empty of other. Here he is speaking of the absolute aspect of the factors conducive to enlightenment, not the relative.

106. *Rnam thar snyoms 'jug dgu*. These nine absorptions are listed in Krang dbyi sun, ed., *Bod*, vol. 1, 524.

107. The three doors of liberation (*rnam thar sgo gsum*) are three meditative concentrations that create liberation. They are emptiness (*stong pa nyid*), signlessness (*mtshan ma med pa*), and wishlessness (*smon pa med pa*).

108. See note 33 immediately above for a list of the ten powers. See Takasaki (1966), 339–41, for a list of the four intrepid factors. Krang dbyi sun, ed., *Bod*, vol. 2, 2958, has an entry for *so so yang dag par rig pa bzhi*, which are four types of specific perfect awareness with which a bodhisattva perceives various phenomena. They are awareness of phenomena, awareness of meaning, awareness of definitions, and awareness of ability. The eighteen exclusive qualities (*ma 'dres bco brgyad*) of a Buddha are described in the *Uttaratantra*, translated in Takasaki (1966), 341–43. According to Krang dbyi sun, ed., ibid., vol. 1, 307, the three knowledges (*mkhyen pa gsum*) are knowledge of the ground, knowledge of the path, and omniscience.

109. See note 92 immediately above. As certain visions, or prognostic images, may only be experienced during the ritual of divination or prognostication, so also the "empty forms" (*śūnyabimba*, *stong gzugs*), which

appear as manifestations of the Buddha-nature during the practice of the Six-branch Yoga, only appear when the mind is resting in a nonconceptual state, although the Buddha-nature is eternally present.

110. The Tibetan text has *kun tu ru*, which is an exact rendering of the Sanskrit word *kunduru*, meaning olibanum or frankincense. This term is used in the tantras as a code word for sexual union.

111. This example is probably from the *Avataṃsaka sūtra*, which is sometimes referred to in Tibetan as the "Sūtra of the Great Roll of Cloth" (*Dar yug chen po'i mdo*).

112. The simile of a treasure beneath the hearth of a pauper's house is found in many scriptures and treatises, such as the *Tathāgatagarbha sūtra*, the *Mahāparinirvāṇa sūtra*, and the commentary to the *Uttaratantra*. See Dol po pa, *Ri chos*, 4–8, where quotations from these and other texts are given which contain this simile. Also see Takasaki (1966), 272–73, for the use of this example in the *Uttaratantra*. The simile of a lamp in a vase is also well known, and is found in such texts as the *Dharmadhātu stotra* of Nāgārjuna.

113. In the tradition of tantra, the ordinary "vital karmic winds" (*karmavāyu, las rlung*) are drawn into the central channel (*avadhūti*) during the practice of yoga, and are thereby transformed into the "vital gnostic wind" (*jñānavāyu, ye shes rlung*). Until this is achieved one remains under the power of ordinary consciousness, which is "mounted" upon the karmic winds. When they have been drawn into the central channel and are transformed into the gnostic wind, this then serves as the support for nonconceptual gnosis.

114. Translation following the 'Dzam thang, 240, reading of *'di las*, "other than this," instead of the Bhutanese reading of *'di la*, "in regard to this."

115. The three pure spheres (*'khor gsum dag pa*) are to be unattached to oneself as the performer of an action, the action itself, and the object or recipient of the action.

116. *Chos spyod rnam bcu*. These ten activities are to copy the scriptures, present offerings, practice generosity, listen to Dharma, uphold it, read it, explain it, recite it, think about the meaning of the Dharma, and meditate upon the meaning of the Dharma. See Krang dbyi sun, ed., *Bod*, vol. 1, 840.

117. During the determined practice (*la zlo*) of meditative equipoise all points of reference, including the teachings of Dharma, must be relinquished in order to correctly experience the nature of reality.

118. Following sessions of meditation, one must analyze or practice discrimination (*shan 'byed*) in regard to the phenomena encountered during ordinary daily activities.

119. *Melting bliss* (*zhu bde*) is a term for the experiences which arise from union with a consort, whether actual or imagined, during the practice of tantric yoga. Common sexual bliss, which is in flux in the sense of leading to an ordinary orgasm, is to be rejected in favor of the immutable bliss experienced as a result of the union of bliss and emptiness without emission of sexual fluids.

120. See chapter 3, section 3, for a discussion of these topics. The idea that the essence of the thoughts or concepts is the buddha-body of reality (*rnam rtog gi ngo bo chos sku red*) is still very widespread in Tibetan Buddhism, especially in the Bka' brgyud traditions. Dol po pa repeatedly criticized this in the strongest terms in a number of his works. Examples of the type of view he is criticizing here and further on in this text are found in the mystical songs of Karma pa Rang byung rdo rje. See Rang byung rdo rje, *Rang*, 58: "These various concepts which arise in the mind dawn as the pure land of the buddhas" (*sems byung rnam rtog sna tshogs 'di/sangs rgyas rnams kyi zhing du shar/*). And see Rang byung rdo rje, *Rang*, 92: "The essence of the six groups [of sense consciousness] is gnosis. Recognition of that is so amazing!" (*tshogs drug rang ngo ye shes yin/de ngo shes pa a re mtshar/*). Even the master Thang stong rgyal po, who would claim to be Dol po pa's rebirth, regarded thoughts as the dynamic energy (*rtsal*) of the buddha-body of reality. See Stearns (1980), 248. This point in Dol po pa's work was certainly not accepted by many later upholders of the *gzhan stong*, especially in the Bka' brgyud tradition.

121. The view that the *essence* of the five poisons of desire, hatred, ignorance, jealousy, and greed are identical to the five forms of gnosis identified with the five Victors, or Buddhas, is accepted by virtually all schools of Buddhism in Tibet, as is the idea that consciousness itself is to be transformed into gnosis. For example, in the Sa skya pa school the main practice of meditation upon Hevajra according to the Lam 'bras system of Virūpa is for the purpose of transforming the five aggregates, the five poisons, and so forth, into the five forms of gnosis personified by the five Buddhas. This issue hinges on different interpretations of what is meant by "transformation" (*gnas 'gyur*).

122. Dol po pa, *Bka' bsdu bzhi pa'i rang 'grel*, 644–45, further elaborates on this scriptural statement by saying that it also means that ultimate reality exists whether individuals realize it or not, see it or not, believe in it or not, attain it or not, and so forth. This is in reference to the mode of existence of the ground of emptiness, the Buddha-nature. Statements about the presence of an absolute reality regardless of whether buddhas appear or not is found in a number of Buddhist scriptures. For example, the "Maitreya Chapter" of the twenty-five-thousand-line *Prajñāpāramitā sūtra* states: "Whether the tathāgatas appear or the tathāgathas do not appear, the true nature [*dharmatā*]

and expanse of the existence of phenomena remains." See Anonymous, *Shes*, 190.2, and Conze (1975), 648. This statement about the appearance of the tathāgatas is, of course, found in other scriptures, such as the *Saṃyutta*, the *Aṅguttara*, the *Śālistamba sūtra*, and the *Laṅkāvatāra sūtra*. See Lamotte (1988), 25, note 25. Significantly for Dol po pa, the *Bṛhaṭṭīkā* (*Yum gsum gnod 'joms*) commentary on the *Prajñāpāramitā sūtra*, often attributed to Vasubandhu, comments that "whether the tathāgatas appear or not" indicates that "the true nature [*dharmatā, chos nyid*] is a nature, but is not impermanent." See Anonymous (Vasubandhu?), *'Phags*, 336.5.5: *chos nyid de ngo bo nyid yin gyi mi rtag pa ni ma yin no/.*

123. In support of this view Dol po pa, *Bka' bsdu bzhi pa'i rang 'grel*, 646, quotes passages found in the *Uttaratantra* commentary by Asaṅga, as translated by Takasaki (1966), 288–90. Dol po pa, ibid., 647–50, also quotes extensively from the *Aṅgulimālīya sūtra* (Peking edition, vol. 34, passages beginning on 309) in regard to absolute reality as the ground, basis, and support of all phenomena. On 651 he comments:

> In many of the exceptional Bodhisattva Commentaries of Shambhala, all such definitive statements of the location of the residence of the Blessed One, the Buddha, [state it to] be the expanse of reality [*dharmadhātu*]. Since precisely that is the ground, location, and support of all phenomena, this falls like lightning upon the tops of the heads of those who assert that everything is groundless and rootless.

124. See notes 27 and 28 immediately above.

125. The phrase "from form to omniscience" (*gzugs nas rnam mkhyen gyi bar*) is a standard phrase referring to all the phenomena that make up the universe. In full form there are 108 categories, beginning with form, the first of the five aggregates, and ending with a Buddha's omniscience.

126. In the Kālacakra system thirty-six phenomena in seven groups are purified through receiving initiation and practicing the meditation. The seven groups are the five constituents, the five aggregates, the ten vital winds, the two channels, the six sense faculties and objects, the six action faculties and activities, and the two factors of pristine consciousness. The practitioner visualizes these as a maṇḍala of deities. See the Dalai Lama and Jeffrey Hopkins (1985), 72–73. As a result, at the time of achieving perfect buddhahood, the deities of this maṇḍala will actualize. Presumably Dol po pa is referring to the abiding reality of these phenomena as deities in the maṇḍala.

127. See note 86 immediately above.

128. Dol po pa, *Bka' bsdu bzhi pa'i rang 'grel*, 653–55, provides the following explanation of this section:

It is a flaw to realize that everything is permanent, because it is refuted by [the fact that] everything composite is impermanent. It is a quality to realize that the absolute buddha-body of reality is permanent, because if buddhahood is realized to always exist, it is understood as the Buddha-nature, and faith is gained.

It is a flaw to realize that everything is impermanent, because everything noncomposite is permanent. It is a quality to realize that everything composite is impermanent, because it is necessary for understanding to correspond to the truth, for adherence to permanence to be refuted, and so forth.

It is a flaw to realize that everything is pure, because it is refuted by [the fact] that everything tainted is impure. It is a quality to realize that the Buddha-nature is pure, because it is necessary to realize the meaning of naturally pure, completely pure, pristine, and extremely pure from the beginning.

It is a flaw to realize that everything is impure, because it is refuted by [the fact] that the expanse of reality [*dharmadhātu*] has always existed as pure from the beginning. It is a quality to realize that the appropriating aggregates are impure, because it fends off obsessive attachment. Meditation on the nine perceptions of ugliness is also taught for that purpose.

It is a flaw to realize that everything is bliss, because it is refuted by [the fact that] saṃsāra is suffering, and because sadness and renunciation of saṃsāra will not be born. It is a quality to realize that the expanse of reality [*dharmadhātu*] is bliss, because the understanding will correspond to the truth, and delight in meditation upon the expanse of reality will be born.

It is a flaw to realize that everything is suffering, because it is refuted by [the fact that] all the profound mode of reality is great bliss. It is a quality to realize that saṃsāra is suffering, because obsessive attachment will be fended off, and renunciation and sadness born.

There is both a flaw and a quality to realizing that a self [*ātman*] exists, because it is a flaw to realize that selves of individuals and phenomena exist, and a quality to realize that a self of thusness exists.

> There is also both a flaw and a quality to realizing that a self [*ātman*] does not exist, because it is a flaw to realize that the pure self does not exist, and a quality to realize that the selves of individuals and phenomena do not exist.
>
> It is a flaw to realize that all relative phenomena exist in reality, and a quality to realize that all absolute phenomena exist in reality.
>
> It is a flaw to realize that the Buddha-nature, which is endowed with many qualities, does not exist, and a quality to realize that the incidental stains do not exist in reality.
>
> It is a flaw to realize that all naturally primordial qualities are nothing in reality, and a quality to realize that all fabricated incidental phenomena are nothing in reality.

129. This is certainly directed at the position of the Sa skya pa school in Tibet. In his *Sdom gsum rab dbye* Sa skya Paṇḍi ta had said:

> The statement in some sūtras, and in the *Mahāyānottaratantra,* that all sentient beings have the essence of buddhahood [*buddhagarbha*], like a jewel within rags, should be understood as provisional.
>
> The intention of that provisional [teaching] is emptiness. It was taught for the purpose of rejecting the five poisons.
>
> The logic which refutes its [existence] as an entity is that if such an expanse of buddhahood [*buddhadhātu*] existed, it would be the same as the self [*ātman*] of the non-Buddhists; it would be a real entity; and it would completely contradict the sūtras of definitive meaning.
>
> Look at the *Tathāgatagarbha parivarta sūtra* concerning the meaning of this. And also know that the master Candrakīrti, in the *Madhyamakāvatāra,* also spoke of the Buddha-nature as provisional in meaning.

See Sa skya Paṇḍi ta, Sdom, 16: . . . *mdo sde 'ga zhig dang / theg pa chen po rgyud bla mar / gos ngan nang na rin chen ltar / sems can rnams la sangs rgyas kyi / snying po yod par gsungs pa ni / dgongs pa yin par shes par bya / de yi dgongs gzhi stong nyid yin / dgos pa skyon lnga spang phyir gsungs / dngos la gnod byed tshad ma ni / de 'dra'i sangs rgyas khams yod na / mu stegs bdag dang mtshungs pa dang / bden pa'i dngos por 'gyur phyir dang / nges pa'i don gyi mdo sde dang / rnam pa kun tu 'gal phyir ro / 'di don de bzhin gshegs pa yi / snying po'i le'u'i mdo sder ltos / slob dpon zla ba grags pas kyang / dbu ma la ni 'jug pa las / bde gshegs snying po drang don du / gsungs pa de yang shes par gyis /.*

130. Translation following the 'Dzam thang, 246, reading of *bgrang yas*, "infinite," instead of the Bhutanese reading of *bgrang yod* "finite." Dol po pa, *Bka' bsdu bzhi pa'i rang 'grel*, 657–58, quotes several scriptures in support of his position. In particular, he quotes the *Uttaratantra*: "Indivisible from the uncreated radiant light, [the Buddha-nature] is endowed with all the phenomena of buddhahood, which exceed the grains of sand on the shore of the river Gaṅga." The two sets of texts mentioned here are listed in notes 12 and 13 in chapter 1.

131. The line "and if the support is negated, the supported is negated," is found only in the 'Dzam thang edition, 247: *rten khegs na yang rten pa khegs phyir dang/.*

132. Dol po pa's point here is that if sentient beings had no intrinsic awareness at all they would be no different than the inanimate gross elements (*mahābhūta*, *'byung chen*) of earth, water, and so forth.

133. Translation according to the 'Dzam thang, 248, reading of *grol*, "liberation," instead of the Bhutanese reading of *gol*, which is an obvious scribal error.

134. This and the previous two lines are missing from the 'Dzam thang edition.

135. Presumably Dol po pa is here referring to different ways in which all, or only two or three of the four alternatives (*catuṣkoṭi*, *mu bzhi*) are to be employed. The four alternatives are whether something exists, does not exist, both exists and does not exist, or neither exists nor does not exist. For a study of the uses of these four positions, see Ruegg (1977). Dol po pa also directs the reader to his *Stong nyid kyi rab tu dbye ba'i bstan bcos* for clarification of this section. See Dol po pa, *Stong*.

136. The three representations (*rten gsum*) are representations of the buddha-bodies of the Buddha, such as images, representations of the enlightened speech, such as written scriptures, and representations of enlightened mind, such as stūpas.

137. These opinions are perhaps representative of the types of arguments used by people who opposed Dol po pa's construction of the great stūpa at Jo nang from 1330–1333. See chapter 1, section 4 above for more details on these events.

138. See note 36 to the verse in the translation of *A General Commentary on the Doctrine,* which deals with this same point.

139. The line "and denigrating also his three representations," is found only in the 'Dzam thang edition, 251: *de yi rten gsum la yang skur btab nas/*.

140. Dol po pa, *Bka' bsdu bzhi pa'i rang 'grel*, 660–61, elaborates on this point:

> For example, when a creature is killed there is the sin of taking a life, but when it dies by itself without being killed there is no sin of taking a life. Therefore, I have not seen it stated that there is a great sin from the natural ruin [of a stūpa]. If you see it, please record it in writing and show it to me also.
>
> Those of the Tretayuga and later [eons] who assert that everything is precisely empty of self-nature, thereby denigrating the Buddha, and on the basis of that also denigrating his three representations, are in agreement with the philosophical systems of some non-Buddhists and those of the barbarians and anti-gods. In the *Viśeṣastava* [*Khyad par du 'phags pa'i bstod pa*] it is stated by the master *Udbhaṭa Siddhasvāmin [Mtho btsun grub rje]:
>
> It is alleged, "The construction of monuments,
> temples, and so forth, is a cause of sin."
> Omniscient One, you have stated, "Precisely that is
> a cause of merit."
>
> In the commentary to it, the master *Prajñāvarman [Shes rab go cha] also makes it totally clear, so after seeing and understanding them, may religious persons benefit everyone, themselves and others.

The master *Udbhata Siddhāsvāmin (Mtho btsun grub rje) is the author of a number of texts in the Tibetan canon. See vol. 46, Peking edition of the *Bstan 'gyur*, pp. 1.1.1–4.3.3., for the text of the *Viśeṣastava*, and 40.2.2–52.5.4., for other texts. According to 'Jam mgon Kong sprul, *Udbhata Siddhāsvāmin was a brahmin who built eight temples at Nālandā and was responsible for first gathering together all the Mahāyāna scriptures there. See 'Jam mgon Kong sprul, *Theg*, vol. 1, 403.

141. Lha'i rgyal mtshan, *Chos*, 32a, mentions that Dol po pa constantly used these verses when making prayers. The same verses are also found at the end of several other texts by Dol po pa. See Dol po pa, *Stong*, 365, *Srid*, 379, *Rang*, 400, and *Dpal*, 138.

142. As emphasized above, since the term *three-natures* (*trisvabhāva*) does occur in the *Prajñāpāramitā sūtras*, as well as a number of other

scriptures generally accepted as Madhyamaka, Dol po pa felt strongly that it was actually a term characteristic of the Great Madhyamaka tradition.

143. For example, according to Nya dbon, *Bstan pa,* 24b, Nāgārjuna himself taught the existence of the universal ground consciousness (*ālayavijñāna*) in his *Byang chub sems 'grel.*

144. The eight groups of consciousness are usually identified with the Yogācāra, or Cittamātra, school. These eight are the universal ground consciousness (*ālayavijñāna*), agitated mentation, mental consciousness, tactile consciousness, gustatory consciousness, olfactory consciousness, auditive consciousness, and visual consciousness.

145. Takasaki (1966), 40, discusses the question of the *icchantika*s, who were said not to belong to any spiritual race (*agotra*) and thus have absolutely no possibility of attaining buddhahood. He sees this as one of the key points for distinguishing the pure *tathāgatagarbha* theory, in which the notion of *agotra* was considered a provisional teaching to convert people, from that of the Vijñānavāda.

146. As noted in chapters 1 and 3 above, Bla ma Dam pa Bsod nams rgyal mtshan was the leader of the Sa skya pa school. See the introduction to the translation of *The Fourth Council* for a discussion of the circumstances in which Bla ma Dam pa made his request to Dol po pa. As mentioned in chapter 3, section 2 above, where its significance was noted, Rton pa bzhi ldan, or "the one endowed with the four reliances," was Dol po pa's favorite pseudonym. He sometimes also signed works as Bstan rtsis chen po Rton pa bzhi ldan, or "the great calculator of the Doctrine, endowed with the four reliances." For example, see Dol po pa, *Chos dbyings*, 755.

Bibliography

European Language Sources

Anacker, Stefan (1984). *Seven Works of Vasubandhu.* Delhi: Motilal Banarsidass.

Bareau, André (1958). *Les Premiers Conciles bouddhiques.* Paris: Presses universitaires de France.

Bernbaum, Edwin (1995). "The Mythic Journey and Its Symbolism: A Study of the Development of Buddhist Guidebooks to Śambhala in Relation to their Antecedents in Hindu Mythology." Ph.D. dissertation. Berkeley: University of California.

Broido, Michael (1989). "The Jo-nang-pas on Madhyamaka: A Sketch." *The Tibet Journal* XIV: pp. 86–90.

Cabezón, José (1990). "The Canonization of Philosophy and the Rhetoric of Siddhānta in Tibetan Buddhism." In *Buddha Nature: A Festschrift in Honor of Minoru Kiyota*, ed. P. Griffiths and J. Keenan, pp. 7–26. Tokyo: Buddhist Books International.

Conze, Edward, and Iida, Shotaro (1968). "'Maitreya's Questions' in the *Prajñāparamitā*." In *Mélanges d'Indianisme a la Mémoire de Louis Renou*, pp. 229–42. Paris: E. de Boccard.

Conze, Edward (1973a). *The Perfection of Wisdom in Eight Thousand Lines & Its Verse Summary.* Bolinas: Four Seasons Foundation.

———. (1973b). *Perfect Wisdom: the Short Prajñāparamitā Texts.* London: Luzac and Co. Ltd.

———. (1975). *The Large Sutra on Perfect Wisdom.* Los Angeles: University of California Press.

Dalai Lama and Jeffrey Hopkins (1985). *The Kalachakra Tantra: Rite of Initiation.* London: Wisdom Publications.

Davidson, Ronald (1981). "The *Litany of Names of Mañjuśrī:* Text and Translation of the *Mañjuśrīnāmasaṃgīti.*" In *Tantric and Taoist Studies in Honour of R. A. Stein*, ed. Michel Strickmann, vol. 1, pp. 1–69. Brussels: Institut Belge des Hautes Études Chinoises.

de La Vallée Poussin, Louis (1908). "Ages of the World (Buddhist)." In *The Encyclopedia of Religion and Ethics*, ed. James Hastings, vol. 12, pp. 187–90. New York: Charles Scribner's Sons, 1921.

de Montaigne, Michel (1993). *The Essays of Michel de Montaigne*. Trans. M. A. Screech. London-New York: Penguin Press.

Decleer, Hubert (n.d.). "The Vajra Throne (Buddhgaya), according to the Sacred Biography of Rwa Lotsāwa." Unpublished paper.

Dreyfus, Georges (1997). *Recognizing Reality: Dharmakīrti's Philosphy and Its Tibetan Interpretations*. Albany: State University of New York Press.

Dudjom Rinpoche, Jikdrel Yeshe Dorje (1991). *The Nyingma School of Tibetan Buddhism: Its Fundamentals and History*. Trans. Gyurme Dorje and Matthew Kapstein. Boston: Wisdom Publications.

Ehrhard, Franz-Karl (1989). "A Renovation of Svayambhunath-Stupa in the 18th Century and its History." *Ancient Nepal* 114 (October–November): pp. 1–8.

———. (1990). "The Stupa of Bodhnath: A Preliminary Analysis of the Written Sources." *Ancient Nepal* 120 (October–November): pp. 1–9.

———. (1994). Review of *The Buddha Within: Tathāgatagarbha Doctrine According to the Shentong Interpretation of the Ratnagotravibhāga*, by S. K. Hookham. *Zeitschrift der Deutschen Morgenländischen Gesellschaft* 144.2: pp. 415–19.

Germano, David (1992). "Poetic Thought, the Intelligent Universe, and the Mystery of Self: the Tantric Synthesis of Rdzogs chen in Fourteenth Century Tibet." Ph.D. Dissertation, Univeristy of Wisconsin.

Griffiths, Paul (1993). Review of *The Buddha Within: Tathāgatagarbha Doctrine According to the Shentong Interpretation of the Ratnagotravibhaga*, by S. K. Hookham. *Journal of the American Oriental Society* 113.2: pp. 317–19.

Grönbold, Günter (1982). "Materialien zur Geschichte des Ṣaḍaṅga-yoga: III. Die Guru-Reihen im buddhistischen Ṣaḍaṅga-yoga." *Zentralasiatische Studien* 16: pp. 337–47.

———. (1983). "Der Sechsgliedrige Yoga des *Kālacakra-tantra.*" *Asiatische Studien/Études Asiatiques* 37: pp. 25–45.

———. (1991). "Das Datum des Buddha nach tantrischen Texten." In *The Dating of the Historical Buddha/Die Datierung des historischen Buddha*, ed. Heinz Bechert, pt. 1, pp. 385–402. Göttingen: Vandenhoeck and Ruprecht.

Harris, Ian (1991). *The Continuity of Madhyamaka and Yogācāra in Indian Mahāyāna Buddhism*. Leiden: E. J Brill.

Hirakawa, Akira (1990). *A History of Indian Buddhism from Śākyamuni to Early Mahāyāna*. Trans. and ed. Paul Groner. Honolulu: University of Hawaii.

Hirsch, Edward (1995). "In the Beginning: A New Translation of the Hebrew Bible Offers a Text for the Ear as Well as the Eye." *The New York Times Book Review*, December 24, pp. 5–6.

Hofinger, Marcel (1946). *Étude sur la concile de Vaiśālī*. Louvain: Bureaux du Muséon.

Hookham, S. K. (1991). *The Buddha Within: Tathāgatagarbha Doctrine According to the Shentong Interpretation of the Ratnagotravibhāga*. Albany: State University of New York Press.

Iida, Shotaro (1980). *Reason and Emptiness*. Tokyo: Hokuseido Press.

Jackson, David (1989). *The Early Abbots of 'Phan-po Na-lendra: The Vicissitudes of a Great Tibetan Monastery in the 15th Century*. Vienna: Arbeitskreis für Tibetische und Buddhistische Studien Universität Wien.

———. (1989b). *The 'Miscellaneous Series" of Tibetan texts in the Bihar Research Society, Patna: A Handlist*. Stuttgart: Franz Steiner Verlag Wiebaden GMbH.

———. (1994). *Enlightenment by a Single Means*. Vienna: Österreichische Akademie der Wissenschaften.

———. (1996). *A History of Tibetan Painting*. Vienna: Österreichische Akademie der Wissenschaften.

Jacobi, H. (1908). "Ages of the World (Indian)." In *The Encyclopedia of Religion and Ethics*, ed. James Hastings, vol 1, pp. 200–202. New York: Charles Scribner's Sons.

Kapstein, Matthew (1991). "New Sources for Tibetan Buddhist History." *China Exchange News* 19, nos. 3 and 4 (Fall/Winter): pp. 15–19.

———. (1992). *The 'Dzam-thang Edition of the Collected Works of Kun-mkhyen Dol-po-pa Shes-rab rgyal-mtshan: Introduction and Catalogue*. Delhi: Shedrup Books.

———. (1992b). "The Illusion of Spiritual Progress." In *Paths to Liberation: The Mārga and Its Transformations in Buddhist Thought*, ed. Robert E. Buswell, Jr., and Robert M. Gimello, pp. 193–224. Honolulu: University of Hawaii Press.

———. (1992c). "Remarks on the *Maṇi bKa'-'bum* and the Cult of Āvalokiteśvara in Tibet." In *Tibetan Buddhism: Reason and Revelation*, ed. Steven D. Goodman and Ronald M. Davidson, pp. 79–94. Albany: State University of New York Press.

———. (1994). "A Golden Age of Understanding? Kun-mkhyen Dol-po-pa (1292–1361) on the *Kṛtayuga* and What Followed." Unpublished paper read at the Congress of the International Association of Buddhist Studies, Mexico City, October 1994.

———. (1996). "*gDams ngag*: Tibetan Technologies of the Self." In *Tibetan Literature*, ed. José Cabezón and Roger Jackson, pp. 275–89. Ithaca: Snow Lion.

———. (n.d.). "From Kun-mkhyen Dol-po-pa to 'Ba'-mda' Dge-legs: Three Jo-nang-pa Masters on the Interpretation of the *Prajñāpāramitā*." Forthcoming in *The Proceedings of the 1995 Meeting of the International Association of Tibetan Studies*, ed. Ernst Steinkellner.

Katz, Nathan (1983). "Tibetan hermeneutics and the *yāna* controversy." In *Contributions on Tibetan and Buddhist Religion and Philosophy*, ed. E. Steinkellner and H. Tauscher, vol. 2, pp. 107–30. Vienna: Arbeitskreis fur Tibetische und Buddhistische Studien.

Kochumuttom, Thomas (1982). *A Buddhist Doctrine of Experience*. Delhi: Motilal Banarsidass.

van der Kuijp, Leonard (1988). "On the Life and Political Career of Ta'i-si-tu Byang-chub rgyal-mtshan (1302–?1364)." In *Tibetan History and Language*, ed. Ernst Steinkellner, pp. 277–327. Vienna: Arbeitskreis für Tibetische und Buddhistische Studien Universität Wien.

———. (1993). "Fourteenth Century Tibetan Cultural History III: The Oeuvre of Bla ma dam pa Bsod nams rgyal mtshan (1312–1375), Part One." *Berliner Indologische Studien* 7: pp. 109–47.

———. (1993b). "*Jambhala: An Imperial Envoy to Tibet During the Late Yuan." *Journal of the American Oriental Society* 113.4: pp. 529–38.

———. (1994). "Fourteenth Century Tibetan Cultural History I: Ta'i-si-tu Byang-chub rgyal-mtshan as a Man of Religion." *Indo-Iranian Journal* 37: pp. 139–49.

———. (1994b). "On the *Lives* of Śākyaśrībhadra (?–?1225)." *Journal of the American Oriental Society* 114.4: pp. 599–616.

Lamotte, Étienne (1988). *History of Indian Buddhism: from the Origins to the Śaka Era*. Trans. Sara Webb-Boin. Louvain: Institut Orientaliste.

Lopez, Donald (1996). "Polemical Literature (*dGag lan*)." In *Tibetan Literature*, ed. José Cabezón and Roger Jackson, pp. 217–28. Ithaca: Snow Lion.

Nagao, Gadjin (1991). *Mādhyamika and Yogācāra*. Trans. Leslie Kawamura. Albany: State University of New York Press.

Need, David (1993). Review of *The Buddha Within: Tathāgatagarbha Doctrine According to the Shentong Interpretation of the Ratnagotravibhāga*, by S. K. Hookham. *Philosophy East & West* XLIII.3, July: pp. 585–88.

Newman, John (1985). "A Brief History of the Kalachakra." In *The Wheel of Time: The Kalachakra in Context,* ed. Geshe Lhundub Sopa, Roger Jackson, and John Newman, pp. 51–90. Madison: Deer Park Books.

———. (1987). "The Outer Wheel of Time: Vajrayāna Buddhist Cosmology in the Kālacakra Tantra." Ph.D. Dissertation, University of Wisconsin.

———. (1988). "Buddhist Sanskrit in the Kālacakra Tantra." *Journal of the International Association of Buddhist Studies* 11.1: pp. 123–40.

———. (1992). "Buddhist Siddhānta in the Kālacakra tantra." *Wiener Zeitschrift für die Kunde Südasiens* 36: pp. 227–34.

Obermiller, E., trans. (1932). *History of Buddhism*. Heidelberg: O. Harrassowitz.

———. (1988). *Prajñāparamitā in Tibetan Buddhism*. Delhi: Classics India Publications.

Onada, Shunzo (1992). *Monastic Debate in Tibet*. Vienna: Arbeitskreis für Tibetische und Buddhistische Studien Universität Wien.

Orofino, Giacomella (1994). "Divination with Mirrors. Observations on a Simile Found in the Kālacakra Literature." In *Tibetan Studies: Proceedings of the 6th Seminar of the International Association for Tibetan Studies*, ed. Per Kvaerne, vol. 2, pp. 612–28. Oslo: The Institute for Comparative Research in Human Culture.

Petech, Luciano (1990). *Central Tibet and the Mongols*. Rome: Istituto Italiano per il Medio ed Estremo Oriente.

Pingree, David (1981). *Jyotiḥśāstra: Astral and Mathematical Literature*. Wiesbaden: Otto Harrassowitz.

Prebish, Charles (1974). "A Review of Scholarship on the Buddhist Councils." *Journal of Asian Studies* 33: pp. 239–54.

Ricca, Franco, and Lo Bue, Erberto (1995). *The Great Stupa of Gyantse*. London: Serindia Publications.

Roerich, George N., trans. (1976). *The Blue Annals*. Delhi: Motilal Banarsidas.

Ruegg, David Seyfort (1963). "The Jo nang pas: A School of Buddhist Ontologists according to the Grub mtha' shel gyi me long." *Journal of the American Oriental Society* 83: pp. 73–91.

———. (1966) *The Life of Bu ston rin po che*. Rome: Instituto Italiano per il Medio ed Estremo Oriente.

———. (1968). "On the Dge lugs pa Theory of the *tathāgatagarbha*." In *Pratidānam*, ed. J. C. Heesterman, G. H. Schokker, and V. I. Subramoniam, pp. 500–509. The Hague–Paris: Mouton.

———. (1969). *La Théorie du Tathāgatagarbha et du Gotra*. Paris: École Française d'Extrême-Orient.

———. (1973). *Le Traité du Tathāgatagarbha de Bu ston Rin chen grub*. Paris: École Française d'Extrême-Orient.

———. (1977). "The Uses of the Four Positions of the *Catuṣkoṭi* and the Problem of the Description of Reality in Mahāyāna Buddhism." *Journal of Indian Philosophy* 5: pp. 1–71.

———. (1981). *The Literature of the Madhyamaka School of Philosophy in India*. Wiesbaden: Otto Harrassowitz.

———. (1988). "A Kar ma Bka' brgyud Work on the Lineages and Traditions of the Indo-Tibetan Dbu ma (Madhyamaka). In *Orientalia Iosephi Tucci Memoriae Dictata*, ed. G. Gnoli and L. Lanciotti, vol. 3, pp. 1249–80. Rome, 1988.

———. (1989). *Buddha Nature, Mind and the Problem of Gradualism in a Comparative Perspective*. London: School of Oriental and African Studies.

———. (1992). "Notes on some Indian and Tibetan Reckonings of the Buddha's Nirvāṇa and the Duration of his Teaching." In *The Dating of the Historical Buddha / Die Datierung des historischen Buddha*, ed. Heinz Bechert, pt. 2, pp. 263–90. Göttingen: Vandenhoeck and Ruprecht.

———. (1995). "Some Reflections on the Place of Philosophy in the Study of Buddhism." *Journal of the International Association of Buddhist Studies* 18.2: pp. 145–81.

Schaeffer, Kurtis (1995). "The Enlightened Heart of Buddhahood: A Study and Translation of The Third Karma pa Rang byung rdo rje's Work on Tathāgatagarbha, The *Bde bzhin gshegs pa'i snying po gtan la dbab pa*." Master's thesis, University of Washington.

Schoening, Jeffrey (1995). *The Śālistamba Sūtra and its Indian Commentaries*. 2 vols. Vienna: Arbeitskreis für Tibetische und Buddhistische Studien Universität Wien.

Schuh, Dieter (1973). *Untersuchungen zur Geschichte der tibetischen Kalenderrechnung*. Wiesbaden: Franz Steiner, Verzeichnis der Orientalischen Handschriften in Deutschland, Supplement Band 16.

Shantideva (1979). *A Guide to the Bodhisattva's Way of Life*. Trans. Stephen Batchelor. Dharamsala: Library of Tibetan Works and Archives.

Smith, E. Gene (1968). Introduction to *The Autobiography and Diaries of Si-tu Paṇ-chen*. New Delhi: International Academy of Indian Culture.

———. (1969). Introduction to *The Autobiography of Paṇ chen Blo-bzang chos-kyi rgyal-mtshan*. New Delhi: Gendan Sungrab Minyam Gyunphel Series.

———. (1970). Introduction to *Kongtrul's Encyclopedia of Indo-Tibetan Culture*. Śatapiṭaka Series 90. New Delhi: International Academy of Indian Culture.

Snellgrove, David (1987). *Indo-Tibetan Buddhism*. Boston: Shambhala Publications.

Stearns, Cyrus (1980). "The Life and Teachings of the Tibetan Saint Thang-stong rgyal po, 'King of the Empty Plain.'" Master's thesis, University of Washington.

———. (1995). "Dol-po-pa Shes-rab rgyal-mtshan and the Genesis of the *Gzhan stong* Position in Tibet." *Asiatische Studien / Études Asiatiques* XLIX, 4: pp. 829–52.

———. (1996). "The Life and Tibetan Legacy of the Indian *Mahāpaṇḍita* Vibhūticandra." *Journal of the International Association of Buddhist Studies* 19.1: pp. 127–71.

Suganuma, Akira (1967). "The Five Dharmas in the Laṅkāvatārasūtra." *Journal of Indian and Buddhist Studies* XV.2: pp. 956–63.

Takasaki, Jikido (1966). *A Study of the Ratnagotravibhāga (Uttaratantra)*. Rome: Istituto Italiano per il Medio ed Estremo Oriente.

Tanabe, George (1992). *Myōe the Dreamkeeper*. Cambridge: Harvard University Press.

Thurman, Robert (1984). *Tsong-kha-pa's Speech of Gold in the Essence of True Eloquence*. Princeton: Princeton University Press.

Tucci, Giuseppe (1973). *Transhimalaya*. Geneva: Nagel Publishers.

———. (1980). *Tibetan Painted Scrolls*. Rome: Libreria Dello Stato. Reprint: Kyoto: Rinsen.

Verhagen, Pieter (1994). *A History of Sanskrit Grammatical Literature in Tibet*. Leiden: E. J. Brill.

Vitali, Roberto (1990). *Early Temples of Central Tibet*. London: Serindia Publications.

Vostrikov, A. I. (1970). *Tibetan Historical Literature*. Calcutta: Soviet Indology Series.

Williams, Paul (1983). "A Note on Some Aspects of Mi bskyod rdo rje's Critique of dGe lugs pa Madhyamaka." *Journal of Indian Philosophy* 11: pp. 125–45.

———. (1989). *Mahāyāna Buddhism*. London: Routledge.

Tibetan and Sanskrit Sources

Anonymous. *Bcom ldan 'das dpal dus kyi 'khor lo'i chos 'byung ngo mtshar rtogs brjod*. Paris: Musée Guimet (#54588), incomplete ms., 52 fols.

———. *'Jam dpal ye shes sems dpa'i don dam pa'i mtshan yang dag par brjod pa (Mañjuśrījñānasattvaparamārthanāmasaṃgīti)*. The Tibetan Tripitaka, ed. D. T. Suzuki, vol. 1, pp. 117.1.1.–124.3.7. Tokyo–Kyoto: Tibetan Tripitaka Research Institute, 1956.

———. *'Phags pa shes rab kyi pha rol tu phin pa khri brgyad stong pa shes bya ba theg pa chen po'i mdo (Āryāṣṭādaśasāhasrikā prajñāpāramitā nāmā mahāyāna sūtra)*. The Tibetan Tripitaka, ed. D. T. Suzuki, vol. 20. Tokyo–Kyoto: Tibetan Tripitaka Research Institute, 1956.

———. *'Phags pa shes rab kyi pha rol tu phin pa lnga brgya pa (Āryāpañcaśatikā prajñāpāramitā mahāyāna sūtra)*. The Tibetan Tripitaka, ed. D. T. Suzuki, vol. 21, pp. 243.3.2.–250.5.2. Tokyo–Kyoto: Tibetan Tripitaka Research Institute, 1956.

———. *Shes rab kyi pha rol tu phyin pa stong phrag nyi shu lnga pa (Pañcaviṃśatisāhasrikā prajñāpāramitā)*. The Tibetan Tripitaka, ed. D. T. Suzuki, vol. 19, pp. 243.3.2.–250.5.2. Tokyo–Kyoto: Tibetan Tripitaka Research Institute, 1956.

Anonymous (Vasubandhu?). *'Phags pa shes rab kyi pha rol tu phyin pa 'bum pa dang nyi khri lnga stong pa dang khri brgyad stong pa'i rgya cher bshad pa (Ārya śatasāhasrikā pañcaviṃśatisāhasrikāṣṭādaśasāhasrikā prajñāpāramitā bṛhaṭṭīkā)*. The Tibetan Tripitaka, ed. D. T. Suzuki, vol. 93: pp. 202.1.1.–339.3.6. Tokyo–Kyoto: Tibetan Tripitaka Research Institute, 1956.

Karma 'phrin las pa. *Dri lan drang ba dang nges pa'i don gyi snang byed ces bya ba ngo gro bla ma'i dris lan*. In *The Songs of Esoteric Practice (Mgur) and Replies to Doctrinal Questions (Dris lan) of Karma-'phrin-las-pa*, pp. 108–39. New Delhi: Ngawang Topgay, 1975.

———. *Dri lan padma dkar po'i chun po zhes bya ba rgya ston dris lan*. In *The Songs of Esoteric Practice (Mgur) and Replies to Doctrinal Questions (Dris lan) of Karma-'phrin-las-pa*, pp. 92–108. New Delhi: Ngawang Topgay, 1975.

———. *Dri lan yid kyi mun sel zhe bya ba lcags mo'i dris lan*. In *The Songs of Esoteric Practice (Mgur) and Replies to Doctrinal Questions (Dris lan) of Karma-'phrin-las-pa*, pp. 88–92. New Delhi: Ngawang Topgay, 1975.

Kalkin Puṇḍarīka. *'Jig rten khams kyi le'u'i 'grel bshad dri ma med pa'i 'od mchan bcas*. Edited and annotated by Bu ston Rin chen grub. In *The Collected Works of Bu-ston*, pt. 2, pp. 301–603. New Delhi: International Academy of Indian Culture, 1965.

———. *Bsdus pa'i rgyud kyi rgyal po dus kyi 'khor lo'i 'grel bshad/rtsa ba'i rgyud kyi rjes su 'jug pa stong phrag bcu gnyis pa dri ma med pa'i 'od*. Sde-dge Bstan-'gyur Series, vol. 10–11. Delhi: Delhi Karmapae Chodhey, 1982.

———. *Vimalaprabhāṭīkā of Kalki Śrī Puṇḍarīka on Śrī Laghukālacakratantrarāja by Śrī Mañjuśrīyaśa*, vol. 1. Edited by Jagannatha Upadhyaya. Bibliotheca Indo-Tibetica Series no. 11. Sarnath: Central Institute of Higher Tibetan Studies, 1986.

Kalkin Yaśas. *Mchog gi dang po'i sangs rgyas las phyung ba rgyud kyi rgyal po chen po dpal dus kyi 'khor lo'i bsdus pa'i rgyud go sla'i mchan bcas*. Edited and annotated by Bu ston Rin chen grub. In *The Collected Works of Bu-ston*, pt. 1, pp. 1–299. New Delhi: International Academy of Indian Culture, 1965.

———. (P). *Mchog gi dang po'i sangs rgyas las phyung ba rgyud kyi rgyal po dpal dus kyi 'khor lo*. The Tibetan Tripitaka, ed. D. T. Suzuki, vol. 1, pp. 127.4.1–174.5.8. Tokyo–Kyoto: Tibetan Tripitaka Research Institute, 1956.

Kun dga' grol mchog, Jo nang rje btsun. *Khrid brgya'i brgyud pa'i lo rgyus*. In *Gdams ngag mdzod*, vol. 12, pp. 309–40. Delhi: N. Lungtok and N. Gyaltsan, 1972.

———. *Lta ba'i gnas la som nyi yi/ 'phyang mor spyod pa las bzlog nas/ 'di nyid rje btsun dgongs pa ces/ mngon sum gsal ba'i nges gsang bzhugs*. Beijing: Cultural Palace of Nationalities, ms., 16 fols.

———. *Paṇdi ta chen po shākya mchog ldan gyi rnam par thar pa zhib mo rnam par 'byed pa*. In *The Complete Works (Gsung-'bum) of Gser-mdog paṇ-chen Shākya mchog-ldan*, vol. 16, pp. 1–233. Thimphu: Kunzang Tobgey, 1975.

———. *Zab khrid brgya dang brgyad kyi yi ge*. In *Gdams ngag mdzod*, vol. 12, pp. 369–595. Delhi: N. Lungtok and N. Gyaltsan, 1972.

———. *Zab lam rdo rje'i rnal sbyor ba yan lag drug gi ngo sprod glur blangs pa thos blo rdeg chen* po. In *Gsung thor bu ba'i bskor*. Beijing: Cultural Palace of Nationalities, ms., fols. 26a–28b.

———. *Zhen pa rang grol gyi lhug par brjod pa'i gtam skal bzang dad pa'i shing rta 'dren byed*. In *The Autobiographies of Jo-nang Kun-dga' grol-mchog and His Previous Embodiments*, vol. 2, pp. 285–534. New Delhi: Tibet House, 1982.

———. *Rigs ldan chos kyi rgyal po rnam rgyal grags pa bzang po'i rnam par thar pa rab bsngags snyan pa'i 'brug sgra*. Kathmandu: Nepal-German Manuscript Preservation Project. Microfilm reel # E-1872/6. Xylograph, 39 fols.

———. *Gsung thor bu ba'i bskor bzhugs pa e ma ho*. Beijing: Cultural Palace of Nationalities, ms., 72 fols.

Kun dga' rdo rje, Tshal pa. *Deb ther dmar po rnams kyi dang po hu lan deb ther 'di*. Beijing: Mi rigs dpe skrun khang, 1981.

Kun dga' bzang po, Ngor chen. *Bstan bcos 'gyur ro 'tshal gyi dkar chag thub bstan rgyas pa'i nyi 'od*. In *The Complete Works of the Great Masters of the Sa skya Sect of Tibetan Buddhism*, vol. 10, pp. 357.4.3–366.4.3.

———. *Lam 'bras bu dang bcas pa'i man ngag gi byung tshul gsung ngag rin po che bstan pa rgyas pa'i nyi 'od*. (Completed by Gung ru ba Shes rab bzang po.) In *The Complete Works of the Great Masters of the Sa skya Sect of Tibetan Buddhism (Sa skya pa'i bka' 'bum)*, vol. 9, pp. 108–26. Tokyo: The Toyo Bunko, 1968.

———. *Sa bzangs bsod nams dpal gyi dris lan*. In *The Complete Works of the Great Masters of the Sa skya Sect of Tibetan Buddhism Buddhism (Sa skya pa'i bka' 'bum)*, vol. 10, pp. 379.4.2–381.4.3.

Kun spangs Chos grags dpal bzang. *Chos rje kun mkhyen chen po'i rnam thar gsal sgron gyi rnam grangs dge legs chen po nor bu'i 'phreng ba*. In *The 'Dzam-thang Edition of the Collected Works (Gsung-'bum) of Kun-mkhyen Dol-po-pa Shes-rab rgyal-mtshan*, vol. 1. Delhi: Shedrup Books, 1992.

Krang dbyi sun, ed. (1993). *Bod rgya tshig mdzod chen mo*. 2 vols. Beijing: Mi rigs dpe skrun khang.

Klong chen rab 'byams pa. *Rgyab chos zab don gnad kyi me long*. In *Zab mo yang tig*, pt. 2, in *Snying thig ya bzhi*, vol. 13. Darjeeling: Taklung Tsetrul Rinpoche Pema Wangyal, 1979.

———. *Rdzogs pa chen po sems nyid ngal gso'i 'grel pa shing rta chen po*. In *Ngal gso skor gsum, rang grol skor gsum, and sngags kyi spyi don*, vol. 1. Gangtok: Ven. Dodrup Chen Rimpoche, 1973.

Dkon mchog bstan pa rab rgyas, Brag dgon pa. *Yul mdo smad kyi ljongs su thub bstan rin po che ji ltar dar ba'i tshul gsal bar brjod pa deb ther rgya mtsho*. Kansu: Mi rigs dpe skrun khang, 1987.

Bkra shis dbang 'dus, ed. *Bod kyi lo rgyus yig tshags dang gzhung yig phyogs bsdus dwangs shel me long*. Beijing: Mi rigs dpe skrun khang, 1989.

Gung ru ba Shes rab bzang po. *Lam 'bras bu dang bcas pa'i man ngag gi byung tshul gsung ngag rin po che bstan pa rgyas pa'i nyi 'od*. (Completing the work of Kun dga' bzang po, Ngor chen). In *The Complete Works of the Great Masters of the Sa skya Sect of Tibetan Buddhism (Sa skya pa'i bka' 'bum)*, vol. 9, pp. 108–26. Tokyo: The Toyo Bunko, 1968.

Go rams pa Bsod nams seng ge. *Lta ba'i shan 'byed theg mchog gnad kyi zla zer*. In *The Complete Works of the Great Masters of the Sa skya Sect of Tibetan Buddhism (Sa skya pa'i bka' 'bum)*, vol. 13, pp. 1.1.1.–24.2.6. Tokyo: The Toyo Bunko, 1968.

Dgra 'dul dbang po, 'Dar stod. *Tha snyad rig gnas lnga ji ltar byung ba'i tshul gsal bar byed pa blo gsal mgrin rgyan legs bshad nor bu'i phreng ba*. In *Bstan rtsis gsal ba'i nyin byed dang tha snyad rig gnas lnga'i byung tshul*, pp. 253–322. Lhasa: Bod ljongs mi dmangs dpe skrun khang, 1987.

'Gos lo Gzhon nu dpal. *Deb ther sngon po*. 2 vols. Chengdu: Mi rigs dpe skrun khang, 1984.

Rgyal ba ye shes. *Kun spangs chos rje'i rnam thar yon tan rab gsal*. Beijing: Cultural Palace of Nationalities, ms., 40 fols.

Ngag gi dbang po. *Khyab bdag 'khor lo'i mgon po rje btsun dam pa blo bzang bstan pa'i rgyal mtshan gyi rnam thar skal bzang dad pa'i shing rta*. In *Life and Works of Jibcundampa I*, pp. 267–409. New Delhi: International Acadamy of Indian Culture, Śata-piṭaka Series, vol. 294, 1982.

Ngag dbang blo gros grags pa. *Dpal ldan jo nang pa'i chos 'byung rgyal ba'i chos tshul gsal byed zla ba'i sgron me*. Koko Nor: Krung go'i bod kyi shes rig dpe skrun khang, 1992.

Ngag dbang blo bzang rgya mtsho, Ta la'i bla ma V. *Za hor gyi ban de ngag dbang blo bzang rgya mtsho'i 'di snang 'khrul ba'i rol rtsed rtogs brjod kyi tshul du bkod pa du kū la'i gos bzang las glegs bam dang po*. Lhasa: Bod ljongs mi dmangs dpe skrun khang, 1989.

———. *Zab pa dang rgya che ba'i dam pa'i chos kyi thob yig ganggā'i chu rgyun las glegs bam bzhi pa*, vol. 4. Delhi: Nechung and Lakhar, 1971.

———. *Rigs dang dkyil 'khor kun gyi khyab bdag rdo rje 'chang blo gsal rgya mtsho grags pa rgyal mtshan dpal bzang po'i rnam par thar pa slob bshad bstan pa'i nyi 'od*. In *Lam-'bras slob-bshad*, vol. 2, pp. 399–637. Dehra Dun: Sakya Centre, 1983.

———. *Lha ldan sprul pa'i gtsug lag khang gi dkar chag shel dkar me long*. Lhasa: Bod ljongs mi dmangs dpe skrun khang, 1987.

Chos kyi rgya mtsho, Kaḥ thog Si tu. *Gangs ljongs dbus gtsang gnas bskor lam yig nor bu zla shel gyi se mo do*. Tashijong: Sungrab Nyamso Gyunphel Parkhang, 1972.

Chos kyi dbang phyug, Brag dkar rta so sprul sku. *Dpal rig 'dzin chen po rdo rje tshe dbang nor bu'i zhabs kyi rnam par thar pa'i cha shas brjod pa ngo mtshar dad pa'i rol mtsho*. In *The Collected Works (Gsung 'bum) of Kaḥ-thog rig-'dzin chen-po Tshe-dbang nor-bu*, vol. 1, pp. 1–376. Dalhousie: Damchoe Sangpo, 1976.

Chos kyi 'byung gnas, Si tu paṇ chen (with 'Be lo Tshe dbang kun khyab). *Bsgrub brgyud karma kam tshang brgyud pa rin po che'i ram par thar pa rab 'byams nor bu zla ba chu shel gyi pheng ba*, vol. 1. New Delhi: D. Gyaltsan and K. Legshay, 1972.

———. *Ta'i si tur 'bod pa karma bstan pa'i nyin byed kyi rang tshul drangs por brjod pa dri bral shel gyi me long*. Published as *The Autobiography & Diaries of Si-tu Paṇ-chen*. New Delhi: International Academy of Indian Culture, 1968.

'Jam mgon Kong sprul, Blo gros mtha' yas. *Theg pa'i sgo kun las btus pa gsung rab rin po che'i mdzod bslab pa gsum legs par ston pa'i bstan bcos shes bya kun khyab*. 3 vols. Beijing: Mi rigs dpe skrun khang, 1982.

———. *Rnal 'byor bla na med pa'i rgyud sde rgya mtsho'i snying po bsdus pa zab mo nang gi don nyung ngu'i tshig gis rnam par 'grol ba zab don snang byed*. Rumtek: 1970.

———. *Gzhan stong dbu ma chen po'i lta khrid rdo rje zla ba dri ma med pa'i 'od zer*. In *The Collected Works of 'Jam-mgon Kong-sprul (Rgya chen bka' mdzod)*, vol. 8, pp. 581–611. Paro: Ngodup, 1976.

'Jam mgon A myes zhabs Ngag dbang kun dga' bsod nams. *Chos rje dpal ldan bla ma dam pas lam 'bras gsung dus kyi gnad kyi zin bris rgyal khang blo gros seng ges mdzad pa zhib tu bshad pa sbas pa mig 'byed*. Ms., 16 fols.

———. *Dpal rdo rje nag po chen po'i zab mo'i chos skor rnams byung ba'i tshul legs par bshad pa bstan srung chos kun gsal ba'i nyin byed*. 2 vols. New Delhi: T. G. Dhongthog Rinpoche, 1979.

'Jam dbyangs mkhyen brtse'i dbang po. *Gzhan stong dbu ma'i rnam gzhag snying por dril ba*. In *The Collected Works (Gsung 'bum) of the Great 'Jam-dbyangs mkhyen-brtse'i dbang-po*, vol. 6, pp. 214–21. Gangtok: 1977.

'Jam dbyangs mkhyen brtse'i dbang phyug. *Rje btsun rdo rje 'chang sgo rum pa chen po kun dga' legs pa'i blo gros rgyal mtshan dpal bzang po'i rigs sngags kyi rtogs pa brjod pa'i gtam ngo mtshar yid bzhin gyi chu gter bzhad pa*. In *Lam-'bras slob-bshad*, vol. 2, pp. 249–397. Dehra Dun: Sakya Centre, 1983.

———. *Gdams ngag byung tshul gyi zin bris gsang chen bstan pa rgyas byed ces bya ba kha'u brag rdzong pa'i bzhed pa ma nor ba ban rgan mkhyen brtse'i nyams len*. In *Lam-'bras slob-bshad*, vol. 14, pp. 1–154. Dehra Dun: Sakya Centre, 1983.

———. *Bla ma rin po che mkhan chen pa'i rnam thar ngo mtshar snye ma zhes bya ba sgro bkur dang bral zhing yid ches la dgod bro ba zhig*. In *Lam-'bras slob-bshad*, vol. 3, pp. 1–250. Dehra Dun: Sakya Centre, 1983.

'Jam dbyangs chos kyi blo gros. *Khyab bdag bla ma 'khor lo'i mgon po padma ye shes rdo rje'i gsang ba'i rnam thar gyi cha shas dad gsum pad dkar bzhad pa'i nyin byed*. In *The Complete Works of Rdzong-gsar mkhyen-brtse rin-po-che 'Jam-dbyangs chos-kyi blo-gros*, vol. 8. Gangtok: Sherab Gyaltsen, 1985.

Nya dbon Kun dga' dpal. *Bstan bcos mngon par rtogs pa'i rgyan 'grel pa dang bcas pa'i rgyas 'grel bshad sbyar yid kyi mun sel*. New Delhi: Ngawang Sopa, 1978.

———. *Bstan pa spyi 'grel zhes bya ba'i gsol 'debs kyi rnam bshad dgongs pa rnam gsal yid kyi mun sel*. Beijing: Cultural Palace of Nationalities, ms., 53 fols.

Tāranātha, Jo nang rje btsun. *Khrid brgya'i brgyud pa'i lo rgyus kha skong*. In *Gdams ngag mdzod*, vol. 12, pp. 341–58. Delhi: N. Lungtok and N. Gyaltsen, 1972.

———. *'Khyog po ri khrod kyi gnas bshad*. Kathmandu: National Archives. Xylograph, 3 fols.

———. *Dge bshes dpal ldan shakya bstan 'dzin gyi dris lan gnad kyi gsal byed*. In *The Collected Works of Jo-nang rje-btsun Tāranātha*, vol. 13, pp. 511–65. Leh: Smanrtsis Shesrig Dpemdzod, 1983.

———. *Rgyal khams pa tā ra nā thas bdag nyid kyi rnam thar nges par brjod pa'i deb ther / shin tu zhib mo ma bcos lhug pa'i rtogs brjod*. Paro: Ngodrup and Sherab Drimay, 1978.

———. *Mthar thug dbu ma chen po 'jig rten 'jig rten 'das pa'i chos thams cad kyi gnad bstan bcos yid bzhin nor bu lta bu snying po nges pa zhes bya ba grub mtha'i mthar thug*. In *The Collected Works of Jo-nang rje-btsun Tāranātha*, vol. 4, pp. 825–45. Leh: Smanrtsis Shesrig Dpemdzod, 1983.

———. *Rdo rje'i rnal 'byor gyi 'khrid yig mthong ba don ldan gyi lhan thabs 'od brgya 'bar*. In *The Collected Works of Jo-nang rje-btsun Tāranātha*, vol. 3, pp. 447–805. Leh: Smanrtsis Shesrig Dpemdzod, 1983.

———. *Dpal dus kyi 'khor lo'i chos bskor gyi byung khungs nyer mkho*. In *The Collected Works of Jo-nang rje-btsun Tāranātha*, vol. 2, pp. 1–43. Leh: Smanrtsis Shesrig Dpemdzod, 1983.

———. *Myang yul stod smad bar gsum gyi ngo mtshar gtam gyi legs bshad mkhas pa'i 'jug ngogs*. Lhasa: Bod ljongs mi dmangs dpe skrun khang, 1983.

———. *Gzhan stong snying po*. In *The Collected Works of Jo-nang rje-btsun Tāranātha*, vol. 4, pp. 491–514. Leh: Smanrtsis Shesrig Dpemdzod, 1983.

———. *Gzhan stong dbu ma'i rgyan*. In *The Collected Works of Jo-nang rje-btsun Tāranātha*, vol. 4, pp. 797–824. Leh: Smanrtsis Shesrig Dpemdzod, 1983.

———. *Gzhan stong dbu ma'i rgyan gyi lung sbyor*. In *The Collected Works of Jo-nang rje-btsun Tāranātha*, vol. 4, pp. 515–54. Leh: Smanrtsis Shesrig Dpemdzod, 1983.

———. *Zab don nyer gcig pa*. In *The Collected Works of Jo-nang rje-btsun Tāranātha*, vol. 4, pp. 781–95. Leh: Smanrtsis Shesrig Dpemdzod, 1983.

———. *Zab mo gzhan stong dbu ma'i brgyud 'debs*. In *The Collected Works of Jo-nang rje-btsun Tāranātha*, vol. 4, pp. 483–89. Leh: Smanrtsis Shesrig Dpemdzod, 1983.

———. *Zab lam rdo rje'i rnal 'byor gyi 'khrid yig mthong ba don ldan*. In *The Collected Works of Jo-nang rje-btsun Tāranātha*, vol. 3, pp. 345–446. Leh: Smanrtsis Shesrig Dpemdzod, 1983.

———. *Gsang ba'i rnam thar*. In *The Collected Works of Jo-nang rje-btsun Tāranātha*, vol. 1, pp. 673–84. Leh: Smanrtsis Shesrig Dpemdzod, 1983.

———. *Gsang ba'i rnam thar*. In *The Collected Works of Jo-nang rje-btsun Tāranātha*, vol. 1, pp. 655–73. Leh: Smanrtsis Shesrig Dpemdzod, 1983.

———. *Untitled*. In *The Collected Works of Jo-nang rje-btsun Tāranātha*, vol. 4, pp. 481–82. Leh: Smanrtsis Shesrig Dpemdzod, 1983.

Bstan pa'i rgyal mtshan, Gshong chen. *Rje btsun rin po che mkhas btsun bstan pa'i rgyal mtshan dpal bzang po'i dgongs bzhed dbu ma chen po'i grub mtha'*. In *The Collected Works (Gsung 'bum) of Thang-stong rgyal-po*, vol. 3, pp. 411–15. Thimphu: Kunsang Topgey, 1976.

Thu'u bkwan Blo bzang chos kyi nyi ma. *Thu'u bkwan grub mtha'*. Kansu: Mi rigs dpe skrun khang, 1984.

Dol po pa Shes rab rgyal mtshan. *Kun mkhyen chen pos mdzad pa'i gshag 'byed bsdus pa*. In *The 'Dzam-thang Edition of the Collected Works (Gsung-'bum) of Kun-mkhyen Dol-po-pa Shes-rab rgyal-mtshan*, vol. 5, pp. 435–71. Delhi: Shedrup Books, 1992.

———. *Kun gzhi rab dbye*. In *The 'Dzam-thang Edition of the Collected Works (Gsung-'bum) of Kun-mkhyen Dol-po-pa Shes-rab rgyal-mtshan*, vol. 5, pp. 349–52. Delhi: Shedrup Books, 1992.

———. *Kun gzhi'i rab tu dbye ba khyad par du 'phags pa*. In *The Collected Works (Gsung 'bum) of Kun-mkhyen Dol-po-pa Shes-rab rgyal-mtshan* (1292–1361)*: Reproduced from the copies of prints from the Rgyal-rtse Rdzong blocks preserved at the Kyichu Monastery in the Paro Valley, Bhutan*, vol. 1, 105–33. Paro/Delhi: Lama Ngodrup and Sherab Drimay, 1984.

———. *Bka' bsdu bzhi pa'i don gtan tshigs chen po*. In *The Collected Works (Gsung 'bum) of Kun-mkhyen Dol-po-pa Shes-rab rgyal-mtshan* (1292–1361)*: Reproduced from the copies of prints from the Rgyal-rtse Rdzong blocks preserved at the Kyichu Monastery in the Paro Valley, Bhutan*, vol. 1, pp. 363–417. Paro/Delhi: Lama Ngodrup and Sherab Drimay, 1984.

———. *Bka bsdus bzhi pa'i don bstan rtsis chen po*. In *The 'Dzam-thang Edition of the Collected Works (Gsung-'bum) of Kun-mkhyen Dol-po-pa Shes-rab rgyal-mtshan*, vol. 5, pp. 207–52. Delhi: Shedrup Books, 1992.

———. *Bka' bsdus bzhi pa'i don bstan rtsis chen po phyogs med ris med ces bya ba'i 'grel pa*. In *The 'Dzam-thang Edition of the Collected Works*

(Gsung-'bum) of Kun-mkhyen Dol-po-pa Shes-rab rgyal-mtshan, vol. 5, pp. 269–329. Delhi: Shedrup Books, 1992.

———. *Bka' bsdus bzhi pa'i bsdus don 'grel pa*. In *The 'Dzam-thang Edition of the Collected Works (Gsung-'bum) of Kun-mkhyen Dol-po-pa Shes-rab rgyal-mtshan*, vol. 5, pp. 253–68. Delhi: Shedrup Books, 1992.

———. *Bka' bsdu bzhi pa'i rang 'grel*. In *The Collected Works* (*Gsung 'bum*) *of Kun-mkhyen Dol-po-pa Shes-rab rgyal-mtshan* (1292–1361)*: Reproduced from the copies of prints from the Rgyal-rtse Rdzong blocks preserved at the Kyichu Monastery in the Paro Valley, Bhutan*, vol. 1, pp. 585–665. Paro/Delhi: Lama Ngodrup and Sherab Drimay, 1984.

———. *Bka' mdo rgyud zab mo kun gyi spyi 'grel gcig shes kun grol*. In *The 'Dzam-thang Edition of the Collected Works (Gsung-'bum) of Kun-mkhyen Dol-po-pa Shes-rab rgyal-mtshan*, vol. 5, pp. 331–34. Delhi: Shedrup Books, 1992.

———. *Ngo sprod khyad 'phags*. In *The 'Dzam-thang Edition of the Collected Works (Gsung-'bum) of Kun-mkhyen Dol-po-pa Shes-rab rgyal-mtshan*, vol. 7, pt. 1, pp. 605–22. Delhi: Shedrup Books, 1992.

———. *Chos kyi sgo chen mang du 'byed pa'i thabs mchog*. In *The 'Dzam-thang Edition of the Collected Works (Gsung-'bum) of Kun-mkhyen Dol-po-pa Shes-rab rgyal-mtshan*, vol. 5, pp. 123–206. Delhi: Shedrup Books, 1992.

———. *Chos dbyings du ma ro cig bde gshegs snying po'i yon tan can gyi mdo sde*. In *The 'Dzam-thang Edition of the Collected Works (Gsung-'bum) of Kun-mkhyen Dol-po-pa Shes-rab rgyal-mtshan*, vol. 5, pp. 739–55. Delhi: Shedrup Books, 1992.

———. *Mchod rten dpal yon can la bstod pa byin rlabs kyi gter chen*. In *The 'Dzam-thang Edition of the Collected Works (Gsung-'bum) of Kun-mkhyen Dol-po-pa Shes-rab rgyal-mtshan*, vol. 7, pt. 2, pp. 836–38. Delhi: Shedrup Books, 1992.

———. *Mchod rten bzhengs tshul la bstod pa 'khor ba dong sprug*. In *The 'Dzam-thang Edition of the Collected Works (Gsung-'bum) of Kun-mkhyen Dol-po-pa Shes-rab rgyal-mtshan*, vol. 7, pt. 2, pp. 831–36. Delhi: Shedrup Books, 1992.

———. *Jo bo ri pa bla ma dkon mchog mgon gyi zhu lan*. In *The 'Dzam-thang Edition of the Collected Works (Gsung-'bum) of Kun-mkhyen Dol-po-pa Shes-rab rgyal-mtshan*, vol. 7, pt. 2, pp. 705–38. Delhi: Shedrup Books, 1992.

———. *Nye gnas dad pa seng ge la gdams pa*. In *The 'Dzam-thang Edition of the Collected Works (Gsung-'bum) of Kun-mkhyen Dol-po-pa Shes-rab rgyal-mtshan*, vol. 7, pt. 1, pp. 631–35. Delhi: Shedrup Books, 1992.

———. *Nye gnas sang rin la gdams pa*. In *The 'Dzam-thang Edition of the Collected Works (Gsung-'bum) of Kun-mkhyen Dol-po-pa Shes-rab rgyal-mtshan*, vol. 7, pt. 1, pp. 635–41. Delhi: Shedrup Books, 1992.

———. *Lta ba shan 'byed yid kyi mun sel*. In *The 'Dzam-thang Edition of the Collected Works (Gsung-'bum) of Kun-mkhyen Dol-po-pa Shes-rab rgyal-mtshan*, vol. 5, pp. 789–810. Delhi: Shedrup Books, 1992.

———. *Stong nyid kyi rab tu dbye ba khyad 'phags*. In *The 'Dzam-thang Edition of the Collected Works (Gsung-'bum) of Kun-mkhyen Dol-po-pa Shes-rab rgyal-mtshan*, vol. 5, pp. 354–65. Delhi: Shedrup Books, 1992.

———. *Ston pa grub bzang la gdams pa*. In *The 'Dzam-thang Edition of the Collected Works (Gsung-'bum) of Kun-mkhyen Dol-po-pa Shes-rab rgyal-mtshan*, vol. 7, pt. 1, pp. 649–58. Delhi: Shedrup Books, 1992.

———. *Bstan pa spyi 'grel zhes bya ba'i gsol 'debs*. In *The Collected Works (Gsung-'bum) of Kun-mkhyen Dol-po-pa Shes-rab rgyal-mtshan* (1292–1361)*: Reproduced from the copies of prints from the Rgyal-rtse Rdzong blocks preserved at the Kyichu Monastery in the Paro Valley, Bhutan*, vol. 1, 686–94. Paro/Delhi: Lama Ngodrup and Sherab Drimay, 1984.

———. *Bstan pa spyi 'grel zhes bya ba'i gsol 'debs*. In *The 'Dzam-thang Edition of the Collected Works (Gsung-'bum) of Kun-mkhyen Dol-po-pa Shes-rab rgyal-mtshan*, vol. 7, pt. 1, pp. 494–501. Delhi: Shedrup Books, 1992.

———. *Bden gnyis gsal ba'i nyi ma*. In *The 'Dzam-thang Edition of the Collected Works (Gsung-'bum) of Kun-mkhyen Dol-po-pa Shes-rab rgyal-mtshan*, vol. 5, pp. 811–49. Delhi: Shedrup Books, 1992.

———. *Dpal yongs grub dgu'i bshad pa khyad 'phags g.yu rnying lta bu*. In *The 'Dzam-thang Edition of the Collected Works (Gsung-'bum) of Kun-mkhyen Dol-po-pa Shes-rab rgyal-mtshan*, vol. 4, pt. 1, pp. 111–40. Delhi: Shedrup Books, 1992.

———. *Dpon byang ba'i phyag tu phul ba'i chos kyi shan 'byed*. In *The 'Dzam-thang Edition of the Collected Works (Gsung-'bum) of Kun-mkhyen Dol-po-pa Shes-rab rgyal-mtshan*, vol. 5, pp. 473–702. Delhi: Shedrup Books, 1992.

———. *'Phags pa shes rab kyi pha rol tu phyin pa khri brgyad stong pa*. In *The 'Dzam-thang Edition of the Collected Works (Gsung-'bum) of Kun-mkhyen Dol-po-pa Shes-rab rgyal-mtshan*, vol. 4, pt. 1, pp. 1–71. Delhi: Shedrup Books, 1992.

———. *'Phags pa shes rab kyi pha rol tu phyin pa khri brgyad stong pa'i mchan bu*. In *The 'Dzam-thang Edition of the Collected Works (Gsung-'bum) of Kun-mkhyen Dol-po-pa Shes-rab rgyal-mtshan*, vol. 3, pt. 1, pp. 11–602. Delhi: Shedrup Books, 1992.

———. *'Phags pa shes rab kyi pha rol tu phyin pa stong phrag nyi shu lnga pa'i bshad pa*. In *The 'Dzam-thang Edition of the Collected Works (Gsung-'bum) of Kun-mkhyen Dol-po-pa Shes-rab rgyal-mtshan*, vol. 3, pt. 2, pp. 603–1022. Delhi: Shedrup Books, 1992.

———. *Bla ma yon tan rgya mtsho'i rnam thar dngos grub 'byung gnas*. In *The 'Dzam-thang Edition of the Collected Works (Gsung-'bum) of*

Kun-mkhyen Dol-po-pa Shes-rab rgyal-mtshan, vol. 7, pt.1, pp. 279–386. Delhi: Shedrup Books, 1992.

———. *Dbu ma'i man ngag khyad 'phags*. In *The 'Dzam-thang Edition of the Collected Works (Gsung-'bum) of Kun-mkhyen Dol-po-pa Shes-rab rgyal-mtshan*, vol. 7, pt. 2, pp. 1171–81. Delhi: Shedrup Books, 1992.

———. *Zhing mchog sham bha la'i bstod pa*. In *The 'Dzam-thang Edition of the Collected Works (Gsung-'bum) of Kun-mkhyen Dol-po-pa Shes-rab rgyal-mtshan*, vol. 7, pt. 2, pp. 853–61. Delhi: Shedrup Books, 1992.

———. *Zhu don gnang ba*. In *The 'Dzam-thang Edition of the Collected Works (Gsung-'bum) of Kun-mkhyen Dol-po-pa Shes-rab rgyal-mtshan*, vol. 5, pp. 343–46. Delhi: Shedrup Books, 1992.

———. *Gzhon nu don grub la gdams pa*. In *The 'Dzam-thang Edition of the Collected Works (Gsung-'bum) of Kun-mkhyen Dol-po-pa Shes-rab rgyal-mtshan*, vol. 7, pt. 2, pp. 679–83. Delhi: Shedrup Books, 1992.

———. *Rang rig rang gsal gyi rab tu dbye ba*. In *The 'Dzam-thang Edition of the Collected Works (Gsung-'bum) of Kun-mkhyen Dol-po-pa Shes-rab rgyal-mtshan,* vol. 5, pp. 381–401. Delhi: Shedrup Books, 1992.

———. *Ri chos nges don rgya mtsho zhes bya ba'i bstan bcos dang bsdus don*. Bir: D. Tsondu Senghe, 1984.

———. *Lo tsā ba shes rab rin chen gyi zhus len*. In *The 'Dzam-thang Edition of the Collected Works (Gsung-'bum) of Kun-mkhyen Dol-po-pa Shes-rab rgyal-mtshan*, vol. 7, pt. 2, pp. 771–74. Delhi: Shedrup Books, 1992.

———. *Shes rab bla ma la gdams pa*. In *The 'Dzam-thang Edition of the Collected Works (Gsung-'bum) of Kun-mkhyen Dol-po-pa Shes-rab rgyal-mtshan*, vol. 7, pt. 1, pp. 623–31. Delhi: Shedrup Books, 1992.

———. *Sriḍ mi srid kyi rab dbye*. In *The 'Dzam-thang Edition of the Collected Works (Gsung-'bum) of Kun-mkhyen Dol-po-pa Shes-rab rgyal-mtshan*, vol. 5, pp. 367–79. Delhi: Shedrup Books, 1992.

———. *Gsung rab spyi'i dkar chag*. In *The 'Dzam-thang Edition of the Collected Works (Gsung-'bum) of Kun-mkhyen Dol-po-pa Shes-rab rgyal-mtshan*, vol. 5, pp. 348–49. Delhi: Shedrup Books, 1992.

———. *Lha rje tshul khrims 'od la gdams pa*. In *The 'Dzam-thang Edition of the Collected Works (Gsung-'bum) of Kun-mkhyen Dol-po-pa Shes-rab rgyal-mtshan*, vol. 7, pt. 2, pp. 668–79. Delhi: Shedrup Books, 1992.

———. *Untitled*. In *The Collected Works (Gsung 'bum) of Kun-mkhyen Dol-po-pa Shes-rab rgyal-mtshan (1292–1361): Reproduced from the copies of prints from the Rgyal-rtse Rdzong blocks preserved at the Kyichu Monastery in the Paro Valley, Bhutan*, vol. 1, pp. 850–54. Paro/Delhi: Lama Ngodrup and Sherab Drimay, 1984.

Gdong thog Theg mchog bstan pa'i rgyal mtshan. *Paṇḍi ta chen po shā kya mchog ldan dri med legs pa'i blo gros kyi gsung rab rin po che par du bskrun pa'i tshul las brtsams pa'i gleng ba bstan pa'i nyi gzhon yid srubs sprin las grol ba'i dga' ston tshangs pa'i bzhad sgra*. Thimphu: Kunzang Tobgey, 1976.

Padma dkar po, 'Brug chen. *Chos 'byung bstan pa'i padma rgyas pa'i nyin byed*. Lhasa: Bod ljongs bod yig dpe rnying dpe skrun khang, 1992.

———. *Mchog gi dang po'i sangs rgyas rnam par phye ba gsang ba thams cad bshad pa'i mdzod*. In *The Collected Works of Kun-mkhyen Padma dkar-po*, vol. 13, pp. 1–533. Darjeeling: Kargyud Sungrab Nyamso Khang, 1974.

———. *Sems dpa' chen po padma dkar po'i rnam thar thugs rje chen po'i zlos gar*. In *The Collected Works of Kun-mkhyen Padma dkar-po*, vol. 3, pp. 330–597. Darjeeling: Kargyud Sungrab Nyamso Khang, 1973.

Padmasambhava. *'Bras bu yongs rdzogs rgyud kyi ti ka gsal byed dri med snying po*, In *Mkha' 'gro snying thig*, pt. 1, in *Snying thig ya bzhi*, vol.10, pp. 57–69. Darjeeling: Taklung Tsetrul Rinpoche Pema Wangyal, 1979.

Dpa' bo Gtsug lag phreng ba. *Chos byung mkhas pa'i dga' ston*. 2 vols. Beijing: Mi rigs dpe skrun khang, 1986.

Dpal ldan Chos kyi bzang po. *Sde pa g.yas ru byang pa'i rgyal rabs rin po che bstar ba*. In *Rare Tibetan Historical and Literary Texts from the Library of Tsepon W. D. Shakabpa*, pp. 166–208. New Delhi, 1974.

Dpal 'byor bzang po. *Rgya bod yig tshang chen mo*. Chengdu: Si khron mi rigs dpe skrun khang, 1985.

Phyogs las rnam rgyal, Jo nang. *Chos kyi rje byang chub sems dpa' chen po'i rnam par thar pa yon tan rin po che'i gter mdzod kun las btus pa*. Beijing: Cultural Palace of Nationalities, ms., 32 fols.

Bu ston Rin chen grub. *Bstan 'gyur gyi dkar chag yid bzhin nor bu dbang gi rgyal po'i phreng ba*. In *The Collected Works of Bu-ston*, pt. 26, pp. 401–644. New Delhi: International Academy of Indian Culture, 1971.

———. *Thams cad mkhyen pa bu ston rin po che'i gsung rab thor bu ba*. In *The Collected Works of Bu-ston*, pt. 26, pp. 143–346. New Delhi: International Academy of Indian Culture, 1971.

———. *Bla ma dam pa rnams kyis rjes su bzung ba'i tshul bka' drin rjes su dran par byed pa*. In *The Collected Works of Bu-ston*, pt. 26, pp. 1–142. New Delhi: International Academy of Indian Culture, 1971.

———. *Gtsang chu mig ring mo'i mkhan po dkon mchog dpal gyis zhus lan mdor bsdus pa*. (Title taken from the colophon.) In *The Collected Works of Bu-ston*, pt. 26, pp. 53–56. New Delhi: International Academy of Indian Culture, 1971.

'Ba' ra ba Rgyal mtshan dpal bzang po. *Skyes mchog chen po 'ba' ra bas/ kun mkhyen dol bu'i bu chen brgyad la lan phyogs cig du btab pa nyi ma'i 'od zer*. In *A Tibetan Encyclopedia of Buddhist Scholasticism*, vol. 11, pp. 637–709. Dehradun, 1970.

———. *Skyes mchog 'ba' ra bas mdzad pa'i/kun gzhi'i rnam shes dang/ ye shes kyi rnam bzhag*. In *A Tibetan Encyclopedia of Buddhist Scholasticism*, vol. 11, pp. 602–37. Dehradun, 1970.

'Be lo Tshe dbang kun khyab (with Si tu paṇ chen Chos kyi 'byung gnas). *Bsgrub brgyud karma kam tshang brgyud pa rin po che'i ram par thar pa rab 'byams nor bu zla ba chu shel gyi pheng ba*, vol. 1. New Delhi: D. Gyaltsan and K. Legshay, 1972.

Byang chub rgyal mtshan, Ta'i si tu. *Rlangs kyi po ti bse ru rgyas pa*. Lhasa: Bod ljongs mi dmangs dpe skrun khang, 1986.

Byang chub rtse mo, Lo chen. *Chos rje bla ma dam pa'i rnam thar thog mtha bar gsum du dge ba*. Beijing: Cultural Palace of Nationalities, ms., 75 fols.

Byams pa thub bstan, Rdzong rtse. *Dga' ldan phun tshogs gling gi thog mtha' bar gsum gyi byung ba yid la dran byed kun khyab snyan pa'i rnga sgra*. Göttingen: Seminars für Indologie und Buddhismuskunde, 1977.

Byams pa dpal, Khro phu Lo tsā ba. *Khro lo chen pos mdzad pa'i dpag bsam 'khri shing*. Beijing: Cultural Palace of Nationalities, ms., 90 fols.

Blo bzang chos kyi rgyal mtshan, Paṇ chen. *Chos smra ba'i dge slong blo bzang chos kyi rgyal mtshan gyi spyod tshul gsal bar ston pa nor bu'i phreng ba*. Lhasa: Bod ljongs mi dmangs dpe skrun khang, 1990.

Blo gsal bstan skyong, Zhwa lu. *Rje btsun tā ra nā tha'i gsung 'bum dang / gzhan yang mkhas grub du ma'i gsung 'bum par khyer zla ba bsgril mdzad pa phun gling par khang du bzhugs pa'i dkar chag*. In *Materials for a History of Tibetan Literature*, ed. Lokesh Candra, pt. 1, pp. 18–33, New Delhi, 1963.

Bhadrabodhi. *Ye shes snying po kun las btus pa zhes bya ba'i bshad sbyar (Jñānasārasamuccayanāmabandhana)*. In *The Tibetan Tripitaka*, ed. D. T. Suzuki, vol. 95, pp. 144.4.3.–153.4.3. Tokyo–Kyoto: Tibetan Tripitaka Research Institute, 1956.

Ma ti paṇ chen 'Jam dbyangs blo gros. *Chos rje thams cad mkhyen pa nyid kyi rgyud sde dang lag len gyi bka' babs pa sa bzang ma ti paṇḍi tas mdzad pa'i blo gros seng ge'i dris lan*. In *The 'Dzam-thang Edition of the Collected Works (Gsung-'bum) of Kun-mkhyen Dol-po-pa Shes-rab rgyal-mtshan*, vol. 7, pt. 2, pp. 1075–85. Delhi: Shedrup Books, 1992.

———. *Chos rje thams cad mkhyen pa'i bstod pa nyid rgyud sde dang lag len gyi bka' babs sa bzang pan di tas mdzad pa*. In *The 'Dzam-thang Edition of the Collected Works (Gsung-'bum) of Kun-mkhyen Dol-po-pa Shes-rab rgyal-mtshan*, vol. 7, pt. 2, pp. 1085–92. Delhi: Shedrup Books, 1992.

———. *Byang chub sems dpa'i spyod pa la 'jug pa'i rnam bshad gzhung don rab gsal snang ba*. Delhi: Tashi Dorje, 1975.

Mang thos klu sgrub rgya mtsho. *Bstan rtsis gsal ba'i nyin byed lhag bsam rab dkar*. Lhasa: Bod ljongs mi dmangs dpe skrun khang, 1987.

Mi bskyod rdo rje, Karma pa. *Dbu ma gzhan stong smra ba'i srol legs par phye ba'i sgron me*. n. p., n.d.

Mi pham Rgya mtsho. *Gzhan stong khas len seng ge'i nga ro*. In *The Collected Works of 'Jam mgon 'Ju Mi pham rgya mtsho*, vol. 3, pp. 359–78. Gangtok: Sonam Topgay Kazi.

Tshar chen Blo gsal rgya mtsho. *Gsung ngag rin po che brgyud pa gsum 'dus kyi bla ma la gsol ba 'debs pa lam rim smon lam dang bcas pa*. In *Lam-'bras slob-bshad*, vol. 14, pp. 235–48. Dehra Dun: Sakya Centre, 1983.

Tshul khrims rin chen, Zhu chen. *Kun mkhyen nyi ma'i gnyen gyi bka' lung gi dgongs don rnam par 'grel ba'i bstan bcos gangs can pa'i skad du 'gyur ro 'tshal gyi chos sbyin rgyun mi 'chad pa'i ngo mtshar 'phrul gyi phyi mo rdzogs ldan bskal pa'i bsod nams kyi sprin phung rgyas par dkrigs pa'i tshul las brtsams pa'i gtam ngo mtshar chu gter 'phel ba'i zla ba gsar pa*. Bod ljongs mi dmangs dpe skrun khang, 1985.

Tshe dbang rgyal, Rta tshag. *Dam pa'i chos kyi byung ba'i legs bshad lho rong chos 'byung ngam rta tshag chos 'byung zhes rtsom pa'i yul ming du chags pa'i ngo mtshar zhing dkon pa'i dpe khyad par can*. Lhasa: Bod ljongs bod yig dpe rnying dpe skrun khang, 1994.

Tshe dbang nor bu, Kaḥ thog rig 'dzin. *Ma bcos pa'i zog po sngags rig 'dzin pa tshe dbang nor bu rang nyid spyad rab chu klung las thig pa tsam kyu ru lugs su smos pa snyim pa'i chu skyes*. In *The Collected Works (Gsung 'bum) of Kaḥ-thog rig-'dzin chen-po Tshe-dbang nor-bu*, vol. 1, pp. 561–612. Dalhousie: Damchoe Sangpo, 1976.

———. *Lha rje mnyam med zla 'od gzhon nu'i bka' brgyud phyag chen gdams pa ji tsam nod pa'i rtogs brjod legs bshad rin chen 'byung khungs*. In *The Collected Works (Gsung 'bum) of Kaḥ-thog rig-'dzin chen-po Tshe-dbang nor-bu*, vol. 2, pp. 155–243. Dalhousie: Damchoe Sangpo, 1976.

Yu mo ba Mi bskyod rdo rje. *Gsal sgron skor bzhi*. Gangtok: Sherab Gyaltsen and Lama Dawa, 1983.

Rang byung rdo rje, Karma pa. *Bde bzhin bshegs pa'i snying po bstan pa zhes bya ba'i bstan bcos*. Published together with the *Zab mo nang don* and the *Rnam shes ye shes 'byed pa*, fols. 35a–39a. Rumtek, 1970.

———. *Zab mo nang gi don zhes bya ba'i gzhung*. Published with the *Bde bzhin bshegs pa'i snying po bstan pa* and the *Rnam shes ye shes 'byed pa*, fols. 1a–32a. Rumtek, 1970.

———. *Rang byung rdo rje'i mgur rnam*. Tashigang, 1983.

Red mda' ba Gzhon nu blo gros. *Dus kyi 'khor lo'i dpyad pa las brtsams te bstan 'dzin rnams la 'phrin du gsol ba nor bu'i phreng ba*. In *Bod kyi rtsis rig kun 'dus chen mo*, 292–303. n.d.n.p.

———. *Dpal dus kyi 'khor lo'i nges don gsal bar byed pa rin po che'i sgron ma*. In *Bod kyi rtsis rig kun 'dus chen mo*, 399–447. n.d.n.p.

———. *'Phrin yig nor bu'i phreng ba'i rang lan*. In *Bod kyi rtsis rig kun 'dus chen mo*, 304–307. n.d.n.p.

Rong ston Shes bya kun rig. *Rong ston thams cad mkhyen pa'i gsung 'bum thor bu*. Ms., 203 fols.

Rong zom Chos kyi bzang po. *Gsang sngags rdo rje theg pa'i tshul las snang ba lhar bsgrub pa rong zom chos bzang gis mdzad pa*. In *Selected Writings (Gsung thor bu) of Rong zom chos kyi bzang po*, pp. 337–59. Leh, 1974.

Rwa Ye shes seng ge. *Mthu stobs dbang phyug rje btsun rwa lo tsa ba'i rnam par thar pa kun khyab snyan pa'i rnga sgra*. Koko Nor: Mtsho sngon mi rigs dpe skrun khang, 1989.

La stod Dbang rgyal. *Dus kyi 'khor lo'i gegs sel mig gi sgron me*. In *Encyclopedia Tibetica: the Collected Works of Bo-dong Paṇ-chen Phyogs-las rnam-rgyal*, vol. 118, pp. 795–834. New Delhi: Tibet House, 1969.

Shākya mchog ldan, Paṇ chen. *Bshes gnyen mus pa rab 'byams pa'i dri lan mthong ba don ldan gyi skor*. In *The Complete Works (Gsung 'bum) of Gser-mdog Paṇ chen Shākya mchog ldan*, vol. 18, pp. 795–834. Thimphu: Kunzang Tobgey, 1975.

———. *Untitled*. In *The Complete Works (Gsung 'bum) of Gser-mdog Paṇ chen Shākya mchog ldan*, vol. 23, pp. 89–92. Thimphu: Kunzang Tobgey, 1975.

Sa skya Paṇḍi ta Kun dga' rgyal mtshan. *Sdom pa gsum gyi rab tu dbye ba'i bstan bcos*. In *Sa paṇ Kun dga' rgyal mtshan gyi gsung 'bum*, vol. 3, pp. 1–101. Lhasa: Bod ljongs bod yig dpe rnying dpe skrun khang, 1992.

Sangs rgyas rgya mtsho, Sde srid. *Bstan bcos bai dur dkar po las dris lan 'khrul snang gya' sel don gyi bzhin ras ston byed*. 2 vols. Dehra Dun: Tau Pon Sakya Centre, 1976.

Sangs rgyas rtse mo. *Dpal ldan red mda' pa chen po'i rnam thar ngo mtshar smad byung*. Beijing: Cultural Palace of Nationalities, ms., 82 fols.

Bsod nams dpal, Chos sgo ba. *Bde gshegs phag mo grub pa'i rnam par thar pa*. In *Bka' brgyud gser 'phreng rgyas pa*, vol. 2, pp. 143–83. Darjeeling: Kargyud Sungrab Nyamso Khang, 1982.

Hao wun zhon and Tou tshun chi, ed., *Bod rgya shan sbyar gyi shes bya'i rnam grangs kun btus tshig mdzod*. 2 vols. Koko Nor: Mtsho sngon mi rigs dpe skrun khang, 1987.

Lha mthongs lo tsā ba Bshes gnyen rnam rgyal, *Lha mthong lo tsa bas bal yul la thegs dus kyi lam yig snyan ngag rtsom 'phro yod*. Ms., 13 fols.

Lha'i rgyal mtshan, Gha rung ba. *Kun mkhyen dol po pa'i rnam thar rgyas pa slar yang bsdus pa lha'i rgyal mtshan gyis bkod pa*. In *The 'Dzam-thang Edition of the Collected Works of Kun-mkhyen Dol-po-pa Shes-rab rgyal-mtshan*, vol. 7, pt. 2, pp. 992–1006. Delhi: Shedrup Books, 1992.

———. *Chos rje jo nang pa kun mkhyen chen po'i rnam thar*. Beijing: Cultural Palace of Nationalities, ms., 57 fols.

Āryadeva. *Ye shes snying po kun las btus pa (Jñānasārasamuccaya)*. In *The Tibetan Tripitaka*, ed. D. T. Suzuki, vol. 95, pp. 143.5.5.–144.4.3. Tokyo–Kyoto: Tibetan Tripitaka Research Institute, 1956.

Index